RESEARCH CENTER

P9-EDP-268

Santa Clara County Free Library

REFERENCE

 58 16

R   CALIF.
352.0073   CALIFORNIA
             COUNTY
             BOUNDARIES

574431

Santa Clara Valley Library System
Mountain View Public Library
Santa Clara County Free Library
California

Alum Rock	Milpitas { Calaveras / Community Center / Sunnyhills
Campbell	
Cupertino	Morgan Hill
Gilroy	Saratoga { Quito / Village
Los Altos	Stanford-Escondido

Research Center-Cupertino
For Bookmobile Service, request schedule

California County Boundaries

California County Boundaries

A Study of the Division of the State into Counties
and the Subsequent Changes in their
Boundaries

WITH MAPS

By OWEN C. COY, Ph.D.,
Director of the Commission

574431

Publication of the
CALIFORNIA HISTORICAL SURVEY COMMISSION
BERKELEY, 1923

Revised Edition

VALLEY PUBLISHERS
FRESNO, CALIFORNIA
1973

SANTA CLARA COUNTY LIBRARY

• 3 3305 00094 3666

SANTA CLARA COUNTY LIBRARY
SAN JOSE, CALIFORNIA

STANDARD BOOK NUMBER: 0-913548-14-6

COPYRIGHT © 1973 BY VALLEY PUBLISHERS

MANUFACTURED IN THE UNITED STATES OF AMERICA

LETTER OF TRANSMITTAL

To His Excellency,

FRIEND W. RICHARDSON, *Governor,*

Sacramento, California.

SIR: Herewith is presented a volume entitled *California County Boundaries* which embraces a history of the division of the state into counties together with a more detailed study of the boundaries of each of the counties. The study covers the action of the legislature from its first session in 1849-50 to and including that of the forty-fifth session in 1923.

Respectfully submitted.

CALIFORNIA HISTORICAL SURVEY COMMISSION.

JOHN F. DAVIS, *Chairman.*
HERBERT E. BOLTON.
EDWARD A. DICKSON.
OWEN C. COY, *Director.*

Berkeley, California, May 15, 1923.

PUBLISHER'S PREFACE

Our goal initially was to reproduce this book exactly as it was published in 1923 so this generation might enjoy what has been a unique, interesting and valuable source of information for over 50 years. As the maps were being prepared for printing, we realized that some adjustments in county boundaries have been made since 1923 which deserve mention. Solicitation of information from the various counties brought an excellent response. We have condensed the information and it is included in an addendum beginning on page 337. Reference to these changes is made on the appropriate county maps.

The maps in this volume are basically the same as those in the original edition. The only change is in the method of designating the original boundaries, changes up to 1923 and the location of subsequent changes described in the addendum.

For readers who wish details about laws concerning county boundaries or the present complete legal description of boundaries, we have supplied the various sections of the Government Code dealing with these subjects in the addendum. Copies of the Code can be found in most public libraries or law libraries.

June 1973

PREFACE

The object of this volume is to present a brief but comprehensive account of the formation of the counties of California, together with a more detailed study of the location and changes in the county boundaries. Beginning with the first legislature, in 1849, which divided the state into twenty-seven counties, the agitation for new counties and for county boundary changes has continued down to the present time, when there are fifty-eight counties, with consequent radical changes in boundary lines.

The work of recording the history of this development was begun while the author was engaged in the survey of the county archives of the state, for he perceived at that time how vitally changes in county boundaries and hence in county jurisdictions affect the scope, location and significance of county archives. For publication in his *Guide to County Archives,* he prepared maps showing the successive boundary changes for each county.

Further study opened up additional problems. It was found that the portion of the Political Code defining county boundaries had not been adequately revised since its adoption in 1872. Data already gathered for the present monograph was therefore used in preparing a bill codifying the county boundary laws, which was introduced into the legislature in 1919. Unfortunately, through a senate amendment, a change in boundary was incorporated, so notwithstanding that the measure became a statute, it was on account of this boundary change declared unconstitutional according to an amendment of 1910 to the constitution of the State of California, which prohibited the formation of new counties and the alteration of county boundary lines except as provided for by general and uniform laws. Another act submitted to the legislature in 1923, received its approval as well as that of the Governor, thus accomplishing the desired codification.

The first portion takes up in chronological order the various changes and proposed changes in the county boundaries and the creation and proposals of new counties. The text is accompanied by eight state maps showing the counties as they existed at eight different periods. The larger part of the volume considers in detail the location of the boundaries of each county and traces all the changes in the boundaries as they have been set forth in legislative acts. For each county there is a colored map showing all significant boundary changes. In an appendix is given a large composite map with a key which makes it possible to determine quickly the various counties which have had jurisdiction over any portion of the state, together with the dates of that jurisdiction.

In the preparation of this work, the author has made careful search of both statutes and legislative journals, thereby tracing through not only actual legislation but also agitation for new counties and boundaries. In the latter connection, also, valuable information has been drawn from old newspaper files. To locate boundary lines it has often been necessary to ferret out old maps and to carry the research into the local county archives and those of the state departments at Sacramento, as well as those of the United States Surveyor General. Every effort has been made to secure accuracy and completeness of detail.

In the earlier years, especially, there were obscurities and inconsistencies in the boundary lines as defined by statute. In such cases, the boundaries have been located on the maps accompanying this volume as nearly as possible in agreement with the legal description and in the light of the descriptions of adjacent county lines and of subsequent legislation whenever it shed illumination on the early obscurities.

A close study of public records and statistics is the first fundamental of all exact history. In California, statistics are almost invariably given in terms of counties, and the county is the important unit in the state hierarchy. Studies of politics, of production, of population, resources and social developments must make use of county archives. But documents can not be located in the county archives, and can not be historically interpreted, unless it is known under what county jurisdiction they were made and filed and of what territory and social components they treat. In view of the fact that there are now more than twice the number of counties that originally existed, and that many radical boundary changes have taken place, it will be seen that the matter of locating and interpreting county documents becomes a complex one. The present volume is offered as a solution of that difficulty; as a key to the interpretation of records and figures otherwise difficult of access.

The author desires to acknowledge his indebtedness to the many persons without whose help this publication would have been impossible. Professor Herbert E. Bolton has ever been an unfailing source of inspiration and guidance. Mr. Ralph S. Kuykendall, formerly associated with the California Historical Survey Commission, rendered valuable service and advice. The authorities of the State Library, through the kindness of Mr. M. J. Ferguson, State Librarian, and Miss Eudora Garroutte, of the California Department, furnished help which was received with appreciation. The courtesy of those in charge of the public archives has also greatly facilitated the work. To Miss Hazel R. Bell and Miss Hester Jordan is due much credit for the careful manner in which they worked on and compared the numerous quotations and references in the earlier stages of the production of this volume; while Miss Jessie H. Davies has assisted most efficiently in the proofreading and has made valuable suggestions during the time the work has been in the press.

OWEN C. COY.

TABLE OF CONTENTS

PART I

THE GENESIS OF CALIFORNIA COUNTIES

THE GENESIS OF CALIFORNIA COUNTIES

So long as California was under Spanish rule this territory was a province of the Castilian empire, and it so continued
until 1822, when it shared in Mexico's independence. The
only known attempt made at establishing any political divisions
of the territory under either the Spanish or Mexican regimes
was that of two grand prefectures, the prefect of the south
residing at Los Angeles and the prefect of the north having
his headquarters at Monterey. Two prefectures were after-
ward established at Santa Barbara and San Jose, and in 1829
ayuntamientos were held at all four. From 1831 to 1840 there
existed five ''districts''—viz., those of San Diego, Los Angeles,
Santa Barbara, Monterey and San Francisco. The exact nature
or boundary of these districts is not certainly known. All
the then settled portion of California was included in a narrow strip along the coast and neighboring valleys, and every-
thing east and north of this was largely *terra incognita*. The
conditions of settlement were decidedly peculiar, the only
moderately well defined divisions being those of the missions,
pueblos and ranchos.

The great change from Mexican to American ownership came
in 1846 and immediately the attempt was made to get something like order out of the chaos—territorial as well as political. The first constitutional convention held at Monterey in
1849 was composed of forty-eight delegates from ten districts,
which as defined by the Governor were those of San Diego,
Los Angeles, Santa Barbara, San Luis Obispo, Monterey, San
Jose, Sonoma, San Francisco, San Joaquin and Sacramento.
The necessity of something more distinct was at once seen, and
one of the first duties of the legislature was to divide the
state into counties. This task was assigned to a committee,
with General Vallejo as chairman. The bulk of the work was
left to the General, who was rightly supposed to be an authority on geography, population and nomenclature.

Report of Committee on Counties, 1850. On January 4,
1850, the committee presented its report.[1] It pointed out some
of the difficulties encountered due to the lack of maps that
correctly indicated the location of rivers, mountains and other
natural landmarks. It admitted that many of the counties

[1]*Senate Journal,* 1st Sess. (1849), 72. The report is given in full in
Appendix E, *Ibid.,* 411-19.

were of great extent, but explained that this was due to the sparse population. It was also pointed out that the committee had avoided forming any counties entirely of mining districts on account of the transitory character of the mining population.

The report of the committee embraced the boundaries of eighteen counties as follows: San Diego, Los Angeles, Santa Barbara, San Luis Obispo, Monterey, San Francisco, San Jose, Mount Diablo, Sonoma, Benicia, Sacramento, Sutter, Butte, Reading, Fremont, San Joaquin, Oro and Mariposa. For the southern half of the state the boundaries of the six counties as proposed were approximately as later adopted by statute. These were San Diego, Los Angeles, Santa Barbara, San Luis Obispo, Monterey and Mariposa. In the north, on the other hand, many changes were made.

The first of these changes were introduced by the committee itself in a subsequent report made after the various delegations of the legislature had presented their wishes and opinions to the committee.[2] Since petitions asking for a separate county had been received from the people of Santa Cruz, upon the recommendation of the delegates from Monterey and San Jose that district was set off as a separate county. The names of several of the proposed counties were also changed as follows: Tuolumne was adopted in place of Oro, Solano for Benicia, Yolo for Fremont, and Shasta for Reading. Several additional counties were also proposed, among them being Coloma, Yubu, Coluse, Trinity, Marin and Mendocino. After passing the Senate other changes were made in the Assembly. The section relating to San Francisco was amended giving to that county jurisdiction over the whole of the bay to low water mark along the Marin and Contra Costa shores. The name Contra Costa was substituted for Mount Diablo, as was El Dorado for Coloma.[3]

The Original Counties, 1850. With these changes the legislature passed an act creating the counties and defining their boundaries which was signed by the Governor, February 18, 1850,[4] and became the fifteenth enactment of the Califor-

---

[2]*Senate Journal*, 1st Sess. (1849), Appendix F, 420-21.
[3]*Assembly Journal*, 1st Sess. (1850), 838–841. Through oversight the west boundary of Contra Costa was left in the middle of the Bay. An attempt was later made to amend this in the interest of San Francisco, but failed. *Ibid.*, 949.
[4]*Statutes*, 1850: 58-63.

CALIFORNIA
1850

TRINITY

SHASTA

MENDOCINO

COLUSA

BUTTE

YOLO

YUBA

SUTTER

NAPA

EL DORADO

SONOMA

SOLANO

SACRAMENTO

CALAVERAS

SAN JOAQUIN

MARIN

CONTRA COSTA

TUOLUMNE

SAN FRANCISCO

SANTA CLARA

SANTA CRUZ

MARIPOSA

MONTEREY

SAN LUIS OBISPO

SANTA BARBARA

LOS ANGELES

SAN DIEGO

nia legislature. By this law twenty-seven counties were created, the list being as follows: San Diego, Los Angeles, Santa Barbara, San Luis Obispo, Monterey, Branciforte, San Francisco, Santa Clara, Contra Costa, Marin, Sonoma, Solano, Yola, Napa, Mendocino, Sacramento, El Dorado, Sutter, Yuba, Butte, Colusi, Shasta, Trinity, Calaveras, San Joaquin, Tuolumne, and Mariposa. In adopting this law many additional counties had been created and the legislature had disregarded in many cases the committee's recommendation that mining districts should not be organized as separate counties. That this act did not please all sections of the state is seen in the effort at amendment which was made almost immediately after it was signed.[5] It was properly claimed that many of the boundaries especially those of Sonoma, Solano and Napa were indefinite and even additional counties were urged. The Senate Committee favored changes relating to San Francisco, Santa Clara, Contra Costa and Yola, but felt that to go further was "unnecessary and inexpedient," for, although the boundaries were indefinite, they were the best that could be done at the time and where they were indefinite the country was sparsely settled, if occupied at all. They felt that the four additional counties proposed—Aveno, Leco, Molino and Plumas—were not justified by the population of the districts.[6] Two amendatory bills were finally passed. One of these changed the names of Branciforte to Santa Cruz, of Yola to Yolo and redefined the boundaries of San Francisco, Santa Clara, Contra Costa and Yolo.[7] The other act changed the county seats in Calaveras and Tuolumne counties.[8]

County Nomenclature. The names of these counties were with two exceptions derived from the Spanish or Indian languages. One of these exceptions, Sutter, was named for the pioneer settler of the Sacramento Valley, General John A. Sutter; the other, Butte, a word of French origin, was applied to the upper Sacramento Valley on account of the Buttes, so called by the French-Canadian trappers of the Hudson Bay Company since about 1829. Realizing the interest that would be taken in knowing why the names of the counties were selected

---

[5]*Assembly Journal*, 1st Sess. (1850), 902, 908, 949, 1144. Yolo was later substituted for "Yola," the form "Colusi" persisted as late as 1857
[6]*Senate Journal*, 1st Sess. (1850), Appendix JJ, 556-558. (Report, March 6, 1850).
[7]*Statutes*, 1850: 155-156.
[8]*Ibid.*, 262-3.

as they were, the senate requested General Vallejo to present to that body a report upon the derivation and definition of the names of the several counties.

This report takes up in detail each of the twenty-seven counties. San Diego (St. James), Los Angeles ([Our Lady of] the Angels), Santa Barbara, San Luis Obispo (St. Luis, the Bishop), Santa Cruz (Holy Cross), San Francisco (St. Francis), and Santa Clara all obtained their names from older Spanish settlements or missions. The religious influence in Spanish nomenclature is also shown in the names Sacramento (Holy Sacrament), San Joaquin (St. Joachim, supposed father of Mary), and Trinity (Trinidad). Others were given Spanish names with some special significance. Among these Monterey (The Royal Forest or Mountain) was named for Count Monterey, viceroy of Mexico. Contra Costa (Opposite Coast) was chosen to describe the shore opposite San Francisco in preference to the name originally suggested, Mount Diablo (the Devil's Mountain). Mendocino was given to the cape in honor of Antonio de Mendoza, viceroy of New Spain. El Dorado (the Golden) was applied by the early Spanish to a fabulous land of gold. The name was quite appropriately applied to that county in which gold was first discovered. Yuba obtained its name from the river which, because of the abundance of wild grapes (*Uvas*) was so named. Calaveras was the name applied to the river by Captain Moraga early in the century because of the great number of skulls found in that vicinity. Mariposa, signifying "Butterfly" was thus named by the Spanish explorers in 1807 because of the great clusters of butterflies found by them in the foothills of the Sierras.

Most of the other names which are not Spanish in origin are derived from the Indian dialects. Marin was the chieftain of the Indians inhabiting the region. Sonoma was the Indian name applied to the valley in which the town of that name was situated. It signified "Valley of the Moon." Solano was the name applied to the most northerly of the Spanish missions and was derived from the name of the chief of the Suisun Indians. Yolo was an Indian term meaning "Abounding in Rushes," similar to the Spanish "*Tulares*" for the marshy district of the southern valley. Napa, Coluse, or Colusi, and Shasta were the names of the Indian tribes occupying those respective districts. Tuolumne is a corruption of the Indian term *tal malamne*, meaning a group of stone wigwams.

New Counties of 1851—Nevada, Placer, Trinity and Klamath. Conditions in 1851 already tended to justify the report of the Committee of 1850, for their statement that they could not then fix all the boundaries in a definite manner was found correct, as was also their suggestion that the increasing population would, by extending the settled area, create a demand for new counties and at the same time assist in determining more definitely the proper location for county boundaries.

During the year 1850 there had been a continuous growth of population in the mining area particularly in the Sierra Nevadas between the American and Yuba rivers and in the mines along the Trinity and Klamath rivers. Early in the session the people of Trinity requested that their county which had been attached to Shasta County be immediately organized as a separate county with the seat of justice at Trinidad. A bill to this purpose was introduced and passed both houses but was later withdrawn because superseded by a more comprehensive county boundary bill.[9] In a similar manner a petition from residents of Yuba County was presented to the assembly requesting the division of that county.[10] Still another petition asked the subdivision of Sutter County.[11]

As the result of this agitation an act was passed providing for the organization of Trinity County and the creation and organization of three new counties, Klamath, Nevada and Placer.[12] Klamath was created from the northern half of Trinity and included all that part of the Klamath Watershed which lies within the boundary of California. Nevada was organized out of the eastern part of Yuba County. Its name ("Snow-covered") is of Spanish origin and was probably taken from the well known mountain range. Placer to the south of Nevada was created from parts of Yuba and Sutter counties. Its name was derived from the Spanish term *placer*, applied to the mines from which the early miners obtained their wealth.

[9] *Legislative Journal*, 2d Sess. (1851), 115, 126, 1051, 1129, 1688.
[10] *Ibid.*, 1103, 1114.
[11] *Ibid.*, 1081.
[12] *Statutes*, 1851: 516. For description of the boundaries of these individual counties see later under each county.

Other Changes, 1851. In addition to the act relating to the four counties named another act defining in full the boundaries of the several counties was passed, revising the law of 1850. In this revision the lines of many of the counties were more or less changed, many of the changes being of little significance. Important changes were, however, made in the boundaries of Los Angeles and Colusi counties. The greatest change was made in Los Angeles County which according to the terms of the act of 1850 had been one of the smaller counties. By the act of 1851 it was greatly enlarged at the expense of both San Diego on the south and Mariposa on the north. Its western and northern boundary was made to include San Fernando, Tejon, and Tehachapi passes while its southern included the settlements around San Juan Capistrano and ran from that point eastward across the desert. The whole of the desert back country to the state boundary was included in Los Angeles County.[13] The territory of Colusi County was changed largely at the expense of her neighbor, Yolo, the boundary between these two counties being shifted southward some twenty-five miles.[14]

Other changes were more by way of definition of boundary lines rather than territorial changes. Among the more important were those of San Luis Obispo which were changed both on the north and south thus affecting Monterey and Santa Barbara, a slight change in the southern line of Shasta, one in the northern line of Sutter, and an adjustment of the line between San Joaquin and Contra Costa counties.[15]

Creation of Siskiyou, Sierra and Tulare Counties, 1852. During the third session of the legislature there was much debate regarding the formation of new counties and the adjustment of county boundaries. Out of a number of counties proposed three new ones were actually created, namely Siskiyou, Sierra and Tulare. Siskiyou was formed by taking from Shasta and Klamath counties. Its chief settled area was along the Klamath River with Scotts Valley and Shasta Plains attached to it. This division was the logical result of the development of mining in those parts, and was made neces-

---

[13]For more exact descriptions see Los Angeles, San Diego and Mariposa counties.
[14]See Colusa County boundaries.
[15]For these changes see the descriptions of the individual counties.

sary by the high Shasta Mountains dividing the Klamath streams from those of the Sacramento. The name was reported to have been derived in the following manner:[16]

> "The French name *Six Cailloux* was given a ford on the Umpqua river, at which place Michael La Frambois, with a party of Hudson Bay trappers, crossed in the year 1832. Six large stones lay in the river where they crossed and they gave it the name of Six Cailloux, or Six Stone Ford; and from this, the mountain took its name —Six Stone Mountain."

Sierra County was created from the eastern or mining district of Yuba County, being therefore the third mining county to be detached entirely or largely from Yuba County.[17] The name with that of its southern neighbor was taken from the mountain range upon whose summit these counties lie. Tulare, the other county created in 1852, was formed by a division of the large Mariposa County, more than one-half of the southern portion of that county being thus separately organized as a new county. This county included all that area north and east of the Coast Range Mountains, and from the Tehachapi Mountains on the south to and including the Kings River watershed on the north.[18] The name was taken from the large lake surrounded by tule marshes which to the Spanish speaking people suggested the name *Tulares* for this region.

Boundary Adjustments, 1852. Several boundaries were shifted in order to make them more definite or because of some local demand for change. The northern boundary of Napa, common to Mendocino, which had been very imperfectly described in 1850 and 1851 was by an act at this session more accurately defined along a line running through Clear Lake.[19] The northern line of Sutter, changed in 1851, was again shifted in 1852 with but slight difference in its location.[20] Another change was made in the northern line of Nevada County, whereby that county was enlarged by a few square miles at the expense of the newly created Sierra

[16]*Senate Journal*, 3d Sess. (1852), 314. A different derivation is given in San Francisco *Alta California*, May 7, 1852.
[17]For description of the boundaries see map and description of Sierra County.
[18]See map and description of Tulare County.
[19]*Statutes*, 1852: 192. See map and description of Napa County.
[20]*Ibid.*, 237. See map and description of Sutter County.

County.[21]   An attempt was made to take Mare Island from Sonoma and place it with Solano, off whose mainland the Island lay, but the act was awkwardly drawn and resulted in excluding it from both counties.[22]   A more definite description involving an unimportant change was made in the line between San Joaquin and Contra Costa,[23] and another in the San Luis Obispo-Santa Barbara boundary.[24]

Pautah County, 1852-1859. That the legislators of California did not consider themselves circumscribed by state boundaries is to be seen in their passage of an act for the creating of Pautah County from territory entirely beyond the bounds of the State of California.   Many settlers from California and others bound for California had taken up their abode in the valleys of the Truckee, Carson and Walker rivers adjoining the eastern boundary of California.   Although this was a part of the territory of Utah, it was near the mining region of California and being on the routes of the overland trails had much in common with this state.   Two measures dealing with this proposed county were introduced into the assembly, one of which became a law and remained upon the statute books until its repeal in 1859.   The boundaries of Pautah County were defined as follows:[25]

> "Commencing at the northeast corner of Sierra County, thence in a southeasterly direction to the northeast extremity of Pyramid Lake; thence in a southeast line to the northwestern boundary of Carson Lake; thence running south to the eastern border of Walker Lake, following said border to the southern limit of said Lake; thence in a southwesterly direction to the southeast corner of Calaveras County; thence following the eastern boundary of Calaveras, El Dorado, Placer, Nevada and Sierra counties to the place of beginning."

The act declared that "Carsonville" should be the seat of justice and further provided that the act should take effect when the Congress of the United States had ceded to the State of California the territory described in the act.

---

[21]*Statutes*, 1852: 190, 191.
[22]*Ibid.*, 236.
[23]*Ibid.*, 178.
[24]*Ibid.*, 218.
[25]*Ibid.*, 1852: 193; 1859: 186.

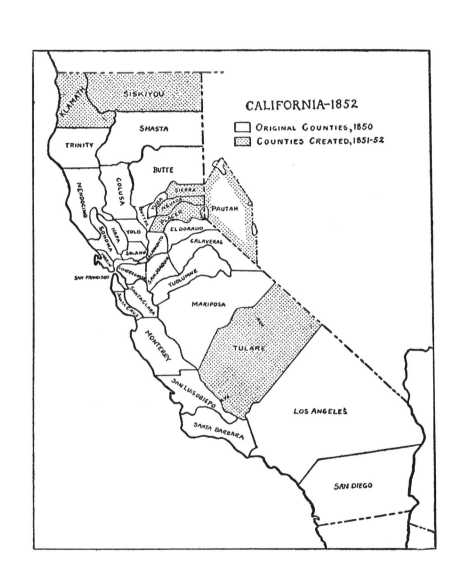

CALIFORNIA–1852

☐ ORIGINAL COUNTIES, 1850
▨ COUNTIES CREATED, 1851-52

KLAMATH

SISKIYOU

TRINITY

SHASTA

MENDOCINO

COLUSA

BUTTE

SIERRA

YUBA

NEVADA

PAUTAH

SONOMA

NAPA

YOLO

BUTTE

PLACER

ELDORADO

MARIN

SOLANO

SACRAMENTO

CALAVERAS

SAN FRANCISCO

CONTRA COSTA

SAN JOAQUIN

TUOLUMNE

SANTA CLARA

SANTA CRUZ

MARIPOSA

MONTEREY

TULARE

SAN LUIS OBISPO

LOS ANGELES

SANTA BARBARA

SAN DIEGO

Petitions for the division of Trinity, Calaveras,[26] and Colusi counties were presented. Bills were introduced in reference to the latter two counties but notwithstanding a determined fight neither of these became laws.[27]

Humboldt, Alameda and San Bernardino Counties, 1853. Three agricultural counties were created by the legislature during its fourth session. The first of these, approved March 19, 1853, formed the county of Alameda out of portions of Contra Costa and Santa Clara, with boundaries essentially as they have since remained.[28] This action was due to the growth of population along the eastern side of San Francisco Bay. The name, meaning "a grove of poplar trees," was first applied by the Spanish explorers to the stream of that name running through the new county. The creation of San Bernardino County was the first subdivision of the southern counties. This action was made necessary by the immigration of a large number of Mormons from Salt Lake and their formation of a colony upon the old San Bernardino rancho, purchased by them in 1851. The territory was taken from Los Angeles, thus reducing it to about one-third of its former size.[29] The discovery and settlement of Humboldt Bay early in 1850 led to the rapid development of the western or coast part of Trinity County and to a decided political rivalry between this district and the mining region on Trinity River. During the spring of 1852 the legislature had been petitioned to divide Trinity County, but without result.[30] A renewal of the agitation the next year led to the creation of Humboldt County in 1853.[31] The name was taken from Humboldt Bay, which had been so named in 1850 in honor of the scientist Alexander von Humboldt.

The boundaries of other counties were under consideration by this legislature but not with important results. Mare Island which had been acted upon in 1852 was by this session definitely placed in Solano County, as had been the intention of the legislation of the previous year.[32] The boundaries of Butte were also more clearly defined.[33] Several unsuccessful

---

[26]*Assembly Journal*, 3d Sess., (1852), 396, 486, 492, 435, 440, 543. *Senate Journal*, 230.
[27]*Assembly Journal*, 72, 147, 247. *Senate Journal*, 150, 192, 445.
[28]*Statutes*, 1853: 56.
[29]*Ibid.*, 1853: 119.
[30]*Senate Journal*, 3d Sess. (1852), 58.
[31]*Statutes*, 1853: 161.
[32]*Ibid.*, 20.
[33]*Ibid.*, 53-4.

attempts were made to secure further changes. Petitions from inhabitants of Butte and Sutter asked that they be annexed to Colusi.[34] Mendocino, still attached to Sonoma, desired separation.[35] The agitation was also continued for the formation of a new county to be formed from portions of Calaveras and other counties, to which was to be applied the name "Mokelumne."[36] A division of Tuolumne and Mariposa was also desired by other petitioners.[37]

Plumas, Amador and Stanislaus, 1854. Three new counties were created in 1854, two mining counties and one an agricultural county. The first of these to be created was Plumas. It was detached from Butte County and included the headwaters of the Feather River. The name was taken from the Spanish name for the river, Rio de las Plumas. The interest of the district was primarily mining. On account of the great growth of the population in the mines of this region and its remoteness from the county seat in the valley it was felt desirable that a new county be formed. The county seat was placed at American Ranch, now known as Quincy.[38]

For several sessions of the legislature a movement had been on foot for the division of Calaveras County. This agitation was pushed with renewed vigor in the session of 1854. There was, however, a lack of unity in the minds of the people of the counties affected. Protests as well as petitions were filed. As introduced the bill asked for the creation of a new county from portions of El Dorado and Calaveras counties under the name of "Washington County." As finally approved the act limited the territory to a part of Calaveras County only and gave the new county the name of "Amador," from one of the Spanish pioneers who came to California in 1771. The seat of justice was placed at Jackson, which from 1850 to 1852 had been the county seat of Calaveras County.[39] Stanislaus the third of the counties created in 1854, was detached from Tuolumne County, and was composed of that part of the county which extended from the Coast Range on the west to the foot-

[34]*Senate Journal,* 4th Sess. (1853), 113, 131.
[35]*Assembly Journal,* 4th Sess. (1853), 385, 414. *Senate Journal,* 381.
[36]*Assembly Journal,* 4th Sess. (1853), 351, 416, 385, 638.
[37]*Senate Journal,* 4th Sess. (1853), 47.
[38]*Assembly Journal,* 5th Sess. (1854), 196, 240. *Senate Journal,* 201. *Statutes,* 1854 : 8.
[39]Washington County, *Assembly Journal,* 5th Sess. (1854), 116, 142, 145, 181, 192, 458. Amador County, *Senate Journal,* 122, 351, 364, 376, 465, 523. *Statutes,* 1854 (Redding) : 46.

hills of the Sierra Nevadas on the east.[40] The county seat was originally placed at Adamsville but soon afterwards moved to Empire City. The name was derived from Estanislao, the name of the famous Indian chief of this region.

Three other boundary changes were made in 1854. Once again an insignificant change was made in the Butte-Sutter line.[41] A change was also made in the line between Santa Barbara and San Luis Obispo.[42] By another act the territory of Marin was enlarged by extending the jurisdiction of the county out into the bay rather than along the low water line as established in 1850.[43]

There were other boundary proposals which were less successful. One proposed to detach a small area from Butte and Sutter and annex it to Colusi,[44] another proposed to form a county to be called "Merced" from portions of Tuolumne and Mariposa;[45] while still a third would have formed a county of "Pajara" from portions of Santa Cruz, Santa Clara and Monterey counties.[46]

Merced County, 1855. Petitions and bills affecting more than a dozen different counties were introduced during the session of 1855 with the result that one new county was created and seven boundary lines modified to a greater or lesser degree. Merced was created from the western or valley portion of Mariposa County. As noticed above an effort had been made to form this county in 1854 from portions of Tuolumne and Mariposa, but since the creation of Stanislaus had taken all the lowland portion of Tuolumne,[47] the new county was limited to a portion of Mariposa, it being given that part lying west of the main road running down the valley at the edge of the Sierra foothills.[48] The name of the county was derived from that of a river, named by Moraga and his party early in the nineteenth century.

Several boundary changes of some importance were made in 1855. The boundaries of Napa, which had been so im-

[40]*Assembly Journal*, 5th Sess. (1854), 278, 335, 482. *Senate Journal*, 254, 273, 356, 452. *Statutes*, 1854 (Redding): 40, 191.
[41]*Statutes*, 1854 (Redding): 26.
[42]*Ibid.*, 148.
[43]*Ibid.*, 121.
[44]*Assembly Journal*, 5th Sess. (1854), 264.
[45]*Ibid.*, 49, 116, 120, 123, 206, 223.
[46]*Ibid.*, 336, 338, 341, 369.
[47]*Ante.*, p. 12.
[48]*Statutes*, 1855: 125. *Senate Journal*, 6th Sess. (1855), 210, 354, 363, 606, 671.

CALIFORNIA–1855

☐	Original Counties, 1850
▨	Counties Created, 1851-52
▨	" " ,1853-55

KLAMATH

SISKIYOU

TRINITY

SHASTA

HUMBOLDT

MENDOCINO

PLUMAS

BUTTE

COLUSA

SIERRA

YUBA

NEVADA

SUTTER

PLACER

YOLO

EL DORADO

NAPA

SONOMA

SOLANO

AMADOR

CALAVERAS

MARIN

SACRAMENTO

SAN JOAQUIN

CONTRA COSTA

TUOLUMNE

SAN FRANCISCO

ALAMEDA

STANISLAUS

SANTA CLARA

MARIPOSA

SANTA CRUZ

MERCED

MONTEREY

TULARE

SAN LUIS OBISPO

SAN BERNARDINO

SANTA BARBARA

LOS ANGELES

SAN DIEGO

perfectly described in the early acts were by a statute of 1856 fixed about as they now stand. The northern boundary, entirely changed on the creation of Lake County sometime later, was at this time pushed further north so as to give Napa full control of Clear Lake.[49] By a change in the boundary between Mendocino and Sonoma the line was placed as it stood until 1917.[50] Amador was granted an increase in area at the expense of El Dorado, the territory between Dry Creek and Cosumnes River being annexed to Amador.[51] By the act creating Klamath in 1851 the northern line of Trinity County had been run due east from the mouth of Mad River to the summit of the Coast Range of mountains. It was later found that this was unsatisfactory since the line cut across many of the streams on the upper Trinity, thus making it necessary for the people on portions of these streams to cross a high range of mountains to get to the county seat. By an act passed in 1855 the dividing line between Trinity and its northern neighbors was placed along the mountain ridge dividing the waters of the Trinity from those of the Klamath.[52]

Buena Vista and Other Proposed Counties, 1855. The fight for additional new counties was carried on during this session. In so far as favorable legislation was concerned one of these attempts was successful although other difficulties which arose later prevented the organization of the county. This was the case of Buena Vista, the forerunner of the present Kern County. A bill was introduced into the assembly providing for the creation of Kern County out of the southern part of Tulare. After amending the bill by substituting the name of "Buena Vista," from a lake in that district, the legislature passed the bill which received the Governor's approval.[53] The act provided that when a majority of the voters of the proposed district, together with a majority of the voters of Tulare County, had signed petitions for the formation of the new county an election should be called for the purpose of choosing county officers. The territory of "Buena Vista County" was defined in the first section of the statute

---

[49]*Statutes*, 1855: 77.
[50]*Ibid.*, 150.
[51]*Ibid.*, 113.
[52]*Ibid.*, 200.
[53]*Assembly Journal*, 6th Sess. (1855), 665, 700, 808, 816. *Senate Journal*, 769.

in these words: "All that portion of the county of Tulare situated south of the township line dividing townships number twenty-one and twenty-two south, shall constitute a new county to be called 'Buena Vista' County."[54]

The proponents of "Pajaro County" again urged their plan of forming a county from portions of Monterey, Santa Cruz and Santa Clara. The petitions for a new county were met by remonstrances against the project. It was argued that the indebtedness of Santa Clara and Monterey prohibited any feasibility of division.[55] The division of San Francisco County was proposed in a bill for the creation of "Remondo County." The bill passed the assembly but was defeated in the senate.[56] Another bill sought to create "Suisun County" by dividing Solano. It however did not obtain the support of the house in which it originated.[57]

San Mateo, Fresno and Tehama, 1856. County boundary legislation in 1856 resulted in the formation of three additional counties: San Mateo, created from San Francisco; Fresno, from Mariposa and Merced; and Tehama, from Colusi, Butte and Shasta. Neither of these counties was essentially a mining county but all represented rather the growth of those parts of the state more adapted to agricultural interests.

In a previous paragraph notice was taken of an unsuccessful attempt in 1855 to divide San Francisco and form from the detached territory a new county to be called "Remondo." In 1856 this agitation was again renewed and resulted in the formation of San Mateo County, thus reducing to approximately its present area, San Francisco, whose government then became consolidated into the city and county of San Francisco.[58] The northern boundary of the new county ran through Shag Rock in San Francisco Bay and the southern end of Laguna de la Merced. The name, meaning St. Matthew, was taken from a stream entering San Francisco Bay in this vicinity. The creation of Fresno County was the third and last important division of the once large Mariposa County. To the part detached from Mariposa was added other terri-

---

[54]*Statutes*, 1855: 203-5.
[55]*Assembly Journal*, 6th Sess. (1855), 397, 529, 622. Sacramento *Union*, March 9, 1855, (3/2).
[56]*Assembly Journal*, 6th Sess. (1855), 727, 791, 806, 826. *Senate Journal*, 829, 834.
[57]*Assembly Journal*, 6th Sess. (1855), 187, 198, 562.
[58]*Statutes*, 1856: 145, 176.

tory taken from Merced and Tulare.[59] The name is the Spanish term for ash tree so common along the banks of the streams
in that region. Tehama County was created in response to a
demand for a county centering around Red Bluff, then the
head of navigation on the Sacramento River. To form this
county territory was taken from Colusi, Shasta and Butte
counties.[60] The name is of Indian origin but its meaning is
uncertain. The boundaries of several counties were modified.
To Colusi was given a small piece of territory lying between
the Sacramento River and Butte Creek. This had previously
been parts of Butte and Sutter counties.[61] The northern
boundary of Nevada was placed along the course of the Middle Yuba River to its source, thus taking a small piece of territory from Sierra.[62] The line between Butte and Sutter was
once again moved, this time at the expense of Butte.[63] An
attempt to redefine the boundaries of Los Angeles County
resulted only in much confusion and will not be discussed
here.[64] Another act amended the northern boundary of
Buena Vista County by placing it along the northern line of
township twenty-one south rather than on its southern line
as established in 1855.[65]

The movement for a new county from portions of Monterey
and Santa Clara was presented in a bill creating ''Aromas
County.'' This measure passed the senate and only failed
in the assembly through a reconsideration of the vote.[66] Petitions from residents of Sierra, Yuba and Plumas counties
asking for the creation of a new county led to the introduc-
tion of a bill providing for the organization of a county
called ''Summit.'' No further action regarding this county
was taken during the session.[67]

Del Norte and Other Boundary Legislation, 1857. During
the eighth session of the legislature nine acts were passed dealing with county boundaries. In only one case, that of Del
Norte, was a new county created. The shifting of the county
seat of Klamath County from Crescent City to Orleans Bar

---

[59]*Statutes*, 1856: 183.
[60]*Ibid.*, 118, 222.
[61]*Ibid.*, 124-5.
[62]*Ibid.*, 143.
[63]*Ibid.*, 231.
[64]*Ibid.*, 53
[65]*Ibid.*, 96.
[66]*Senate Journal*, 7th Sess. (1856), 552, 813, 858. *Assembly Journal,*
856, 858.
[67]*Assembly Journal*, 7th Sess. (1856), 190, 191, 208, 257, 265.

in 1856 gave rise to the agitation of the people of the former place for the creation of a new county. Early in the session a bill was introduced providing for the creation of a new county to be known as "Buchanan." In this form it passed the assembly but in the senate the name was amended to read "Del Norte." On account of errors this bill was vetoed by the Governor but was followed by another which received his approval and became a statute.[68] The name was applied to this county because of its extreme northern position.

The boundaries of several counties were changed. Those of Tehama were redefined in full with modifications in both the Shasta line on the north and the Colusi line on the south.[69] The former of these added to Tehama the territory between the south and middle forks of Cottonwood Creek; the other was unimportant. A slight change was made in the northern line of Amador, placing it along the Cosumnes River which it has since followed;[70] and another change in the Solano-Yolo boundary placed it in its present position.[71] Three other acts defining the boundaries of Sacramento, San Bernardino and San Mateo did but little more than make more definite boundaries which had been already established.[72]

As usual there were many more projects for new counties or shifting of boundaries which did not secure approval. A bill was introduced for the creation of a new county to be known as "Mokelumne" from portions of San Joaquin, Calaveras, Amador and Sacramento counties.[73] Another which sought the formation of a new county from parts of Placer and Sacramento counties secured the approval of both houses.[74] A bill relating to the organization of "Buena Vista County" passed the assembly;[75] while still another bill would have created the county of "Eureka" from the northern portion of El Dorado.[76]

Boundary Legislation, 1858. The legislation of the ninth session in so far as county boundaries is concerned amounted to but one act more clearly defining, but not changing, the

[68]*Assembly Journal*, 8th Sess. (1857), 167, 202, 291, 437, 438, 448. *Statutes*, 1857: 35.
[69]*Ibid.*, 109, 25.
[70]*Ibid.*, 251.
[71]*Ibid.*, 108.
[72]*Ibid.*, 132, 165, 222.
[73]*Assembly Journal*, 8th Sess. (1857), 529.
[74]*Ibid.*, 545, 581, 638.
[75]*Ibid.*, 545, 674. *Senate Journal*, 8th Sess. (1857), 645–6.
[76]*Assembly Journal*, 8th Sess. (1857), 568, 677, 699–701.

boundaries of Del Norte County, which had been created the previous year.[77] A further attempt was made to organize "Buena Vista County" by extending the time for its organization to 1859.[78] The governments of the city and county of Sacramento were consolidated by another act,[79] which also gave rise to the agitation for a new county, called "Folsom," to be composed of the rural sections of the county.[80] Petitions were received and an effort made to form a new county from portions of Sierra, Butte, Plumas and Yuba counties. A bill to that end was introduced into the assembly assigning to the proposed county the name of "Summit," which a substitute bill changed to "Altura" and later to "Alturas" but the measure was lost in the assembly.[81] Another bill sought to divide Tuolumne County and to create a new county to be known as "Yo Semite."[82]

Other boundaries were considered but without resultant legislation. Among these were the western and northern line of Butte,[83] the Klamath-Humboldt boundary,[84] the line between Placer and Sutter[85] and that between Los Angeles and San Bernardino.[86]

Mendocino Organized, 1859. Four acts relating to county boundaries were passed in 1859. The most important of these was the act which provided for the separate organization of Mendocino County which since its creation in 1850 had been administered as a part of Sonoma County. The boundaries of Mendocino were kept about as they had been except for a change in the south with Sonoma and a slight change in the north which was apparently an error in drawing the act.[87] By another act the southern boundary of Tehama was modified. In that part common to Butte a change was made whereby the line was placed farther north, while the boundary with Colusa was described in a more definite manner.[88] Another act redefined the boundaries of Tuolumne but without noticeable change.[89] The fourth act

[77]*Statutes*, 1858: 21.
[78]*Ibid.*, 36.
[79]*Ibid.*, 267, *seq.*
[80]Sacramento *Union*, March 1, 1858 (2/4).
[81]*Assembly Journal*, 9th Sess. (1858), 390, 417, 449, 452-3, 487-8.
[82]*Ibid.*, 419, 425, 595.
[83]*Ibid.*, 562, 611.
[84]*Senate Journal*, 391, 482, 565, 604.
[85]*Assembly Journal*, 426, 442, 541, 579.
[86]*Ibid.*, 420, 595. *Senate Journal*, 79.
[87]*Statutes*, 1859: 98.
[88]*Ibid.*, 359. Henceforth the name appears as "Colusa" in the Statutes.
[89]*Ibid.*, 213.

required the Surveyor General to run the line between Butte and Yuba and establish it as the legal boundary.[90]

The fight for the creation of "Mokelumne County" was again taken up by citizens of Sacramento and San Joaquin counties who desired the new county.[91] The boundaries of the proposed county were to run from[92]

> "the Sacramento river, where the section line running east and west through the townships 7 north, Mount Diablo meridian crosses said stream; thence east, along said section line, until it intersects the Daylor or Omachumes Grant: thence along the north line of said grant to its northeast corner, and thence due east to the boundary line between El Dorado and Sacramento counties; thence southerly, following the western boundaries of El Dorado, Amador and Calaveras counties, to the section line running east and west through the centers of townships 3 north; thence due west, along said section line, to the San Joaquin River; thence down the center of the San Joaquin River to its junction with the waters of the Sacramento; thence up the center of the Sacramento river to the place of beginning."

Remonstrances presented by others opposed to the formation of the county[93] resulted in a modification of boundaries by the committee to which it was referred so as to exclude a large part of those opposed to the new county.[94] In this form the bill passed the assembly but by a narrow margin failed to pass the senate.[95]

San Joaquin was beset by divisionists upon both sides, for in addition to those who sought to create "Mokelumne County," others desired to be detached from San Joaquin and annexed to Stanislaus County. This movement seems to have been engineered by those interested in the success of the town of Knights Ferry, which it was hoped might be a successful rival for the rather migratory county seat of Stanislaus

[90]*Statutes*, 1859 : 225.
[91]*Assembly Journal*, 10th Sess. (1859), 225, 236, 275, 464. Sacramento *Union*, January 27 (2/2) ; February 7, (3/2), 1859.
[92]*Ibid.*, March 14, 1859 (2/3).
[93]*Assembly Journal*, 10th Sess. (1859), 432. Sacramento *Union*, April 4, 1859 (2/2).
[94]*Assembly Journal*, 10th Sess. (1859), 464. Sacramento *Union*, March 21 (2/3) ; 30 (3/3), 1859.
[95]*Senate Journal*, 10th Sess. (1859), 733, 738.

County. San Joaquin strongly protested against any division of her territory and was joined in this by others who opposed the annexation to Stanislaus.[96] At this session petitions were again presented from residents of Sierra, Yuba, Butte and Plumas counties asking that the creation of "Alturas" or "Summit" County be considered again. A bill to this effect passed the assembly but failed in the senate.[97] Divisionists were also found in Santa Barbara,[98] Sonoma,[99] and Fresno counties. In the latter county a petition, signed by 103 residents of that county, asked to be transferred to Tulare but on account of the protest of many others the petition was denied.[100]

During the eleventh session (1860) the legislation dealing with county boundaries was productive of few changes. Four boundary acts were passed. Three of these, relating to Mendocino,[101] Marin [102] and Butte,[103] had for their purpose the fixing of lines as nearly as possible in accordance with previous legislation. The act relating to Stanislaus resulted from an agitation carried forward from the previous session. This bill as introduced proposed to annex to Stanislaus portions to be detached from Tuolumne, Calaveras and San Joaquin counties. Amendments were made in both the assembly and senate with the result that the only part still under consideration was a triangular portion at the eastern end of San Joaquin County.[104] This territory which included Knights Ferry was now transferred to Stanislaus.[105] Two years later Knights Ferry became the seat of justice of the county of its adoption.

Other county division agitations were less successful. "Alturas" proponents again urged the division of Sierra County and once again succeeded in getting their measure passed in the assembly.[106] Certain residents in northern El

[96]*Assembly Journal*, 10th Sess. (1859), 195, 231, 262, 339, 439, 461, 499. *Senate Journal*, 526, 606.
[97]*Assembly Journal*, 10th Sess. (1859), 417, 432, 458, 464. *Senate Journal*, 653, 696, 731.
[98]*Senate Journal*, 114.
[99]*Assembly Journal*, 541.
[100]*Ibid.*, 390, 367.
[101]*Statutes*, 1860: 334. The northern line had in 1859 inadvertently been changed. This act replaced it to its former position.
[102]*Ibid.*, 269.
[103]*Ibid.*, 115.
[104]*Assembly Journal*, 11th Sess. (1860), 223, 313, 314, 345. *Senate Journal*, 284, 289, 296.
[105]*Statutes*, 1860: 34.
[106]*Assembly Journal*, 11th Sess. (1860), 215, 411. *Senate Journal*, 379, 564.

Dorado sought separation and the organization of a new county to be named "Marshall" in honor of the discoverer of gold. Petitions to this effect were presented and a bill introduced detaching from El Dorado that portion north of the south fork of the American River.[107] The movement for the formation of "Mokelumne County" again made itself manifest. A bill was introduced into the assembly seeking the creation of the county from portions of San Joaquin and Sacramento counties.[108] The project was both strongly supported and bitterly opposed by petitions and remonstrances. Although the Committee on Counties and County Boundaries reported adversely, the bill was recommitted to the county delegation,[109] a majority of whom presented a report favoring a substitute bill.[110] Even this was strongly opposed by the representative of San Joaquin County, who presented a full report of his arguments against the proposed county. He showed that the transfer of a part of San Joaquin's territory to Stanislaus had already reduced the size and resources of the former so that any further division of the county would be disastrous. A bill for the division of Napa County and the formation of a new county to be called "Lake" was adversely reported by the assembly committee.[111] Bills were passed seeking to define the Plumas-Sierra boundary,[112] and to alter the Tehama boundaries[113] but they did not secure the approval of the senate. Other bills were introduced defining the boundaries of Sutter[114] and those of Sacramento.[115]

Washoe County, 1860. Mining operations east of the Sierras attracted many settlers from California and elsewhere giving rise to agitation for changes to accommodate this new condition. Mention has been made in an earlier paragraph of the proposed county of Pautah lying east of the state boundary.[116] A similar move was agitated in 1860 in the form of a joint resolution asking Congress to cede to California

[107]*Assembly Journal*, 11th Sess. (1860), 537, 540, 622. Sacramento *Union*, March 17 (2/5), 23 (1/4), 1860.
[108]*Assembly Journal*, 11th Sess. (1860), 227.
[109]*Ibid.*, 307, 309, 322. Sacramento *Union*, February 10, 1860 (1/6).
[110]*Assembly Journal*, 11th Sess (1860), 350, 376-80. Sacramento *Union*, February 17 (1/4), 24, March 7 (2/2), 1860.
[111]*Assembly Journal*, 11th Sess. (1860), 482, 563.
[112]*Ibid.*, 291, 346. *Senate Journal*, 310, 564.
[113]*Assembly Journal*, 625.
[114]*Senate Journal*, 149, 278.
[115]*Ibid.*, 192.
[116]*Ante*, 9.

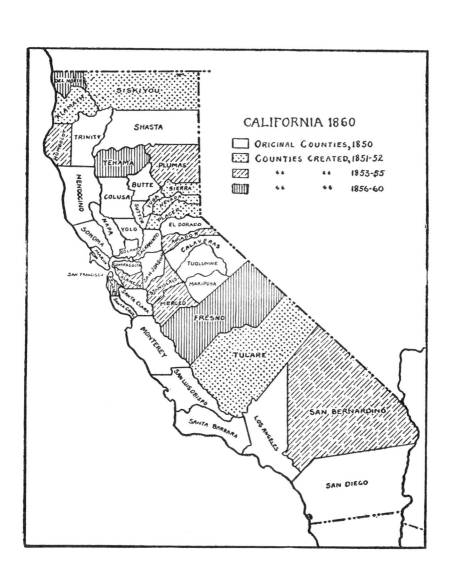

CALIFORNIA 1860

☐ ORIGINAL COUNTIES, 1850
▨ COUNTIES CREATED, 1851-52
▨ " " 1853-55
▥ " " 1856-60

DEL NORTE

SISKIYOU

KLAMATH

TRINITY

SHASTA

HUMBOLDT

TEHAMA

PLUMAS

MENDOCINO

BUTTE

SIERRA

COLUSA

YUBA

NEVADA

SUTTER

PLACER

NAPA

YOLO

EL DORADO

SONOMA

SOLANO

SACRAMENTO

AMADOR

CALAVERAS

MARIN

CONTRA COSTA

SAN JOAQUIN

TUOLUMNE

SAN FRANCISCO

ALAMEDA

STANISLAUS

MARIPOSA

SANTA CLARA

SANTA CRUZ

MERCED

FRESNO

MONTEREY

TULARE

SAN LUIS OBISPO

SAN BERNARDINO

SANTA BARBARA

LOS ANGELES

SAN DIEGO

certain territory lying in the present state of Nevada. This then was to be organized as "Washoe County." According to the plan the boundaries were to run as follows:[117]

"Commencing at the point of intersection of the forty-second degree of north latitude with the one hundred and eighteenth degree of longitude west from Greenwich, and running south on the line of one hundred and eighteenth degree of west longitude until it intersects the easterly boundary of this state; thence northerly and along the boundary line of the State of California to its northeast corner; thence on the line of the forty-second degree of north latitude to the place of beginning."

The new territory was to be attached to El Dorado County until organized. The argument in favor of this was that the new mining interests had so increased the population of the district that it already had 10,000 people, one-half of whom were Californians, while within a few months the population would be four or five times that number, most of them Californians.[118] A bill was introduced and passed the assembly altering the El Dorado-Amador boundary but the measure was lost in the senate.[119]

Creation of Mono and Lake, 1861. The first of the mining counties east of the Sierra Nevadas was created by a division of Calaveras County in 1861. During the session of 1860 a petition had been presented to the senate from citizens of Mariposa, Tulare, Fresno, and Calaveras counties for the creation of a new county to be called "Mono."[120] Early in the twelfth session the project was again presented, this time in the form of a bill providing for the formation of "Esmeralda County."[121] There was little or no opposition to the measure owing to the rapid growth of the region brought about by the development of the silver mines. The assembly committee reported the immediate necessity of passing the measure, but amended the bill by substituting the name "Mono" for "Esmeralda." In this form it was accepted by the senate and became a statute.[122] The name Mono was taken from that

---

[117]Sacramento *Union*, March 6, 1860 (1/2).
[118]*Ibid.*, April 4, 1860 (1/5).
[119]*Assembly Journal*, 11th Sess. (1860), 537, 696, *et seq. Senate Journal*, 746, 772.
[120]*Senate Journal*, 317.
[121]*Ibid.*, 12th Sess. (1861), 312. A similar bill was introduced in the Assembly; *Journal*, 243, 270.
[122]*Assembly Journal*, 319, 348, 606, 615. *Senate Journal*, 312, 343, 546. *Statutes*, 1861: 235.

of the important lake in the region. It is probably of Indian origin.

Lake County was also created in 1861, by detaching a portion of the northern end of Napa County. During the previous session of the legislature a petition had been submitted asking for the formation of this new county. The project was again presented to the legislature in 1861 with the result that an act was passed creating the county.[123] The name was naturally suggested from Clear Lake, the most prominent physical feature of the county.

Other boundary acts passed in 1861 dealt with Sacramento, Butte, Monterey, Sonoma and the counties surrounding them. A change in the channel of the Mokelumne River required a more explicit reference to its branches in order to maintain the then existing boundary between Sacramento and San Joaquin.[124] The boundary between Monterey and San Luis Obispo had been changed many times but was still unsatisfactory. In 1861 it was shifted northward and placed on a line three miles north of the sixth standard south of Mount Diablo base-line.[125] The act redefining the Butte-Yuba boundary came through a dispute over the location of the "Woodville House." By the act this house and outbuildings were placed in Yuba County.[126]

Many other bills dealing with county boundaries were introduced but failed of passage. One sought to secure the creation of "Alturas County," a project which had been presented and defeated each session since 1858.[127] San Joaquin endeavored to repeal or modify the act of 1860 granting to Stanislaus a portion of its territory.[128] By means of petitions an agitation was begun looking for the annexation to San Mateo of territory belonging to Santa Cruz County,[129] and another would have annexed to Santa Clara a portion of Alameda.[130] The boundaries of Amador,[131] Mendocino, [132] and Sonoma[133] were the subjects of other bills; while still

---

[123]*Assembly Journal,* 12th Sess. (1861), 475, 650, 833. *Statutes,* 1861: 560.
[124]*Statutes,* 1861: 221. See below, Sacramento boundaries.
[125]*Ibid.,* 349.
[126]*Ibid.,* 167.
[127]*Assembly Journal,* 12th Sess. (1861), 230.
[128]*Ibid.,* 845.
[129]*Senate Journal,* 136, 137.
[130]*Ibid.,* 167.
[131]*Assembly Journal,* 283.
[132]*Ibid.,* 484, 674, 715.
[133]*Ibid.,* 670, 782, 809, 811.

another would have created a new county to be known as "Tejon."[134] In the northern part of the state there was an agitation for a division of Shasta County. The object appears to have been to set off that part of the county lying east of the Sacramento River into a separate county to be known as "Reading" in honor of P. B. Reading, a pioneer trapper and settler in the region. The stronger agricultural interests in the region seeking to be detached seem to have been the motive for division. Millville was mentioned as the probable county seat.[135]

The legislature in 1862 passed but one act dealing with county boundaries. This was an act which defined but did not change the boundaries of Humboldt County.[136] This lack of boundary legislation was not on account of the absence of the usual number of petitions and bills dealing with the subject, for many projects for new counties and changes in boundaries of old ones were brought before the legislature. Among others "Alturas County" once again made an unsuccessful fight for existence.[137] By another bill a second county east of the Sierras would have been organized under the name of "Coso." This measure received the support of the delegations from Los Angeles, San Bernardino and Tulare but upon the recommendation of the Committee on Counties and County Boundaries was indefinitely postponed.[138] "Chico County" would have been created from the western half of Butte had bills introduced into both houses been passed. The agitation for this division represented two elements: the local rivalry between towns as to the county seat and the difference in economic interests between the agricultural and mining districts. It was argued that the new county would embrace an area of some eight hundred square miles containing five thousand people, leaving Butte County one thousand square miles and nine thousand people. Although the fight was intense the recommendation of the committee was taken and in both houses the bills were indefinitely postponed.[139] Another bill provided

[134]*Assembly Journal*, 12th Sess. (1861), 485.
[135]Sacramento *Union*, March 26, 1861.
[136]*Statutes*, 1862: 6.
[137]*Assembly Journal*, 13th Sess. (1862), 144, 236–9, 248. *Senate Journal*, 321, 378, 445.
[138]*Senate Journal*, 389, 391, 392, 414, 485.
[139]*Assembly Journal*, 13th Sess. (1862), 221, 282–4, 313. *Senate Journal*, 393, 414, 418, 424. Sacramento *Union*, February 10, 17 (8/4) ; March 3 (3/3), 7 (4/4), 9 (4/1), 25 (2/1), 1862.

for the creation of a new county by the division of Sonoma.[140]
This agitation was probably a part of a fight begun the year
before when an unsuccessful attempt was made to remove the
county seat from Santa Rosa to Petaluma.[141]   Because of uncertainty in the act of 1855 defining the boundaries of Napa
County a dispute had arisen between Napa and Solano regarding their common boundary which depended upon the fixing of
the mouth of the Guichica Creek.   By a recent survey the state
Surveyor General had determined this point some three miles
farther south than had earlier surveys, thus apparently adding territory to Napa County at the expense of Solano.   A
bill was introduced to fix this boundary along the line as
earlier observed but the committee was divided in its recommendation and the bill was laid upon the table.[142]

Other bills which did not obtain approval sought to amend
the boundary between Monterey and San Luis Obispo,[143]
Tehama and Shasta[144] and to alter and define the boundaries
of Lake[145] and Sutter.[146]

During the fourteenth session (1863) four boundary acts
became statutes.   The first of these acts more clearly defined
and altered the boundary between Sierra and Plumas.   The
change gave to Sierra a narrow strip of territory along its
northern border.[147]   Two of the acts related to the boundaries
of El Dorado County, one of them giving to Amador that portion of El Dorado lying east of the mountains and drained by
Carson River.[148]   This territory was soon after detached from
Amador as Alpine County.   The other act added to El Dorado's territory at the expense of Placer County.[149]   This legislation resulted from an uncertainty left in earlier acts regarding which branch of the Middle Fork of the American River
should serve as boundary, together with the desire of residents
of the Lake region to be joined to El Dorado.   The fourth act
adjusted once again the Monterey-San Luis Obispo line which
so many times had undergone change.   By this act the boundary was placed upon the sixth standard south of Mount

[140]*Assembly Journal*, 526.
[141]Sacramento *Union*, April 1, 1861 (4/1).
[142]*Assembly Journal*, 381, 444, 445, 481, 698.
[143]*Ibid.*, 332, 351, 393, 615.
[144]*Senate Journal*, 414, 430, 532.
[145]*Ibid.*, 415, 484.
[146]*Ibid.*, 295, 369. *Assembly Journal*, 538.
[147]*Statutes*, 1863: 114.
[148]*Ibid.*, 231.
[149]*Ibid.*, 349.

Diablo, where it has subsequently remained.[150] Two other measures failed of passage. One of them sought to alter and define the boundaries of Tehama County. It was passed by both houses but was not signed by the Governor.[151] The other dealt with the boundaries of Lake County.[152]

Alpine, Lassen and Coso Counties, 1864. During the spring of 1864 three new counties were created, all of them lying east of the Sierras. The first of these was Alpine, formed from portions of El Dorado, Amador, Calaveras, Tuolumne and Mono.[153] The name was doubtless suggested by the mountainous nature of the country. The second of these counties was in the Honey Lake region. The people of this district had long maintained a spirit of independence regarding California and in fact considered and acted in the belief that they were outside the jurisdiction of this state. In 1856 a number of settlers near Honey Lake organized an independent territory called by them Nataqua.[154] The boundaries of this proposed territory included more populous regions farther south and east, whose people had but little, if any, knowledge or interest in ''Nataqua Territory'' so the project was allowed to rest. There was, however, strong opposition on the part of a portion of the Honey Lake settlers to any supervision by Plumas County, created by the California legislature in 1856, with the result that when the supervisors of that county took steps to provide for the administration of that part of the county they met resistance.[155] Upon the creation in 1861 of Nevada territory which claimed as its western boundary the summit of the Sierras this territory was organized as a part of Roop County (Nevada). This action brought on a clash with the officials of Plumas County, which became known as the Sage Brush or Border Line War. After a resort to arms and some bloodshed an agreement was reached to appeal to the governments of California and Nevada to have the boundary line determined by a joint survey.[156]

---

[150]*Statutes*, 1863 : 358.
[151]*Assembly Journal*, 14th Sess. (1863), 429, 475, 623.
[152]*Ibid.*, 479.
[153]*Assembly Journal*, 15th Sess. (1863-64), 230, 383, 394, 536. *Statutes*, 1863-4 : 178.
[154]Fairchild, *Lassen County*, 46-50.
[155]*Ibid.*, 78-82. At other times, however, they appealed to Governor Johnson of California for protection from Indians. *Ibid.*, 86-7.
[156]*Ibid.*, 311-324.

This survey showed Honey Lake to lie well within the boundary of California and therefore within Plumas County. The feelings of the Honey Lake people were however to be considered and since the district was claimed to contain a thousand people the legislature was induced to pass an act creating the county of Lassen from that portion of Plumas lying east of the summit of the mountains to which was also added the eastern half of Shasta.[157] The name was taken from that of Peter Lassen, a pioneer who was one of the first to open an emigrant route through the region and whose grave is within its borders.

Another act passed and approved by the Governor created a third new county to be known as "Coso County." This county was to be formed from portions of Tulare and Mono counties. Coso County lay east of the Sierras and owed its rise to importance to the mining development in that region. The act defined the boundaries of Coso County as follows:[158]

> "Commencing at the point where the southern boundary line of Tulare County is intersected by the eastern boundary line of the State of California, and running in a westerly direction along said county boundary line to the summit of the Sierra Nevada Mountains; thence in a northerly direction along said summit, to the head waters of Big Pine Creek; thence in an easterly direction down the middle of the channel of said Big Pine Creek, to its mouth; thence due east to the state line; thence in a southerly direction along the state boundary line, to the place of beginning."

The seat of justice was to be at Bend City.

Other acts related to the boundaries of Lake and Sutter counties. In the case of Lake a considerable portion of territory on the headwaters of Eel River was added to it from Mendocino and a slight change was also made in the southern boundary.[159] The act defining Sutter's boundaries described them more precisely in terms of the United States surveys but did not materially change the position of the lines.[160]

---

[157]*Assembly Journal,* 15th Sess. (1863-4), 388, 430, 551, 677. *Statutes,* 1863-4: 264.
[158]*Statutes,* 1863-4: 528.
[159]*Ibid.,* 111.
[160]*Ibid.,* 301.

Other measures sought to clear up difficulties in existing boundary lines. An act was passed authorizing and requiring the supervisors of San Joaquin and Calaveras to survey and mark the line between those two counties,[161] while bills which failed to become statutes aimed to define the boundaries of Sacramento County,[162] the boundary between Los Angeles and Santa Barbara,[163] and that between Monterey on the west and Merced and Stanislaus on the east.[164]

Inyo and Kern Counties, 1866. During the session of 1865–66 acts were passed which resulted in the organization of two counties each of which had been created by previous statutes under other names but neither had been organized. The first of these was Inyo. As early as 1862 the project for the formation of a county near Owens Lake east of the Sierras had been brought before the legislature, the name "Coso" being given to the proposed county. Two years later the agitation had been successful in so far as the legislature was concerned and "Coso County" was created.[165] For some reason, the organization was never completed so in 1866 the matter was again presented and an act passed creating it as Inyo County. This new county included that part of Tulare lying east of the Sierras together with a portion of Mono County. The name is of Indian origin, but its meaning is uncertain.

In a similar manner Kern County was created. This county had previously been authorized by statute embracing practically this same territory but designated in the act as "Buena Vista County." Although the terms of the earlier act were such that they could not be met and "Buena Vista County" remained unorganized, newspaper references and even official reports refer to this district under that name.[166] By the act of 1866 a new county was created outright, the name being changed to that of Kern, a pioneer explorer who accompanied Fremont and for whom Kern River was named. The impetus for the creation of the county was a combination of both mining and agricultural interests, the predominance

---

[161]*Statutes*, 1863–4: 262.
[162]*Senate Journal*, 15th Sess. (1863–4), 278, 308.
[163]*Assembly Journal*, 565, 584, 667, 689.
[164]*Senate Journal*, 266, 308.
[165]*Ante*, 28.
[166]*Statutes*, 1855: 203–5; 1856: 96; 1858: 36.

of the mining interests being seen in the fact of the location of the county seat at Havilah, a mining center.[167]

Several other acts were passed in 1866 altering and defining county boundaries. In the case of Sierra two changes were made. By the first Sierra gained from Yuba County a small piece of territory lying between the north fork of the Yuba River and Cañon Creek;[168] by the other act she lost a more valuable piece of territory at her northwest corner which was given to Plumas.[169] This was a portion of the district which for a number of years had been trying to secede from Sierra and with parts of other counties would have formed the proposed county of "Summit" or "Alturas." This act therefore gave to Plumas a portion of the Slate Creek Valley. Another act conferred upon the board of supervisors of Merced County certain powers which upon examination are found to be the authorization to have surveyed the boundaries between that county and Stanislaus in a manner which added materially to Merced County, the line being made to run directly across the valley much farther north than the previous line.[170] Acts were also passed more clearly defining the boundaries of Mono,[171] Placer,[172] Yolo,[173] and Lassen.[174]

Granite or Natoma County Proposed, 1866. As in previous sessions several bills dealing with county boundaries failed of passage. Probably the most ambitious of these was a bill which would have created a new county to be called "Granite" from territory taken from Sacramento together with portions from El Dorado and Placer.[175] The boundaries of the proposed county were described in the bill as follows:[176]

"Commencing at the northeast corner of fractional section 4, in township 10 north, range 6 east, Monte Diablo base and meridian; thence running on and along the sectional line directly south to Dry Creek (in Dry Creek township), County of Sacramento; thence on and along

---

[167]*Statutes*, 1865-6: 796. The name Havilah is derived from the biblical reference to Havilah as the city of gold.
[168]*Ibid.*, 228.
[169]*Ibid.*, 605.
[170]*Statutes*, 1865-66: 172. *Assembly Journal*, 16th Sess. (1865-66), 373, 386, 397, 441. *Senate Journal*, 353, 356.
[171]*Statutes*, 1865-66: 144.
[172]*Ibid.*, 223.
[173]*Ibid.*, 162.
[174]*Ibid.*, 453.
[175]*Assembly Journal*, 16th Sess. (1865-66), 535.
[176]Sacramento *Union*, March 13, 1866 (1/7).

the county line of Sacramento County in a southeast
direction to the county line of Amador and El Dorado
counties; thence in a northwesterly direction to the Consumnes River at Michigan Bar; thence in a northerly
direction up said river five miles; thence northwesterly in
a direct line to the east side of the Natoma Ditch and
Water Company's dam, on the south fork of the American
River, about two and a half miles north of Salmon Falls,
in El Dorado County; thence down the center of said
river to the second standard line north, Monte Diablo
base and meridian; thence along the second standard line
to the place of beginning.''

When reported back from the Committee on Counties and
County Boundaries a substitute bill was submitted limiting
the territory to that within the limits of Sacramento County
and giving it the name ''Natoma,'' an Indian word meaning
''sparkling water.''[177]   The Sacramento delegation were, with
one exception, strongly opposed to the bill. The substitute
measure was for a time accepted but the bill was finally
defeated.[178]   Other bills were introduced dealing with the
Fresno-Mariposa boundary,[179] the Marin-Sonoma line,[180] the
boundary between Butte and Colusa;[181] as well as one to alter
and define the boundary of San Mateo County.[182]

Five other county boundary acts were passed during the
seventeenth session (1868) of the legislature. Two of them
made noticeable changes in boundaries. One materially
increased the area of San Mateo by adding new territory at the
expense of Santa Cruz.[183]   Another redefined the boundaries of
Lake County so as to include within its borders Long Valley,
the watershed of one of the branches of Cache Creek.[184]   Two
other acts modified or repealed legislation passed at the previous session. In the case of the Plumas-Sierra boundary the
latter was again given a portion of the territory taken from it
in 1866, the boundary being placed along Slate Creek.[185]
Another act repealed, in so far as it concerned Stanislaus, the

---

[177]Sacramento *Union,* March 23, 1866 (1/6).
[178]*Ibid.,* March 24, 1866 (1/6). *Assembly Journal,* 16th Sess. (1865-6),
621, 644, 655, 662.
[179]*Assembly Journal,* 654.
[180]*Ibid.,* 566.
[181]*Senate Journal,* 164, 430, 492.
[182]*Assembly Journal,* 327.
[183]*Statutes,* 1867-68: 174.
[184]*Ibid.,* 269.
[185]*Ibid.,* 462.

act passed in 1866 affecting the boundaries of Merced.[186]   The fifth act redefined the northern boundary of San Diego.[187]

Other proposed measures were not successful. One bill introduced by Roberts of Nevada County sought the creation of a new county to be known as "Alta County." This bill failed to secure the approval of the Committee on Counties and County Boundaries.[188]   Butte[189] and Alpine[190] each unsuccessfully sought to amend recent legislation dealing with their boundaries. Likewise an attempt to change the Santa Barbara-San Luis Obispo line failed of passage[191] as did also legislation relating to Kern[192] and Marin.[193]

No important boundary acts were passed by the legislature at its eighteenth session. One act enlarged Inyo at the expense of Mono giving to the former a strip of territory some twenty miles wide running across the county.[194]   By another act the Mariposa-Fresno line was changed from a direct course to a line along the summit of the divide between the Merced and San Joaquin rivers.[195]   Another act redefined the boundaries of Sacramento County without change except as was made necessary by the changing channels of the Sacramento River and its sloughs. Sutter Slough appears for the first time in describing the western boundary of Sacramento County.[196]

New Counties Proposed, 1870.   No less than six prospective counties presented claims to the legislature at its eighteenth session showing why they should be created. The list includes Anaheim, Donner, Orestimba, Summit, San Benito and Ventura. "Anaheim County" was to be created from the southern and eastern portion of Los Angeles County. The measure passed the assembly but the senate felt that it was somewhat premature and furthermore that because of the drought of that year in Southern California the measure might well be laid over until a later session.[197]

---

[186]Statutes, 1867–68 : 56.
[187]Ibid., 604.
[188]Senate Journal, 17th Sess. (1867-8), 303, 424.
[189]Assembly Journal, 17th Sess. (1867-8), 451, 995 ; 241, 395.
[190]Ibid., 480, 687.
[191]Senate Journal, 245, 657, 698.
[192]Ibid., 237, 247, 324.   Assembly Journal, 366.
[193]Senate Journal, 194, 286, 627, 753.
[194]Statutes, 1869-70 : 20, 421.
[195]Ibid., 449.
[196]Ibid., 294.
[197]Assembly Journal, 18th Sess. (1869-70), 316, 445, 481.   Senate Journal, 585.   This was the beginning of the agitation resulting in the formation of Orange County.

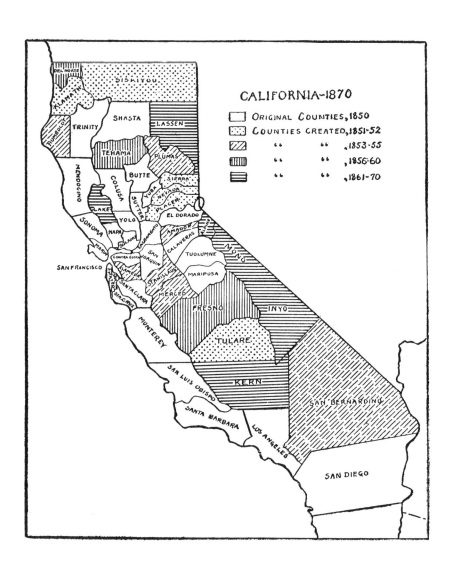

CALIFORNIA–1870

☐ ORIGINAL COUNTIES, 1850
▨ COUNTIES CREATED, 1851-52
▨ " " , 1853-55
▨ " " , 1856-60
▤ " " , 1861-70

DEL NORTE
SISKIYOU
KLAMATH
HUMBOLDT
TRINITY
SHASTA
LASSEN
MENDOCINO
TEHAMA
PLUMAS
BUTTE
COLUSA
SIERRA
YUBA
NEVADA
SUTTER
PLACER
LAKE
YOLO
EL DORADO
SONOMA
NAPA
AMADOR
CALAVERAS
MONO
MARIN
SACRAMENTO
SAN JOAQUIN
TUOLUMNE
CONTRA COSTA
SAN FRANCISCO
ALAMEDA
STANISLAUS
MARIPOSA
SANTA CLARA
MERCED
SANTA CRUZ
FRESNO
INYO
MONTEREY
TULARE
SAN LUIS OBISPO
KERN
SANTA BARBARA
SAN BERNARDINO
LOS ANGELES
SAN DIEGO

"Donner County" was urged by the people of the trans-mountain district of Sierra, Nevada, and Placer. It was claimed to have an area of three hundred and fifty square miles and ample population and resources for a separate county. According to the bill the boundaries of the proposed county were to run as follows:[198]

> "Commencing at the northeast corner of Alpine County, on the state line; thence north along the state line to 40 degrees north latitude; thence west along the fortieth parallel to a point due north of the west boundary of Sierra and Beckwourth valleys, in Plumas County; thence southerly to the Nevada County line; thence west along the Nevada County line to the northeast corner of Eureka township; thence southerly along the line of Eureka and Washington townships to the Placer County line; thence southeast to the El Dorado County line, where the same crosses the summit of the Sierra Nevada; thence along the summit to the north boundary of Alpine County; thence easterly along the north line of Alpine County to the place of beginning."

The opposition of the delegations from counties whose territory would be diminished by the bill resulted in its defeat.[199]

The development of the San Joaquin Valley led to the agitation for a new county to be created out of that portion of Stanislaus and Merced counties lying west of the rivers which during the season of high water formed a barrier between the people of this district and their county seats. Two names were proposed for the new county, "Jefferson"[200] and "Orestimba," the latter being that of an old Mexican grant in the region. Hills Ferry across from the mouth of the Merced River aspired to be the county seat. The senate gave its approval to the measure but it was blocked in the assembly.[201]

The agitation for "Summit" County was the beginning of a movement which four years later resulted in the formation of Modoc County from the eastern half of Siskiyou. The measure, introduced by Senator Irwin of Siskiyou, failed to pass

---

[198]Sacramento *Union*, December 15 (1/7), 16 (2/2), 1869; January 21 (1/6), 1870.

[199]*Assembly Journal*, 18th Sess. (1869-70), 247, 404.

[200]Sacramento *Union*, January 28, 1870 (2/3).

[201]*Senate Journal*, 18th Sess. (1869-70), 611, 650, 717. *Assembly Journal*, 839, 846.

the senate in 1870.[202]   Two other propositions relating to the creation of San Benito[203] and Ventura[204] counties to be created from portions of Monterey and Santa Barbara counties respectively succeeded in winning approval in the assembly, but were refused passage in the senate.

Codification of Boundary Legislation, 1872. The nineteenth session of the legislature was of greater importance than usual because at that time the various laws upon the statute books were brought together under subject headings and arranged into codes. One part of the Political Code was devoted to county boundaries. This codification comprised one comprehensive act whereby all the county boundaries were by it redefined in full, the first act of this character since 1851. Although it was the purpose of the code commission to bring into harmony and juxtaposition existing laws rather than to alter county boundaries, there were made several unimportant changes as well as one or two of greater significance. Most of the changes arose from the attempt to define the boundaries more clearly. Such changes were made in the boundaries between Butte and Colusa, Del Norte and Siskiyou, Placer and Sutter, Plumas and Shasta, San Diego and San Bernardino and between Santa Barbara and San Luis Obispo. A more important change was that affecting the southern boundary of Tulare and Inyo. This was placed upon the sixth standard south of Mount Diablo, thus drawing across the state a direct line which still forms the northern boundary of San Luis Obispo, Kern and San Bernardino counties. By this act Inyo gained a large area of desert which had formerly been a part of San Bernardino. Another change of even greater importance was made in the western boundary of Los Angeles. This line had formerly run from the summit of the Santa Susana Hills to the northwest corner of the Castac Rancho subsequently detached by the organization of Kern County. By the code in 1872 the line was made to run to the southwest corner of Kern County which elsewhere is defined as the point where the south line of Kern reaches the summit of the coast range of mountains. This then moved the northwest corner

---

[202]*Senate Journal* 18th Sess. (1869-70), 453, 739. This should not be confused with the agitation for a "Summit" county from western Sierra.
[203]*Assembly Journal*, 222, 386, 432. *Senate Journal*, 633.
[204]*Assembly Journal*, 461, 587, 604.

of Los Angeles County some sixteen miles farther west giving to Los Angeles a large area of mountainous land formerly belonging to Santa Barbara County.[205]

Ventura and Other Changes, 1872. The code was to be considered as having preceded all other legislation of that session and therefore was to be superseded by any other acts passed during the session. There were six such special acts dealing with county boundaries passed during the session; the most important of these created a new county from the eastern part of Santa Barbara and assigned to it the name of "Ventura" from that of its chief town and the Mission San Buenaventura.[206] By another act the boundaries of Lake County were redefined and changed, Knox township on the south being reannexed to Napa.[207] At the previous session the Mariposa-Fresno line had been modified giving to the former county the Merced watershed. By act of this session this was again changed to approximately its former position with the exception that the Mariposa Big Tree grant was left with Mariposa.[208] Other acts were passed seeking to make definite the location of the Siskiyou-Lassen line[209] and to provide for the actual survey of the lines between Mendocino and Humboldt, Trinity and Klamath[210] and the boundary between Lake and Yolo.[211]

Measures were again introduced calling for the formation of "Donner"[212] and "San Benito"[213] counties but they failed of passage as did bills relating to the boundaries between Inyo and Mono,[214] and Sacramento and Yolo counties.[215] A petition from citizens of eastern Siskiyou asking for a new county to be created from portions of Siskiyou, Lassen and Shasta to be called "Surprise County" was presented but no action taken.[216]

---

[205]For full discussion of this see Los Angeles County boundary. The Los Angeles authorities never took advantage of the annexation of this territory.
[206]*Statutes*, 1871-72: 484. *Assembly Journal*, 19th Sess. (1871-72), 294, 418, 632.
[207]*Statutes*, 305.
[208]*Ibid.*, 891.
[209]*Ibid.*, 886.
[210]*Ibid.*, 766.
[211]*Ibid.*, 903.
[212]*Assembly Journal*, 19th Sess. (1871-72), 315, 418, 650, 744.
[213]*Ibid.*, 154, 345. *Senate Journal*, 479, 557.
[214]*Senate Journal*, 19th Sess. (1871-72), 404, 418, 478.
[215]*Assembly Journal*, 359, 625, 796, 825.
[216]Sacramento *Union*, February 2, 1872 (3/3).

Klamath Abolished; Modoc and San Benito Created, 1874.

The twentieth session of the legislature abolished one county, Klamath, and created two new counties, Modoc and San Benito, besides passing measures modifying the boundaries of several others.

Klamath County had been created in 1851 because of the interest in mining upon the Klamath, Salmon, and Trinity rivers. Originally large in territory it had been reduced in size by annexations to Siskiyou, Trinity, and Del Norte until there was but little left besides rugged mountains whose diminishing mineral wealth formed the main support of its population. Miners were a shifting class of residents and mining property difficult to assess, the result therefore was that Klamath's indebtedness rose while its assessed valuation declined. In view of this situation the legislature in 1874 passed an act authorizing the dissolution of Klamath and annexation of portions of it to Humboldt and Siskiyou counties respectively. The act provided that the issue should be submitted to the vote of the people of the counties concerned and that if a favorable result was obtained the dissolution should be completed.[217]

The creation of San Benito County, which had been agitated for some time was finally authorized by an act of this session, the territory for the new county being taken from Monterey.[218] In like manner Modoc was created from the eastern portion of Siskiyou. The measure as at first drawn sought to create a new county known as "Canby" from portions of Siskiyou and Lassen. Since it proposed to include a considerable part of the population and wealth of the latter county the measure met strong opposition.[219] Recognizing the inability to carry the measure in that form a further bill was introduced calling for the division of Siskiyou County, the detached portion to be organized as "Summit County." Since this bill eliminated the objectional features of the previous measure it was approved by the committee and passed the assembly. In the assembly the bill was also approved with an amendment substituting the name "Modoc" for "Summit." In this form it

---

[217]Statutes, 1873-74: 755. Senate Journal, 20th Sess. (1873-74), 743.
[218]Statutes, 1873-74: 95. Assembly Journal, 20th Sess. (1873-74), 368, 418, 463, 550, 611. Senate Journal, 367.
[219]Assembly Journal, 361, 439. Sacramento Union, January 23, 1874.

secured the Governor's approval and thus became a law.[220]
Several modifications in boundaries were made at this session;
none, however, were of great significance. Fresno County's
boundaries both on the north and south were again defined,
the former was merely a reënactment of a bill passed in 1872
while the latter placed the Fresno-Tulare boundary along
township and section lines rather than along the mountain
ridge as theretofore.[221] The northern line of Sierra was also
placed upon township and section lines without noticeable
change in location.[222] In the case of Alameda County a
change was made necessary in order to prevent the long wharf
recently erected by the Central Pacific Railroad Company
from being intersected by the county boundary. By a statute
the western boundary of Alameda County was made to run
five hundred feet west of the wharf mentioned.[223]

Many other measures were considered but failed of passage.
One of these which secured the support of both houses would
have formed a new county named "Vallejo" by a division of
Solano County. Since it failed to secure the Governor's signa-
ture it did not become a law.[224] Bills to create a new county
named "Orange" were introduced into both the senate and
assembly but on account of opposition were indefinitely postponed by each house.[225] A senate bill proposed the organization of a new county to be called "Manache" by subdividing
Tulare County, but the measure was opposed by committee.[226]
Another bill introduced pending the outcome of the measure
creating San Benito County sought to annex to Santa Cruz a
portion of Monterey County,[227] but this bill as well as others
relating to the Shasta-Tehama[228] and Nevada-Placer[229] boundaries failed of passage.

Twenty-First Session, 1875-76. At its twenty-first session
the legislature passed but one act changing the boundaries of

[220]*Assembly Journal,* 462, 467, 528, 612, 656. *Senate Journal,* 436. *Statutes,*
1873-74: 124.
[221]*Statutes,* 1873-74: 700.
[222]*Code Amendments,* 1873-74: 166.
[223]*Ibid.,* 168.
[224]*Senate Journal,* 20th Sess. (1873-74), 459, 495, 599, 607-10, 653, 759.
Assembly Journal, 1040.
[225]*Senate Journal,* 665, 763. *Assembly Journal,* 646, 818. See *ante,* 33,
for agitation favoring Anaheim County in 1870.
[226]*Senate Journal,* 381, 522. Sacramento *Union,* February 3, 1874 (1/6).
[227]*Assembly Journal,* 727, 818.
[228]*Ibid.,* 350, 547.
[229]*Ibid.,* 463, 1197.

the counties. This act referred to the line between Fresno and Tulare counties and was but a small change from the boundary adopted at the previous session. This new line returned to Fresno some five square townships and has remained the boundary between the two counties since that date.[230] Two other measures amended acts relating to the creation of San Benito County[231] and the abolition of Klamath County[232] but did not affect these boundaries. Other bills seeking to amend the boundaries of Alameda[233] and to establish more clearly the Santa Clara-Santa Cruz line[234] failed of passage.

Twenty-Second Session, 1877-78. In 1878 two acts relating to county boundaries were passed. The first of these referred to the southern boundary of Sacramento County and was necessitated by the changes in the channel of the Mokelumne River which since 1850 had cut a new channel and hence required a change in the law if the main channel were to be accepted as the line between San Joaquin and Sacramento counties. By this act the western branch of the river was defined as the boundary.[235] The other act made a slight change in the San Mateo-Alameda line by providing that the boundary follow the ship channel in the bay from the initial point to a position opposite Dumbarton Point.[236]

Two new counties sought to be created. The first of these was "Purisima." This proposed county was to be formed from the northern portion of Santa Barbara and would contain about eleven hundred square miles with a population of four thousand. Lompoc was the chief center of population.[237] The other proposed county was to be formed by dividing Butte, the new county to be called "Chico." The fight was vigorous between the friends of the proposed county and the defenders of the old one, and many disputed statistics were presented on each side. The fight seems to have been primarily the old feud between Chico and Oroville which was

---

[230]*Statutes*, 1875–76 : 397.
[231]*Ibid.*, 177.
[232]*Ibid.*, 603.
[233]*Assembly Journal*, 21st Sess. (1875–76), 307, 351. *Senate Journal*, 479.
[234]*Assembly Journal*, 378, 483.
[235]*Political Code* (1877–78), 3928.
[236]*Ibid.*, 3951.
[237]*Assembly Journal*, 22nd Sess. (1877–78), 201, 455. Sacramento *Union*, January 14, 1878 (1/7).

increased by the growing difference in interests between the agricultural and mining elements represented by each of these centers. The bill failed to pass the assembly.[238] Likewise two other measures dealing with the Los Angeles-San Bernardino line[239] and the boundaries of San Luis Obispo[240] failed of passage.

Twenty-Third to Twenty-Fifth Sessions. The three sessions of the legislature from 1880 to 1883, inclusive, passed no acts relating to county boundaries. In the twenty-third session several measures were considered; one dealing with the boundary of San Joaquin,[241] one with the definition of the western boundary of Lake County[242] and another authorizing the survey of the boundary of Calaveras and Alpine counties,[243] but none received the support of the committees to whom they were referred.

During the twenty-fourth session (1881) four measures were under consideration. One of these resulted from a revival of the agitation for the creation of "Orange" County,[244] another from a petition signed by residents in northern San Diego County who asked that they be annexed to San Bernardino, doubtless the beginning of the movement later resulting in the formation of Riverside County.[245] The two other bills related to the boundaries of Sacramento County[246] and to a change in the Calaveras-San Joaquin boundary.[247]

During the twenty-fifth session a number of county boundary measures were introduced, among them a general bill providing for the formation of new counties.[248] None, however, were passed. As during previous sessions, new counties clamored for recognition. The formation of "Orange County" was the subject of many petitions and protests but no action was taken.[249] "Los Alamos County" presented

[238]*Assembly Journal*, 255, 310. Sacramento *Union*, January 25, 1878 (1/5); February 5 (3/4); February 6 (1/6); February 14 (1/5), 1878.
[239]*Senate Journal*, 423.
[240]*Assembly Journal*, 519, 760.
[241]*Senate Journal*, 23rd Sess. (1880), 557, 666.
[242]*Assembly Journal*, 158, 709.
[243]*Ibid.*, 106, 227.
[244]*Senate Journal*, 24th Sess. (1881), 265. *Assembly Journal*, 115, 256.
[245]*Assembly Journal*, 49, 176.
[246]*Senate Journal*, 33, 68.
[247]*Ibid.*, 273. *Assembly Journal*, 309.
[248]*Assembly Journal*, 25th Sess. (1883), 203, 348, 550. *Senate Journal*, 85, 379.
[249]*Assembly Journal*, 25th Sess. (1883), 22, 105, 112, 112, 154, 173.

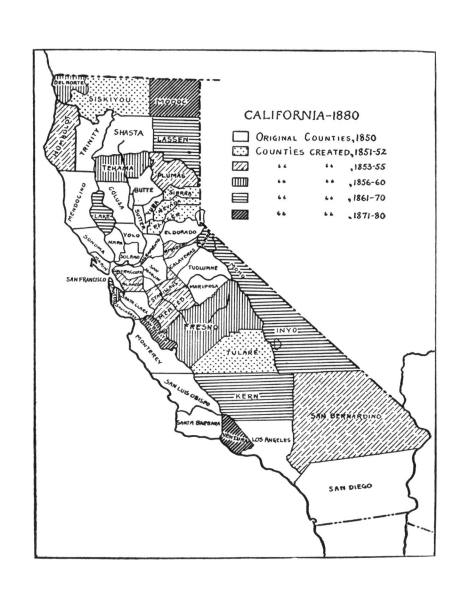

CALIFORNIA-1880

☐ ORIGINAL COUNTIES, 1850
▦ COUNTIES CREATED, 1851-52
▨ " " , 1853-55
▥ " " , 1856-60
▤ " " , 1861-70
▧ " " , 1871-80

DEL NORTE
SISKIYOU
MODOC
HUMBOLDT
TRINITY
SHASTA
LASSEN
TEHAMA
PLUMAS
MENDOCINO
COLUSA
BUTTE
SIERRA
YUBA
NEVADA
SUTTER
LAKE
PLACER
NAPA
YOLO
EL DORADO
SONOMA
SOLANO
AMADOR
MARIN
SACRAMENTO
SAN JOAQUIN
CALAVERAS
SAN FRANCISCO
CONTRA COSTA
ALAMEDA
STANISLAUS
TUOLUMNE
MONO
SANTA CLARA
MARIPOSA
SANTA CRUZ
MERCED
FRESNO
MONTEREY
INYO
TULARE
SAN LUIS OBISPO
KERN
SANTA BARBARA
SAN BERNARDINO
VENTURA
LOS ANGELES
SAN DIEGO

its claims for organization out of northern Santa Barbara, but because of the general bill then pending the committee refused to give it favorable consideration.[250] Bills modifying the boundaries of Merced[251] as well as the El Dorado-Amador[252] and Siskiyou-Del Norte[253] boundaries also failed of passage.

Twenty-Sixth Session. But one change in county boundaries was made by the legislature during its twenty-sixth session and that was of little significance. Since the act of 1850 the boundary between San Luis Obispo and the counties to the east had run along the summit of the coast range. In keeping with the general trend of legislation this was now modified and described by means of United States township and section lines.[254] Other measures less successful related to changes in the boundaries of San Benito[255] and Lake counties.[256] Three new counties sought recognition without success. These were "Orange,"[257] "Los Alamos" from a portion of Santa Barbara[258] and one to be set off from San Bernardino County.[259] Another attempt to pass a general act providing for the formation of new counties was also unsuccessful.[260]

Del Norte and San Benito, 1887. Two acts of some importance relating to county boundaries were passed by the legislature in 1887. One of these transferred from Del Norte to Siskiyou all the territory held by the former along the upper waters of the Klamath River.[261] The other act considerably increased the area of San Benito County by adding to it portions of Fresno and Merced counties.[262]

In addition to these changes three new counties sought organization. These were "Glenn," "San Leandro," and "Lorraine." The bill for the creation of "Glenn County"

[250]*Assembly Journal*, 25th Sess. (1883), 209, 440. *Senate Journal*, 81.
[251]*Assembly Journal*, 50.
[252]*Ibid.*, 106, 329, 650, 656.
[253]*Ibid.*, 241, 277, 650.
[254]*Statutes*. 1885 : 139.
[255]*Senate Journal*, 26th Sess. (1885), 121, 306, 478.
[256]*Assembly Journal*, 15, 152, 219. *Senate Journal*, 267, 342.
[257]*Assembly Journal*, 26th Sess. (1885), 184, 255, 463. *Senate Journal*. 478.
[258]*Assembly Journal*, 254, 266, 388, 450. *Senate Journal*, 228, 548.
[259]*Assembly Journal*, 340.
[260]*Ibid.*, 16, 91, 133. *Senate Journal*, 119, 478.
[261]*Statutes*. 1887 : 106.
[262]*Ibid.*, 103.

from the northern portion of Colusa was presented early in the session and secured the approval of the assembly but did not pass the senate.[263] The bill for the creation of "Lorraine" was introduced by Assemblyman Butler of Tulare who later withdrew it.[264] Bills for the creation of "San Leandro County" from a portion of Alameda were introduced into both houses but failed to secure favorable action in either.[265]

Orange County, 1889. After a fight lasting nearly twenty years the people residing in the southeastern part of Los Angeles County were given their own county government under the name of Orange County. This was the first new county to be created during a period of fifteen years, notwithstanding urgent petitions and other efforts to secure county organizations. As early as 1870 the movement for the organization of such a county under the name of "Anaheim" had begun, and had continued more or less persistently under the name of "Santa Ana" or "Orange" until its creation under the latter name in 1889.[266]

By another act a slight verbal change was made in the description of the boundaries of Placer County but no noticeable change was made in the location of its boundaries.[267]

Three other districts sought the formation of new counties but with not great success. Bills to create "Glenn County" were introduced into both houses and the assembly bill received the approval of both bodies but was not approved by the Governor.[268] Other bills would have created "Pomona County" from a portion of San Bernardino County. Many protests against the formation of the county were filed with the result that no legislation resulted.[269] "Natoma County" was another seeking organization. This would have embraced territory taken from eastern Sacramento, western El Dorado and a portion of Placer County and was important because of its rising fruit industry.[270]

---

[263]*Assembly Journal*, 27th Sess. (1887), 79, 227, 230, 372. *Senate Journal*, 75, 276.
[264]*Assembly Journal*, 204, 334.
[265]*Senate Journal*, 254, 290. *Assembly Journal*, 329, 503.
[266]*Statutes*, 1889 : 123. *Assembly Journal*, 28th Sess. (1889), 45, 111, 134, 173, 235, 264, 304, 356. *Senate Journal*, 169, 304, 406, 540, 572, 623, 825.
[267]*Statutes*, 1889 : 402.
[268]*Assembly Journal*, 40, 81, 210. *Senate Journal*, 157, 440, 833, 839, 840.
[269]*Assembly Journal*, 181, 331, 305, 458. *Senate Journal*, 197, 623.
[270]*Assembly Journal*, 149, 305. Sacramento *Union*, February 4, 1889 (3/1).

Still other bills which failed of passage referred to changes in the boundaries of Butte,[271] Del Norte and Siskiyou;[272] while one sought to annex to Amador a portion of El Dorado.[273]

Glenn County Created, 1891. In 1891 the efforts to create Glenn County came to fruition when the legislature passed an act dividing Colusa into two parts, the northern portion to be known as "Glenn County."[274] An effort to create another new county in Southern California was unsuccessful because of a difference of opinion among the proponents of county division. A bill to create "Pomona County"[275] was introduced early in the session but it was soon followed by bills proposing the formation of "San Jacinto"[276] and "Riverside" counties.[277] The San Jacinto bill passed the assembly by a large vote but failed in the senate, while the latter was supported in the senate but failed in the assembly. Other measures attempted changes in the Colusa-Butte boundary,[278] the Tulare-Fresno[279] line and in the boundaries of Sutter County.[280]

Madera, Kings and Riverside. 1893. The thirtieth session of the legislature is one to be remembered because of its readiness to create new counties. At this session bills were proposed which if passed would have created no less than a dozen different new counties. As it was three of these counties were authorized, namely Madera,[281] from Fresno County; Kings,[282] from Tulare; and Riverside[283] from San Diego and San Bernardino. One further act was passed amending the southern boundary of Glenn, whereby the town of Princeton was returned to Colusa County.[284]

The other proposed measures were in some cases clearly related to the counties actually created. For example the movement for Riverside was doubtless a part of the same agitation which manifested itself both in the demand for the

---

[271]*Assembly Journal*, 28th Sess. (1889), 150, 283. *Senate Journal*, 310, 623.
[272]*Assembly Journal*, 71, 248.
[273]*Ibid.*, 39, 151. *Senate Journal*, 36.
[274]*Statutes*, 1891 : 98. *Assembly Journal*, 29th Sess. (1891), 71, 307, 489. *Senate Journal*, 67, 274, 518–9.
[275]*Assembly Journal*, 37, 307. *Senate Journal*, 43, 224, 274.
[276]*Assembly Journal*, 123, 307, 490. *Senate Journal*, 143, 274.
[277]*Assembly Journal*, 246, 307. *Senate Journal*, 195, 274, 653.
[278]*Assembly Journal*, 297, 432.
[279]*Senate Journal*, 58.
[280]*Assembly Journal*, 87, 432, 957. *Senate Journal*, 45, 352, 866.
[281]*Statutes*, 1893 : 168.
[282]*Ibid.*, 176.
[283]*Ibid.*, 159.
[284]*Ibid.*, 158.

creation of "San Antonio County" from the eastern portion
of Los Angeles County with Pomona as county seat,[285] and
in that for the creation of "San Jacinto"[286] and "Escon-
dido"[287] counties. A further bill sought merely to define more
clearly the northern boundary of San Diego and the southern
boundary of San Bernardino counties.[288]

In the lower San Joaquin Valley "Kings County" was
created, but closely associated with this demand was that for
three other counties, namely "Putnam,"[289] from Tulare, with
Porterville as the center; "Buena Vista"[290] also from Tulare
with Tulare city as a prospective county seat; and also "Tehachapi County."[291] The demand for a new county in the
northern Santa Barbara region was again manifest in the agitation for "Santa Ynez"[292] and "Santa Rita"[293] counties.

In northern California Butte County alone experienced the
epidemic for county division. From there the divisionists
once again urged the formation of a new county to be named
"Bidwell,"[294] after the pioneer settler of the district. Two
other bills relating to boundaries were introduced but not
approved. These concerned the boundaries of Del Norte[295]
and the line between Sacramento and Yolo.[296] Four separate
bills were introduced providing for a general law to deal with
the question of new counties. None of these were approved
by the committee.[297]

Constitutional Amendment, 1894. In reaction from the
demand which swept the legislature into creating so many

[285]*Assembly Journal*, 30th Sess. (1893), 87, 335, 336, 747. *Senate Journal*,
77. Sacramento *Union*, March 9, 1893 (5/3).
[286]*Assembly Journal*, 185, 336. *Senate Journal*, 90.
[287]*Assembly Journal*, 87.
[288]*Ibid.*, 586.
[289]*Ibid.*, 41, 337. *Senate Journal*, 62, 282. Sacramento *Union*, January
12, 1893 (5/1).
[290]*Assembly Journal*, 41, 336. *Senate Journal*, 63, 282. Sacramento
Union, January 12, 1893 (5/1).
[291]*Assembly Journal*, 503.
[292]*Ibid.*, 142, 210, 217, 229, 266, 327, 342, 391, 436, 797. *Senate Journal*,
166, 417, 518. Sacramento *Union*, February 10, March 10, 1893 (5/7).
[293]*Assembly Journal*, 213, 399. *Senate Journal*, 194, 313, 399, 417.
[294]*Assembly Journal*, 132, 294, 306, 356. *Senate Journal*, 116, 299, 309
337. Sacramento *Union*, January 17, 1893 (1/6).
[295]*Assembly Journal*, 60.
[296]*Ibid.*, 104, 416. *Senate Journal*, 241, 472.
[297]*Assembly Journal*, 41, 179, 212. *Senate Journal*, 120, 235.

new counties in 1893 an amendment was proposed to the state
constitution (Art. XI, Sec. 3) the text of which is as follows:

"Sec. 3. The legislature, by general and uniform laws,
may provide for the formation of new counties; *provided,
however,* that no new county shall be established which
shall reduce any county to a population of less than eight
thousand; nor shall a new county be formed containing a
less population of less than five thousand; nor shall any
line thereof pass within five miles of the county seat of
any county proposed to be divided. Every county which
shall be enlarged or created from territory taken from
any other county or counties, shall be liable for a just
proportion of the existing debt and liabilities of the
county or counties from which such territory shall be
taken."

This was submitted to referendum and adopted by the
people November 6, 1894. Thus was the legislature deprived
of the right of creating new counties by special acts as had
been done in each case before that date.

Although the constitutional amendment of 1894 did not
restrict the power of the legislature in altering county boundaries, practically no boundary legislation was passed during
either the thirty-first, thirty-second or thirty-third sessions
of the legislature. The thirty-first session (1895) spent much
time working over a bill of a general character which would
satisfy the requirements of the constitution, but the bill did not
pass either house.[298] Other proposed bills sought to change
the boundaries of Alpine[299] and Contra Costa[300] and to amend
the Political Code by adding a section defining the boundaries
of Orange County.[301]

The thirty-second session took up again the matter of a
general act but both houses disapproved of the features of the
bills as proposed.[302] Changes in county boundaries were
sought in the cases of Madera[303] and Ventura; in the latter
case the Conejo Rancho was to be thrown entirely into Ven-

---

[298]*Assembly Journal,* 31st Sess. (1895), 64, 180, 185, 199, 208, 300, 321,
322, 363. *Senate Journal,* 197, 198, 395, 873, 1074.
[299]*Assembly Journal,* 31st Sess. (1895), 148, 363. *Senate Journal,* 503,
1074.
[300]*Assembly Journal,* 472, 592, 610.
[301]*Ibid.,* 319, 610. *Senate Journal,* 411, 523, 1074.
[302]*Assembly Journal,* 32d Sess. (1897), 348, 772. *Senate Journal,* 331,
1119.
[303]*Assembly Journal,* 435, 500, 772.

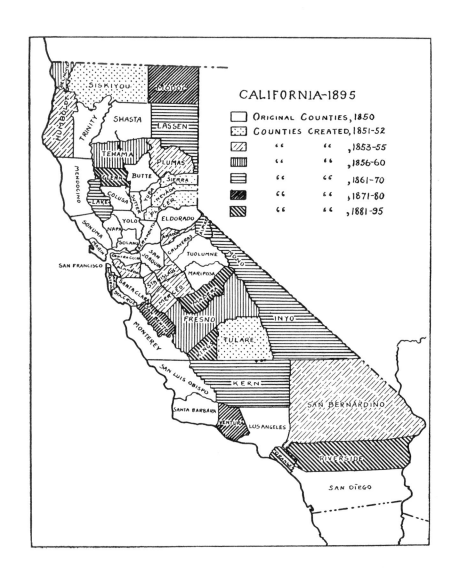

CALIFORNIA-1895

☐ ORIGINAL COUNTIES, 1850
▨ COUNTIES CREATED, 1851-52
▨ " " , 1853-55
▥ " " , 1856-60
▤ " " , 1861-70
▨ " " , 1871-80
▨ " " , 1881-95

tura County.[304]   Another bill would have changed the
El Dorado-Amador line.[305] The only legislation adopted, however, was a redefinition of the Butte-Yuba boundary.[306]

During the thirty-third session there was much ineffective
debate in reference to boundary matters. Plumas caused
much of this on account of her flock of a half dozen bills redefining her boundaries. On account of the mountainous character of the region practically all of the boundaries of Plumas
County had been placed along ridges or in terms of natural
physical features. It was now proposed to define the boundaries by means of the United States survey lines and to that
end a separate bill was introduced to deal with the boundary
between Plumas and each of the adjacent counties.[307] The
northern boundary of Mendocino also demanded its share of
attention. By an act of 1872, a survey of this line, which
ran along the 40th parallel north, was authorized by statute, it
being stipulated that the line as surveyed should be the legal
boundary. In accordance with this act the boundary was
fixed, but was later found not to have followed the 40th parallel
but to have been located further south. An alteration of
this line to the 40th parallel was now proposed, but the measure
was not adopted.[308] Other bills related to the northern line of
San Mateo,[309] the line between Shasta and Lassen,[310] the one
between Amador and El Dorado,[311] and the Solano-Yolo boundary.[312] A general bill dealing with the boundary matters
passed the assembly but none passed the senate.[313]

More Exact Descriptions, 1901. The thirty-fourth session
of the legislature passed five acts defining county boundaries.
In none of these cases was a change in boundary proposed,
but merely a better definition of boundaries in terms of the
regular United States surveys. Three of these acts related
to Plumas County and defined the boundaries between that

[304]*Assembly Journal*, 32d Sess. (1897), 734, 926.
[305]*Ibid.*, 735, 821, 1215. *Senate Journal*, 1081, 1119.
[306]Statutes, 1897 : 22. *Senate Journal*, 302, 431, 479.
[307]*Assembly Journal*, 33d Sess. (1899), 410, 772. Butte, Yuba, Tehama,
Lassen, and Shasta were the other counties affected.
[308]*Ibid.*, 78, 323, 379, 585. *Senate Journal*, 46, 344.
[309]*Assembly Journal*, 473, 772, 1119. *Senate Journal*, 1085.
[310]*Assembly Journal*, 237, 323, 396. *Senate Journal*, 889.
[311]*Assembly Journal*, 896, 1023, 1611.
[312]*Ibid.*, 522. *Senate Journal*, 457, 458, 671.
[313]*Assembly Journal*, 450, 772, 1467, 1500. *Senate Journal*, 401, 608.

county and Lassen,[314] Butte,[315] and Shasta.[316] One of the others redefined the boundary between Humboldt on the south and Del Norte and Siskiyou on the north[317] while the other concerned the line between San Mateo and Alameda.[318]

Other proposed legislation dealt with the boundaries of Fresno, Tulare and Kings,[319] and with the Trinity-Mendocino line.[320] The general county boundary bill again passed the assembly but met defeat in the senate.[321]

The thirty-fifth (1903) and thirty-sixth (1905) sessions made no changes in county boundaries. In 1903 but two changes were proposed. One of these dealt with the line between El Dorado and Placer counties;[322] the other with the Mendocino-Glenn County boundary.[323] The thirty-sixth session passed one act which dealt with the boundary between Sacramento and San Joaquin but apparently made no change in its location.[324] Four other boundary measures were considered. One of these was an attempt to amend the act of 1887 whereby portions of Fresno and Merced counties had been annexed to San Benito.[325] Two others proposed to make such changes in the Political Code as would incorporate the modification in county boundaries made by the creation of Glenn County.[326] The fourth measure was in reference to a general county boundary law. A bill of this nature passed the senate and in an amended form also passed the assembly but the two houses were unable to agree upon its final form.[327]

A General Act—Imperial Created, 1907. The legislature during its thirty-seventh session (1907) passed a general act setting forth a general method of procedure whereby new counties might be formed. The general features of the act

---

[314]*Statutes*, 1901: 76.
[315]*Ibid.*, 549.
[316]*Ibid.*, 560.
[317]*Ibid.*, 600.
[318]*Ibid.*, 291.
[319]*Assembly Journal*, 34th Sess. (1901), 87.
[320]*Ibid.*, 312, 380.
[321]*Ibid.*, 88, 305, 749. *Senate Journal*, 906.
[322]*Assembly Journal*, 35th Sess. (1903), 762, 1061. *Senate Journal*, 500, 594.
[323]*Assembly Journal*, 793.
[324]*Statutes*, 1905: 164. *Assembly Journal*, 36th Sess. (1905), 68, 147, 176, 1584. *Senate Journal*, 1219. A careful reading of this statute fails to show in what manner it differs from a code amendment adopted in 1878. *Code Amendments*, 1877–78, 70–71.
[325]*Senate Journal*, 833.
[326]*Assembly Journal*, 485, 1101. *Senate Journal*, 416.
[327]*Senate Journal*, 125, 691, 1061–62, 1182, 1231, 1311, 1373, 1486. *Assembly Journal*, 1768, 1801–02, 1866.

were that if fifty per cent of the voters of a district petitioned the board of supervisors of a county for organization as a separate county the board should call an election upon the issue and for the necessary officers and if sixty-five per cent of the voters voted in favor of the formation of a new county the clerk of the board was required to certify to that fact to the secretary of state or to issue writs of election to the officers chosen. If districts of more than one county were to be included in the new county petitions from fifty per cent of the voters in each of these districts were to be presented and sixty-five per cent of the votes in each district was to be necessary for an affirmative decision. The act laid down certain general restrictions outside of which no county should be created. They were that such change should not reduce any existing county to less than twenty-five thousand population nor to an area less than twelve hundred square miles; the new county should have a population of at least six thousand and no boundary line should be made to run within five miles of the county seat of the county to be divided, furthermore the new county was to be liable for its just share of the indebtedness of the old county.[328] Notwithstanding the many features of this act which would seem to prohibit the formation of a new county, it did enable the people of Imperial Valley to petition for and effect a separation from San Diego County. Imperial County was thus created August 15, 1907.

In addition to this general law under which Imperial County was created, two other acts dealing with county boundaries were passed. The first concerned the boundaries of Glenn, Mendocino and Lake counties, where instead of following the mountain ridges as theretofore the lines were placed upon United States survey lines.[329] The other act referred to the boundary between Kings and Fresno. This act provided that there should be added to Kings County that portion of southwestern Fresno which lies south of the fourth standard south of Mount Diablo base line. It being, however, provided that a commission be appointed from electors within the district proposed to be transferred and that they

[328]*Statutes*, 1907 : 275.
[329]*Ibid.*, 135.

should provide for and conduct an election whereby the voters of the territory might express their desires as to the proposed transfer.[330] At the polls the people of the territory did not approve of the change.

Other bills proposed changes in the boundaries of San Benito,[331] Los Angeles[332] and Del Norte.[333] There was also presented a petition from taxpayers of the southern part of Santa Clara County protesting against any attempt to divide that county.[334]

Annexation to Kings, 1909. Since the act passed in 1907 giving to Kings County that part of Fresno County lying south of the fourth standard line was not ratified by the voters of the district involved, the question was again before the legislature at its thirty-eighth session (1909). A much modified annexation to Kings was then proposed and adopted. This addition included a small triangular piece lying south of townships seventeen south and east of range two east of Mount Diablo Base and Meridian.[335] Two other boundaries were redefined and placed upon township and section lines or otherwise more definitely located. These were the lines between Lake and Glenn[336] and the Nevada-Sierra County line.[337]

The general law for creating new counties again came up for consideration in 1909. The previous session as noted above had drawn up and adopted an act providing a means whereby under very rigid restrictions a new county might be formed. In spite of these apparently insurmountable obstacles the people of Imperial Valley had dissolved their connection with San Diego and formed a new county. Apparently alarmed by the fact that this had been successful, amendments to the act were proposed and adopted making the creation of new counties even more difficult if not prohibitive. The most drastic of these changes was that which required that the petitions calling for an election must be signed by sixty-five per cent of the qualified voters in the district affected by the

[330]*Statutes*, 1907 : 260–63.
[331]*Assembly Journal*, 37th Sess. (1907), 555, 1844. *Senate Journal*, 545, 681. 833, 1643.
[332]*Assembly Journal*, 592, 1301. *Senate Journal*, 558, 1218, 1402.
[333]*Assembly Journal*, 251, 1844.
[334]*Senate Journal*, 37th Sess. (1907), 709.
[335]*Statutes*, 1909 : 827, 828.
[336]*Ibid.*, 326.
[337]*Ibid.*, 86. As amendment to *Political Code*, § 3921.

change and also by fifty per cent of the voters of the remainder of the county. If more than one county was concerned in the change then similar separate petitions were to be presented from each district and each county.[338]

Constitutional Amendment, 1910. At this session a further amendment was proposed to article XI, section 3, of the state constitution providing that the alteration of county boundaries as well as the formation of new counties should be made by general and uniform laws passed by the legislature. It further provided that any new county must have at least eight thousand population rather than five thousand, as previously, and that the formation of such a county must not reduce any existing county to less than twenty thousand, instead of eight thousand as the earlier section provided. This amendment was submitted to popular vote and ratified, November 8, 1910.

Placer-El Dorado Line Redefined, 1913. Following the constitutional amendment of 1910 there was a decided falling off in proposed as well as actual legislation dealing with county boundaries. No such bills were introduced during the thirty-ninth session (1911) and but few during the fortieth session. One of these, an amendment to section 3924 of the Political Code, redefined the line between Placer and El Dorado counties. The main purpose of this act doubtless was to define the boundary more accurately by means of reference to the United States survey lines but it should be noted that a slight but real change was made by giving to Placer a small portion of El Dorado lying on the south side of a bend in the American River.[339] Other bills as introduced dealt with the boundaries of Santa Clara, Santa Cruz, and San Benito[340] and with the Tuolumne-Mariposa line.[341] The latter passed both houses to be pocketed by the Governor.

---

[338]*Statutes,* 1909 : 194–203.
[339]*Ibid.,* 1913 : 603, 604.
[340]*Assembly Journal,* 40th Sess. (1913), 532, 2993. This bill sought to define more carefully the common corner on the Pajaro River but appears to have been hastily and improperly drawn.
[341]*Senate Journal,* 1275, 1734, 2006, 2910. *Assembly Journal,* 2240, 2373, 2965. This bill passed both houses but was not signed by the governor. The purpose seems to have been to define by means of the United States survey lines the Tuolumne–Mariposa boundary. By the use of an antiquated section of the Political Code it did materially change the Mariposa–Madera boundary, re-enacting an act passed in 1870. Subsequent to the adoption of the Code (1872) three other acts had been passed dealing with the boundary in question but these evidently had been overlooked.

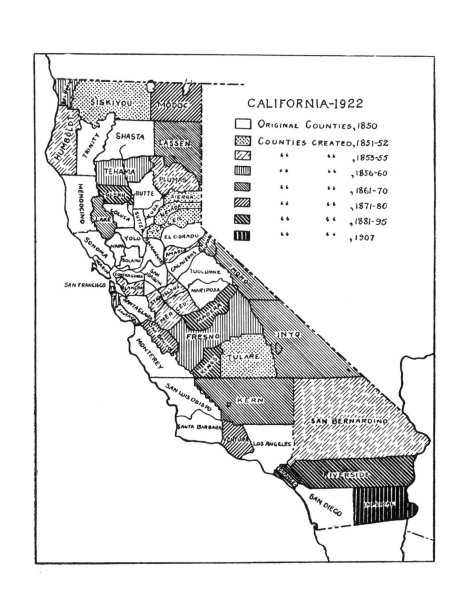

CALIFORNIA-1922

☐ ORIGINAL COUNTIES, 1850
▨ COUNTIES CREATED, 1851-52
◫ " " , 1853-55
⬚ " " , 1856-60
◩ " " , 1861-70
◪ " " , 1871-80
◨ " " , 1881-95
▥ " " , 1907

SISKIYOU
MODOC
HUMBOLDT
TRINITY
SHASTA
LASSEN
TEHAMA
PLUMAS
MENDOCINO
GLENN
BUTTE
SIERRA
COLUSA
SUTTER
YUBA
NEVADA
LAKE
PLACER
YOLO
EL DORADO
SONOMA
NAPA
SOLANO
AMADOR
CALAVERAS
MARIN
ALPINE
CONTRA COSTA
SAN JOAQUIN
TUOLUMNE
MONO
SAN FRANCISCO
ALAMEDA
STANISLAUS
MARIPOSA
SAN MATEO
SANTA CLARA
MERCED
MADERA
SANTA CRUZ
INYO
FRESNO
MONTEREY
TULARE
KINGS
SAN LUIS OBISPO
KERN
SAN BERNARDINO
SANTA BARBARA
VENTURA
LOS ANGELES
RIVERSIDE
ORANGE
SAN DIEGO
IMPERIAL

Boundary Adjustments, 1915-1917. During the forty-first session (1915) three bills dealing with county boundaries were introduced. Two of these were companion bills relating to the line between Glenn and Butte, the other was an attempt to amend the general act relating to the formation of new counties and altering county boundaries. The first of these was adopted and became a statute. The change was slight and merely made the boundary more definite by defining it in terms of the United States survey of the Aguas Frias Rancho.[342]

A proposed general act would have made it much easier for certain counties to be divided as the existing law with its rigid restriction was to be repealed and a new method substituted. Since it applied to counties whose county seats contained more than fifty thousand and where fifty per cent of the population resided within five miles of the county seat, it appears to have been drawn for a specific purpose.[343] Both bills were reported by their respective committees without recommendation and no further action was taken upon them.

During the forty-second session (1917) bills were introduced redefining or altering some five county boundaries in addition to a proposed amendment to the general act. There were adopted three of these boundary acts, dealing with the Mendocino-Lake,[344] the Mendocino-Sonoma[345] and the Kern-San Bernardino boundaries.[346] In the case of the Mendocino boundaries the legislature merely meant to define the lines by reference to the nearest and most appropriate United States survey lines. The Kern-San Bernardino bill was introduced because of long continued failure on the part of the officials of the two counties to see that the line as surveyed and observed was the same as the line defined in the statute books. The discovery of wealthy mineral deposits along the line in question brought on the issue, which resulted in this legislation, which fixed the line more nearly as defined in the early statutes. Two other bills relating to boundary matters were

---

[342]*Statutes*, 1915 : 898.
[343]*Senate Journal*, 41st Sess. (1915), 442, 2536. *Assembly Journal*, 417, 2507.
[344]*Statutes*, 1917 : 1635.
[345]*Ibid.*, 1396.
[346]*Ibid.*, 301.

not passed. One of these sought to provide a method whereby certain portions of San Mateo County might be annexed to San Francisco.[347] The other was a new description with a more definite location of the northern line of Riverside County, a change made urgent because of lawlessness in this border district and the impracticability of locating the line as then described. The bill was passed by both houses but pocketed by the Governor.[348] Proposed changes in the general law would have enabled sixty per cent of the voters of a district desiring to be formed into a new county to petition the board of supervisors to call an election for that purpose. If sixty per cent of the voters of the district affected and thirty per cent of the voters of the remainder of the county favored the action the new county would be formed. The other restriction as to size and population remained unchanged.[349]

Codification of Boundary Laws, 1919. During the forty-third session (1919) some four bills were introduced relative to the question of county boundaries. The first three dealt with the Los Angeles-Ventura line, the Los Angeles-Orange County line and with the boundary between San Bernardino and Riverside counties. There was also a comprehensive bill prepared by the Historical Survey Commission bringing together into the proper part of the Political Code all the statutes and code provisions defining the boundaries of the counties. Since this bill could be made to include the features of the others it was given precedence and with many amendments was enacted into a law. The bill as originally proposed, prepared by the Historical Survey Commission, merely codified the laws which described the county boundaries as they then existed. Several of the amendments submitted by county authorities aimed at better definitions and some slight changes were made in boundaries. The only change of decided character was the line between Los Angeles and Ventura. This had been introduced in a separate bill at the instigation of the officials of the two counties affected in an attempt to clear up an uncertainty regarding the location of the boundary which

---

[347] *Assembly Journal*, 42d Sess. (1917), 73, 2317.
[348] This line was a segment of the old northern line of San Diego which presumably ran parallel with the Mexican boundary. *Ibid.*, 976, 1050, 1080. 1104. 1643. 2329, 2490.
[349] *Ibid.*, 263, 2313.

appears to have existed ever since the line was surveyed in 1881,[350] since the line surveyed and subsequently recognized as the boundary is clearly not the line evidently defined in the Political Code. The line between Orange and Los Angeles was more clearly described by defining the course of Coyote Creek which an earlier statute had determined as the boundary. The Riverside-San Bernardino line was redefined in the manner urged by the county authorities of both counties in the past two sessions of the legislature. This act repealed all the section defining county boundaries and enacted new sections considering the counties in their alphabetical order.

Supreme Court Decision, 1920. Because of the fact that the act of 1919 actually changed the boundary between Los Angeles and Ventura counties the issue of the constitutionality of the measure was brought before the Supreme Court for decision. The decision as announced by Justice Olney and concurred in by the full court was that the act, although it included all the counties, was a series of special enactments rather than a general act and since it did in the case in question change the existing boundary it was not in accordance with article XI, section 3, of the constitution which reads "the legislature by general and uniform laws may provide for the alteration of county boundary lines and for the formation of new counties," inasmuch as the section, although reading in the form of a permission, was in reality a prohibition upon the power of the legislature to alter the county boundaries by any other method.[351]

The reading of the constitution and the decision of the court are clear that county boundaries may not be altered by special legislation. The constitution does not specify and the Supreme Court has not decided that the legislature may not more clearly define and establish existing lines which because of vague

---

[350]For full discussion of this point see the description of the Los Angeles boundary.
[351]*Mundell* v. *Lyons*, 59 Cal. 213–216.

descriptions still remain uncertain. Upon this point the decision just referred to goes on to state:

"We would add that what we have said would by no means necessarily apply to an act which merely established and made certain boundaries theretofore uncertain. The question as to the validity of such an act is not presented, and, concerning it, we express no opinion."

In view of this fact it would appear that had the bill codifying the boundary laws been passed as originally drawn by the Historical Survey Commission it would have been within the constitutional powers of the legislature.

Codification Act of 1923. In accordance with the views expressed in the preceding paragraph and after consultation with the Attorney General's office another bill was prepared by the Historical Survey Commission and presented to the legislature in 1921. This bill defined the Los Angeles-Ventura line as it had been surveyed in 1881 and observed since that date and made other corrections in the wording of two sections of the act of 1919. This bill was passed by both houses and presented to the Governor, but did not secure his approval.[352]

In 1923 a further attempt was made to secure the desired legislation. The measure as drawn up was the result of the work of the former sessions of the legislature together with much consultation with county officials. A new section, submitted by the Imperial County officials, was substituted for the one previously describing the boundaries of that county, thus giving it an opportunity to claim certain lands along the state border, otherwise the bill was practically identical with the earlier proposed measure. The legislature approved the act and it was subsequently signed by the governor. Thus for the first time since its adoption, fifty-one years ago (1872), does the Political Code in its consideration of county boundaries bring into harmony the various effective laws dealing with county boundaries.[353]

[352]*Senate Bill* No. 285, (1921).
[353]Ventura county created during the session when the code was adopted (1872), was not given place in the code.

PART II

HISTORY OF THE BOUNDARIES BY COUNTIES

ALAMEDA COUNTY

Original Boundary. Alameda County was organized under an act passed on March 25, 1853, its territory being taken from Contra Costa and Santa Clara counties. Its boundaries as then defined have, with minor changes, remained essentially the same. They were as follows:[1]

"Beginning at a point at the head of a slough, which is an arm of the Bay of San Francisco, making into the main land in front of the Gegara ranches; thence to a lone sycamore tree that stands in a ravine between the dwellings of Fluhencia and Valentine Gegara; thence up said ravine to the top of the mountains; thence on a direct line eastwardly, to the junction of the San Joaquin and Tuolumne counties. From thence northwestwardly on the west line of San Joaquin County, to the slough known as the Pescadora; thence westwardly in a straight line until it strikes the dividing ridge, in the direction of the house of Joel Harlan, in Amador Valley; thence westwardly along the middle of said ridge, crossing the gulch one-half mile below Prince's Mill; thence to, and running upon, the dividing ridge between the redwoods, known as the San Antonio and Prince's woods; thence along the top of said ridge to the head of the gulch or creek that divides the ranches of the Peralta's from those known as the San Pablo ranches; thence down the middle of said gulch to its mouth; and from thence westwardly, to the eastern line of the county of San Francisco; thence along said last mentioned line to the place of beginning."

Without material change these lines were redefined in section 3953 of the Political Code as it was adopted in 1872. This section reads as follows:[2]

"Beginning at the southwest corner, being common corner of San Mateo, Santa Clara, and Alameda, as established in section 3951; thence easterly on northern line of Santa Clara, as established in section 3952, to common corner of San Joaquin, Stanislaus, Santa Clara, and Alameda, as established in section 3932; thence northwesterly on the west line of San Joaquin County to the slough known as the Pescadora (being the west channel or old San Joaquin River); thence westerly in a straight line until it strikes the dividing ridge in the direction of the house of Joel Harlan, in Amador Valley; thence westerly along said ridge, crossing the gulch one-half mile

---

[1]*Statutes*, 1853: 56.
[2]*Political Code*, (1872): § 3953.

below Prince's Mill; thence to and running upon the dividing ridge between the redwoods known as the San Antonio and Prince's Woods; thence along said ridge to the head of the gulch or creek (Cerrito Creek) that divides the ranches of the Peraltas from the San Pablo ranches; thence down said gulch to its mouth; thence westerly to the easterly line of San Francisco, as established in section 3950; thence southeasterly along the eastern line of San Francisco and San Mateo to the place of beginning.''

The Western Boundary. Because of the building of the Oakland mole and long wharf by the Central Pacific Railroad Company, it became necessary in 1874 to shift the San Francisco-Alameda boundary further west in order that the wharf might be entirely within Alameda County. This amended line ran from the corner common to Contra Costa, San Francisco and Alameda,[3]

"thence southerly to a point in the bay of San Francisco that would intersect a line parallel with the north line of the Central Pacific Railroad Company's wharf (as it now is), if extended westerly five hundred feet towards Yerba Buena Island; thence southeasterly in a line parallel with the east line of the city and county of San Francisco (which is the line now dividing said city and county from the county of Alameda), to its intersection with the south line of said city and county, as established in section three thousand nine hundred and fifty; thence easterly along said last-mentioned line to the northeast corner of San Mateo; and thence southeasterly along the eastern line of San Mateo to the place of beginning."

In 1878 the line common to San Mateo County was changed to a position "in the center of the ship channel in the Bay of San Francisco, west of and opposite to Dumbarton Point."[4]

Just as the building of the Central Pacific Company's wharf in 1874 required a shifting in the line of Alameda County in order to avoid the confusion incident to having it intersected by the county boundary line, so the removal of that wharf in 1919 required a redefinition of the boundary line in terms of more permanent landmarks. By this act the line is defined in its same relative position, but in its relationship to the lighthouse on Yerba Buena Island rather than the railroad wharf.

Boundary of 1923. By the act of 1919 the boundaries

---

[3]*Political Code* (1874), § 3953, as given in *Code Amendments* 1873–74: 168.

[4]*Political Code* (1878), § 3951.

of Alameda County were redefined in section 3909 of the
Political Code. A change in the terms whereby the western
line was described has been noted in the preceding paragraph.
In the interest of a clearer definition the line between Alameda
and Santa Clara was redescribed as will appear in the section
devoted to Santa Clara. This change was made necessary on
account of the fact that the terms found in the act then in
force were extremely indefinite. The boundaries of 1923 are
as follows:[5]

"3909. *Alameda.* Beginning at the southwest corner,
being the common corner of San Mateo, Santa Clara, and
Alameda, as established in section three thousand nine
hundred fifty-one; thence easterly along the northerly
boundary of Santa Clara County as defined in said section
to the corner common to Santa Clara, San Joaquin, Stanislaus, and Alameda counties; thence northwesterly and
northerly along the boundary line between Alameda and
San Joaquin counties, as described in the field notes of
the survey of said line, as adopted by the board of supervisors of Alameda County, California, on February 6,
1869, to the corner common to Alameda, Contra Costa
and San Joaquin counties; thence in a general westerly
direction along the boundary line between Alameda and
Contra Costa counties, as described in field notes of the
survey of said boundary line, filed November 19, 1877,
in the office of the clerk of Alameda County, California,
to the most westerly point where said line is coincident
with the line dividing the Rancho San Pablo from the
Rancho San Antonio; thence westerly along the northerly
boundary line of the Rancho San Antonio to the initial
point of the description thereof, as recorded in Liber 'B'
of patents, page 30, records of Alameda County, California; thence southwesterly in a direct line to a point in
San Francisco bay, said point being four and one-half
statute miles due southeast of the northwest point of
Golden Rock (also known as Red Rock); thence southeasterly in a direct line to a point from which the lighthouse on the most southerly point of Yerba Buena Island
bears south seventy-two degrees west, four thousand seven
hundred feet; thence southeasterly in a direct line to a
point on the southerly line of township two south, range
four west, Mount Diablo base and meridian, distant thereon two statute miles west of the southeast corner of said
township, forming corner common to San Francisco, San
Mateo and Alameda; thence southeasterly along the eastern line of San Mateo County to the place of beginning."

[5]*Political Code* (1919), § 3909; (1923), § 3909.

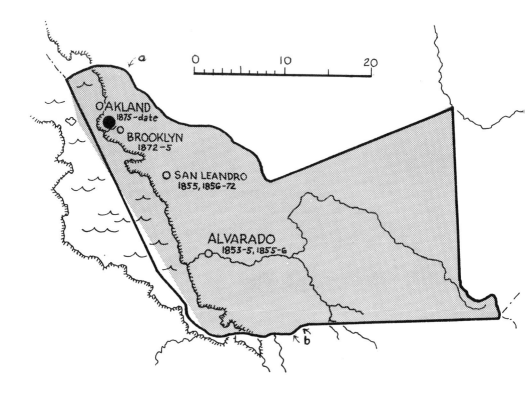

Alameda County

Solid   Stats.   1853; 56; Pol. Code (1872), Sec. 3953.
Shaded   Pol. Code (1874), Sec. 3953; (1919), Sec. 3909.
  a   See Addendum, Page 338
  b   See Addendum, Page 338
Solid bold line designates original boundary. Changes are
lettered (a, b, c, etc.). Shading denotes present county
boundaries.

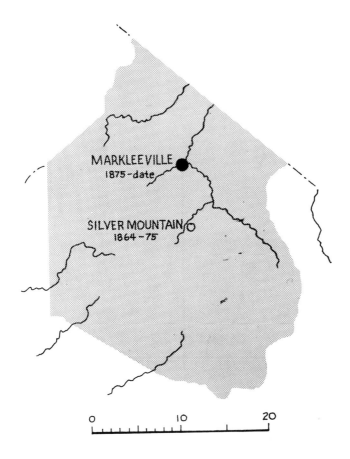

MARKLEEVILLE
1875-date

SILVER MOUNTAIN
1864-75

0   10   20

Alpine County

Statutes   1863-4: 178.
Political Code (1872), Sec. 3921 (1923), Sec. 3910.
Solid bold line designates original boundary. Changes are
lettered (a, b, c, etc.). Shading denotes present county
boundaries.

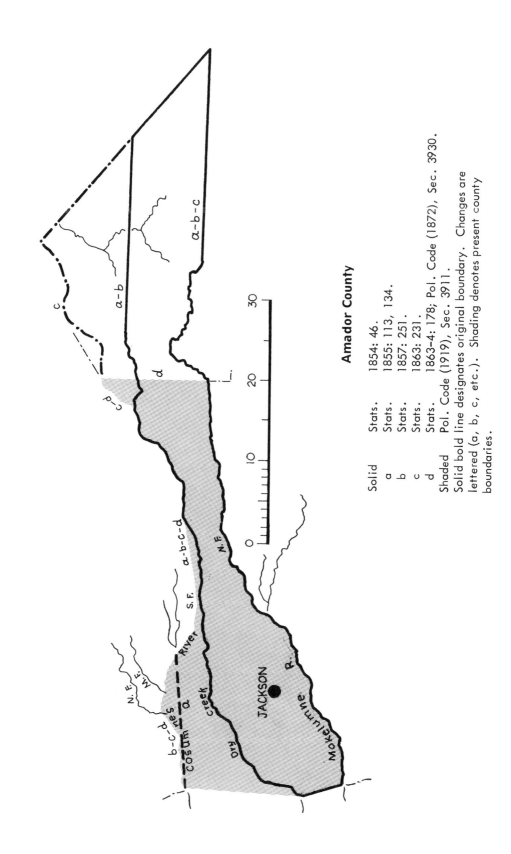

Amador County

Solid	Stats.	1854: 46.
a	Stats.	1855: 113, 134.
b	Stats.	1857: 251.
c	Stats.	1863: 231.
d	Stats.	1863-4: 178; Pol. Code (1872), Sec. 3930.

Shaded   Pol. Code (1919), Sec. 3911.
Solid bold line designates original boundary. Changes are lettered (a, b, c, etc.). Shading denotes present county boundaries.

ALPINE COUNTY

Alpine County was created on March 16, 1864, from territory which had previously been portions of El Dorado, Amador, Calaveras and Tuolumne counties. Since that time the boundaries have never been changed.[1] As described in the Political Code they are as follows:[2]

"Beginning at north corner, at a point where the state line crosses the east summit of the Sierra Nevada Mountains, being the most easterly corner of El Dorado; thence southwesterly along said summit to a point two miles west of James Green's house in Hope Valley called Thompson's Peak; thence southwesterly in a direct line to a point on the Amador and Nevada turnpike road in front of Z. Kirkwood's house, being common corner of Amador, Alpine, and El Dorado; thence south across the north fork of the Mokelumne River to the road leading from West Point, in Calaveras, to Big Tree road, near the Big Meadows; thence easterly along said West Point road to the Big Tree road; thence easterly in a direct line to where the Sonora trail strikes the middle fork of the Stanislaus River; thence easterly along said trail to the summit of the Sierra Nevada Mountains; thence northerly along said summit to the dividing ridge between West Walker and Carson Rivers; thence northeasterly along said dividing ridge to the state line, forming easterly corner of Alpine and northerly corner of Mono; thence northwest along said state line to the place of beginning."

[1]*Statutes*, 1863–64: 178.
[2]*Political Code* (1872), § 3931; (1923), § 3910.

AMADOR COUNTY

Original Boundary, 1854. Amador County was formed on May 10, 1854, being originally composed of that part of Calaveras County lying north of the Mokelumne River. As created its boundaries were as follows:[1]

> "Beginning in the middle of Mokelumne River, on the eastern boundary of San Joaquin County, thence up the middle of the channel of said river to the sources of the north fork of the same, thence due east to the eastern boundary of the state, thence northwesterly to the southeast corner of El Dorado County, thence along the southern boundary of El Dorado County, to the eastern line of Sacramento County, thence southerly along the eastern boundary of Sacramento and San Joaquin counties, to the place of beginning."

Additions from El Dorado, 1855, 1857, 1863. Although Calaveras alone had contributed to the original territory of Amador County, El Dorado was later to be drawn upon to add to this area. The first addition from El Dorado was made in 1855, when

> "all that portion of El Dorado County lying south of a line beginning at a point in the middle of the Consumnes River, at the eastern boundary of Sacramento County, running thence in an easterly direction, on an air line, to the mouth of the South Fork of the South Fork of the Consumnes River, thence up the middle of the South Fork of the South Fork of Consumnes River to its source, and thence due east to the present county line dividing El Dorado County from the county of Amador is hereby detached from the county of El Dorado, and attached to, and made a part of Amador County."[2]

In 1857 a slight change was made in the Amador-El Dorado line, the line being made to follow the channel of the Cosumnes River down from its South Fork rather than the "air line," as previously described.[3]

The development of the county lying east of the Sierras in the early sixties caused numerous changes in county juris-

[1]*Statutes*, 1854: 157.
[2]*Ibid.*, 1855: 113, 134.
[3]*Ibid.*, 1857: 251.

dictions. One phase of this is seen in the shifting of the El Dorado-Amador line in 1863, whereby a part of eastern El Dorado was given to Amador County. The Amador and Nevada wagon road, which here became the boundary, probably also helps to explain why this territory was placed under the jurisdiction of Amador County. The line between the two counties in 1863 ran as follows:[4]

"Beginning in the centre of the Cosumnes River at the point where said river enters Sacramento County; thence up the middle of the channel of said river to the South Fork of said river; thence up the centre of the channel of said South Fork to the South Fork of the South Fork of said river; thence up said South Fork of the South Fork to its source; thence due east to the Amador and Nevada wagon road; thence along the line of said road to its junction with the Big Tree and Carson Valley road, in Hope Valley; thence, from said junction, along the line of the road leading down said valley, through Carson Cañon, to the eastern boundary of this state. Said roads, when marking the boundary line of said counties as provided in this act, shall be included within the boundaries of Amador County."

Alpine County Detached, 1864. The same movement which led to the addition of territory to Amador in 1863, caused a loss of more than one-third of the area of the county the next year. This was the result of the organization of Alpine County.[5] Since that time there has been no change in the boundaries of Amador County.

Present Boundaries, 1923. The boundaries of 1864 were defined in the Political Code in 1872 and were incorporated in the revisions of the code in 1919 and 1923. The boundaries of Amador County are defined as follows:[6]

"Beginning at southwest corner, in the Mokelumne River, on the eastern boundary of San Joaquin, as established in section three thousand nine hundred and forty-seven, thence up said river to its junction with the north fork of the same; thence up the said north fork to the line of Alpine, being at a point south of common corner of Amador, Alpine, and El Dorado, which is in the center of the Amador and Nevada road, in front of Z. Kirk-

[4]*Statutes*, 1863:231.
[5]*Ibid.*, 1863:178.
[6]*Political Code* (1872), § 3930; (1919), § 3911; (1923), § 3911.

wood's house, as established in section three thousand nine hundred and ten; thence north by the line of Alpine to said common corner; thence westerly along said road to a point east of the source of the south fork of the south fork of the Cosumnes River; thence west to said source; thence down the south fork of the south fork and the south fork and the main Cosumnes River to the easterly line of Sacramento, as established in section three thousand nine hundred and forty-two; thence by eastern lines of Sacramento and San Joaquin to the place of beginning.''

BUTTE COUNTY

Original Boundaries, 1850. Butte was one of the original counties created and organized in 1850. Like most of these counties, its area was then much larger than at present, Plumas County being made up entirely of territory once belonging to Butte, which also at one time claimed large portions of Lassen and Tehama. Its original boundaries were as follows:[1]

"Beginning on the Sacramento River at the Red Bluffs, in latitude forty degrees thirty-two minutes and twenty-three seconds north, and running thence due east to the dividing ridge which separates the waters flowing into the Sacramento River below the Red Bluffs, and into Feather River, from those flowing into the Sacramento above the Red Bluffs; thence following the top of said ridge to the Sierra Nevada; thence due east to the boundary of the state; thence due south, following said boundary, to the northeast corner of Yuba County; thence following the northwestern boundary of Yuba County to Feather River; thence due west along the northern boundary of Sutter County to the Sacramento River; thence running up the middle of said river to the place of beginning."

Since the southern boundary is here described in terms of Yuba and Sutter counties, it will be necessary to note where their boundaries lay. As described in Sec. 20 of the act which also created Butte County, the northern boundary of Yuba is described as

"beginning at the mouth of Honcut Creek, and running up the middle of the same to its source; thence following the dividing ridge between Feather and Yuba rivers to the summit of the Sierra Nevada; thence east to the boundary of the state."[1]

The northern line of Sutter is defined in Sec. 19 of the same act as running from a point in the Sacramento River

"due west of the mouth of Honcut Creek; thence due east to the mouth of said creek."[2]

Butte-Sutter Line, 1851-1856. The south boundary of Butte, separating that county from Sutter, was subject to

---

[1]*Statutes*, 1850 : 62.
[2]*Ibid.*, 1850 : 62.

many changes during the early years. The first of these came in 1851, when the boundary was changed from the line just described and placed upon a line running from

> "a point due west of the north point of the three Buttes; thence due east to the middle of Feather River."[3]

The next year the line was again changed and made to run from:

> "a point due west of the north point of the three Buttes; thence in a southeasterly direction to a point at the base of the Buttes, due west of the south point of the same; thence in a northeasterly direction to a point in the middle of Feather River, opposite the mouth of Honcut Creek."[4]

In 1854 another change was made, the line this time running from the same initial point in the Sacramento River west of the north Butte

> "thence due east to the said north point of the three Buttes; thence in a straight line to a point in the middle of Feather River opposite the mouth of Honcut Creek."[5]

In 1856 still another change was made. The boundary was this time shifted further north, and the southeast corner of Butte County placed upon Butte Creek rather than the Sacramento River, as formerly. It ran from a point in Butte Creek lying

> "due west of a point of timber half a mile north of James E. Edwards' house; thence due east to said point of timber; thence in a straight line to a point in the middle of Feather River opposite the mouth of Honcut Creek."[6]

The line was here at last located practically as it is at present.[7] The description, however, was indefinite, so in 1864 it was redefined in the terms of the township line as it now appears in the code.[8]

Separation of Plumas, 1854. In the meanwhile other changes had been taking place; the most radical of all, how-

[3] *Statutes,* 1851 : 176.
[4] *Ibid.,* 1852 : 237.
[5] *Ibid.,* 1854 : 19.
[6] *Ibid.,* 1856 : 231.
[7] Edwards' House is shown on the Official Map of Butte County, 1861.
[8] *Statutes,* 1863–64 : 301.

ever, came in 1854 when more than half of the original area
was set off as Plumas County. The line between Plumas and
Butte counties was defined as follows:[9]

> "commencing at the Buckeye House on the line between
> Yuba and Butte, and running in a right line crossing
> the southern portion of Walker's Plains and Feather
> River, to the summit of the dividing ridge, dividing the
> waters of the west branch and the main Feather River;
> thence following the said divide, to the summit of the
> main divide, separating the waters of the Sacramento
> and the main North Feather; thence following said divide
> to the line of Shasta County."

The Butte-Tehama Line. The northwestern boundary of
Butte County has also been shifted many times. As stated
above, in 1850 the northwest corner of the county was in the
Sacramento River at the Red Bluffs. In 1851 it was moved
a little further south to a point "opposite the mouth of Red
Bluff Creek," thence due east to the ridge as before.[10]

The boundary remained along this line until 1856 when
Tehama County was created, at which time the territory of
Butte was levied upon to help make up the new county. The
line in question began in the Sacramento River at the mouth
of Mud Creek and ran

> "thence up the middle of Mud Creek, to the line which
> divides the counties of Butte and Plumas."[11]

This would infer that Mud Creek reached to the Butte-
Plumas line, which was not the fact. Since by later interpretation the line between those points has been made a direct
line, it has been so placed in considering the meaning of this
act. In 1857 a slight change was made in this line near the
Sacramento River, it being described as running westward
from the place "where it [Mud Creek] disappears" in a direct
line to the river.[12]

---

[9]*Statutes.* 1854 : 8. Most of these points are shown clearly on the Official
Map of Butte County, 1861.
[10]*Ibid.,* 1851 : 176.
[11]*Ibid.,* 1856 : 222.
[12]*Ibid.,* 1857 : 109. The point on the Sacramento River is indefinite,
since it is described as being located on "the first section line north of
Ragers' House." *See* below, 88, note 15.

The boundary between the counties was placed upon the present line in 1859. This act describes it as going from the common corner of Butte, Plumas and Tehama County,

> "thence, in direct line, to the headwaters of Rock Creek; thence down the middle of the channel of said creek, to township-line twenty-three; thence along said line, to the middle of the Sacramento River."[13]

Colusa Line. The line separating Butte from Colusa County was changed several times before it was finally determined by the Political Code in 1872. As originally defined it lay along the Sacramento River, but in 1856 it was amended to read as running from

> "a point one hundred yards south of Regan's Ranch, on the Sacramento River; thence down the middle of the Sacramento River to Placer City; thence easterly to Watson's Bridge, on Butte Creek, and in Butte County; thence down the middle of Butte Creek."[14]

The line here described remained unchanged until 1872 when it was placed upon its present location which is described as running from a point in the Sacramento River, on the south line of township twenty-three;

> "thence down said river to the southwest corner of the Llano Seco grant; thence northeasterly along said grant line to its intersection with the northern boundary of township nineteen north; thence east to Butte Creek; thence down Butte Creek."[15]

Butte-Yuba Line, 1860 and 1861. In 1860 and 1861 slight changes were made in the wording of the description of the line between Butte and Yuba counties. The first of these explicitly placed Strawberry Valley in Yuba County. It reads as follows:[16]

> "Beginning at the highest point in the present county line, within three hundred yards east of the village of Strawberry Valley, and running thence in a right line to a point in the present county line two thousand feet distant from the place of beginning, and on the western and

[13]*Statutes*, 1859 : 359.
[14]*Ibid.*, 1856 : 124. The location of Regan's Ranch is more fully discussed in note 15, p. 88.
[15]*Political Code* (1872), § 3916.
[16]*Statutes*, 1860 : 115.

opposite side of said village of Strawberry Valley, so as to leave the said village of Strawberry Valley wholly in Yuba County.''

The second of these acts, placing the Woodville House in Yuba County, describes the line as follows:[17]

"Beginning at a station tree on the established line between said counties, about twenty-six chains easterly from the house known as the 'Woodville House,' thence, on a right line fifty chains, more or less, to the third station tree, westerly from the said Woodville House, on the said established line, said right line passing about three chains northerly of said house, and leaving the same, with all of the out-buildings, in Yuba County.''

Inasmuch as the amount of territory here described is so small, and the effect of the acts was rather to define than amend the boundaries in question, these acts have not been indicated upon the map.

The Line of the Political Code, 1872. At the time of the adoption of the code in 1872 the entire boundary was redefined. A slight inconsistency in the line with Colusa led to an amendment in 1874 which defined the boundaries of Butte County as follows:[18]

"Beginning at the northwest corner of Yuba, in Feather River, at the mouth of Honcut Creek; thence northeasterly up the Honcut Creek and the north or Natchez branch of the same, to its source, on line established by Surveyor General, on survey of Westcoatt and Henning, eighteen hundred and fifty-nine; thence to the summit line of the ridge dividing the waters of the Yuba and Feather rivers; thence northeasterly up said ridge, on line of said survey, to the third station tree westerly from the Woodville House; thence in a right line, fifty chains more or less, to a station tree easterly from said house about twenty-six chains—said right line passing about three chains northerly of said house; thence northeasterly on said ridge and survey, to a point on line of said survey a little westerly from the village of Strawberry Valley—which point is two thousand feet distant westerly, in right line from point of highest altitude on line of said survey east, and within three hundred yards of the village of Strawberry Valley; thence to the common corner of Plumas, Butte, and Yuba, as established in section three thousand

[17]*Statutes*, 1861: 167.
[18]*Code Amendments*, 1873–74: 167.

nine hundred and twenty; thence northwesterly on south-westerly line of Plumas, as established in said section, to the most eastern southeastern corner of Tehama, as established in section three thousand nine hundred and fifteen, forming also the north corner of Butte; thence southwest-erly on the southeasterly line of Tehama to the southeast corner of Tehama, at point of intersection of Rock Creek and southern line of township twenty-four north, Mount Diablo base; thence west on said township line to the Sacramento River; thence down said river to the south-west corner of the Llano Seco grant; thence northeasterly along said grant line to its intersection with the northern boundary of township nineteen north; thence east to Watson's bridge, on Butte Creek; thence on Colusa County east line, down Butte Creek, to the northwest corner of Sutter County, as established in section three thousand nine hundred and twenty-six; thence east on north line of Sutter County to Feather River; thence down Feather River to place of beginning.''

Boundary Adjustments, 1897, 1901, 1915. During re-cent years there has been a growing tendency to define county boundaries in terms of the United States land surveys. In accordance with this idea the line between Yuba and Butte counties was so defined in 1897[19] and the Plumas-Butte line in 1901.[20] No changes in general location of the lines were made beyond the necessary shifting to the nearest United States survey lines. In 1915 the boundary with Glenn was further defined as follows:[21]

> ''From the point where the line between township 19 north, range 1 east and township 20 north, range 1 east intersects the line between sections three and four of the Aguas Frias Rancho according to the La Croze survey of the said Aguas Frias Rancho, said point being on the line between Butte and Glenn counties, running thence south along the said line between the said sections three and four to its point of intersection with the center line of Butte Creek, said point of intersection being on the present line between Butte and Glenn counties.''

Present Boundary, 1923. The statute of 1919 attempted to codify the laws then in force relating to county bound-aries.[22] Through an oversight the act of 1897 mentioned

[19]*Statutes,* 1897 : 22.
[20]*Ibid.,* 1901 : 549.
[21]*Ibid.,* 1915 : 898.
[22]*Political Code* (1919), § 3912.

above was omitted. An effort to remedy this error was made during the next two sessions of the legislature. In 1923 an act was passed defining the boundaries as follows:[23]

"3912. *Butte.* Beginning at the northwest corner of Yuba, in the center line of the Feather River, opposite the mouth of Honcut Creek; thence northeasterly up the Honcut Creek and the South Honcut Creek, following their various meanders and along the boundary line as surveyed in the year one thousand nine hundred one by B. L. McCoy, county surveyor of Butte County, and Jason R. Meek, county surveyor of Yuba County, to its intersection with the south line of section thirty-one, of township nineteen north, range six east, Mount Diablo Base and Meridian, and running thence east to the southwest corner of the southeast one-quarter of the southeast one-quarter of section thirty-one, said township and range; thence north three-quarters of a mile; thence east one-quarter of a mile; thence north one-quarter of a mile, to corner common to sections twenty-nine, thirty, thirty-one, and thirty-two, said township and range; thence east one-half mile to the one-quarter section corner between sections twenty-nine and thirty-two, said township and range; thence north one-half mile to the center of section twenty-nine; thence east one-half mile to the one-quarter section corner between sections twenty-eight and twenty-nine, said township and range; thence north three-quarters of a mile; thence east one-quarter of a mile; thence north three-quarters of a mile; thence east one-quarter of a mile to the one-quarter section corner between sections sixteen and twenty-one, said township and range; thence north one and one-half miles to the center of section nine, said township and range; thence east one and one-half miles to the one-quarter section corner between sections ten and eleven, said township and range; thence south one-half mile to the corner common to sections ten, eleven, fourteen, and fifteen, said township and range; thence east two miles to the corner common to sections twelve and thirteen, township nineteen north, range six east, and sections seven and eighteen, township nineteen north, range seven east, Mount Diablo Base and Meridian; thence north one mile to the corner common to sections one and twelve, township nineteen north, range six east, and sections six and seven, township nineteen north, range seven east, Mount Diablo Meridian; thence east three miles to the corner common to sections three, four, nine,

[23]*Political Code* (1923), § 3912.

and ten, township nineteen north, range seven east, Mount Diablo Meridian; thence south one-half mile to one-quarter section corner between sections nine and ten, said township and range; thence east one and one-half miles to the center of section eleven said township and range; thence north one-half mile to the one-quarter section corner between sections two and eleven, said township and range; thence east one-half mile to the corner common to sections one, two, eleven and twelve, said township and range; thence north two miles to the corner common to sections twenty-five, twenty-six, thirty-five, and thirty-six, township twenty north, range seven east, Mount Diablo Meridian; thence east one-half mile to one-quarter section corner between sections twenty-five and thirty-six, said township and range; thence north one-half mile to the center of section twenty-five, said township and range; thence east one and one-half miles to the one-quarter section corner between sections twenty-nine and thirty, township twenty north, range eight east, Mount Diablo Meridian; thence north one-quarter of a mile; thence east one-half of a mile; thence north one and one-quarter miles to the one-quarter section corner between sections seventeen and twenty, said township and range; thence east one and one-half miles to the corner common to sections fifteen, sixteen, twenty-one, and twenty-two, said township and range; thence northerly to the common corner of Plumas, Butte and Yuba, as established in section three thousand nine hundred forty; thence northerly to the northeast corner of the southeast quarter of the southeast quarter of section nine, township twenty north, range eight east; thence west one-half mile; thence north three-quarters of a mile to the quarter section corner between sections four and nine, said township and range; thence west to the corner common to sections four, five, eight and nine, said township and range; thence north one-half mile to the quarter section corner between said sections four and five; thence west one mile to the quarter section corner between sections five and six, said township and range; thence north one-half mile, more or less, to the north corner of sections five and six, said township and range; thence west on township line one and a quarter miles, more or less, to the southwest corner of section thirty-one, township twenty-one north, range eight east, Mount Diablo Base and Meridian; thence north on township line, two miles to the east corner of sections twenty-four and twenty-five, township twenty-one north, range seven east, Mount Diablo Base and Meridian; thence west one mile to the corner common to sections twenty-three, twenty-four, twenty-five and twenty-six, said township and range; thence north one-half mile to the quarter section corner between sections twenty-three and twenty-four, said township and range; thence west one-half mile to the center of said section twenty-three; thence north one-half mile to the quarter section corner between sections fourteen and twenty-three, said township and range; thence west one-half mile to the corner common to sections fourteen, fifteen, twenty-two and twenty-three, said township and range; thence north one mile to the corner common to sections ten, eleven, fourteen and fifteen, said township and range; thence west one mile; thence north one mile; thence west one mile; thence north two miles; thence west one mile; thence north one mile; thence west one mile, to the east corner of sections twenty-four and twenty-five, township twenty-two north, range six east, Mount Diablo Base and Meridian; thence north, on township line, one mile to the east corner of sections thirteen and twenty-four, said township and range; thence west one mile to the corner common to sections thirteen, fourteen, twenty-three and twenty-four, said township and range; thence north one mile to the corner common to sections eleven, twelve, thirteen and fourteen, said township and range; thence west one mile to the corner common to sections ten, eleven, fourteen and fifteen, said township and range; thence north one mile to the corner common to sections two, three, ten and eleven; thence west one-quarter mile; thence north one-quarter mile; thence west one-quarter mile; thence north one-quarter mile to the center of section three, said township and range; thence west three-quarters of a mile; thence north one-half mile to the north boundary of section four, said township and range; thence west on township line one-half mile; thence north one mile; thence west three-quarters of a mile to the quarter section corner between sections twenty-nine and thirty-two, township twenty-three, north, range six east, Mount Diablo Base and Meridian; thence north one mile to the quarter section corner between sections twenty and twenty-nine, said township and range; thence west one mile to the quarter section corner between sections nineteen and thirty, said township and range; thence north one mile to the quarter section corner between sections eighteen and nineteen, said township and range; thence west one-half mile to the west corner of said sections eighteen and nineteen; thence north, on township line, one mile to the east corner of sections twelve and thirteen, township twenty-three¹ north, range five east; thence west one mile to the corner common to sections eleven, twelve, thirteen and fourteen, said township and range; thence north one-half mile to the quarter section corner between said sections eleven and twelve; thence west one mile to the quarter section corner between sections ten and eleven, said township and range; thence north one-half mile to the corner common to sections two, three, ten, and eleven, said township and range; thence west one mile to the corner common to sections three, four, nine, and ten, said township and range; thence north one mile to the north corner of said sections three and four, two miles to the corner common to sections twenty-seven, twenty-eight, thirty-three, and thirty-four, township twenty-four north, range five east, Mount Diablo Base and Meridian; thence west one mile to the corner common to sections twenty-eight, twenty-nine, thirty-two, and thirty-three, said township and range; thence north one mile to the corner common to sections twenty, twenty-one, twenty-eight, and twenty-nine, said township and range; thence east one mile to the corner common to sections twenty-one, twenty-two, twenty-seven, and twenty-eight, said township and range; thence north one mile to the corner common to sections fifteen, sixteen, twenty-one, and twenty-two, said township and range; thence west one-half mile to the quarter section corner between said sections sixteen and twenty-one; thence north two miles to the quarter section corner between sections four and nine, said township and range; thence east one-half mile to the corner common to sections three, four, nine, and ten, said township and range; thence north one mile to the north corner of sections three and four, said township and range, two miles to the corner common to sections twenty-seven, twenty-eight, thirty-three, and thirty-four, township twenty-five north, range five east, Mount Diablo Base and Meridian; thence west one-half mile to the quarter section corner between said sections twenty-eight and thirty-three; thence north two miles to the quarter section corner between sections sixteen and twenty-one, said township and range; thence east one-half mile to the corner common to sections fifteen, sixteen, twenty-one, and twenty-two, said township and range; thence north one mile to the corner common to sections nine, ten, fifteen, and sixteen, said township and range; thence east one half mile to the quarter section corner between said sections ten and fifteen; thence north one and one-half miles to the center of section three, said township and range; thence east one mile to the center of section two, said township

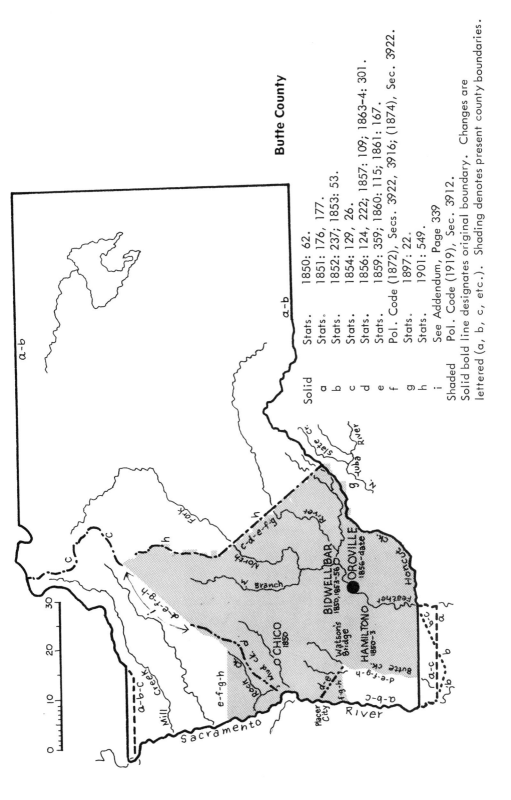

Butte County

Solid		Stats.	1850: 62.
a		Stats.	1851: 176, 177.
b		Stats.	1852: 237; 1853: 53.
c		Stats.	1854: 129, 26.
d		Stats.	1856: 124, 222; 1857: 109; 1863-4: 301.
e		Stats.	1859: 359; 1860: 115; 1861: 167.
f		Pol. Code (1872), Secs. 3922, 3916; (1874), Sec. 3922.
g		Stats.	1897: 22.
h		Stats.	1901: 549.
i		See Addendum, Page 339

Shaded   Pol. Code (1919), Sec. 3912.
Solid bold line designates original boundary. Changes are lettered (a, b, c, etc.). Shading denotes present county boundaries.

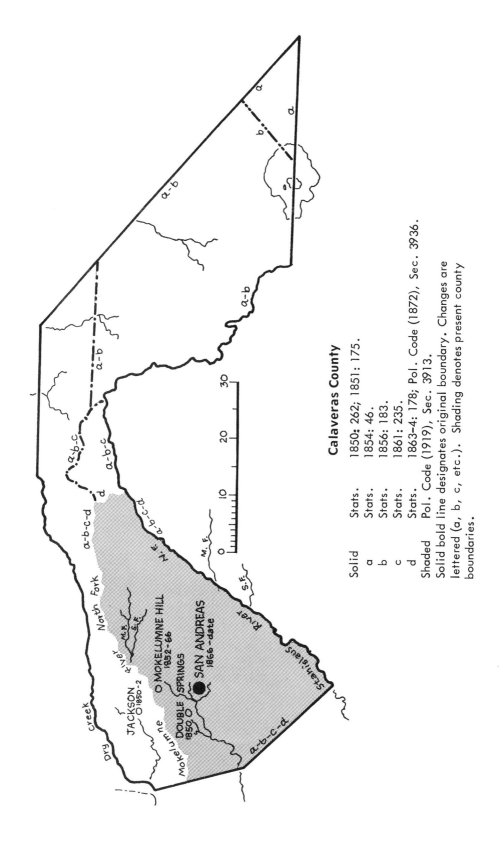

Calaveras County

Solid	Stats.	1850: 262; 1851: 175.
a	Stats.	1854: 46.
b	Stats.	1856: 183.
c	Stats.	1861: 235.
d	Stats.	1863-4: 178; Pol. Code (1872), Sec. 3936.

Shaded Pol. Code (1919), Sec. 3913.

Solid bold line designates original boundary. Changes are lettered (a, b, c, etc.). Shading denotes present county boundaries.

and range; thence north one-half mile, more or less, to the quarter section corner on north boundary of said section two; thence east on township line to the quarter section corner on south boundary of section thirty-five, township twenty-six north, range five east, Mount Diablo Base and Meridian; thence north one mile to the quarter section corner between sections twenty-six and thirty-five, said township and range; thence east one-half mile to the corner common to sections twenty-five, twenty-six, thirty-five, and thirty-six, said township and range; thence north one mile to the corner common to sections twenty-three, twenty-four, twenty-five, and twenty-six, said township and range; thence west one-half mile to the quarter section corner between said sections twenty-three and twenty-six; thence north one and one-half miles to the center of section fourteen, said township and range; thence west one-half mile to the quarter section corner between sections fourteen and fifteen, said township and range; thence north one-half mile to the corner common to sections ten, eleven, fourteen, and fifteen, said township and range; thence west one mile to the corner common to sections nine, ten, fifteen, and sixteen, said township and range; thence north two and one-half miles to the quarter section corner between sections thirty-three and thirty-four, township twenty-seven north, range five east, Mount Diablo Base and Meridian; thence west one and three-quarters miles, more or less, to the Chico and Humboldt road at the corner common to Plumas, Butte, and Tehama counties; thence southwesterly on the southeasterly line of Tehama to the southeast corner of Tehama, at point of intersection of Rock Creek and southern line of township twenty-four north, Mount Diablo Base; thence west on said township line to the Sacramento River; thence down said river to the southwest corner of the Llano Seco grant; thence northeasterly and southeasterly along the eastern boundary of Glenn County as established in section three thousand nine hundred nineteen to the northeastern corner of Colusa County; thence on Colusa County east line, down Butte Creek, to the northwest corner of Sutter County, as established in section three thousand nine hundred fifty-nine; thence east on north line of Sutter County to Feather River; thence down Feather River to place of beginning.''

CALAVERAS COUNTY

Original Boundary. Calaveras was one of the counties created by the first legislature in 1850. Its area as it was originally created was nearly four times its present size. During the first two years three acts were passed in an effort to define the boundaries of this county. The last of these, passed in 1851, gives the clearest definition of the lines as they were originally intended. It reads:

> "Beginning at the corner of Sacramento and San Joaquin counties; thence up the middle of Dry Creek to its source; thence following the summit of the dividing ridge between Moquelumne and Cosumne rivers; thence due east to the state boundary line; thence in a southeasterly direction along the boundary line of the state to the parallel of thirty-eight degrees of north latitude; thence due west to the summit of the Sierra Nevada; thence in a westerly direction along said summit to the north fork of the Stanislaus River; thence down the north fork of the Stanislaus River to a point one mile north of Knights Ferry; thence along the eastern boundary of San Joaquin County to the place of beginning."[1]

The only portion here requiring further consideration is that part in common with San Joaquin County. This line is defined elsewhere as running from the southeastern corner of Sacramento County in Dry Creek

> "thence south to a point one mile north of Lemon's Ranch; thence south to a point one mile north of Knights Ferry on the Stanislaus River."[2]

Amador Line, 1854. The creation of Amador County in 1854 deprived Calaveras of a large strip of territory along its north border. The line between the two counties ran as follows:[3]

> "Beginning in the middle of Mokelumne River, on the eastern boundary of San Joaquin County, thence up the middle of the channel of said river to the sources of the north fork of the same, thence due east to the eastern boundary of the state."

---

[1]*Statutes,* 1851 : 175 ; the other acts were 1850 : 63, 262.
[2]*Ibid.,* 1850 : 63, § 26.
[3]*Ibid.,* 1854 : 157.

The Mokelumne River, as here described, forms the present boundary between these counties.

Fresno County, 1856. A slight change in the southern boundary of Calaveras was made by the creation of Fresno County in 1856. That line was described as running due southwest from a point on the state line to Newtons Crossing on the Chowchilla River.[4] The change here made was of little importance às it included only a small triangular area lying east of Mono Lake.

The Eastern Boundary: Mono and Alpine. A much larger reduction in the area of Calaveras County was made in 1861 when Mono County was created, taking with it all that part of Calaveras lying east of the main summit of the Sierra Nevadas.[5]

The last step in bringing Calaveras County to its present limits was made at the time of the creation of Alpine County in 1864. The line separating the two counties now stands as it was at that time defined.[6]

Present Line, 1923. The boundary of Calaveras as adopted in the Political Code in 1872 embodied the changes made up to that date.[7] There has been no amendment to the boundaries since that time. An error in referring to the ''easterly'' line of Alpine as being the boundary adjacent to Calaveras was corrected when the portion of the Political Code referring to county boundaries was amended in 1919. Except for this correction and changes in the section numbers the description given below is the same as the one adopted in 1872.[8]

> ''3913. *Calaveras.* Beginning at southern corner, at a point in the Stanislaus River where it intersects the eastern line of Stanislaus County, as established in section three thousand nine hundred fifty-eight, being a point one mile north of Knights Ferry, and being the western corner of Tuolumne County; thence up said river and north fork thereof, to the westerly line of Alpine as established in section three thousand nine hundred ten; thence northerly, on the line of Alpine, to the southeast corner of

---

[4]*Statutes*, 1856 : 183. This line may still be traced from portions of the present line between Mariposa and Madera counties.
[5]*Ibid.*, 1861 : 235.
[6]*Ibid.*, 1863–64 : 178.
[7]*Political Code* (1872), § 3936.
[8]*Ibid.*, (1919), § 3913; (1923), § 3913.

Amador, as established in section three thousand nine hundred eleven and section three thousand nine hundred ten; thence southwesterly, on the southern line of Amador, down the Mokelumne River, to the southwest corner of Amador, on eastern line of San Joaquin County; thence southerly and southeasterly, on line of San Joaquin and Stanislaus, as established in sections three thousand nine hundred forty-seven and three thousand nine hundred fifty-eight, to the place of beginning.''

COLUSA COUNTY

None of the fifty-seven other counties of the state have had, in respect to their boundaries, a history similar to that of Colusa County (originally Colusi), for with the exception of a small strip, about six miles in width, extending across the northern part of the county, its present territory has nothing in common with its original limits. All that part of Tehama south and west of Red Bluff and the whole of Glenn County were at one time included within the bounds of Colusa, while on the other hand the greater part of the present Colusa was originally within Yolo County.

Original Boundaries, 1850. Colusi County was created, although not separately organized, in 1850. Its boundaries as described in the law ran as follows:[1]

> "Beginning at a point on the summit of the Coast Range due west from the Red Bluffs, and running thence due east to said Bluffs on the Sacramento River; thence down the middle of said river to the northwest corner of Sutter County; thence due west, along the northern boundary of Yolo County, to the summit of the Coast Range; thence in a northwesterly direction, following the summit of said range, to the point of beginning."

The southern line was, as stated, determined by the northern boundary of Sutter and Yolo which ran due west from the mouth of Honcut Creek.

The county was left unorganized by the legislature at its first session which provided that until the time of its organization it should be attached to Butte County.

Line of 1851, 1856. Early in the year 1851 Colusi County was organized with its county seat at Monroeville, at the mouth of Stony Creek near the northern end of the county. The legislature was at this time in session and had under consideration the redefinition of county boundaries. Several changes were made in the boundaries of the counties, among them being the northern and southern boundaries of Colusi County. The former was defined as running from the Sacramento River at the mouth of Red Bluff Creek, up that creek to its source and

---

[1]*Statutes,* 1850 : 62. As late as 1857 the name Colusi is used.

thence west to the summit of the Coast Range. This new line was some distance south of the original boundary. A greater change was made in the Yolo-Colusi county line, the northern boundary of Yolo being defined thus:[2]

> "on the summit of the Coast Range at a point due west from a point in the Sacramento River ten miles below the head of 'Sycamore Slough,' and running due east to the Sacramento River."

It has been impossible to determine the exact location of this line. It seems, however, to have been near the present boundary and has been shown accordingly upon the map.

The Western Boundary. On account of the unknown character of the country during the early years descriptions of county boundaries were often extremely vague and sometimes entirely misleading. A case in hand is that of the western boundary of Colusa County before it was finally established in 1868. In 1851 this boundary was defined as running "in a southeasterly direction following the summit of the Coast Range."[3] Since the summit of this range was also the eastern boundary of Mendocino County the boundaries of the two were therefore in this region identical. A study of the two boundaries taken together may therefore help to determine the location of the line. Elsewhere under the discussion of Mendocino County it has been shown that the terms "summit of the Coast Range" may not be interpreted literally,[4] for that watershed lies west of Clear Lake and such an interpretation would be inconsistent with other provisions in the Mendocino descriptions. The "summit" then must have been somewhere east of the lake. Unfortunately, there are east of the lake two ridges either of which might, from the reading of the statute, have been the one referred to. According to one interpretation the territory drained by the north fork of Cache Creek, known as the Long Valley region, would be in Mendocino County; according to the other it would be in Colusa.

The statute defining the boundaries of Colusi County in 1856 appear at first reading to solve the question, or at any rate to determine definitely which of these two ridges was

[2]*Statutes,* 1851: 179.
[3]*Ibid.,* 1851: 179.
[4]*See* discussion of Mendocino boundary.

then accepted as the western boundary of Colusa. It provided that the Colusi line should run west from the Sacramento River on the line between townships twelve and thirteen north

> "to the first ridge of the Coast Range, up said ridge to the summit of the Coast Range, up said summit to a point five miles south of Thames Creek."[5]

Since the description reads westward it is natural to suppose that the "first ridge" is the one lying east of Long Valley and west of Bear Creek. From a study of the boundaries of the adjacent counties and in view of the nature of the geography of this region it appears unreasonable to consider that this was the case. The question then arises as to whether the "first ridge of the Coast Range" mentioned in the act of 1856 was not in reality the same as the ridge referred to in the description of the Napa boundary in 1855, namely one lying further west. For it should be noticed that in 1855 the northern line of Napa County had been redefined, that part which extended north from the outlet of Clear Lake being described as follows:[6]

> "thence easterly to the top of the mountains dividing Clear Lake Valleys from Sacramento Valley; thence northerly along the top of said mountains to the head of Clear Lake."

Now, while it is possible that the eastern line of Napa extended as far east as to include Long Valley, in view of the fact that the boundary touched at the outlet of the lake it is more probable that this line went north along the nearest ridge, that is, the one lying between Clear Lake and Long Valley. Also it should be noted that since the waters of Long Valley empty not into Clear Lake, but into Cache Creek and then into the Sacramento Valley, it can scarcely be argued that Long Valley was one of the Clear Lake valleys. If this reasoning is correct the Napa boundary ran northerly along the ridge immediately east of Clear Lake and did not include Long

[5]*Statutes*, 1856 : 124.
[6]*Ibid.*, 1855 : 77.

Valley. Similarly it may be argued that the Colusi line was in this region the same as the Napa boundary.

In 1864 further legislation was adopted which assists greatly in defining these lines, for in that year the eastern line of Lake County, which when created in 1861 had fallen heir to this part of Napa County, was described in a manner which does not allow of differences in interpretation as did the act of 1855. The portion of the description referred to places the line

> "along the main ridge of mountains dividing the waters of Long Valley on the east, and Clear Lake on the west; thence up said ridge to the summit of the Coast Range."[7]

Although this act materially extended the territory of Lake County at the expense of Mendocino it is nowhere referred to as an attempt to change the boundary in this particular region. In view of the ambiguity and uncertainty of former descriptions it seems safe to conclude that in reference to this line the attempt was to define rather than to alter. This then helps to interpret the location of the Colusa line, for if the western boundary of that county coincided with the eastern line of Lake County it was at last definitely described. If, on the other hand, as might be contended, the Colusa line ran east of Long Valley, a most extraordinary condition would have resulted from this act, for the intervening territory would be a detached portion of Mendocino County. This, however, seems absurd and it appears clear that the "first ridge of the Coast Range" mentioned in 1856 was the same as the ridge mentioned in the Lake County boundary act of 1864, and that this was also "the summit of the Coast Range" mentioned in the earlier acts of 1850 and 1851.[8]

Notwithstanding that the act of 1864 definitely fixed the eastern limits of Lake County and would appear also to have designated the location of the western line of Colusa as well, this interpretation was not accepted by the people of Lake

---

[7] *Statutes.* 1863–64 : 112.
[8] It is not held that these conclusions are proved. They do appear to be the more reasonable interpretation of the statutes and have been adopted upon the maps. It has been the accepted rule that when it is impossible to determine the location of a line from a statute, and when a later act is adopted not clearly inconsistent with or altering the former line, then the later description should be accepted as giving the location of the former line.

County, who still contended that the Colusa line lay to the east of Long Valley and that the legislation should specifically fix the boundary on the eastern line and give to Lake County the intervening territory.[9] Whatever the merits of the case may have been,[10] the champions of Lake County were successful in having an act approved by the legislature in 1868 fixing the easternmost line as the boundary between the two counties. Since that date no change has been made in this line.

Colusa-Tehama Boundary, 1856-1891. The creation of Tehama County in 1856 took away about one-fourth of the area of Colusa. On account of the indefinite manner in which the lines are described it is impossible to determine accurately the location of the boundary between Tehama and Colusa until 1872. The statute of 1856 defines the line between the two counties as running from a point on the summit of the Coast Range

> "five miles below Thame's Creek; thence easterly, to a point one hundred yards south of Regan's Ranch, on the Sacramento River."[11]

During the year 1857 in a further attempt to define the line it was described thus:[12]

> "Beginning at the first section line north of Ragers' House, on the Sacramento River, and running west on that line to where it is crossed by Stony Creek; thence up the middle channel of said creek, to the mouth of the North Fork of said creek; up the middle channel of the said North Fork, to the summit of the Coast Range."

In 1859 it was again redescribed as follows:[13]

> "beginning at the first section line north of Rogers' house, on the Sacramento River, and running west on said line to the summit of the Coast Range."

---

[9]Lakeport, Clear Lake *Courier*, March 3, 1867.

[10]It is possible to argue that this was merely a correction of an error made in 1864, when the western line was accepted as the boundary of Lake County. This was the contention of the writer referred to in the Clear Lake *Courier*, cited above. The Colusa *Sun*, on the other hand, argues that the law meant to give Colusa all the territory to the western ridge as this was the first ridge which the southern boundary would intercept. (Colusa *Sun*, February 9, 1867). After the adoption of the law of 1868, a writer who signs himself a resident of Long Valley, asks for the annexation of Long Valley to Colusa "where it formerly was before the creation of Lake County." (Colusa *Sun*, February 10, 1872).

[11]The name of the creek is variously spelled in three acts passed in 1856, each attempting to define this line, viz: Thome's, Thames, and Thom's creek. *Statutes*, 1856: 118, 124, 222.

[12]*Statutes*, 1857: 109.

[13]*Ibid.*, 1859: 359.

At the time the code was adopted in 1872 the location of the boundary was fixed by defining it in these words:[14]

> "Beginning at the point of intersection of Sacramento River with south line of Township twenty-three north, Mount Diablo Base; thence west, on said line, being northern line of Colusa, to the summit of the Coast Range."

The line of 1872 is described in a manner which permits it to be definitely located, but the same can not be said of the previous descriptions, the chief difficulty being to determine the location of Regan's Ranch and then to know whether this ranch was identical with Ragers' or Rogers' house referred to in the later acts. In view of the careless manner in which names were used in the early statutes, together with the similarity in these names, and also the fact that nowhere have the different names been found together, which would have indicated that they were distinct places, it seems safe to assume that they were identical.[15]

It must therefore be concluded that, notwithstanding frequent changes in wording, no significant territorial changes were effected by the statutes cited but that they show various attempts to define the line and were not alterations of boundary.

The Colusa-Butte Boundary, 1856-1872. At the time Colusa County was organized the Sacramento River was the eastern boundary. In 1856, however, a change was made whereby the line was shifted further east to Butte Creek giving to Colusa considerable territory lying between the two streams. By the act of 1856 the eastern boundary is described in these words:[16]

> "thence down the middle of the Sacramento River to Placer City; thence easterly to Watson's Bridge, on Butte

---

[14]*Political Code* (1872), § 3915.

[15]The name Rogers does not appear on any of the available maps, while that of Regan is shown upon later maps, although Rogers rather than Regan was the term used in the statutes to determine the line. The most reliable authority is the official plat and field notes of the survey of the Capay Rancho, made in April and May, 1858, on file in the archives of United States Surveyor General, San Francisco. They show Reager's House to be located on the left bank of the Sacramento River just south of the line between townships 22 and 23 north of Mount Diablo base line. I have therefore taken the name Reager for the map in preference to either of the names mentioned in the statutes.

[16]*Statutes*, 1856: 125. Henning, Map of Butte County, 1862, shows this line definitely.

Creek, and in Butte County; thence down the middle of Butte Creek to its junction with Butte Slough; thence down Butte Slough to its mouth on the Sacramento River.''

At the time of the codification of the laws in 1872, a slight change was made in this line. Since then, with the exception of the change brought about by the formation of Glenn County, there has been practically no change in this line. The line of 1872 ran from the

> "south line of township twenty-three; thence down said (Sacramento) river to the southwest corner of the Llano Seco grant; thence northeasterly along said grant line to its intersection with the northern boundary of township nineteen north; thence east to Butte Creek; thence down Butte Creek to Butte Slough; thence up Butte Slough to Sacramento River; thence down Sacramento River to the place of beginning.''[17]

Glenn County Line, 1891, 1893. In 1891 Glenn County was detached from Colusa County. The original boundary between the two counties was defined as follows:[18]

> "Beginning at a point on the boundary line between the counties of Colusa and Lake, as now established by law, at the northwest corner of the southwest quarter of section thirty, township eighteen north, range eight west, Mount Diablo Base and Meridian; running thence east along the half section line, and one and one-half miles north of the line dividing townships seventeen and eighteen north, of Mount Diablo Base and Meridian, to Butte Creek, the boundary line between Colusa and Butte counties.''

Since this included within the new county the town of Princeton on the west bank of the Sacramento River the line was unsatisfactory, so a change was made at the next session of the legislature, returning to Colusa the town of Princeton and adjacent country.[19]

---

[17]*Political Code* (1872), § 3916.
[18]*Statutes*, 1891 : 98.
[19]*Ibid.,* 1893 : 158.

Present Boundary. By an act of the legislature approved on May 24, 1919, these recent changes were incorporated as section 3914 of the Political Code which reads as follows:[20]

"Beginning at southeast corner, being northeast corner of Yolo, in Sacramento River, at its intersection with the south line of township thirteen north, Mount Diablo Base; thence west, on said township line to the ridge dividing the waters flowing into Bear Creek and Stony Creek, from those flowing west into the north fork of Cache Creek and Clear Lake; thence northerly, along said ridge to the summit line of the Coast Range, being the eastern line of Lake, forming southwest corner of Colusa and northwest corner of Yolo; thence northerly on said eastern boundary of Lake, to the southwest corner of Glenn; thence easterly on southern line of Glenn to Butte Creek; thence down Butte Creek to Butte Slough; thence up Butte Slough to Sacramento River; thence down Sacramento River to the place of beginning."

[20]*Political Code* (1919), § 3914; (1923), § 3914.

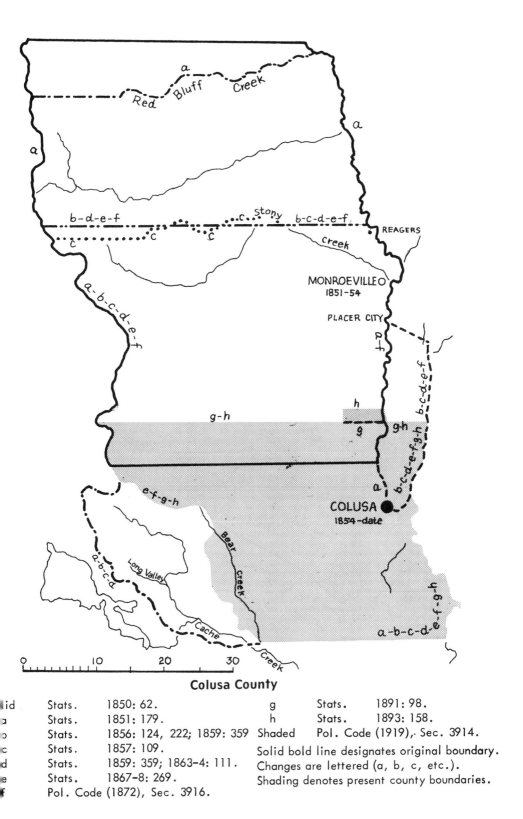

Colusa County

lid	Stats.	1850: 62.
a	Stats.	1851: 179.
b	Stats.	1856: 124, 222; 1859: 359
c	Stats.	1857: 109.
d	Stats.	1859: 359; 1863-4: 111.
e	Stats.	1867-8: 269.
f	Pol. Code (1872), Sec. 3916.

g	Stats.	1891: 98.
h	Stats.	1893: 158.
Shaded	Pol. Code (1919), Sec. 3914.

Solid bold line designates original boundary.
Changes are lettered (a, b, c, etc.).
Shading denotes present county boundaries.

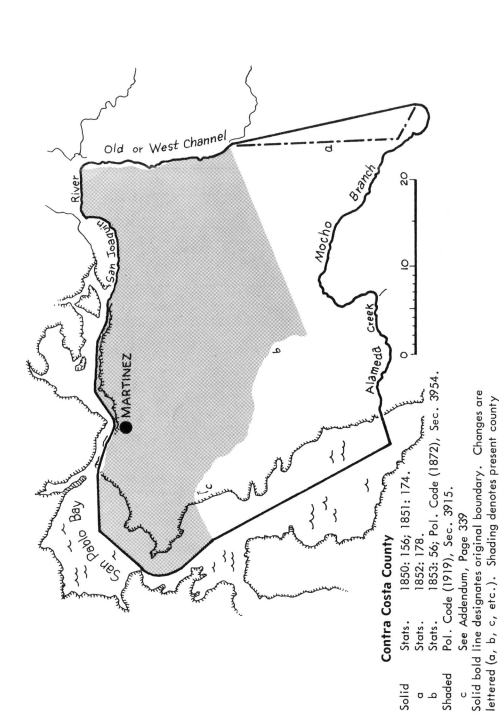

Contra Costa County

Solid	Stats.	1850: 156; 1851: 174.
a	Stats.	1852: 178.
b	Stats.	1853: 56; Pol. Code (1872), Sec. 3954.
Shaded	Pol. Code (1919), Sec. 3915.
c	See Addendum, Page 339

Solid bold line designates original boundary. Changes are lettered (a, b, c, etc.). Shading denotes present county boundaries.

CONTRA COSTA COUNTY

Original Boundary. Contra Costa was one of the original counties created in 1850. At that time it included about two-thirds of the present Alameda County as well as what it now has. The name Contra Costa was at that time, therefore, entirely appropriate for it held the opposite shore from San Francisco. Its original boundaries were as follows:[1]

> "Beginning at the mouth of Alameda Creek, and running to the southeast corner of San Francisco County to Golden Rock; thence up the middle of the Bay of San Pablo to the Straits of Carquinez; thence up the middle of said straits and Suisun Bay to the mouth of the San Joaquin River; thence up the middle of said river to the place known as the Pescadero or Lower Crossing; thence in a direct line to the summit of the Coast Range at the head of Alameda Creek; thence down the middle of said creek to its mouth, which was the place of beginning."

Alameda Creek here referred to is defined more definitely in a later act as being the Mocho branch of the Alameda Creek.[2]

In 1852 the limits of the county were redefined, the eastern and southern boundaries being given in these words:

> "thence up the middle of San Joaquin River to the confluence of the west channel of the San Joaquin River, with the main San Joaquin River, as laid down in Gibbe's map; thence up the middle of said west channel to a point about ten miles below Moore and Rhodes' Ranch, at a bend where the said west channel running downward, takes a general course north; thence due south in a direct line to the summit of the Coast Range; thence to the head of Mocho Creek, in a direct line; thence down the middle of said creek to its confluence with Alameda Creek; thence down the middle of said creek to the place of beginning."

Alameda County Created, 1853. In 1853 the southern third of the county was detached and, together with a portion of Santa Clara County, was organized as Alameda

---

[1] *Statutes,* 1850 : 156 ; 1851 : 174.
[2] *Ibid.,* 1852 : 178.

County. This placed the southern Contra Costa boundary upon the present line between the two counties.[3]

Line of Political Code, 1872. The change of 1853 was incorporated in the description of the boundaries as given in the Political Code for 1872. Section 3954 describes the boundaries of Contra Costa as follows:

> "Beginning in Bay of San Francisco, at the northwest point of Red Rock, being the common corner of Marin, Contra Costa, and San Francisco, as established in section 3950; thence up the Straits and Bay of San Pablo, on eastern boundary of Marin, to point of intersection with line bearing south twenty-six and one-half degrees east, and about six and one-quarter miles distant from southwest corner of Napa County, as established in section 3958, forming common corner of Marin, Solano, Sonoma, and Contra Costa, as established in section 3955; thence to the Straits of Carquinez; thence up said straits and Suisun Bay, to the mouth of the San Joaquin River; thence up said river, to the confluence of the west and main channel thereof, as laid down on Gibbe's map; thence up the said west channel to a point about ten miles below Moore and Rhodes' Ranch, at a bend where the said west channel, running downward, takes a general course north, the point being on the westerly line of San Joaquin County, and forming the northeast corner of Alameda and southeast corner of Contra Costa; thence on the northern line of Alameda, as laid down on Horace A. Higley's map, and as established in section 3953, to the easterly line of San Francisco City and County, as established in section 3950; thence due northwest, along said easterly line of San Francisco, four and one-half miles, more or less, to the place of beginning."

Present Boundary, 1923. A change in the definition of the Alameda-Contra Costa line in 1919 was incorporated in section 3915 of the code as amended in that year. This new section, which defines the boundaries of Contra Costa County as they now exist, reads as follows:[4]

> "3915. *Contra Costa.* Beginning in Bay of San Francisco, at the northwest point of Red Rock, being the common corner of Marin, Contra Costa, and San Francisco, as established in section three thousand nine hundred forty-six; thence up the Straits and Bay of San Pablo, on eastern boundary of Marin, to point of intersection

---

[3]*Statutes,* 1853: 56.
[4]*Political Code* (1919), § 3915; (1923), § 3915.

with line bearing south twenty-six and one-half degrees east, and about six and one-quarter miles distant from southwest corner of Napa County, as established in section three thousand nine hundred thirty-six, forming common corner of Marin, Solano, Sonoma, and Contra Costa as established in section three thousand nine hundred fifty-seven; thence to the Straits of Carquinez; thence up said straits and Suisun Bay, to the mouth of the San Joaquin River; thence up said river, to the confluence of the west and main channels thereof, as laid down on Gibbe's map; thence up the said west channel, to a point about ten miles below Moore and Rhodes' Ranch, at a bend where the said west channel, running downward, takes a general course north, the point being on the westerly line of San Joaquin County, and forming the northeast corner of Alameda and southeast corner of Contra Costa; thence westerly on the northern line of Alameda, as established in section three thousand nine hundred nine, to the easterly line of San Francisco City and County, as established in section three thousand nine hundred forty-six; thence due northwest, along said easterly line to San Francisco, four and one-half miles, more or less, to the place of beginning.''

DEL NORTE COUNTY

Original Boundary. Del Norte County, located in the extreme northeast corner of the state, was created on March 2, 1857, from a portion of Klamath County. Its original boundary was defined in these words:

> "commencing at a point in the Pacific Ocean, three miles from shore, on the forty-second parallel of north latitude, and running thence southerly three miles from shore to a point one mile south of the mouth of Klamath River; thence easterly, on a line parallel with said Klamath River, to a point one mile south of the mouth of Blue Creek; thence in a northeasterly direction, to the summit of the Siskiyou Mountains; thence in an easterly direction, following the ridge that divides the waters of Clear Creek from the waters of Dillon's Creek, to the Klamath River, at a point equi-distant from the mouth of said Dillon's Creek and the mouth of said Clear Creek; thence across the Klamath River, and in an easterly and northerly direction to said Klamath River, at the head of the cañon, (said cañon being about five miles above the mouth of Indian Creek, and between Eagle Ranch and Johnson's Ranch,) following the ridge of the mountain, and heading the waters that flow into said Klamath River, on the south side, between the two points last before mentioned; thence crossing the river, and in a northerly direction, following the ridge dividing the waters that flow into the river above from the waters that flow into the river below the place of crossing, to a point on the forty-second parallel of north latitude, due north from the head of said cañon; and thence west to the place of beginning."[1]

The Eastern Boundary. During the next thirty years the eastern boundary was changed three times. The first was in 1858 when that part lying near the northeastern corner was modified to read as follows:[2]

> "across the Klamath River, and in an easterly and northerly direction, following the ridge of the mountain, and heading the waters that flow into said Klamath River on the south side, above the point last above mentioned, to

---

[1]*Statutes*, 1857 : 35. The location of the lines here described may be found by consulting Randall's Map of Del Norte County, 1866, in the archives at Crescent City; and early state maps.
[2]*Ibid.*, 1858 : 21.

(94)

said Klamath River, at the head of the cañon, (said cañon being about five miles above the mouth of Indian Creek, and between Eagle Ranch and Johnson's Ranch,) and crossing said Klamath River at a point three miles south of Johnson's dwelling-house; thence due west to the summit of the ridge between the place of crossing and the mouth of said Indian Creek; thence northerly, following said last mentioned ridge, to a point on the forty-second parallel of north latitude due north from the place of crossing last mentioned.''

Again in 1872 when the code was adopted occasion was taken to change the wording describing this part of the boundary. It reads thus:[3]

''thence across Klamath River and east to the summit of Salmon Mountains, forming the southeast corner; thence northerly in a direct line to the head of the cañon on said river, about five miles above the mouth of Indian Creek; thence north, crossing Klamath River, to a point on the forty-second parallel of north latitude, forming northeast corner.''

These changes were of little significance; however, in 1887 a more radical amendment was made, whereby the whole of the eastern boundary was moved further west, the new boundary being located as follows:[4]

''along the northern boundary of Humboldt County, to the summit of a spur of the Siskiyou range of mountains; thence northerly, following the summit of said spur of the Siskiyou range of mountains, to the forty-second parallel of north latitude.''

Humboldt County Boundary. The section just quoted defines the southern boundary in terms of the lines of Humboldt County. It should, therefore, be noted that at the time of the dissolution of Klamath County in 1874 that portion of the northern line of Humboldt which affects this discussion was defined as follows:[5]

''commencing at the point where the present boundary of Klamath and Del Norte crosses the Klamath River; thence running easterly in a direct line to where the Salmon River enters the Klamath River.''

[3]*Political Code* (1872), § 3909.
[4]*Statutes and Amendments to the Codes of California,* 1887 : 106, § 3909.
[5]*Statutes,* 1873–74 : 756.

In 1901, in accordance with the tendency of recent legislation to define county boundaries in terms of the lines of the United States surveys, this line between Del Norte and Humboldt was also amended to read:[6]

"Commencing at the point where the north line of township twelve north, range one east, Humboldt Meridian, intersects with the Pacific Ocean; thence east on said township line to the northeast corner of township twelve north, range three east, Humboldt Meridian; thence south to the southeast corner of said township twelve north, range three east, Humboldt Meridian; thence east on the north boundary line of township eleven north."

Present Boundary, 1923. In 1919 section 3909 of the Political Code was amended to conform to the actual legal boundaries of the county, the section being given the new number of 3916. This section defines the present boundaries of Del Norte as follows:[7]

"3916. *Del Norte.* Situated in the northwest corner of the State of California, beginning at a point in the Pacific Ocean, on the forty-second parallel of north latitude, three miles from shore, being on the southern line of Oregon; thence running southerly, three miles from the ocean shore, to the northern line of Humboldt County; thence easterly, along the northern boundary of Humboldt County to the summit of a spur of the Siskiyou range of mountains; thence northerly, following the summit of said spur of the Siskiyou range of mountains, to the forty-second parallel of north latitude; thence due west to the place of beginning."

[6]*Statutes*, 1901: 600.
[7]*Political Code* (1919), § 3916; (1923), § 3916.

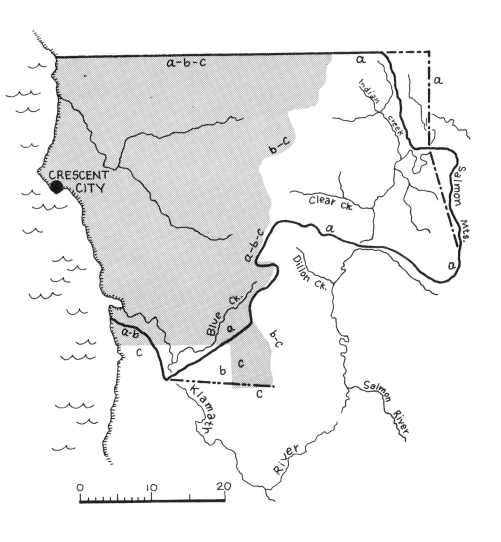

Del Norte County

Solid	Stats.	1857: 35; 1858: 21.
a	Pol. Code (1872), Sec. 3909.
b	Pol. Code (1887), Sec. 3909.
c	Stats.	1901: 600.
Shaded	Pol. Code (1919), Sec. 3916.

Solid bold line designates original boundary. Changes are lettered (a, b, c, etc.). Shading denotes present county boundaries.

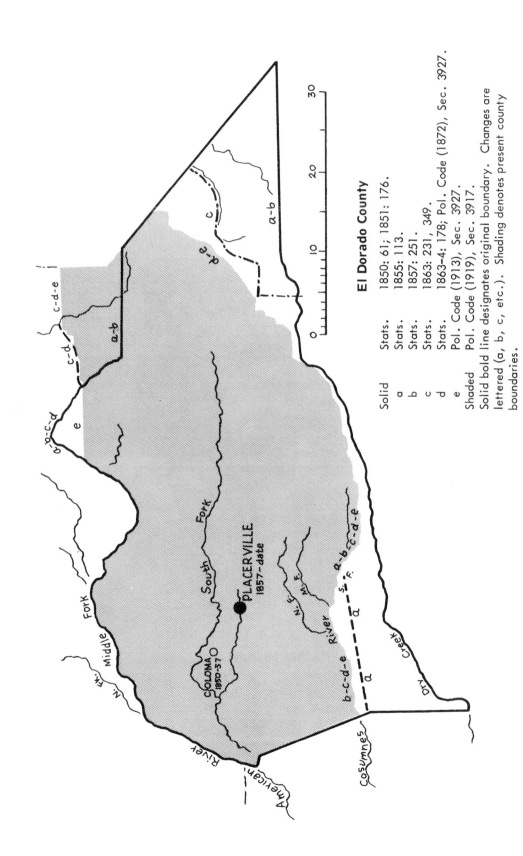

El Dorado County

Solid	Stats.	1850: 61; 1851: 176.
a	Stats.	1855: 113.
b	Stats.	1857: 251.
c	Stats.	1863: 231, 349.
d	Stats.	1863-4: 178; Pol. Code (1872), Sec. 3927.
e		Pol. Code (1913), Sec. 3927.
Shaded		Pol. Code (1919), Sec. 3917.

Solid bold line designates original boundary. Changes are lettered (a, b, c, etc.). Shading denotes present county boundaries.

EL DORADO COUNTY

Original Boundary, 1850. El Dorado, the county including within its limits the place of the original gold discovery, was naturally one of the first counties of the state to be created. Several changes have subsequently been made in the boundaries whereby El Dorado has contributed to Amador, Alpine and Placer counties. Originally its boundaries were described thus:[1]

> "Beginning at the junction of the north and south forks of the American River, and running thence up the middle of the north fork to the mouth of the middle fork; thence up the middle of said fork to its source; thence in a due easterly direction to the boundary of the state; thence in a southeasterly direction, following the boundary of the state, to the northeast corner of Calaveras County; thence in a westerly direction along the northern boundary of said county to the southeast corner of Sacramento County; thence in a northerly direction along the boundary of said county to the south fork; and thence down the middle of said fork to its mouth, which was the place of beginning."

The northern boundary of Calaveras County is elsewhere shown to run from the corner of Sacramento and San Joaquin counties

> "up the middle of Dry Creek to its source; thence following the summit of the dividing ridge between Moquelumne and Cosumne rivers; thence due east to the state boundary line;"[2]

Amador Line, 1854. Amador County, which had been created in 1854 from the northern part of Calaveras, was soon enlarged at the expense of El Dorado. Three changes were made in the line between the two counties before it was finally adjusted in 1863. The first of these was made in 1855 and read as follows:

> "All that portion of El Dorado County lying south of a line beginning at a point in the middle of the Consumnes

---

[1]*Statutes*, 1850: 61. The north boundary, which here does not specify which branch of the middle fork was intended, is made more definite by the act of 1863, noted below.
[2]*Ibid.*, 63.

River, at the eastern boundary of Sacramento County, running thence in an easterly direction, on an air line, to the mouth of the south fork of the south fork of the Consumnes River, thence up the middle of the south fork of the south fork of Consumnes River to its source, and thence due east to the present county line dividing El Dorado County from the county of Amador is hereby detached from the county of El Dorado, and attached to, and made a part of Amador County.''[3]

In 1857 a slight change was made in this line. it being made to follow the channel of the Cosumnes River down from its south fork rather than the ''air line,'' as previously described.[4]

The development of the country lying east of the Sierras in the early sixties caused numerous changes in county jurisdictions. One phase of this is seen in the shift of the El Dorado-Amador line in 1863, whereby a part of eastern El Dorado was given to Amador County. The Amador and Nevada wagon road, which here became the boundary, probably also helps to explain why this territory was placed under the jurisdiction of Amador County. The line between the two counties in 1863 ran as follows:[5]

> ''Beginning in the centre of the Cosumnes River at the point where said river enters Sacramento County; thence up the middle of the channel of said river to the south fork of said river; thence up the centre of the channel of said south fork to the south fork of the south fork of said river; thence up said south fork of the south fork to its source; thence due east to the Amador and Nevada wagon road; thence along the line of said road to its junction with the Big Tree and Carson Valley road, in Hope Valley; thence, from said junction, along the line of the road leading down said valley, through Carson Canon, to the eastern boundary of this state. Said roads, when marking the boundary line of said counties as provided in this act, shall be included within the boundaries of Amador County.''

Alpine County, 1864. In 1864 Alpine County was organized and took from El Dorado a small strip of territory in addition to that added to Amador the previous year.[6]

---

[3]*Statutes*, 1855 : 113.
[4]*Ibid.*, 1857 : 251.
[5]*Ibid.*, 1863 : 231.
[6]*Ibid.*, 1863–64 : 178.

Since that time there has been no change in the southern boundary of El Dorado County.

The Northern Boundary, 1863 and 1913. Before 1863 the northern line of El Dorado County was not clearly described, since the law did not definitely specify which of the branches of the middle fork of the American River should be followed. In 1863 this difficulty was settled by an act which declared that the north boundary of El Dorado should run

> "up the middle of the north fork [of the American River] to the mouth of the middle fork; thence up the middle of the middle fork to Junction Bar; thence up the middle of the main south fork of the said middle fork to the point where the same south fork is intersected by the George- town and Lake Bigler trail; thence along said trail to Sugar Pine Point, on the western shore of Lake Bigler; and thence due east."[7]

In 1913 another change was made in this line between El Dorado and Placer, whereby a small piece of territory lying south of the south fork of the middle fork of the American River was taken from El Dorado and given to Placer County. This act,[8] which defined the boundaries as they now are, was incorporated without change, except in section numbers, in the Political Code as amended in 1919. Below is given the description as found in section 3917 of the Political Code for 1923:

> "3917. *El Dorado.* Beginning at the junction of the north and south forks of the American River, which is the extreme west corner; thence up the north fork of the American River to the point of confluence of the middle fork of the American River; thence up the middle fork of the American River to the point of confluence of the south fork of middle fork of the American River at Junction Bar; thence up said last-named fork, now known as the Rubicon River, to a point where the same is inter- sected by the section line between sections twenty-nine and thirty-two, township fourteen north, range fourteen east, Mount Diablo Base and Meridian; thence east on the

---

[7]*Statutes*, 1863:349. A study of the early maps showing the El Dorado County boundary indicates that this was the line observed in the years before 1863 and not a change of boundary. For example see Britton & Rey, *Map of California*, 1860.
[8]*Ibid.*, 1913:603.

section line through township fourteen north, ranges
fourteen and fifteen east to the northeast corner of section thirty-five, township fourteen north, range fifteen
east; thence north on range line to southwest corner of
section thirty, township fourteen north, range sixteen
east; thence east on section line to the southeast corner of
section thirty, township fourteen north, range sixteen
east; thence north to the one-quarter section corner
between sections twenty-nine and thirty, township fourteen north, range sixteen east; thence through the centers
of sections twenty-nine, twenty-eight and twenty-seven,
to the one-quarter section corner between sections twenty-
six and twenty-seven, township fourteen north, range sixteen east; thence north on section line to the northwest
corner of section twenty-six; thence east on section line
to the northeast corner of section twenty-six; thence north
on section line to the one-quarter section corner between
sections twenty-three and twenty-four; thence east
through the center of section to the one-quarter corner
between sections nineteen and twenty-four, township fourteen north, range sixteen east and township fourteen
north, range seventeen east; thence north on the range
line to the one-quarter section corner between sections
thirteen and eighteen; thence east to the legal center of
section eighteen, township fourteen north, range seventeen east; thence north to the one-quarter section corner
between sections seven and eighteen, township fourteen
north, range seventeen east; thence east on the section
line to the western shore line of Lake Bigler, now called
Lake Tahoe; thence east in said lake to the state line;
thence south and southeasterly on the state line to the
northern corner of Alpine County, being a point where the
state line crosses the eastern summit line of the Sierra Nevada mountains; thence southwesterly along the west line
of Alpine County, as established in section three thousand
nine hundred ten, to the common corner of Alpine, Amador, and El Dorado counties, as established by said section; thence westerly on the northern line of Amador
County, as established in section three thousand nine
hundred eleven, and down the Cosumnes River and south
fork thereof, to the eastern line of Sacramento County, as
established in section three thousand nine hundred forty-
two; thence northerly by the eastern line of Sacramento
County to the south fork of the American River; thence
down the latter to the place of beginning.''

FRESNO COUNTY

Original Boundary, 1856. Fresno County was created on April 19, 1856, from territory which previously composed the southern part of Merced and the southern and eastern part of Mariposa. Its creation reduced both of these counties to approximately their present limits. The boundaries of 1856 are given in the act as follows:

"Beginning at a point where the Stockton road to Miller-town crosses the Chowchilla, known as Newton's Crossing; thence down said stream, on the north side, with the high water mark to the sink of the same at the lower molt of cottonwood timber; thence south, forty-five degrees west to the south boundary of Merced County; thence in a southeasterly direction with the present southwestern boundary of Merced and Tulare counties, to a point in the southwestern boundary of Tulare County south, forty-five degrees west from the point on Kings River, where the line dividing townships fifteen and sixteen south, crosses the same; thence north, forty-five degrees east to said point on Kings River; thence east with the line dividing townships fifteen and sixteen south, to the dividing ridge between the waters of Kings River and the Kawdah; thence with the said dividing ridge to the summit of the Sierra Nevada; thence north, forty-five degrees east to the eastern boundary of the State of California; thence in a north-western direction with said state line to a point north forty-five degrees east from the place of beginning; thence south, forty-five degrees west to the place of beginning."[1]

Mono Line, 1861. The creation of Mono County in 1861 took from Fresno all that portion of its territory lying east of the summit of the Sierra Nevadas.[2]

Mariposa Line Readjusted, 1870, 1872. In 1870 a portion of the line between Fresno and Mariposa was modified, a small part of Fresno being given back to Mariposa. The act making this change reads as follows:[3]

"The line at present known as the boundary line between Mariposa and Fresno counties, from the westerly point of junction of said counties, running easterly to the south-

[1]*Statutes,* 1856 : 183.
[2]*Ibid.,* 1861 : 235.
[3]*Ibid.,* 1869–70 : 449.

west corner of section eleven (11) and the northwest corner of section fourteen (14), in township six (6) south, range twenty (20) east, of Mount Diablo Meridian, shall hereafter be known as the established boundary line between the said counties. From the southwest corner of section eleven (11) and the northwest corner of section fourteen (14), in township six (6) south, range twenty (20) east, of Mount Diablo Meridian, a new line shall be surveyed and established as follows: Running east, following the section lines to the top of the main ridge between the waters of Big Creek and the Fresno; thence eastwardly on the main ridge which divides the waters of the Merced and the San Joaquin rivers, to the eastern boundary of Fresno County.''

The description of the line as here given found its way into the Political Code in 1872, notwithstanding the fact that during this same session of the legislature an amended line had been adopted whereby the Mariposa-Fresno boundary was located as it has since remained.[4] By the creation of Madera County in 1893 this became the line between Mariposa and Madera.

Fresno-Tulare Line, 1874, 1876. During the legislative session of 1873–74 the line between Fresno and Tulare was again defined and almost wholly changed from its original location. The act describes the boundary in these words:

''Commencing on the sixth standard south from Mount Diablo Meridian, at the southwest corner of township number seventeen (17) east, and running from thence north on the range line between townships sixteen and seventeen east, to the northwest corner of township number twenty-two south, range seventeen east; thence east on the township line between townships twenty-one and twenty-two south, to the southeast corner of township number twenty-one south, range eighteen east; thence north on the range line between townships eighteen and nineteen east to the northwest corner of township number twenty south, range number nineteen east; thence east on the township line between townships number nineteen and twenty south, to the southeast corner of section thirty-three, in township nineteen (19) south, range nineteen (19) east; thence north on section lines one mile, east one mile, north one mile and east one mile, north one mile and east one mile, to the southwest corner of section eighteen

---

[4]*Statutes*, 1871–72: 891; 1873–74: 100.

(18) in township nineteen (19) south, range twenty east; thence north one mile and east to the northeast corner of said section eighteen, township nineteen south, range twenty east; thence north one mile, east one mile, north one mile and east one mile to the southeast corner of section thirty-three, in township number eighteen south, range number twenty east; thence north one mile, east one mile, north one mile, east one mile, north one mile, east one mile, north one mile, and east to the southeast corner of section seven (7) in township eighteen south, range twenty-one east; thence north one mile, east one mile, north one mile, east one mile, to the southwest corner of section thirty-four (34), in township seventeen (17) south, range twenty-one east; thence north one mile, east one mile, north one mile, east one mile, north one mile, east one mile, north one mile and east to the southeast corner of section seven (7), in township number seventeen (17) south, range number twenty-two (22) east; thence north one mile, east one mile, north one mile and east to the southeast corner of section thirty-three (33), in township number sixteen (16) south, range number twenty-two east; thence north one mile, east one mile, north one mile, east one mile; thence north one mile, east one mile, north one mile and east to the northeast corner of section eighteen (18), in township number sixteen (16) south, range number twenty-three (23) east; thence north one mile, east one mile and north on section line to the township line between townships fifteen and sixteen south; thence east on said township line to the southeast corner of township number fifteen south, range twenty-four east; thence north on the range line between ranges twenty-four and twenty-five east to the northwest corner of township number fifteen south, range twenty-five east; thence east on the township line between townships fourteen and fifteen south, to the northeast corner of township number fifteen south, range number twenty-seven east; thence north six miles to the northwest corner of township number fourteen south, of range number twenty-eight east; thence east to the southeast corner of township number thirteen (13) south, range number twenty-eight east; thence north on the range line to the third standard line south from Mount Diablo Meridian, and from thence east on township line between townships thirteen and fourteen south to the present county line of Inyo County.''[5]

[5]*Statutes,* 1873–74 : 700.

For some reason this line, so carefully and elaborately defined in the act of 1874, was not satisfactory. The legislature at its next session, therefore, again amended it, placing the boundary between Fresno and Tulare on its present location.[6] The amended description reads thus:[7]

> "Commencing at a point on the eastern boundary line of Monterey County, as described in section three thousand nine hundred and forty-eight of Political Code, being on the summit of Coast Range, which point is south forty-five degrees west from the point on Kings River where the northern line of township sixteen south crosses the same; thence north forty-five degrees east to said point on Kings River; thence east along northern line of township sixteen south and continuing on said line to the northwest corner of township sixteen south, range twenty-five (25) east; thence north to the northwest corner of township fifteen (15) south, range twenty-five (25) east; thence east to the northeast corner of township fifteen south, range twenty-seven (27) east; thence north to the northeast corner of township fourteen south of range twenty-seven east; thence east on the line between township thirteen and fourteen south to the summit of Sierra Nevada, being the western line of Inyo County."

San Benito Line, 1887. In 1887 a change was made by which the eastern line of San Benito County was placed further east and described in the terms of the United States surveys. That part of the new boundary of San Benito affecting Fresno County ran from the corner common to Monterey, San Benito and Fresno counties as follows:[8]

> "thence northerly, following the summit of said mountains to where the range line between townships eighteen south, of ranges twelve and thirteen east, Mount Diablo Meridian, crosses the same; thence northerly along said range line to the northeast corner of township eighteen south, range twelve east; thence northerly along said township line to the southeast corner of township sixteen south, range twelve east, Mount Diablo Base and Meridian; thence northwest in a straight line to the northeast corner of township fourteen south, range nine east; thence in a straight line northwesterly, running toward the northeast

---

[6]This remark does not apply to that part of the line now forming the boundary of Kings County.
[7]*Statutes*, 1875–76 : 397.
[8]*Statutes and Amendments to the Code*, 1887 : 103.

corner of township thirteen south, range seven east, to a point where said line intersects the present boundary line between the counties of San Benito and Merced."

Madera County, 1893. In 1893 Madera, a new county, was formed from the northern part of Fresno. Its southern boundary is described as running from a point where the Fresno-Merced line

"is intersected by the San Joaquin River; . . . thence up the middle of said river, following the meanderings thereof southeasterly and northeasterly, to the point where said river crosses the south boundary line of township six south, of range twenty-four east, Mount Diablo Base and Meridian; thence running northeast to the boundary line of Mono County."[9]

Kings County Line, 1909. In 1907 an unsuccessful effort was made to have the northern boundary of Kings placed upon the fifth standard south, Mount Diablo Base, that is directly west along the most northerly line of Kings County. This would have taken from Fresno a large triangular piece of territory lying in its southwest corner. Since the law required a referendum vote of the people of the district affected it was defeated.[10] In 1909 a less radical change was carried through the legislature, giving to Kings a small piece of territory lying along the Kings River, the new boundary being thus described:[11]

"Beginning at the corner common to the counties of Kings, Monterey and Fresno; thence in a northeasterly direction along the boundary line between Fresno and Kings county as now established by law, to the corner common to sections thirteen (13) and twenty-four (24) in township twenty (20) south, range eighteen (18) east, Mount Diablo Base and Meridian and sections eighteen (18) and nineteen (19) in township twenty (20) south, range nineteen (19) east, Mount Diablo Base and Meridian, the same being the northwest corner of section nineteen (19) in township twenty (20) south, range nineteen (19) east, Mount Diablo Base and Meridian; thence north fifteen (15) miles to the southwest corner of section thirty-one (31) in township seventeen (17) south, range nineteen (19) east, Mount Diablo Base and Merid-

[9]*Statutes*, 1893 : 168.
[10]*Ibid.*, 1907 : 260.
[11]*Ibid.*, 1909 : 828.

ian; thence east along the township line a distance of eleven and one-half miles more or less to a point where said township line intersects the center line of the main channel of Kings River; thence northeasterly and easterly following the meander of said center line of the main channel of Kings River to the point where said center line of the main channel of Kings River intersects the boundary line between the county of Fresno and the county of Kings as now established by law; thence northeasterly along said boundary line to the corner common to the counties of Tulare, Fresno and Kings.''

Present Boundary, 1923. In 1923 these acts were codified in section three thousand nine hundred and eighteen of the Political Code. It defines the boundaries of Fresno County as follows:[12]

"3918. *Fresno.* Beginning on the south line of Merced county at a point where said line crosses the San Joaquin River; thence south, forty-five degrees west, and on line of Merced, to the eastern boundary line of San Benito; thence southeasterly along said boundary line to the eastern boundary of Monterey, and continuing along said Monterey boundary in a southeasterly direction, to a point in the same, which point is south forty-five degrees west from the point on Kings River where northern line of township sixteen south crosses the same; said point being the common corner of Fresno, Monterey, and Kings counties; thence northeasterly on the northwestern boundary of Kings and Tulare counties to said point on the Kings River where the northern line of township sixteen south crosses the same; thence east along northern line of township sixteen south and continuing on said line to the north-west corner of township sixteen south, range twenty-five east; thence north to the northwest corner of township fifteen south, range twenty-five east; thence east to the northeast corner of township fifteen south, range twenty-seven east; thence north to the northeast corner of township fourteen south of range twenty-seven east; thence east on the line between townships thirteen and fourteen south to the summit of Sierra Nevada, being the western line of Inyo County; thence northwesterly, on the summit line and lines of Inyo and Mono, to the common corner of Mono, Madera, and Fresno; thence westerly and south-westerly on the southern line of Madera to the place of beginning.''

---

[12]*Political Code* (1919), § 3918; (1923), § 3918.

Fresno County

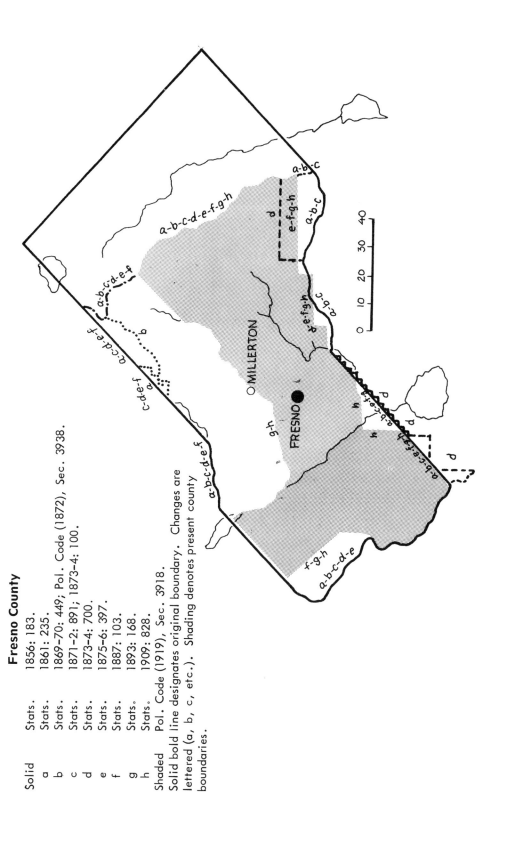

Solid	Stats.	1856: 183.
a	Stats.	1861: 235.
b	Stats.	1869–70: 449; Pol. Code (1872), Sec. 3938.
c	Stats.	1871–2: 891; 1873–4: 100.
d	Stats.	1873–4: 700.
e	Stats.	1875–6: 397.
f	Stats.	1887: 103.
g	Stats.	1893: 168.
h	Stats.	1909: 828.

Shaded   Pol. Code (1919), Sec. 3918.

Solid bold line designates original boundary. Changes are lettered (a, b, c, etc.). Shading denotes present county boundaries.

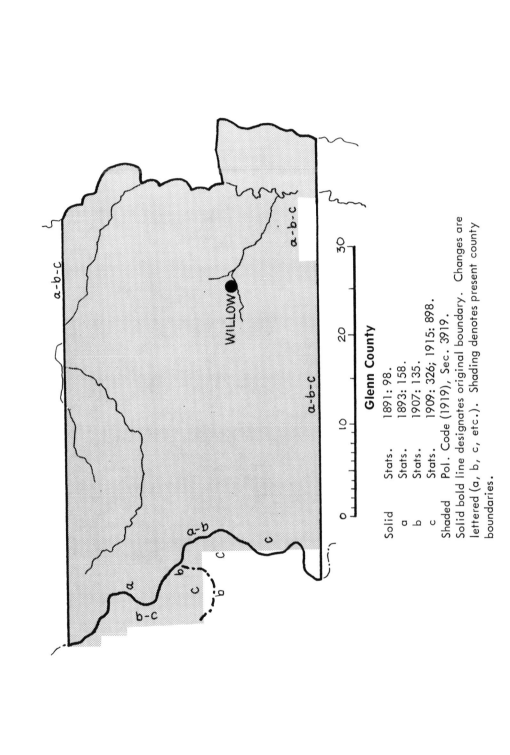

Glenn County

Solid	Stats.	1891: 98.
a	Stats.	1893: 158.
b	Stats.	1907: 135.
c	Stats.	1909: 326; 1915: 898.
Shaded	Pol. Code (1919), Sec. 3919.

Solid bold line designates original boundary. Changes are lettered (a, b, c, etc.). Shading denotes present county boundaries.

GLENN COUNTY

Original Line, 1891. Glenn County was created on March 11, 1891, from territory which had previously been included in Colusa County. Its boundaries as it was originally created are described in the statute in these words:[1]

> "Beginning at a point on the boundary line between the counties of Colusa and Lake, as now established by law, at the northwest corner of the southwest quarter of section thirty, township eighteen north, range eight west, Mount Diablo Base and Meridian; running thence east along the half section line, and one and one-half miles north of the line dividing townships seventeen and eighteen north, of Mount Diablo Base and Meridian, to Butte Creek, the boundary line between Colusa and Butte counties; thence northerly along said Butte Creek, with said county line, to a point where the north line of township nineteen north intersects said Butte Creek; thence westerly along the boundary line between the counties of Butte and Colusa as now established by law, to the center of the Sacramento River; thence northerly, and following the meanderings thereof, along the center of said Sacramento River, to a point where the north line of township twenty-two intersects the center of the Sacramento River, being the initial point of Tehama County, as established by law; thence west along the north line of township twenty-two north, to the southwest corner of Tehama County, as established in section three thousand nine hundred and fifteen of the Political Code; thence southerly on the summit of the Coast Range mountains, on the established line between Mendocino and Lake and Colusa counties, to the place of beginning."

The Line of 1893. In 1893 a small change was made in the southeast corner of Glenn County whereby the town of Princeton and a portion of the surrounding territory were taken from Glenn and placed again in Colusa County. The new boundary was made to run from a point on the old line located at the intersection of that line with the range line separating townships 18 north, 2 west, from 18 north, 3 west;

> "running thence north two miles to northeast corner of southeast quarter of section thirteen, township eighteen

[1]*Statutes,* 1891 : 98.

north, range three west; running thence east along the
half section line to the center of the Sacramento River;
thence down the center of the said Sacramento River, in
a southeasterly course, to a point where a line between
Glenn and Colusa counties crosses the said Sacramento
River.''[2]

Boundary Adjustments, 1907, 1909, 1915. In 1907 the eastern boundary of Mendocino County, which is also the western
boundary of Glenn, was modified by placing it upon township
and section lines as at present. By this change a strip of
territory lying on the west of the summit of the mountains,
formerly belonging to Mendocino, was given to Glenn County.[3]

In 1909 the boundary line between Glenn and Lake counties,
which had previously been located upon the ridge of mountains, was likewise defined in terms of townships and sections.[4]

During the session of 1915 a redefinition of the Glenn-Butte
line was adopted as follows:[5]

"From the point where the line between township 19
north, range 1 east and township 20 north, range 1 east,
intersects the line between sections three and four of the
Aguas Frias Rancho according to the La Croze survey of
the said Aguas Frias Rancho, said point being on the line
between Butte and Glenn counties, running thence south
along the said line between the said sections three and
four to its point of intersection with the center line of
Butte Creek, said point of intersection being on the present line between Butte and Glenn counties.''

Present Boundary, 1923. Previous to 1919 the description of the boundaries of Glenn County had not been given a
place in the Political Code. During the session of the legislature in that year a new section was incorporated into the code
defining these boundaries as they had been established by
earlier laws. The description is as follows:[6]

"3919. *Glenn.* Beginning at a point on the eastern
boundary line of Lake, as established in section three
thousand nine hundred twenty-five at the northwest corner
of the southwest quarter of section twenty-six, township eighteen north, range eight west, Mount Diablo
Base and Meridian; running thence east along the

---

[2]*Statutes,* 1893 : 158.
[3]*Ibid.,* 1907 : 135.
[4]*Ibid.,* 1909 : 327.
[5]*Ibid.,* 1915 : 898.
[6]*Political Code* (1919), § 3919 ; (1923), § 3919.

half-section line, and one and one-half miles north of the line dividing townships seventeen and eighteen north, of Mount Diablo Base and Meridian, to the range line separating townships eighteen north, range two west, from eighteen north, range three west; thence running north two miles to northeast corner of southeast quarter of section thirteen, township eighteen north, range three west; running thence east along the half-section line to the center of the Sacramento River; thence down the center of the said Sacramento River, in a southeasterly course, to the point of intersection with the half-section line, one and one-half miles north of the line dividing townships seventeen and eighteen north, Mount Diablo Base and Meridian; thence east on said half-section line to its intersection with Butte Creek, said point of intersection lying on the western boundary of Butte County and being the southeastern corner of Glenn and the northeastern corner of Colusa; thence northerly along the middle of the channel of said Butte Creek to the point of intersection with the line between sections three and four of the Aguas Frias Rancho as surveyed by La Croze; thence north along the said line between the said sections three and four to its point of intersection with the line between township nineteen north, range one east and township twenty north, range one east; thence west along said line to its intersection with the southern boundary of the Llano Seco grant, on the north line of section two in township nineteen north, range one west; thence southwest along said grant line to the southwest corner of said grant in the center of the Sacramento River; thence northerly and following the meanderings thereof, along the center of said Sacramento River, to a point where the north line of township twenty-two intersects the center of the Sacramento River, being the initial point of Tehama County, as established by law; thence west along the north line of township twenty-two north, to the southwest corner of Tehama County, as established in section three thousand nine hundred sixty of the Political Code; thence southerly on the established line between Mendocino and Lake counties, to the place of beginning.''

HUMBOLDT COUNTY

Original Boundary, 1853. Humboldt County was created March 12, 1853, from territory which previously had been a part of Trinity County. Its original boundaries were defined as follows:[1]

> "Commencing on the north at a point in the ocean three miles due west of the mouth of Mad River; thence due east from the point of beginning to the Trinity River; thence up the Trinity River to the mouth of the south fork of said Trinity River, running along the eastern side of the said south fork, one hundred feet above high water mark to the mouth of Grouse Creek; and thence in a due south direction to the fortieth degree of north latitude; and thence due west to the Pacific Ocean, and three miles therein; and thence north to the point of beginning."

Mendocino Boundary, 1859, 1860. In 1859 Mendocino County, which up to that time had been joined to Sonoma County, was separately organized and its boundaries were redefined. A small change in the northern boundary of this county encroached upon the territory of Humboldt County, for instead of the line being placed upon the fortieth parallel of latitude as previously, it was now located along "the line of the fifth standard north of the Mount Diablo Meridian,"[2] which was three or four miles north of the earlier line. This modification of the boundary, since it gave to Mendocino the harbor at Shelter Cove, was met by a protest from the people of Humboldt County. As a result, the legislature in 1860 once again placed the boundary line on the fortieth parallel.[3]

A statute passed in 1862 and the Political Code of 1872[4] both merely redefined the boundaries upon the old line of 1853 and 1860.

Annexation from Klamath County, 1875. In 1875 Klamath County, which had originally included a great part of the northwestern portion of the state, was dissolved. This was in consequence of the act of March 28, 1874.[5] In accordance

---

[1]*Statutes*, 1853 : 161.
[2]*Ibid.*, 1859 : 98.
[3]*Ibid.*, 1860 : 334.
[4]*Ibid.*, 1862 : 6; *Political Code* (1872), § 3914.
[5]*Statutes*, 1873–74 : 756.

with this act Humboldt County received all that part of Klamath County lying south and west of a line

"commencing at the point where the present boundary of Klamath and Del Norte crosses the Klamath River; thence running easterly in a direct line to where the Salmon River enters the Klamath River; thence in a southerly direction, following the ridge of the mountain that divides the waters of the Salmon and its tributaries from the waters of Klamath and Trinity rivers, and their tributaries, to the northern boundary line of Trinity County."

The Northern Boundary, 1901. The last step in establishing the present boundary of Humboldt County was made in 1901 when the line with Del Norte and Siskiyou was placed upon township lines. The act reads as follows:[6]

"Commencing at the point where the north line of township twelve north, range one east, Humboldt Meridian, intersects with the Pacific Ocean; thence east on said township line to the northeast corner of township twelve north, range three east, Humboldt Meridian; thence south on the southeast corner of said township twelve north, range three east, Humboldt Meridian; thence east on the north boundary line of township eleven north, range four east, eleven north five east, and eleven north six east, Humboldt Meridian, to the Klamath River; thence following said Klamath River in a southerly direction to the mouth of Salmon River, the point which now is the northeast corner of Humboldt County; thence following the line already established."

Present Boundary, 1923. When the portion of the Political Code defining county boundaries was amended in 1919 the changes in the boundaries of Humboldt County were incorporated in section 3920, which reads as follows:[7]

"*Humboldt.* Commencing at the point where the north line of township twelve north, range one east, Humboldt Meridian, intersects with the Pacific Ocean; thence east on said township line to the northeast corner of township twelve north, range three east, Humboldt Meridian; thence south to the southeast corner of said township twelve north, range three east, Humboldt Meridian; thence east on the north boundary line of township eleven north, range four east, eleven north, five east, and eleven north,

[6]*Statutes,* 1901 : 600.
[7]*Political Code* (1919), § 3920; (1923), § 3920.

six east, Humboldt Meridian, to the Klamath River; thence following said Klamath River in a southerly direction to the mouth of the Salmon River; thence in a southerly direction, following the ridge of the mountain that divides the water of the Salmon and its tributaries from the waters of Klamath and Trinity rivers, and their tributaries to the northern line of Trinity County; thence southwesterly on the line of mountain, being the northern line of Trinity, to a point in the Trinity River directly east of the mouth of Mad River; thence southeasterly, up Trinity River, to the mouth of its south fork; thence southeasterly, along the eastern side of said south fork, one hundred feet above high water mark, to the mouth of Grouse Creek; thence south, to a point on the fortieth degree of north latitude, being on northern line of Mendocino, and forming southeast corner of Humboldt; thence west on said line, to the Pacific Ocean; thence northerly, along the ocean shore to the place of beginning.''

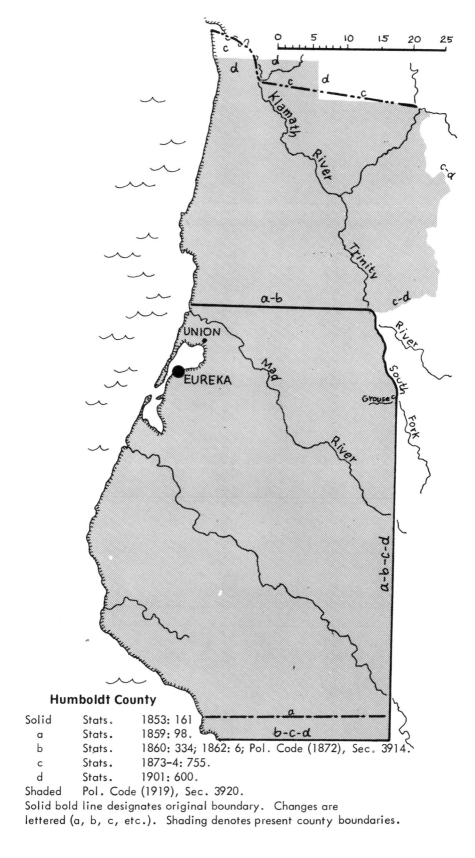

Humboldt County

Solid	Stats.	1853: 161
a	Stats.	1859: 98.
b	Stats.	1860: 334; 1862: 6; Pol. Code (1872), Sec. 3914.
c	Stats.	1873-4: 755.
d	Stats.	1901: 600.
Shaded	Pol. Code (1919), Sec. 3920.	

Solid bold line designates original boundary. Changes are
lettered (a, b, c, etc.). Shading denotes present county boundaries.

Imperial County

Political Code (1919), Sec. 3921.

a   See Addendum, Page 339

Solid bold line designates original boundary. Changes are lettered (a, b, c, etc.). Shading denotes present county boundaries.

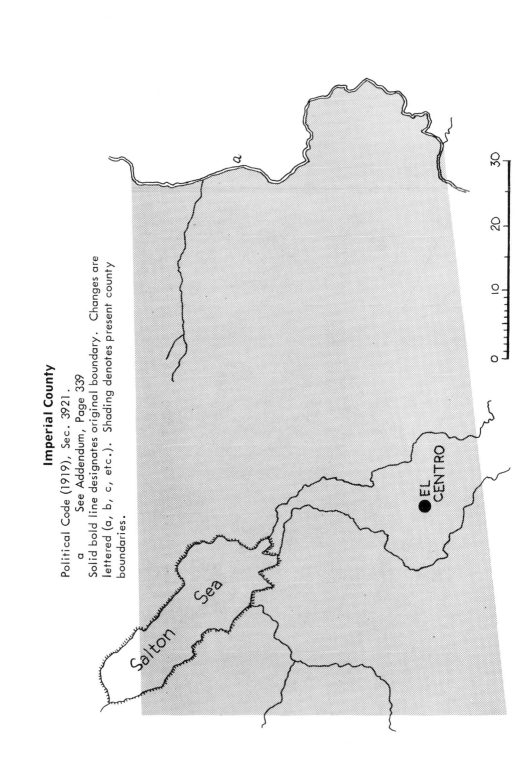

IMPERIAL COUNTY

Imperial County was created in 1907 under the provision of a general law providing for the creation of new counties.[1] Since it was established in this manner the boundaries were not set forth in any legislative act until the revision of this portion of the Political Code in 1919. The county boundaries were there defined as follows:

"3921. *Imperial.* Beginning on the second standard parallel south of San Bernardino Base and Meridian, at the common corner of township nine south, range nine east and township nine south, range eight east, said corner being the northwest corner of Imperial and the northeast corner of San Diego; thence east on the said second standard parallel to the state line on the Colorado River; thence down said river to its junction with the boundary line between the United States and Mexico; thence westerly, following that boundary to its intersection with the township line between and dividing townships eight and nine east, San Bernardino Meridian; thence north along said township line to the place of beginning."

Because of a question regarding the interstate boundary line, the authorities of Imperial County submitted a new definition of the boundaries which was incorporated into the Political Code in 1923. It reads as follows:[2]

"3921. *Imperial.* Beginning on the second standard parallel south of San Bernardino base and meridian, at the common corner of township nine south, range nine east and township nine south, range eight east, said corner being the northwest corner of Imperial County and the northeast corner of San Diego County; thence south on the range line between ranges eight east and nine east to the boundary line between the United States and Mexico; thence easterly following the boundary line between United States and Mexico as fixed by the treaty of Guadalupe Hidalgo to the junction of the Colorado River with the mouth of the Gila; thence up the Colorado River following the said boundary to its intersection with the line of the second standard parallel south of the San Bernardino meridian; thence westerly and following the said second standard parallel to the place of beginning."

[1]*Statutes,* 1907: 275.
[2]*Political Code* (1923), § 3921.

INYO COUNTY

Original Boundary. During the decade of the sixties several counties were organized on the eastern side of the Sierra Nevada Mountains. One of these was Inyo, created by an act of March 22, 1866. Its boundaries were defined in these words:

> "Commencing at the point where the southern boundary line of Tulare County is intersected by the eastern boundary line of the State of California, and running in a southwesterly direction along said county boundary line to the summit of the Sierra Nevada mountains; thence in a northerly direction along the said summit to the headwaters of Big Pine Creek; thence in an easterly direction down the middle of the channel of said Big Pine Creek to its mouth; thence due east to the state line; thence in a southerly direction along the state boundary line to the place of beginning."[1]

Mono Line, 1870. By a subsequent change in boundaries the area of the county was greatly increased. Through an act passed in 1870 the line between Mono and Inyo was shifted further north running from a

> "point where the main summit of the Sierra Nevada mountains is intersected by the line between townships numbered five and six south, of Mount Diablo Base Line; thence running due east in said township line to the eastern boundary of the State of California. All the territory lying between the line herein established and the line heretofore dividing said counties is hereby declared to form a portion of and be included in the County of Inyo."[2]

Present Boundary, 1923. In 1872 a change was made at the time the Political Code was adopted,[3] the southern boundary being moved south to the sixth standard. Except for changes in section numbers, the description of 1872 was incorporated in section 3922 of the Political Code as amended in

[1]*Statutes,* 1865–66 : 355.
[2]*Ibid.,* 1869–70 : 421.
[3]*Political Code* (1872), § 3942.

1919.[4] The section, which defines the present boudaries of Inyo County, reads as follows:[5]

"3922. *Inyo.* Beginning at the southeast corner of Tulare, as established in section three thousand nine hundred sixty-two, being the point of intersection of sixth standard south, Mount Diablo Base, with summit line of Sierra Nevada mountains; thence east, by said standard and extension thereof, to the eastern line of the state, forming southeast corner; thence northwesterly, on state line, to the southeast corner of Mono, as established in section three thousand nine hundred thirty-four; thence west on the southern line of Mono to the summit of the Sierra Nevada mountains, being on the eastern line of Fresno, and forming the southwest corner of Mono and northwest corner of Inyo; thence southeasterly on said summit line to the place of beginning."

[4]*Political Code* (1919), § 3922.
[5]*Ibid.,* (1923), § 3922.

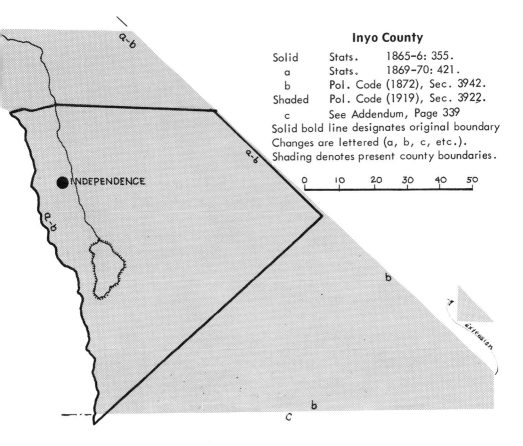

Inyo County

Solid	Stats.	1865–6: 355.
a	Stats.	1869–70: 421.
b	Pol. Code (1872), Sec. 3942.
Shaded	Pol. Code (1919), Sec. 3922.
c	See Addendum, Page 339

Solid bold line designates original boundary
Changes are lettered (a, b, c, etc.).
Shading denotes present county boundaries.

0 10 20 30 40 50

INDEPENDENCE

KERN COUNTY

Original Boundaries, 1866. Kern County was created in 1866 from territory which previous to that time was portions of Tulare and Los Angeles counties. Its original boundaries were described as follows:[1]

> "Commencing at a point on the western boundary line of Tulare County, two miles due south of the sixth standard south of the Mount Diablo Base Line; thence due east to the western boundary line of Inyo County; thence southerly and easterly, following the western boundary of Inyo County and northern boundary of Los Angeles County, to the northeast corner of Los Angeles County; thence south along the eastern boundary of Los Angeles County to the line between townships eight and nine, north of the San Bernardino Base Line; thence due west to the Tulare County line; thence southerly along the said Tulare County line to the southwest corner of Tulare County; thence northerly following along the western boundary of Tulare County to the place of beginning."

On account of the uncertain location of the boundary between Los Angeles and Tulare counties there may be some confusion in regard to the description of the eastern portion of the northern boundary of Kern County, for there may be a doubt as to whether this line struck the summit of the Sierras as far south as "two miles due south of the sixth standard south." If it did, the description as quoted above is perfectly proper. If not, then that portion of the act which describes the line as running "southerly and easterly, following the western boundary of Inyo County" is incorrect.

The northern line of Los Angeles County previous to the organization of Kern is described in the Statutes of 1851 and 1856[2] as running northeast from the "northeasternmost corner" of the Tejon Rancho. Since the territory here involved was not surveyed until a period later than that under consideration, it is doubtful whether the confusion in regard to the location of the line was at that time apparent.[3]

---

[1]*Statutes*, 1865–66 : 796.
[2]*Ibid.*, 1851 : 172 ; 1856 : 53.
[3]The Tejon Rancho was surveyed in 1862 and the northeast corner of Kern County lying west of the summit of the Sierras was not surveyed until a much later date.

The Northern Boundary, 1868. At the next session of the legislature following the creation of Kern County the northern boundary was placed one and one-half miles further north, running due east from "a point on the western boundary line of Tulare County one-half mile due north of the sixth standard south, of the Mount Diablo base line."[4]

Code Line of 1872. In 1872, at the time of the adoption of the Political Code, changes were made in the northern and southern boundaries of the county, the north line then being placed upon the sixth standard south of the Mount Diablo Base Line, on which line it has since remained. The southern line, which had extended westward along the northern boundary of Los Angeles County, was now continued further west along the extension of that same line to the summit of the Coast Range, which point is elsewhere described as forming the southwest corner of Kern County and the northwest corner of Los Angeles County. The full section reads as follows:[5]

> "Beginning at northwest corner, being common corner of San Luis Obispo, Monterey, Tulare, and Kern, as established in section 3940; thence east, on sixth standard south, Mount Diablo Base, to the northwest corner of San Bernardino, as established in section 3943; thence south, on the westerly line of San Bernardino, to southern line of township nine north, San Bernardino Base, forming southeast corner; thence west along said line and extension thereof to the summit of the Coast Range, being on the line of Santa Barbara, forming southwest corner; thence northwesterly, on said summit line, being eastern line of Santa Barbara and San Luis Obispo, to the place of beginning."

The Western Boundary, 1884. In 1884 that portion of the western boundary which was common to Kern and San Luis Obispo counties was amended and, whereas it had previously followed the summit of the Coast Range mountains, it was now placed upon the lines of the United States government survey. This line of 1884 still forms the boundary between San Luis Obispo and Kern counties.[6]

---

[4]*Statutes,* 1867–68: 40.
[5]*Political Code* (1872), § 3941.
[6]*Statutes,* 1885: 139. The detailed description may be seen in the later acts quoted below.

Eastern Boundary, 1917. Owing to uncertainty regarding the location of the western boundary of San Bernardino County[7] and to the rapid development of mines along this border an effort was made by the legislature in 1917 to fix the line in a satisfactory manner. The line is defined as follows:[8]

> "Beginning at the northwest corner of township eight north, range seven west, San Bernardino Meridian, being the northeast corner of Los Angeles County; thence east along the township line to the section line between sections thirty-two and thirty-three, township nine north, range seven west, San Bernardino Meridian; thence north, following section lines, to the eighth standard parallel south of Mount Diablo Base; thence east along said standard parallel to the southwest corner of township thirty-two south, range forty-one east, Mount Diablo Meridian; thence north along township lines to the seventh standard parallel south of Mount Diablo Base; thence along said standard parallel to the southwest corner of section thirty-six, township twenty-eight south, range forty east, Mount Diablo Meridian; thence north along section lines to the northwest corner of section one, township twenty-five south, range forty east, Mount Diablo Meridian, said point being hereby established as the northeast corner of Kern County and the northwest corner of San Bernardino County."

Present Boundary, 1923. At the time of the recodification of the county boundaries in 1919 these recent changes were incorporated in the act, together with slight readjustment of the boundary joining upon Ventura County. The section defining the present boundaries reads as follows:[9]

> "3923. *Kern.* Beginning at northwest corner, being common corner of San Luis Obispo, Kings, and Kern, as established in section three thousand nine hundred sixty-two; thence east, on the sixth standard south of Mount Diablo Base, to the northwest corner of section one, township twenty-five south, range forty east, Mount Diablo Meridian, said point being the northeast corner of Kern County and the northwest corner of San Bernardino County; thence south on the westerly line of San Bernardino as established in section three thousand nine hundred forty-four to the southeast corner of section thirty-

[7]See under Los Angeles County.
[8]*Statutes,* 1917 : 301.
[9]*Political Code* (1919), § 3923; (1923), § 3923.

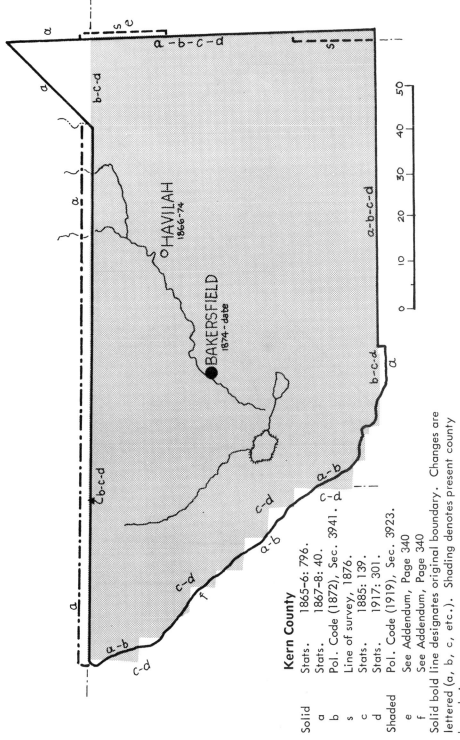

Kern County

Solid	Stats.	1865-6: 796.
a	Stats.	1867-8: 40.
b	Pol. Code (1872), Sec. 3941.
s	Line of survey, 1876.
c	Stats.	1885: 139.
d	Stats.	1917: 301.
Shaded	Pol. Code (1919), Sec. 3923.
e	See Addendum, Page 340
f	See Addendum, Page 340

Solid bold line designates original boundary. Changes are
lettered (a, b, c, etc.). Shading denotes present county
boundaries.

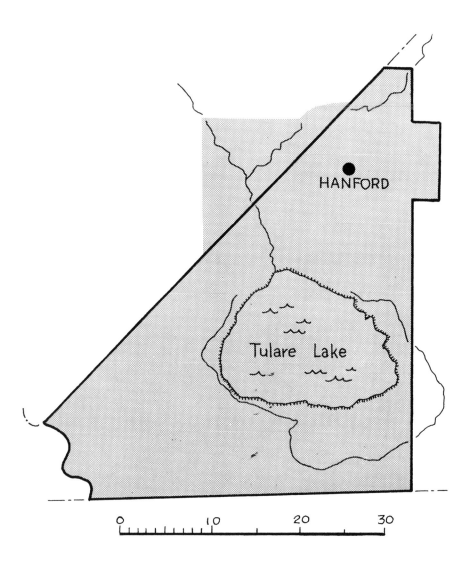

Kings County

Solid   Stats.   1893: 176.
Shaded   Stats.   1909: 827; Pol. Code (1919), Sec. 3924.
Solid bold line designates original boundary. Changes are
lettered (a, b, c, etc.). Shading denotes present county
boundaries.

two, township nine north, range seven west, San Bernardino Base and Meridian, forming the southeast corner of
Kern County; thence west along the range line between
ranges eight and nine north of San Bernardino Base to
the northeast corner of section five, township eight north,
range nineteen west, San Bernardino Base and Meridian,
said point being at the corner common to Ventura, Los
Angeles and Kern counties, as established in section three
thousand nine hundred sixty-four; thence westerly and
northwesterly along the northern boundary of Ventura as
defined in said section to the corner common to Santa Barbara, Ventura and Kern; thence along the northern boundary of Santa Barbara to the corner common to San Luis
Obispo, Santa Barbara and Kern; thence northerly along
the eastern boundary of San Luis Obispo to the place of
beginning.''

KINGS COUNTY

Original Boundaries, 1893. Kings County was created on March 22, 1893, from territory which had previously been a portion of Tulare County. Its boundaries, as they were at that time, are described in the act as follows:[1]

> "Beginning at the point where the fourth standard line south of Mount Diablo Base Line intersects or crosses the boundary line as now established by law between Tulare and Fresno counties; thence east to the northeast corner of section one, in township seventeen south, of range twenty-two east, Mount Diablo Base and Meridian; thence south six miles; thence east three miles; thence south nine miles to the southeast corner of section sixteen, in township nineteen south, range twenty-three east, Mount Diablo Base and Meridian; thence west three miles to the southeast corner of section thirteen, township nineteen south, range twenty-two east, Mount Diablo Base and Meridian; thence south nine miles to the southeast corner of township twenty south, range twenty-two east, Mount Diablo Base and Meridian; thence west to the northeast corner of township twenty-one south, range twenty-two east, Mount Diablo Base and Meridian; thence south twenty-four miles to the boundary line between Kern and Tulare counties as now established by law; thence west along the said boundary line between Kern and Tulare counties, to the corner common to the counties of Tulare, Monterey, San Luis Obispo, and Kern, as now established by law; thence in a northwesterly direction along the boundary line between the counties of Monterey and Tulare, as now established by law, to the corner common to the counties of Tulare, Monterey, and Fresno; thence in a northeastern direction along the boundary line between Fresno and Tulare counties, as now established by law, to the place of beginning."

Annexation from Fresno County, 1909. In 1907 an act was passed proposing to change the boundary line between Fresno and Kings County so as to place it upon the fourth standard south, Mount Diablo Base. This would have added to Kings County a large portion of territory previously belonging to Fresno County. The act provided that the pro-

---

[1]*Statutes,* 1893 : 176.

posed change should be submitted to the vote of the people living within the territory affected.[2]

This proposed change was not ratified, so at the next session of the legislature, in 1909, a less radical revision of the Fresno-Kings County line was made. According to the terms of this act the east and south boundaries of Kings County were to remain the same as they had been under the law of 1893, the northwestern boundary being the only one affected. It was to run as follows:[3]

"Beginning at the corner common to the counties of Kings, Monterey and Fresno; thence in a northeasterly direction along the boundary line between Fresno and Kings County as now established by law, to the corner common to sections thirteen (13) and twenty-four (24) in township twenty (20) south, range eighteen (18) east, Mount Diablo Base and Meridian, and sections eighteen (18) and nineteen (19) in township twenty (20) south, range nineteen (19) east, Mount Diablo Base and Meridian, the same being the northwest corner of section nineteen (19) in township twenty (20) south, range nineteen (19) east, Mount Diablo Base and Meridian; thence north fifteen (15) miles to the southwest corner of section thirty-one (31) in township seventeen (17) south, range nineteen (19) east, Mount Diablo Base and Meridian; thence east along the township line a distance of eleven and one-half miles more or less to a point where said township line intersects the center line of the main channel of Kings River; thence northeasterly and easterly following the meander of said center line of the main channel of Kings River to the point where said center line of the main channel of Kings River intersects the boundary line between the county of Fresno and the county of Kings as now established by law; thence northeasterly along said boundary line to the corner common to the counties of Tulare, Fresno and Kings."

Present Boundary, 1923. At the revision of the code in 1919 a new section was added defining the boundaries of Kings County as they had been set forth in the acts above cited. The description is as follows:[4]

"3924. *Kings.* Beginning at the northeast corner of section one in township seventeen south, range twenty-

[2]*Statutes*, 1907 : 260.
[3]*Ibid.*, 1909 : 828.
[4]*Political Code* (1919), § 3924; (1923), § 3924.

two east, Mount Diablo Base and Meridian; thence south six miles; thence east three miles; thence south nine miles to the southeast corner of section sixteen in township nineteen south, range twenty-three east, Mount Diablo Base and Meridian; thence west three miles to the southeast corner of section thirteen in township nineteen south, range twenty-two east, Mount Diablo Base and Meridian; thence south nine miles to the southeast corner of township twenty south, range twenty-two east, Mount Diablo Base and Meridian; thence west to the northeast corner of township twenty-one south, range twenty-two east; thence south twenty-four miles to the north boundary of Kern County, as now established by law; thence west along said north boundary of Kern County to the corner common to the counties of Monterey, San Luis Obispo, and Kern, as now established by law; thence in a northwesterly direction along the line between the counties of Monterey and Kings, as now established by law, to the corner common to the counties of Kings, Monterey, and Fresno; thence in a northeasterly direction along the boundary line between Fresno and Kings counties, as now established by law, to the corner common to sections thirteen and twenty-four in township twenty south, range eighteen east, Mount Diablo Base and Meridian, and sections eighteen and nineteen in township twenty south, range nineteen east, Mount Diablo Base and Meridian, the same being the northwest corner of section nineteen in township twenty south, range nineteen east, Mount Diablo Base and Meridian; thence north fifteen miles to the southwest corner of section thirty-one in township seventeen south, range nineteen east, Mount Diablo Base and Meridian; thence east along the township line a distance of eleven and one-half miles, more or less, to the point where said township line intersects the center line of the main channel of Kings River; thence northeasterly and easterly following the meander of the said center line of the main channel of Kings River to the point where said center line intersects the boundary line between the county of Fresno and the county of Kings, as now established by law; thence northeasterly along said boundary line to the corner common to the counties of Tulare, Fresno, and Kings; thence east along the fourth standard parallel line south, Mount Diablo Base and Meridian, to the point of beginning.''

KLAMATH COUNTY

Klamath bears the unenviable distinction of being the only county of the state which has completely disappeared. Many other counties were never organized although they had been created by law, but no other county having once been organized has ceased to exist as a political unit. Klamath County was created April 25, 1851, and was dissolved under an act passed March 28, 1874.

Its original territory may briefly be described as composing that part of the state lying north of a line drawn east from the mouth of Mad River and west of the summit of the Coast Range mountains. The section of the act reads as follows:[1]

> "Beginning at the point in the ocean, three miles due west of the mouth of Mad River, and running thence due east along the north line of Trinity County to the summit of the Coast Range; thence in a northerly direction along the summit of said Coast Range to the parallel of forty-two degrees north latitude; thence due west to the ocean, and three miles therein; thence in a southeasterly direction parallel with the coast to the place of beginning."

The location of the eastern boundary "along the summit of the Coast Range" is not readily apparent, on account of the uncertain direction the mountains take in the northern part of the state. Facts seem, however, to make it certain that all of the Klamath watershed, west of Rhett Lake was in Klamath County.[2]

Siskiyou Organized, 1852. In 1852 a new county was created along the northern state line. This was Siskiyou, composed of a part of Shasta County and the Shasta and Scott's River valleys of Klamath County. The line between Klamath and Siskiyou was defined as running from a point on the northern boundary of the state

> "due north of the mouth of Indian Creek, (being the first large creek adjoining the Indian territory, at a place

[1]*Statutes,* 1851 : 180.
[2]Shasta Plains, evidently Shasta Valley, was a voting precinct in Klamath County in 1851 as shown in Klamath County Archives. See also the decision of the Assembly in the case of the contested election *Coates* vs. *Hawkes,* decided in favor of Coates of Klamath County. *Assembly Journal,* 3d Sess. (1852), 99, 114.

known as Happy Camp, which empties into the Klamath River, on the opposite side below the mouth of Scott's River,) and from thence across Klamath River, running, in a southeasterly course along the summit of the mountains dividing the waters of Scott's and Salmon rivers, to the place of beginning."[3]

The place of beginning here mentioned was described earlier as the Devil's Castle near the Soda Springs, a point which still helps to determine the line of Siskiyou.

Trinity Line Adjusted, 1855. At the time of creation of the county the nature of the country included in the new county was but little known. There can be little wonder then that it was soon discovered that parts of it belonged more naturally to adjacent counties. The arbitrary southern line, running east nearly to the Sacramento River, cut off from the remainder of Trinity County all that region lying along the headwaters of the main Trinity and its northern tributaries. The distance to the county seat (Crescent City, 1854–56) made it almost impossible for the population living there to attend to their legal business. In 1855 an attempt was made to remedy this condition. The new line between Trinity and Klamath counties was described as running from[4]

"the northeast corner of Humboldt County, on the Trinity River, at the point where the boundary line between said county of Humboldt and the county of Klamath crosses said river; thence northeasterly up the principal ridge to the summit of the range of mountains dividing the waters of the Trinity River from the waters of Salmon River; thence following the said summit in an easterly direction to the summit of the range that divides the waters of the Sacramento from the waters that flow westwardly through the Klamath into the Pacific."

Del Norte County Created, 1857. Klamath County, as just stated, lacked unity. This was noticeable in the difficulties regarding the location of the county seat. Trinidad, located on the coast just north of Humboldt Bay, at one time an important depot for miners' supplies, first held the honor. The rise of Crescent City further north led to a demand for a change of the local capital to that place in 1854. This was

[3]*Statutes,* 1855 : 200.
[4]*Ibid.,* 1855 : 200.

not satisfactory to the part of the county south and east of the Klamath River and doubtless was an important factor in the change of the Klamath-Trinity line just noted. By 1856 the demand that the county seat be more centrally located resulted in a third change, this time to Orleans Bar on the Klamath River.

As result of their loss of the county seat the people of Crescent City were much aroused and a movement was begun which led in 1857 to the separate organization of that part of the county as a new county known as Del Norte. The southern boundary of Del Norte County was defined in these words:

> "Commencing at a point in the Pacific Ocean three miles from shore, on the forty-second parallel of north latitude, and running thence southerly three miles from shore to a point one mile south of the mouth of the Klamath River; thence easterly, on a line parallel with the Klamath River, to a point one mile south of the mouth of Blue Creek; thence, in a northeasterly direction, to the summit of the Siskiyou mountains; thence, in an easterly direction, following the summit of the ridge that divides the waters of Clear Creek from the waters of Dillon's Creek, to the Klamath River, at a point equi-distant from the mouth of said Clear Creek and the mouth of said Dillon's Creek; thence across the Klamath River, and in an easterly and northerly direction, following the ridge of the mountain, and heading the waters that flow into said Klamath River on the south side, above the point last above mentioned."[5]

Line of 1872. The separation of Del Norte in 1857 was the last change in the boundaries of Klamath County before its dissolution in 1875. As defined in the Political Code of 1872 the boundaries were as follows:[6]

> "Beginning at southwest corner of Del Norte, as established in section 3909; thence southerly, by ocean shore, to a point west from the mouth of Mad River, forming southwest corner; thence east to a point on Trinity River, which forms common corner of Humboldt, Klamath, and Trinity; thence northeasterly to and along Scott's Mountain to its point of intersection with the ridge dividing the waters which flow into Scott's, Shasta, and Sacramento rivers on the north from the waters which flow into Salmon and

---

[5]*Statutes*, 1857:35; 1858:21. The act of 1858 defines this line more clearly and is here used in the quotation.
[6]*Political Code* (1872), § 3910.

Klamath rivers on the south, forming the common corner
of Siskiyou, Klamath, and Trinity; thence northerly to
and along the last mentioned ridge to the southeast corner of Del Norte, as established in section 3909; thence
westerly along the southern line of Del Norte to the place
of beginning.''

The southern line of Del Norte here referred to was practically the same as the line described in the acts of 1857 and
1858.

Dissolution of the County, 1874-75. Klamath County had
never flourished: its territory was badly cut up into isolated
districts by mountain ranges; and its population, mostly
miners, lacked the stability necessary for a well organized
government; furthermore, they did not possess property which
could easily be drawn upon for the support of the government. The natural result was that the debt of the county
increased rapidly, the government became less efficient, and
the discontent among the people rose in like proportion. In
1874 an act was passed whereby the county was to be dissolved, the debt and territory to be divided between Humboldt
and Siskiyou counties. The provisions of this act were carried out in 1875. The act decreed as follows:

"All that part of the territory now composing the
county of Klamath, situate and lying north and easterly
of the following line and boundary, to wit: commencing
at the point where the present boundary of Klamath and
Del Norte crosses the Klamath River; thence running
easterly in a direct line to where the Salmon River enters
the Klamath River; thence in a southerly direction, following the ridge of the mountain that divides the waters
of the Salmon and its tributaries from the waters of
Klamath and Trinity rivers, and their tributaries, to the
northern boundary line of Trinity County; shall be and
compose a part of the county of Siskiyou, and shall be
within the jurisdiction thereof, and of the courts and
officers of said county; and all that part of the territory
now composing the county of Klamath, situate and lying
south and westerly of the above described boundary and
line, shall be a part of Humboldt County, and within the
jurisdiction thereof, and of the courts and officers of the
county.''[7]

---

[7]*Statutes*, 1873–74 : 756. This line is indicated upon the map of
Klamath County.

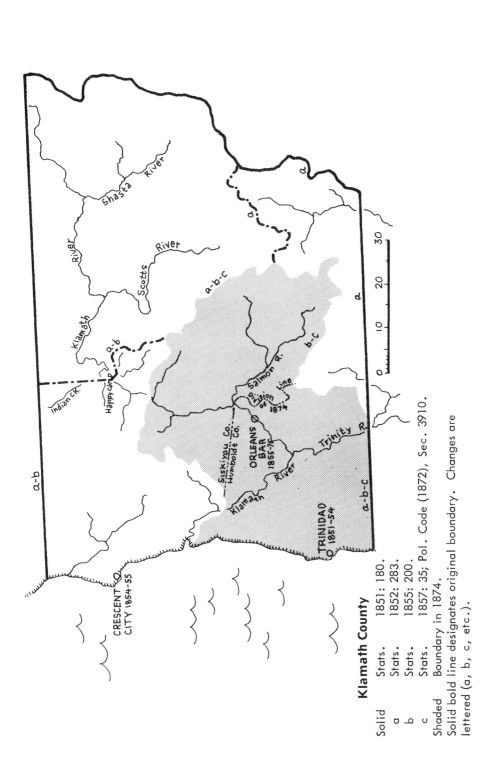

Klamath County

Solid	Stats.	1851: 180.
a	Stats.	1852: 283.
b	Stats.	1855: 200.
c	Stats.	1857: 35; Pol. Code (1872), Sec. 3910.

Shaded   Boundary in 1874.

Solid bold line designates original boundary. Changes are
lettered (a, b, c, etc.).

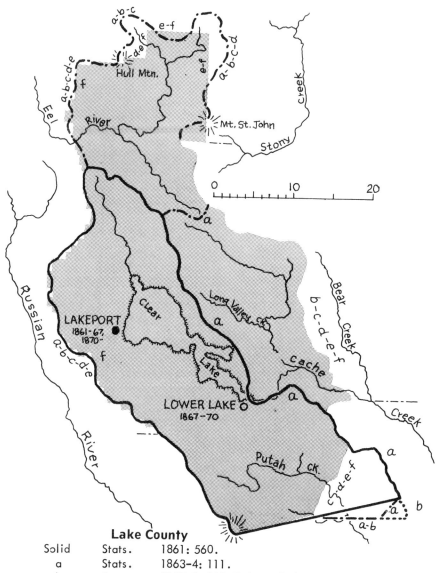

Lake County

Solid	Stats.	1861: 560.
a	Stats.	1863-4: 111.
b	Stats.	1867-8: 269; Pol. Code (1872), Sec. 3917.
c	Stats.	1871-2: 305, 903.
d	Stats.	1907: 135.
e	Stats.	1909: 326.
f	Stats.	1917: 1635.
Shaded	Pol. Code (1919), Sec. 3925.	

Solid bold line designates original boundary. Changes are
lettered (a, b, c, etc.). Shading denotes present county
boundaries.

LAKE COUNTY

Original Line, 1861. In 1861 that part of Napa County lying around Clear Lake was created into a separate county known as Lake County. Its boundaries at that time were as follows:[1]

> "Commencing at the southeastern corner of Mendocino County; thence running in an easterly direction along the dividing ridge between Russian River and Knight's Valley on the west, and Clear Lake and Coyote Valley on the east, to the highest point of Mount St. Helena; thence easterly in a direct line to the point where the second standard line north (United States survey), crosses the line dividing Yolo and Napa counties; thence along the line of Yolo County to the Mendocino County line; thence along said Mendocino County line to the place of beginning."

From the description as given in the act, the line is not difficult to locate and, with the exception of the eastern portion, does not involve any complications. On the east, trouble arises because of the definition of the line in terms of the boundaries of Yolo and Mendocino counties, no mention being made of Colusa County. Elsewhere it has been shown, however, that this line ran just east of the Lake and west of Long Valley,[2] that valley being a part of Colusa County, and that the failure to mention Colusa County in describing the eastern boundary of Lake County must have been an oversight on the part of those who prepared the act.

Line of 1864. In 1864 the whole boundary of Lake County was redefined and several changes were made, especially on the south and north. The full description is as follows:[3]

> "Commencing at the southeastern corner of Mendocino County, thence running in an easterly direction along the dividing ridge between Russian River and Knight's Valleys on the west, and Clear Lake and Loconoma Valleys on the east, to the highest point of Mount St. Helena; thence along the present line to the Butts' Cañon road;

---

[1] *Statutes*, 1861:560.
[2] *See* description of Colusa and Mendocino counties.
[3] *Statutes*, 1863–64:111.

thence eastwardly to the most northern point of the Los Putas Rancho, commonly known as the "Berryessa Rancho;" thence easterly in a direct line to a point where the second standard line north (United States survey) crosses the line dividing Yolo and Napa counties; thence northerly along the highest ridge of mountains dividing the waters of the Sacramento on the east, and the Berryessa on the west, until it intersects the line dividing Yolo and Colusa counties; thence along the main ridge of mountains dividing the waters of Long Valley on the east, and Clear Lake on the west; thence up said ridge to the summit of the Coast Range; thence along the summit to Hull's Mountain; thence west on a direct line to Mount St. Hedson; thence southerly on the ridge dividing the waters of Russian River on the west, and Clear Lake on the east, to the place of beginning."

The first change to be noted here is the description of the south or Napa boundary, which, instead of running directly from Mount St. Helena to the point where the second standard north intersects the Napa and Yolo line, it was made to follow the old line to Butts' Cañon and then to turn east to the northern end of the Los Putos Rancho, and then to the same point on the Yolo boundary as previously described. The line northward is now described more definitely and runs between Clear Lake and Long Valley, thus helping to confirm the location of the line previously described. At the upper end of the lake another important change is to be noted, for, instead of turning immediately west around the head of Clear Lake, the boundary is now described as running

"along the summit to Hull's Mountain."

This, it will be seen by glancing at the map, increased the size of the county about twenty-five per cent by adding a portion of the headwaters of Eel River, for Mount Hull lies not on the main summit of the Coast Range but on a spur dividing two branches of upper Eel River.

From Hull's Mountain, the description must not be construed too literally, as it is quite evident that the local topography was not familiar to those who prepared the act. It, however, turned westward along the watershed to Mount St. Hedson [Sanhedrin] and thence south across Eel River to the ridge which had previously formed the boundary, thence by this line to the starting place.

Annexation of Long Valley, 1868. In 1868 the boundaries of Lake County were again amended. The first change was a slight modification of the southern boundary which, instead of running as before from the most northern point of the Los Putos Rancho "easterly in a direct line to a point where the second standard line north (United States survey) crosses the line dividing Yolo County and Napa County," it now ran

> "easterly, along the northern line of said rancho to the northeast corner thereof, thence east to the line between Yolo and Napa counties."

Northward from this point the line is not only described anew but is located further to the east, placing Long Valley, which hitherto had been in Colusa, into Lake County. The section of the act reads thus:[4]

> "thence northerly, along the summit of the range of mountains dividing the waters of the Sacramento River from those flowing into or through Berryessa and Morgan Valleys on the west, to Cache Creek; thence east, to the summit of the spur of the Coast Range which divides the waters flowing east into Bear Creek and Stony Creek and those flowing west into the north fork of Cache Creek; thence northerly, along the said dividing ridge, following the divide of said waters to the summit of the Coast Range of mountains; thence northerly, along the said summit to the highest point of Hull's Mountain;"

The line here established on the east still remains the boundary between Lake and Colusa counties.

The Line of 1872. Three separate attempts to define or amend the boundaries of Lake County were made during the session of the legislature which met in 1871–72. The first of these was by the adoption of section three thousand nine hundred and seventeen of the Political Code. In it no effort was made to change existing boundaries, the whole, however, being redefined. The section reads as follows:[5]

> "Beginning at the summit of Mount Hull, near Mount St. John, on the western line of Colusa, and forming the northeast corner of Lake and east corner of Mendocino;

[4]*Statutes,* 1867–8 : 269.
[5]*Political Code* (1872), § 3917.

thence southerly and circuitously, by the summit line of the Mayacmas Range, being the dividing ridge between the waters flowing into the Russian and Eel rivers and those flowing easterly into Clear Lake, to the summit of Mount St. Helena; thence easterly along the line heretofore established to the Buttes Cañon road; thence easterly in a right line, to the most northern point of the Berryessa Rancho; thence easterly along the northern line of said rancho to the northeast corner thereof; thence east to the western line of Yolo County, as established in section 3929; thence northerly, on the western line of Yolo and Colusa counties, to the place of beginning.''

At the same session, although the act was not incorporated into the code, the Napa-Lake county boundary was again modified so as to give to Napa County a large district along upper Putah Creek which was subsequently organized as Knox township of Napa County. The description of this boundary is as follows:[6]

''The northern boundary line of Napa and the southeasterly boundary line of Lake counties shall commence at the highest point of the Mount St. Helena; thence running in an easterly direction along the present boundary line between said counties to the Buttes Cañon road; thence northeasterly in a direct line to the junction of Jericho and Putah creeks; thence up Jericho Creek to the junction of Hunting Creek, in Jericho Valley; thence up Hunting Creek to a large pile of rocks on the southeasterly side of the county road, at the lower and most easterly end of Hunting Valley; thence in a straight line in the direction of the intersection of Bear and Cache creeks to the county line of Yolo County; thence along the line of Yolo County in a southeasterly direction to the present county line dividing Yolo and Napa counties.''

Another act passed by the legislature at the same session confirmed the survey of the line with Yolo County as run by H. H. Sanford, Deputy Surveyor General. It made no change in the previous line.[7]

Recent Changes, 1907, 1909 and 1917. After 1872 no legislative action was taken in reference to the boundaries of Lake County until 1907. Since then three acts have been passed, all having as their purpose a clearer definition of the boundary lines by describing their location by means of United

[6]*Statutes*, 1871–72 : 305.
[7]*Ibid.*, 1871–72 : 903.

States survey lines. The first of these was adopted in 1907 and defined anew the eastern boundary of Mendocino, north of Mount Hull.[8] The second, in 1909, defined the line between Lake and Glenn counties,[9] and the third, in 1917, described the Lake and Mendocino boundary lying south of Mount Hull.[10]

Present Boundary. These changes were made a part of the Political Code when in 1919 that portion of the code defining county boundaries was brought down to date. Section 3925 of the code as adopted in 1923 gives the present boundaries of Lake County as follows:[11]

"3925. *Lake.* Beginning at the monument on top of Mount Hull, established by T. P. Smythe and R. P. Hammond and party on October 20, 1885, and approved by H. J. Willey, surveyor general of the State of California, on December 23, 1885; thence due north to the half section line running east and west through section two, township nineteen north, range ten west, Mount Diablo Base and Meridian; thence east along said half section line through sections two and one of said township, range, base and meridian, and then through section five to the southeast corner of the northeast quarter of said section five, township nineteen north, range nine west, Mount Diablo Base and Meridian; thence north along the line between and dividing sections four and five of said township, range, base and meridian, and continuing north along the line between and dividing sections thirty-two and thirty-three, twenty-eight and twenty-nine, twenty and twenty-one to the common section corner of sections sixteen, seventeen, twenty, and twenty-one, township twenty north, range nine west, said section corner being on the eastern boundary of Mendocino County and being also the common corner of Lake and Glenn counties; thence east between sections sixteen, twenty-one, fifteen, twenty-two, fourteen, twenty-three, thirteen, twenty-four, of township twenty north, range nine west, Mount Diablo Meridian, and sections eighteen, nineteen, seventeen, twenty, sixteen, twenty-one, fifteen, twenty-two, township twenty north, range eight west, Mount Diablo Meridian, to corner of sections fourteen, fifteen, twenty-two, twenty-three, township twenty north, range eight west, Mount Diablo Meridian; thence south between sections twenty-two, twenty-three, twenty-six, twenty-seven, thirty-four, thirty-five, township twenty

[8]*Statutes*, 1907: 135.
[9]*Ibid.*, 1909: 326.
[10]*Ibid.*, 1917: 1635.
[11]*Political Code* (1919), § 3925; (1923), § 3925.

north, range eight west, Mount Diablo Meridian, and sections two, three, ten, eleven, fourteen, fifteen, twenty-two, twenty-three, twenty-six, twenty-seven, thirty-four, thirty-five, township nineteen north, range eight west, Mount Diablo Meridian, and sections two, three, ten, eleven, fourteen, fifteen, twenty-two, twenty-three, twenty-six, twenty-seven, to one-quarter section corner on section line dividing sections twenty-six and twenty-seven, township eighteen north, range eight west, Mount Diablo Meridian; said point being on boundary line between the county of Glenn and the county of Colusa as established by 'An act to change and permanently locate the boundary line between the counties of Glenn and Colusa, approved March 11, 1893'; thence running westerly along the half section line and one and one-half miles north of the line dividing townships seventeen and eighteen of Mount Diablo Base and Meridian, to the northwest corner of the southwest one-quarter of section thirty, township eighteen north, range eight west, Mount Diablo Base and Meridian, said corner being also the northwest corner of Colusa County; thence southerly on the western line of Colusa and Yolo counties to the point on said Yolo County line, where said line is intersected by the boundary line between Napa and Lake counties as defined in 'An act to define the northern boundary line of Napa County, adjoining Lake and Yolo counties,' approved March 8, 1872; thence southwesterly in a straight line to a large pile of rocks on the southeasterly side of the county road at the lower and most easterly end of Hunting Valley; thence down Hunting Creek to its junction with Jericho Creek in Jericho Valley; thence down Jericho Creek to its junction with Putah Creek; thence southwesterly in a direct line to the Buttes Cañon road at a point near the northwest corner of section nineteen, township ten north, range five west, said point being on the line between Lake and Napa counties as established in 'An act to define the boundaries and provide for the organization of Lake County,' approved May 20, 1861; thence westerly on the line established by said act to the summit of Mount St. Helena; thence northwesterly along the summit of the Mayacmas range, being the dividing ridge between the waters flowing into Russian River and those flowing into Clear Lake, to the southeast corner of Mendocino and the northeast corner of Sonoma counties as established in section three thousand nine hundred thirty-one; thence northerly along the eastern line of Mendocino County as established in said section, to the place of beginning.''

LASSEN COUNTY

Original Boundary, 1864. Lassen was created on April 1, 1864, from territory previously belonging to Plumas and Shasta counties. Its original boundaries were as follows:[1]

"Commencing on the boundary line dividing Sierra and Plumas counties, at a point on the summit of the ridge which crosses said boundary line, and which divides Long Valley from Sierra Valley; thence following the summit of said ridge (northwesterly) which separates the waters of Feather River from those which flow into the Great Basin and Honey Lake Valley, to a point due south from the town of Susanville; thence due south to the summit of the ridge separating the waters which flow into the east branch of the north fork of Feather River, running through Indian Valley, from those which flow into the north fork of Feather River, running through the Mountain Meadows; thence following the summit of said ridge to a point due south from a point where the old and present travelled road from the Big Meadows, via Hamilton's Ranch, first crosses the said north fork of Feather River; thence due north to the southern boundary line of Shasta County; thence west along said boundary line to a point due south of the Black Butte Mountain; thence due north to the southern boundary line of Siskiyou County; thence east along said boundary line to the eastern boundary of the state; thence south along said state line to the southeast corner of Plumas County; thence west along the boundary line of Sierra and Plumas counties to the place of beginning."

Lines of 1866 and 1872. This act was amended in 1866 and in a little different form was adopted in the Political Code of 1872, reading as follows:[2]

"Beginning at southwest corner, on the northern line of Sierra, as established in section 3921, at a point on the summit of the ridge which crosses said line, and which divides Long Valley from Sierra Valley; thence northwesterly, following said ridge, to a point due south from the town of Susanville; thence westerly, along the ridge separating the waters which flow into the east branch of the north fork of Feather River, running through Indian

---

[1] *Statutes,* 1863–64 : 264.
[2] *Political Code,* 1872, § 3912 ; *Statutes,* 1865–66 : 453.

Valley, from those which flow into the north fork of
Feather River, running through Mountain Meadows, to a
point on said ridge south from the point where the old
and present traveled road from the Big Meadows, via
Hamilton's ranch, first crosses the said north fork; thence
north, to a point east of the southeast corner of Shasta;
thence west, along said extension line, to a point due south
of Black Butte Mountain, being southeast corner of
Shasta; thence north, to a point on southern line of Siskiyou marked by a rock mound, being northwest corner of
Lassen and northeast corner of Shasta; thence east, along
said line, to the eastern boundary of the state; thence
south, along said state line, to the northeast corner of
Sierra, as established in section 3921; thence west, along
the line of Sierra, to the place of beginning.''

Plumas Boundary, 1901. In 1901 the boundary between
Lassen and Plumas was amended by being placed upon lines
of the United States surveys rather than ''along the ridge''
which it had previously followed.[3]

Present Boundary, 1923. The line of 1901 was incorporated into the code in 1919, the description of Lassen County
boundaries being as follows:[4]

''3926. *Lassen.* Beginning at the southwest corner, on
the northern line of Sierra, located on the south boundary
of township twenty-two north, range sixteen east, Mount
Diablo Base and Meridian, at the corner common to sections thirty-five and thirty-six, and running thence north
two miles to the corner common to sections twenty-three,
twenty-four, and twenty-six, said township and range;
thence east one mile to the east boundary of said township and range at the corner common to sections twenty-
four and twenty-five; thence north one mile to the west
corner of sections eighteen and nineteen, township twenty-
two north, range seventeen east, Mount Diablo Base and
Meridian; thence east one-half mile to the quarter section
corner between said sections eighteen and nineteen; thence
north one mile to the quarter section corner between sections seven and eighteen, said township and range; thence
east one-half mile to the corner common to sections seven,
eight, seventeen and eighteen, said township and range;
thence north on section lines to the south corner of sections
thirty-one and thirty-two, township twenty-three north,
range seventeen east, Mount Diablo Base and Meridian;

---

[3]*Statutes,* 1901: 76.
[4]*Political Code* (1919), § 3926; (1923), § 3926.

thence north six miles to the south corner of sections thirty-one and thirty-two, township twenty-four north, range seventeen east, Mount Diablo Base and Meridian; thence east one-half mile; thence north two miles; thence west one-half mile; thence north two miles; thence west one mile, to the east corner of sections twelve and thirteen, township twenty-four north, range sixteen east, Mount Diablo Base and Meridian; thence north one-half mile to the quarter section corner on east side of said section twelve; thence west one-half mile to the center of said section twelve; thence north one-half mile to the quarter section corner between sections one and twelve, said township and range; thence west one-half mile to the corner common to sections one, two, eleven, and twelve, said township and range; thence north one-half mile to the quarter section corner between said sections one and two; thence west one-half mile to the center of said section two; thence north one-half mile to the quarter section corner on north boundary of said section two; thence west on township line one-half mile to the south corner of sections thirty-four and thirty-five, township twenty-five north, range sixteen east, Mount Diablo Base and Meridian; thence north one mile to the corner common to sections twenty-six, twenty-seven, thirty-four, and thirty-five, said township and range; thence west one-half mile to the quarter section corner between said sections twenty-seven and thirty-four; thence north one mile to the quarter section corner between sections twenty-two and twenty-seven, said township and range; thence west one-half mile to the corner common to sections twenty-one, twenty-two, twenty-seven, and twenty-eight, said township and range; thence north one mile to the corner common to sections fifteen, sixteen, twenty-one, and twenty-two, said township and range; thence west one mile to the corner common to sections sixteen, seventeen, twenty, and twenty-one, said township and range; thence north two miles to the corner common to sections four, five, eight, and nine, said township and range; thence west one-half mile to the quarter section corner between said sections five and eight; thence north three miles to the corner common to sections nineteen, twenty, twenty-nine, and thirty, said township and range; thence west two miles to the corner common to sections twenty-three, twenty-four, twenty-five, and twenty-six, township twenty-six north, range fifteen east, Mount Diablo Base and Meridian; thence north one and one-half miles to the quarter section corner between sections thirteen and fourteen, said township and

range; thence west one mile to the quarter section corner
between sections fourteen and fifteen, said township and
range; thence north one-half mile to the corner common
to sections ten, eleven, fourteen, and fifteen, said township and range; thence west four miles to the west corner
of sections seven and eighteen, said township and range;
thence north, on township line, one-half mile to the quarter
section corner, on east boundary of section twelve, township twenty-six north, range fourteen east, Mount Diablo
Base and Meridian; thence west one mile to the quarter
section corner between sections eleven and twelve, said
township and range; thence north one-half mile to the
corner common to sections one, two, eleven and twelve,
said township and range; thence west one mile to the corner common to sections two, three, ten and eleven, said
township and range; thence north three-quarters of a mile
to the southwest corner of lot five in section two and
the southeast corner of lot seven in section three, said
township and range; thence west one mile to the southwest
corner of lot five in section three and the southeast corner
of lot seven in section four, said township and range;
thence north one-half mile to the north corner of sections
three and four, said township and range; thence west on
township line one-half mile to the quarter section corner
on south boundary of section thirty-three, township
twenty-seven north, range fourteen east, Mount Diablo
Base and Meridian; thence north one mile' to the quarter
section corner between sections twenty-eight and thirty-
three, said township and range; thence west one-half mile
to the corner common to sections twenty-eight, twenty-nine,
thirty-two and thirty-three, said township and range;
thence north one-half mile to the quarter section corner
between said sections twenty-eight and twenty-nine; thence
west one mile to the quarter section corner between sections twenty-nine and thirty, said township and range;
thence north one-half mile to the corner common to sections nineteen, twenty, twenty-nine and thirty, said
township and range; thence west one-half mile to the
quarter section corner between said sections nineteen and
thirty; thence north one mile to the quarter section corner between sections eighteen and nineteen, said township and range; thence west one-half mile to west corner
of said sections eighteen and nineteen; thence north
on township line one mile to the east corner of sections
twelve and thirteen, township twenty-seven north, range
thirteen east, Mount Diablo Base and Meridian; thence
west one and one-half miles to the quarter section corner
between sections eleven and fourteen, said township and

range; thence north one mile to the quarter section corner between sections two and eleven, said township and range; thence west one-half mile to the corner common to sections two, three, ten and eleven, said township and range; thence north one mile to the north corner of said sections two and three; thence west on township line one mile to the south corner of sections twenty-three and thirty-four, township twenty-eight north, range thirteen east, Mount Diablo Base and Meridian; thence north one mile to the corner common to sections twenty-seven, twenty-eight, thirty-three and thirty-four, said township and range; thence west one mile to the corner common to section twenty-eight, twenty-nine, thirty-two, and thirty-three, said township and range; thence north one-half mile to the quarter section corner between said sections twenty-eight and twenty-nine; thence west one mile to the quarter section corner between sections twenty-nine and thirty, said township and range; thence north one-half mile; thence west one and one-half miles to the quarter section corner between sections twenty-four and twenty-five, township twenty-eight north, range twelve east; thence north one and one-half miles to the center of section thirteen, said township and range; thence west two and one-half miles to the quarter section corner between sections fifteen and sixteen, said township and range; thence north one-half mile to the corner common to sections nine, ten, fifteen, and sixteen, said township and range; thence west one mile to the corner common to sections eight, nine, sixteen, and seventeen, said township and range; thence north one-half mile to the quarter section corner between said sections eight and nine; thence west one-half mile to the center of said section eight; thence north one-half mile to the quarter section corner between sections five and eight, said township and range; thence west four miles to the quarter section corner between sections three and ten, township twenty-eight north, range eleven east, Mount Diablo Base and Meridian; thence north one-half mile to the center of said section three; thence west two miles to the center of section five, said township and range; thence south one-half mile to the quarter section corner between sections five and eight, said township and range; thence west one-half mile to the corner common to sections five, six, seven, and eight, said township and range; thence south one-half mile to the quarter section corner between said sections seven and eight; thence west one mile, more or less, to the quarter section corner on the west boundary of said section seven;

thence south on township line to the east corner of sections thirteen and twenty-four, township twenty-eight north, range ten east, Mount Diablo Base and Meridian; thence west one mile to the corner common to sections thirteen, fourteen, twenty-three, and twenty-four, said township and range; thence south one-half mile to the quarter section corner between said sections twenty-three and twenty-four; thence west one mile to the quarter section corner between sections twenty-two and twenty-three, said township and range; thence south one mile to the quarter section corner between sections twenty-six and twenty-seven, said township and range; thence west one-half mile to the center of said section twenty-seven; thence south one-half mile to the quarter section corner between sections twenty-seven and thirty-four, said township and range; thence west one-half mile to the corner common to sections twenty-seven, twenty-eight, thirty-three and thirty-four, said township and range; thence south one-half mile to the quarter section corner between said sections thirty-three and thirty-four; thence west one mile to the quarter section corner between sections thirty-two and thirty-three, said township and range; thence south three miles to the quarter section corner between sections sixteen and seventeen, township twenty-seven north, range ten east, Mount Diablo Base and Meridian; thence west one mile to the quarter section corner between sections seventeen and eighteen, said township and range; thence south one-half mile to the corner common to sections seventeen, eighteen, nineteen and twenty, said township and range; thence west two miles to the corner common to sections thirteen, fourteen, twenty-three and twenty-four, township twenty-seven north, range nine east, Mount Diablo Base and Meridian; thence north one mile to the corner common to sections eleven, twelve, thirteen and fourteen, said township and range; thence west one mile to the corner common to sections ten, eleven, fourteen and fifteen, said township and range; thence north one mile to the corner common to sections two, three, ten and eleven, said township and range; thence west three miles to the corner common to sections five, six, seven and eight, said township and range; thence north one mile to the section corner common to sections thirty-one and thirty-two, township twenty-eight north, range nine east; thence west on township line two miles to the south corner of sections thirty-five and thirty-six, township twenty-eight north, range eight east, Mount Diablo Base and Meridian; thence north one and one-half miles to the

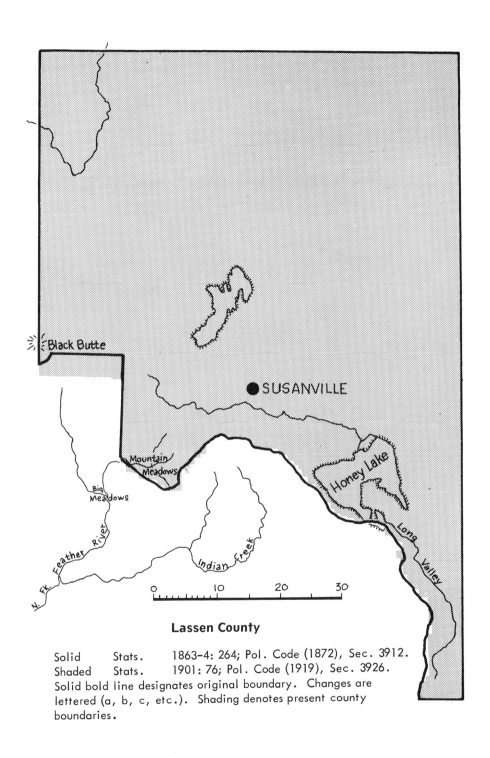

Lassen County

Solid   Stats.   1863-4: 264; Pol. Code (1872), Sec. 3912.
Shaded   Stats.   1901: 76; Pol. Code (1919), Sec. 3926.
Solid bold line designates original boundary. Changes are
lettered (a, b, c, etc.). Shading denotes present county
boundaries.

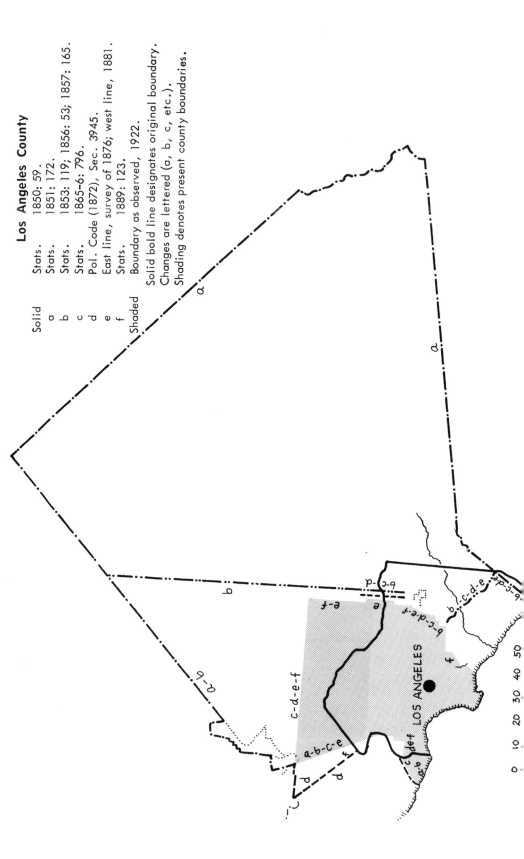

Los Angeles County

Solid		
a	Stats.	1850: 59.
b	Stats.	1851: 172.
c	Stats.	1853: 119; 1856: 53; 1857: 165.
d	Stats.	1865-6: 796.
e	Pol. Code (1872), Sec. 3945.
f	East line, survey of 1876; west line, 1881.
	Stats.	1889: 123.
Shaded	Boundary as observed, 1922.

Solid bold line designates original boundary.
Changes are lettered (a, b, c, etc.).
Shading denotes present county boundaries.

LOS ANGELES

0 10 20 30 40 50

quarter section corner between sections twenty-five and twenty-six, said township and range; thence west one mile to the quarter section corner between sections twenty-six and twenty-seven, said township and range; thence north thirteen miles, more or less, to the quarter section corner between sections twenty-two and twenty-three, township thirty north, range eight east, Mount Diablo Base and Meridian; thence west fourteen miles, more or less, to the corner common to Shasta, Lassen and Plumas, said corner being the southeast corner of Shasta County and situated in the west half of section twenty-one, township thirty-one north, range six east, Mount Diablo Base and Meridian; thence north on the eastern line of Shasta to the southern line of Modoc marked by a rock mound, being northwest corner of Lassen and northeast corner of Shasta; thence east, along said line, to the eastern boundary of the state; thence south, along said state line, to the northeast corner of Sierra, as established in section three thousand nine hundred fifty-four; thence west, along the line of Sierra, to the place of beginning.''

LOS ANGELES COUNTY

Original Boundary, 1850. Los Angeles was one of the original counties into which the state was divided in 1850. Although adjoining Santa Barbara, Mariposa and San Diego counties, its area was then small as compared with the territory which was included within its borders during the succeeding years. Its boundaries then were as follows:

> "Beginning on the coast of the Pacific at the southern boundary of the farm called Trumfo, and running thence along the summit of the ridge of hills called Santa Susana to the northwestern boundary of the farm called San Francisco; thence along the northern and northeastern boundary of said farm of San Francisco to the farm called Piro; thence in a line running due northeast to the summit of the Coast Range; thence along the summit of said range to the western boundary of San Diego County,"[1]

which it followed to the ocean, thence northwest to the starting point, including Santa Catalina and San Clemente islands.

When an attempt is made to plot this line in accordance with modern geographical knowledge, many difficulties arise. The first of these is met in the endeavor to identify the "farm called Trumfo," which nowhere appears upon the maps under this title. There is, however, a rancho, Las Virgenes, through which runs the Triunfo Creek which has since an early date been accepted as identical with the rancho referred to.[2] This rancho, as now surveyed, does not reach the ocean; it is therefore necessary to run an arbitrary line from the southern corner of this rancho to the ocean in order to ascertain the point of beginning. In the second place, from the Triunfo Ranch the line was defined as running along the "summit of the ridge of hills called Santa Susana." Here again trouble is encountered, unless one is willing to interpret the law not too strictly in accordance with modern names. A study of early

---

[1]*Statutes,* 1850 : 59.
[2]All later acts define the boundary in terms of Triunfo Rancho, and in all the maps the line is run by Las Virgenes. There is a Triunfo Creek and canyon within the limit of this rancho, which probably gave it this name. This name is variously spelled Trumfo, Triumpo, Triumfo, and Triunfo. First surveyed in 1865; approved survey in 1881.

maps indicates that the name Santa Susana was applied rather generally, including the hills on the south side of the Simi Valley, as well as those on the north of this valley. Under these conditions, then, the present Simi and Susana hills and Oak Ridge might all have been included under the one name. The line then would go north from the Las Virgenes Rancho to the Simi Hills, thence to the eastward around the end of the Simi Valley and westward along the Santa Susana Hills and Oak Ridge to the San Francisco Rancho, and along this rancho to Temescal Rancho,[3] thence northeast, to the summit of the Coast Range, and eastward along the summit to the San Diego boundary line.[4]

The Line of 1851. In 1851 the former act was replaced by a new one whereby the county boundaries were redefined in full. By this act a radical change was made in the territory of Los Angeles County, through the annexation to Los Angeles of the territory including the present San Bernardino County. The western and northern boundary of Los Angeles as then defined ran from

> "the coast of the Pacific, at a point parallell with the northern boundary of the Rancho, called Malaga; thence in a direction so as to include said Rancho, to the north-west corner of the Rancho, known as Triumpo, running on the northerly line of the same to the north-east corner; thence to the summit of the ridge of hills called Santa Susanna; thence in a direct line to the Rancho of Casteque and Lejon and along their northern line to the north-eastern corner, and from thence in a north-east line to the eastern boundary of the State."[5]

Since this line stood for many years and a portion of it is still retained as the boundary of the county, its proper location is of greater historical importance than the line of 1850.

From the coast to the northeast corner of the Triunfo Rancho, the line of 1851 has come down, without legislative change, to the present day. In absence of contradictory evi-

---

[3]Temescal is taken for the Piru rancho of the act. The Piru Creek runs through this rancho. The reference to the northeast boundary of San Francisco rancho was evidently due either to oversight or to ignorance of the geography of the region.
[4]The San Diego line in 1850 ran from the ocean up San Mateo Creek to its source, and thence due north to the state line.
[5]*Statutes*, 1851 : 172.

dence, then, the presumption is that the line, as it runs at present, is the same as the line of 1851. If this be the case, two points are cleared up: first, the Malaga Rancho referred to is identical with the present Malibu Rancho;[6] and, second, the Triumpo Rancho is the same as the Las Virgenes Rancho. The line of 1851 conforms therefore in general to the present boundary as far as this northeastern corner of Las Virgenes Rancho.

From the Las Virgenes (Triumpo) Rancho to the Rancho of Casteque (Castac Rancho) the location of the line is more or less uncertain because of lack of definiteness as to the location of the intermediate point, lying on the "summit" of the Santa Susana Hills. That the term, Santa Susana Hills, at that time included more than the ridge to which the name is now applied was shown in discussing the line of 1850. By the same process of reasoning, the point in question must lie at some place on a line following the summit of the Simi Hills to Santa Susana Hills, and thence to Oak Ridge. Since all subsequent acts in reference to this boundary have defined it in terms of this same point or a point similarly described a study of the present line may assist in determining the location of the point.

From a casual examination, the conclusion is naturally drawn that the present irregular line is not in harmony with the act of 1851, but if this line is followed to its first intersection with the summit line above described, this is found to be at a point at or near the Santa Susana Pass on the road leading from San Fernando Valley westward through Simi Valley. Further evidence lends support to the conclusion that this is the point also intended by the act of 1856, and in the code of 1872. Since this is not the nearest nor highest point on the summit of the ridge, nor the most direct in line between the Las Virgenes and the Castac ranchos, it may be questioned whether this is the point defined in the act. In other words, is it reasonable to suppose that the point was located so far east of the other points referred to in the act? An examination of the topography shows that, with the exception of the Simi Valley, the greater part of this territory is mountainous

---

[6]Rancho Topanga Malibu Sequit, commonly called Malibu Rancho.

land, and therefore would be considered of little value in determining to which county it should belong. Under the interpretation of the law of 1850, Simi Valley was shown to be in Santa Barbara County. It would be in keeping with that act that the new line should leave it there. That is the result if the point at or near the Santa Susana Pass is accepted. On the other hand, to run the line directly northward would result in dividing the Simi Valley and rancho between the two counties. On this point it is to be observed that the legislators were inclined to follow boundary lines of ranchos rather than cut across them. The conclusion therefore is that the point "on the summit of the ridge of hills called Santa Susana" was located in the near vicinity of Santa Susana Pass.[7]

A study of maps in the archives of Los Angeles County shows that in early years the line from Malibu Rancho to the northwest corner of Las Virgenes was merely extended in a straight line northeasterly until it intersected the summit at the point first described.[8] In 1881, however, the line was surveyed as shown on the present maps. Although it would appear that the line from the northeast corner of Las Virgenes (Triunfo) Rancho to the point near the Santa Susana Pass is very irregular and not in harmony with the code line, a closer examination indicates that the later surveyors, instead of going in a direct line across the mountains, chose to follow the eastern boundary of the Simi Rancho, which had already been surveyed, to the point desired.[9]

After leaving the point upon the summit of the Santa Susana Hills, the line ran to the Castac Rancho,[10] thence along the western and northern sides of this rancho and the Tejon Rancho, so as to include them within Los Angeles County,[11] thence in a direct line northeasterly to the eastern boundary of the state and southward to the San Diego line. This

---

[7]Since this was the point where the road between San Fernando and Simi valleys crossed the hills it was naturally called the "summit."
[8]This completely ignored that clause in the act which describes the line as "running on the northerly line of the same (Triunfo Rancho) to the northeast corner."
[9]The full notes and plat of the surveys of 1881 are in the office of the County Surveyor, Los Angeles.
[10]"Rancho of Casteque and Lejon." The act of 1856 specifies the northwest corner of this rancho.
[11]A more complete discussion regarding this portion of the act will appear in connection with the consideration of the act of 1856.

San Diego line, as defined in a previous section of the
act, ran easterly from the coast at San Mateo Point along the
north and western sides of Santa Margarita Rancho to the
western corner of Rancho San Jacinto Nuevo; along its northern side to the northeast corner, and thence, in a line parallel
with the southern boundary of the state, to the Colorado
River.[12]

San Bernardino Line, 1853. After the act of 1851 the
next change in the boundary of Los Angeles County was made
in 1853, when the eastern portion of the county was separately
organized as San Bernardino County. From the date of its
organization the line between that county and Los Angeles has
remained essentially the same; although, as will presently be
noted, the line as surveyed in 1878 does not conform strictly
to the legislative acts upon which it is based.

The southern part of this line of 1853 now forms the boundary between San Bernardino and Orange counties, the latter
county having been set off from Los Angeles in 1889. In
reference to this boundary some difficulty was encountered
before 1872 on account of the manner in which the southern
part of the line was described. The description read:[13]

> "Beginning at a point where a due south line drawn
> from the highest peak of the Sierra de Santiago inter-
> sects the northern boundary of San Diego County; thence
> running along the summit of said Sierra to the Santa
> Ana river."

It will be noticed that the act fails to state how the line
was to reach the "highest peak of the Sierra de Santiago"
from the point designated as the place of beginning. It is
natural to suppose that this line ran due north to the peak
described, but, on the other hand, if reliance can be placed
upon early maps, which also seem to be confirmed by the code
in 1872, this north and south line was entirely disregarded
and the boundary made to follow the ridge northwesterly from

---

[12]For more complete account of this line see under San Diego County.
[13]*Statutes*, 1853 : 119.

its point of intersection with the San Diego boundary, a point some distance northeast of the place described in the act.[14]

From the Santiago ridge northward, the boundary is the same as the present line. No difficulty is encountered until the Cucamonga Rancho is reached. Here confusion arises because of uncertainty regarding the topographical features mentioned in the act. Since this line as established in the act of 1853 serves as the basis for the present boundary between San Bernardino and Los Angeles counties, and similarly for the line between Kern and San Bernardino, an effort has been made to examine carefully the historical evidence in reference to it. The portion of the act in question reads:

> "thence along the eastern boundaries of said (San Jose) Ranch and of San Antonio, and the western and northern boundary of Cucaimonga ranch to the ravine of Cucaimonga."[15]

The confusion arises either because the surveyors who originally located the line failed to run it in accordance with the act, and later efforts have been made to interpret the act in agreement with the line surveyed; or because of subsequent changes in nomenclature, whereby the name Cucamonga has been transferred to a ravine other than the one intended in the statute. The question is, whether the "ravine of Cucaimonga" mentioned in the act is identical with the San Antonio Ravine on the western boundary of Cucamonga Rancho, or is it the smaller ravine or cañon lying some two miles further east to which the name is at present applied? The surveyors of Los Angeles and San Bernardino counties have accepted the San Antonio Ravine as the original "ravine of Cucaimonga," and as authority state that this was the original name for the ravine as shown upon early maps.[16] Other evidence, however, does not support this contention, for, since 1865 at latest, the United States surveyors have uniformly applied the name San Antonio and Cucamonga to the ravines now bearing those

---

[14]The maps examined are: Kiepert-Eddy, *Karte des States California*, Berlin, 1856 ; Britton and Rey, *Map of the State of California*, by Geo. E. Goddard, C. E., issued after the adjournment of the legislature, 1860, third edition ; Farley's *Map of the newly discovered Tramontaine Silver Mines in Southern California* (1861) ; Ransome and Doolittle, *New map of the State of California*, 1863.
[15]*Statutes*, 1853 : 119.
[16]See correspondence January, 1916, in Archives of County Surveyor, Los Angeles.

names.[17] Furthermore, this more easterly point is in keeping with the strict reading of the act, for the line was to proceed along the ''western and northern boundary of Cucaimonga Ranch to the ravine of Cucaimonga.'' The San Antonio Ravine lies along the western side of the rancho, and to go up this ravine would make it impossible to follow along the ''northern boundary of Cucaimonga Ranch.'' But the ravine or cañon now named Cucamonga meets this requirement. Therefore, notwithstanding the fact that the established line is based upon the assumption that the ravine now called San Antonio is identical with the ''ravine of Cucaimonga'' mentioned in the act, the weight of evidence does not support this interpretation, but indicates clearly that the present Cucamonga cañon was the one intended by the statute.[18]

It having been determined which of these ravines was the one intended by the act, there can be no question as to the further course of this boundary. The law reads:

> ''thence up said ravine to its source in the Coast Range; thence due north to the northern boundary of Los Angeles County.''[19]

The Acts of 1856 and 1857. In 1856 an act was passed amending the act of 1851. The entire boundary of the county was then redefined, in an attempt to clear up some of the uncertainties in the earlier act. This statute made no change in the description of the line as far as the point upon the summit of the Santa Susana Hills; from there, however, it was to run

> ''in a direct line to the north-westernmost corner of the tract of land called Castec, where it approaches nearer to, or touches, the tract of land called Tejon; thence along the limits of the rancho or tract of land called the Tejon, up and along its western to the north-westernmost corner thereof; thence along the northern line of the said tract

---

[17]The Cucamonga Rancho, as shown by plat in the U. S. Land Office, was surveyed in May, 1865, and shows the names as at present. The surrounding land was surveyed into townships and sections in 1865 and 1884 and the township plats also show the names as now used.

[18]An examination of the surveyor's report and field notes, 1876, does not indicate any effort on his part to determine these topographical features mentioned in the act.

[19]The present boundary is legally based upon this line. Attention will be directed later to the lack of harmony between the line of survey and the statute line.

of land called the Tejon to its north-easternmost corner; thence in a northeast line to the eastern boundary of the State.''[20]

There can be no question that the two tracts of land here referred to are the same as the present Castac and Tejon ranchos. Although those ranchos were not surveyed until a much later date and were therefore but indefinite tracts, the location of the boundary line has been determined for the purposes of this study, according to the later approved surveys.

The remaining clauses of this statute present glaring inconsistencies and as they stand are meaningless, for the ideas of two distinct and conflicting legislative acts have here been combined.[21] In the first place the boundaries of the county are described as running from the Tejon Rancho northeast to the state line and thence southeast to the northern line of San Diego County, and thence westerly. In this the act has completely ignored the existence of San Bernardino County created in 1853. Later clauses, however, indicate that this was not the real intention of the legislators, for the act further says that from the Colorado River the line was to run

> "along the boundary line of San Diego County to the Coast Range, *to the boundary line of San Bernardino County; thence down and along the boundary line of said San Bernardino County to the boundary line of San Diego County;* thence to the Pacific Ocean."

The only reasonable explanation of this confusion is that it was the purpose of the person who drew up this act further to amend the law of 1851 by describing the eastern boundary of the county in terms of San Bernardino County, which had been created in 1853. He inserted the words in italics in the above quotation, but neglected to eliminate the preceding inconsistent clauses. If these had been omitted, the act would have been definite and consistent. In order to make sure of its limits San Bernardino County had its boundaries

---

[20]*Statutes*, 1856: 54.
[21]*Ibid.*, 1851: 172; 1853: 119. The former defined the boundaries of Los Angeles County in 1851; the latter detached the eastern portion, making it into San Bernardino County.

fully redefined, though unchanged, in an act passed at the next session of the legislature.[22]

Kern County Line, 1866. The territory of Los Angeles County was next modified by an act passed in 1866 by which Kern County was created. This county was formed in part from Tulare County and in part from Los Angeles County. The northern boundary of Los Angeles was therefore shifted south to "the line between townships eight and nine, north of the San Bernardino base line."

Boundary of the Political Code, 1872. At the time of the adoption of the Political Code in 1872, the boundaries of Los Angeles County were again defined in full. In general the former lines were adopted; however, on the west one change was made. Here the boundary followed the line adopted in 1856 as far as the point on the summit of the Santa Susana Hills. After leaving the Santa Susana Hills the next portion of the line is defined in these words:

> "thence in a direct line northwesterly, to the southwest corner of Kern, as established in Section 3941, forming the northwest corner of Los Angeles."[23]

The point of difference between this and the line of 1856 is the location of the northwest corner of the county. Upon an examination of the section referred to, that defining the southwest corner of Kern, this corner is found to be located at the point where the southern line of township nine north, San Bernardino base, intersects the summit of the Coast Range. If the point on the summit of the Santa Susana is the same as that previously accepted, and there is no reason to think otherwise, in view of the known topographical conditions, there can be no dispute as to the proper location of this boundary. The line ran from the point at the Santa Susana Pass to the place where the southern line of Kern County strikes the summit of the Coast Ridge. The United States topographical maps designate this as Sawmill Mountain, a short distance

[22]*Statutes*, 1857 : 165.
[23]*Political Code*, 1872. § 3945.

west of Mount Pinos.[24] From the point just considered, the boundary of the county followed lines already established, running along the southern line of Kern to San Bernardino, then south along the western boundary of that county to San Diego County and thence southwest to the Pacific Ocean.

Eastern Boundary Survey, 1876. In 1876 the supervisors of Los Angeles County authorized the surveyor to make a survey of the eastern boundary of the county.[25] This was done the following year and the report submitted February 5th, 1877.[26] Since that time this line as surveyed has been observed as the county boundary. A comparison of the records of this survey together with the legislative acts upon which it was presumed to be based shows a careless disregard for the latter, probably due in part to difficulties in identifying the places named. This line as defined in the Political Code (1872) is based upon the act of 1853, whereby San Bernardino County was created. The difference in opinion regarding the identity of "the ravine Cucaimonga" has been noted in discussing the act of 1853. The surveyors who located and marked the present boundary may have assumed that San Antonio Ravine was the ravine referred to in the act. Even if this assumption be accepted as correct, a conclusion which the evidence does not seem to justify, the remainder of the boundary still is not in harmony with the statute provisions, for, instead of running due north from the source of this ravine, as provided in the act, the boundary as surveyed proceeds in a straight line along the general course of the San Antonio Ravine to Mount San Antonio, thence northwesterly to the southeast corner of township five north, range eight west, and thence north along the range line. This is not a due north line. In 1917 through a dispute between San Bernardino and Kern counties that line, originally a

---

[24]This point lies approximately 16 miles west of the northwest corner of the county as at present recognized. The topographical sheets of the U. S. Geological Survey, prepared during the summer of 1903, give a full and accurate description of all the points in question, as they were known at that time. It is probable that the name Santa Susana mountains is now applied in a more limited manner than formerly, but otherwise the points can differ but little. The second, and revised edition of State Geological Survey Map of California and Nevada, issued by authority of the regents of the University in 1874, shows Mount Pinos to lie within Los Angeles County.
[25]Los Angeles County Archives, Minutes of Supervisors, VI, 301.
[26]*Ibid.*, 426-438.

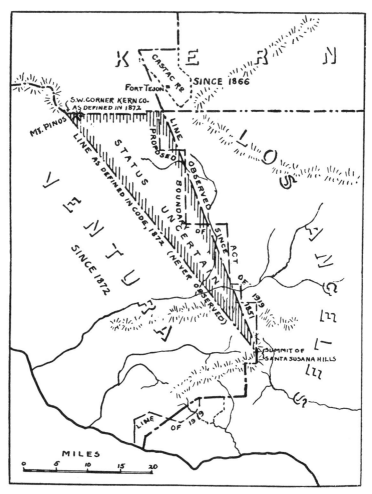

Los Angeles-Ventura Boundary

continuation of the Los Angeles-San Bernardino boundary, was placed further east and more strictly in accordance with the original intention of the act.

Ventura Boundary Survey, 1881. The location of the western boundary has been considered in dealing with earlier legislation. It has been shown that this line as far north as the northeast corner of the Rancho Las Virgenes (Triunfo) was first established in 1851, and since that time has been unchanged by subsequent legislation. From the Las Virgenes Rancho to the northwest corner of the county, the line has been redefined and modified several times. In the discussion of the lines of 1851 and 1856, their location was quite fully considered, especially in reference to the location of the point on the summit of the Santa Susana Hills. The evidence seems to indicate that this point, near the Santa Susana Pass, adopted by the act of 1851, has remained relatively a fixed point to the present day. Unfortunately, however, the same thing can not be said of those parts of the line north and south of this point. In 1881 the surveyors of the two contiguous counties surveyed and marked the line as it has since been observed. From the Las Virgenes Rancho this line instead of running in a direct line follows the southern and eastern boundary of the Simi Rancho, as previously surveyed, to the Santa Susana Pass. Continuing, however, from this point to the northwest corner of the county, the legal basis for the line seems to have been ignored. Had the line been made to follow the directions as given in the Political Code the northwest corner of the county would have been located some sixteen miles further west than at present, thus adding to Los Angeles County territory aggregating approximately 300 square miles. The report of the survey as preserved in the county archives indicates that the surveyors did not endeavor to follow the line as defined by the Political Code in 1872, but relied upon their knowledge of the location of the line, which, however, was the line defined by the earlier act of 1856.[27] The line as surveyed, following the line of 1856, was subsequently approved by the supervisors

---

[27]Los Angeles County Archives, Minutes of Supervisors, VII, 383-393.

and has since been the recognized boundary line, the provisions of the code being entirely ignored.

Orange County Line, 1889. The section of the political Code as adopted in 1872 has in general remained unchanged except in so far as it has been superseded by legislation creating Orange County,[28] the northern line of that county then becoming the southern boundary of Los Angeles County. Beginning in the Pacific Ocean at the mouth of Coyote Creek this boundary was defined as proceeding northeasterly up this creek until its intersection with the line between townships three south, ten and eleven west; thence north on this line to the northwest corner of section six, township three south, range ten west, thence east on the northern line of township to the San Bernardino boundary. At the time of the codification of the county boundary laws in 1919 the Los Angeles-Orange county line was described in a more precise manner.[29]

Proposed Change in Ventura Boundary, 1919. The act of 1919, codifying the boundary laws, as first prepared fixed the Ventura-Los Angeles line along the survey of 1881, thereby endeavoring to make the statutory line agree with the actual boundary. By amendment this boundary was changed in accordance with the expressed wishes of the boards of supervisors of the two counties. The line adopted in 1919 ran as follows:[30]

"3927. *Los Angeles.* Beginning at the intersection of the southwesterly boundary line of the State of California with a line drawn normal to the shore of the Pacific Ocean from the southwesterly corner of fractional section twenty-seven, township one south, range twenty west, San Bernardino Base and Meridian; thence northerly in a straight line three miles to the southwesterly corner of said fractional section twenty-seven; thence north along the west lines of fractional section twenty-seven and sections twenty-two, fifteen, ten and three, township one south, range twenty west, San Bernardino Base and Meridian, to line number three of the boundary of the Rancho El Conejo; thence northeasterly, southeasterly,

---

[28]*Statutes,* 1889:123.
[29]*Political Code* (1919), §3938.
[30]*Ibid.,* § 3927.

northeasterly and northerly along lines numbers three, four, five, six and seven of the boundary of the Rancho El Conejo to a point in said line number seven, being corner number seven of the boundary of the Rancho Simi; thence easterly along line number seven, northerly along line number eight, easterly along line number nine and northerly along line number ten of the boundary of the Rancho Simi to corner number eleven of the Rancho Simi, being in the southerly boundary line of the Rancho San Francisco; thence westerly along the southerly boundary line of the Rancho San Francisco to a point in said line due south of the southwest corner of fractional section twenty, township four north, range seventeen west, San Bernardino Base and Meridian; thence due north to the southwest corner of said fractional section twenty, said last mentioned corner being in the northerly boundary line of the Rancho San Francisco; thence westerly along the northerly line of the Rancho San Francisco to the range line between ranges seventeen and eighteen west, San Bernardino Base and Meridian; thence north along said range line to the northeast corner of township five north, range eighteen west, San Bernardino Base and Meridian; thence west along the township line between townships five and six north to the southwest corner of township six north, range eighteen west, San Bernardino Base and Meridian; thence north along the range line between ranges eighteen and nineteen west, San Bernardino Base and Meridian, to the corner common to townships seven and eight north, ranges eighteen and nineteen west, San Bernardino Base and Meridian; thence west along the south line of township eight north, range nineteen west, to the southwest corner of section thirty-three, township eight north, range nineteen west, San Bernardino Base and Meridian; thence north along the west lines of sections thirty-three, twenty-eight, twenty-one, sixteen, nine and four, township eight north, range nineteen west, San Bernardino Base and Meridian, to the northwest corner of said section four, said corner being a point common to the boundaries of the counties of Kern, Ventura and Los Angeles. . . .''

Because of the fact that this was clearly a change in boundary between two counties the Supreme Court declared the action beyond the power of the legislature and therefore void.[31]

---

[31]*Mundell* vs. *Lyons,* 182 Cal., 289.

Proposed Boundary, 1921. There was passed by the legislature in 1921 a bill presented by Senators Lyon and Arbuckle establishing the boundaries of Los Angeles County in a manner believed to be in conformity with the constitutional powers of the legislature since it did not seek to change the boundaries. Its purpose was to define clearly the boundaries of the county as they have hitherto been recognized by the authorities of Los Angeles and the surrounding counties. The line on the west was defined as surveyed by E. T. Wright and J. T. Stow during the year 1881, and the San Bernardino line as surveyed in 1876. Notwithstanding that the authorities of both counties favored the act and it was passed by both houses of the legislature, it did not secure the approval of the Governor.[32]

Present Boundary, 1923. Legislation adopted in 1923 at last defined the boundaries of Los Angeles County in a manner harmonizing with the *de facto* boundaries. The section of the Political Code relating to Los Angeles County reads as follows:[33]

> "Beginning at a point in the southwesterly boundary line of the State of California, said point being on the southerly prolongation of the westerly boundary line of Rancho Topanga Malibu Sequit; thence northerly along said prolongation and westerly line of said rancho to the northwesterly corner thereof; thence northeasterly in a direct line to corner number seven of the boundary of Rancho Simi; thence easterly along line number seven, northerly along line number eight, easterly along line number nine of the boundary of Rancho Simi to corner number ten of the boundary of Rancho Simi; thence following the boundary line as surveyed by E. T. Wright and J. T. Stow, county surveyors, in June and July, 1881, as shown on map recorded in book 43, page 25 et seq., miscellaneous records of Los Angeles County as follows: North one hundred five and one-hundredth chains to a point; thence north seven degrees twenty-nine minutes west, one hundred fifty-seven and fifty-hundredths chains to a point; thence north twenty-one degrees fifty-seven minutes west, to a point in the north line of section four, township eight north, range nineteen west, San Bernardino Base and Meridian, distant westerly along said north line one thousand four hundred feet, more or less, from the northeast corner of said section four, said point being

[32]*Senate Bill* No. 285 (1921).
[33]*Political Code* (1923), § 3927.

common to the boundaries of the counties of Kern, Ventura and Los Angeles; thence east along the north line of township eight north, San Bernardino Base and Meridian, to the northeast corner of township eight north, range eight west, San Bernardino Base and Meridian, said corner being a point common to the boundaries of the counties of San Bernardino, Kern and Los Angeles; thence south along the range line between ranges seven and eight west to the southeast corner of township six north, range eight west, San Bernardino Base and Meridian; thence east along the township line between townships five and six north to the northeast corner of township five north, range eight west, San Bernardino Base and Meridian; thence south along the range line between ranges seven and eight west to a point in the east line of section twelve, township four north, range eight west, San Bernardino Base and Meridian, distant southerly nine hundred forty feet, measured along said east line from the northeast corner of said section twelve; thence southerly in a direct line to the summit of San Antonio peak; thence southwesterly in a direct line to the northwest corner of Rancho Cucamonga; thence southwesterly along the northwesterly boundary line of Rancho Cucamonga to the most westerly corner of Rancho Cucamonga; thence southwesterly in a direct line to the northeast corner of Rancho San Jose; thence southwesterly and westerly along the easterly and southerly boundary lines of Rancho San Jose to the range line between ranges eight and nine west in township two south, San Bernardino Base and Meridian; thence south along the range line between ranges eight and nine west, to the southeast corner of section twelve, township two south, range nine west, San Bernardino Base and Meridian, said corner being an angle point in the boundary line of the Rancho Santa Ana del Chino; thence westerly, southwesterly, southerly, easterly and southerly along the boundary line of the Rancho Santa Ana del Chino to the southwest corner of the Rancho Santa Ana del Chino, said corner being the center of section thirty-five, township two south, range nine west, San Bernardino Base and Meridian; thence southeasterly in a straight line to a point in the south line of section thirty-six, township two south, range nine west, San Bernardino Base and Meridian, distant fifty-two and eighty-four-hundredths feet easterly thereon from the southwest corner of said section thirty-six, said point being common to the boundaries of the counties of San

Bernardino, Orange and Los Angeles; thence westerly along the northern line of Orange County as defined in section three thousand nine hundred thirty-eight to the southwesterly boundary line of the State of California; thence northwesterly along the southwesterly boundary line of the State of California to the point of beginning. Also the islands of Santa Catalina and San Clemente.''

Madera County

Statutes   1893: 168.
Political Code (1919), Sec. 3928.
Solid bold line designates original boundary. Changes are lettered (a, b, c, etc.). Shading denotes present county boundaries.

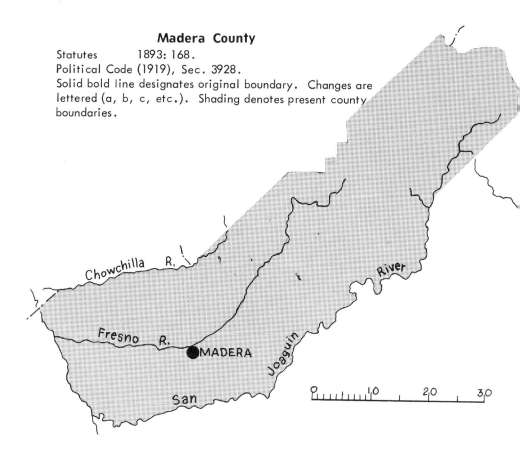

MADERA COUNTY

On March 11, 1893, Madera County was created from that part of Fresno County lying north and west of the San Joaquin River. Its boundaries, which have not been changed since the time of the creation of the county, as incorporated into the Political Code in 1919, are described as follows:[1]

"3928. *Madera.* Beginning at a point where the third standard line south of Mount Diablo Base Line crosses the San Joaquin River; thence up the middle of said river, following the meanderings thereof southeasterly and northeasterly, to the point where said river crosses the south boundary line of township six south, of range twenty-four east, Mount Diablo Base and Meridian; thence running northeast to the boundary line of Mono County; thence following the western line of Mono County and southern line of Tuolumne, to the corner common to the counties of Tuolumne, Mariposa, and Madera; thence following the southern line of Mariposa, to the southeast corner of Merced; thence westerly, following the southern line of Merced to a point where said line is intersected by the San Joaquin River; thence following up the middle of said river to the point of beginning."

[1]*Political Code* (1919), § 3928; (1923), § 3928.

MARIN COUNTY

Marin County was created in 1850. According to the act its boundaries were as follows:[1]

> "Beginning at the seacoast, at the mouth of the inlet called Estero Americano, and running up the middle of said Estero to its head; thence following the road which leads from Bodega to San Rafael, passing between the two rocks known by the name of Dos Piedros, to the Laguna of San Antonio; thence through the middle of said Laguna to its outlet, which forms the creek of San Antonio; thence following down the middle of said creek to its entrance into Petaluma Creek; thence following down the middle of said creek to the bay of San Pablo, and into said bay to the boundary of Contra Costa County; thence following said county boundary to the boundary of San Francisco County; thence along the boundary of said county to the mouth of the bay of San Francisco, and three English miles into the ocean; thence in a northerly direction, parallel with the coast, to the place of beginning, including two small islands called Dos Hermanos and Marin islands."

San Francisco Line. The only part of this description which requires explanation is that portion bordering on San Francisco County, for instead of this line being placed in the middle of the bay, as might be expected, it was defined as

> "Beginning at low water mark on the north side of the entrance of the Bay of San Francisco, and following the line of low water mark along the northern and interior coast of said bay to a point due northwest of Golden Rock."[2]

The only important change in the boundaries of Marin County was made in 1854 when the line in San Francisco Bay was modified. The boundary was to run from the mouth of Petaluma Creek to the Contra Costa line in the middle of San Pablo Bay and along this line

> "to the Invincible Rock, situated in the bay of San Francisco, near the entrance of the straits of San Pablo; thence southwardly by a direct line, so as to include the island of Los Angelos, to a point in the bay of San Francisco equi-

---

[1]*Statutes,* 1850:60; 1851:177.
[2]*Ibid.,* 1850:156. Golden Rock is identified with Red Rock.

distant between said island and Bird Island; thence by a direct southwardly line to its intersection with the present line of the county of San Francisco, at the mouth of the bay; thence with said county line three miles into the ocean."[3]

The Invincible Rock mentioned in the act is shown upon old maps of San Francisco Bay to lie near and just south of The Brothers in San Pablo Straits;[4] while Bird Island is without doubt to be identified with Alcatraz (Pelican) Island.

Further confusion in reference to the San Francisco-Marin boundary arose in 1857 when an act was passed defining the boundary of San Francisco County. The principal purpose of this act was to define closely the line between San Mateo and San Francisco. The act as drawn up did not take into consideration the Marin County act of 1854, but followed the former San Francisco description of 1851, thus placing the boundary once again at the low water line of the Marin shore.[5] This had to be remedied by enacting a new definition of Marin's boundaries in 1860,[6] placing the line once more in the position adopted in 1854.

A further slight change in the line in San Francisco Bay, made in 1868, was the last change made in the boundaries of Marin County. By this act the line was defined to run from Invincible Rock

"in a right line, to Red Rock; thence, running from the northwest point of said Red Rock in a direct southeasterly course, to the extreme southeasterly point of Angel Island; thence, in a direct course southwesterly, to the extreme end of Point Cavallo at low water mark; thence, along the line of low water mark, along the western shore of the bay, to Point Bonita and three miles into the Pacific Ocean."[7]

The Sonoma Line. In 1861 the Sonoma line was redefined along the line of a survey made in 1856 rather than by reference to the Bodega-San Rafael Road as it had been

---

[3]*Statutes,* 1854 (Redding) : 121.
[4]Hoffman, Map of the region adjacent to the Bay of San Francisco, 1867.
[5]*Statutes,* 1857 : 209.
[6]*Ibid.,* 1860 : 269.
[7]*Ibid.,* 1867–8 : 347.

described theretofore.[8] The act defines the line as running from the head of the Estero Americano

> "in a direct line to the head of San Antonio Creek, on the line surveyed and established by Wm. Mock, under the direction of the surveyor general, in the year eighteen hundred and fifty-six."

Present Boundaries, 1923. The boundaries as they now stand are defined in the Political Code as follows:[9]

> "3929. *Marin.* Beginning in the Pacific Ocean at southwestern corner of Sonoma; thence southeasterly along southern line of Sonoma, as established in section three thousand nine hundred fifty-seven, to the mouth of Petaluma Creek; thence to common corner of Marin, Sonoma, Contra Costa, and Solano, in San Pablo Bay, as established in section three thousand nine hundred fifty-seven; thence southerly along the western boundary of Contra Costa, in the bay of San Pablo, to the middle of the straits of San Pablo; thence southerly, in a direct line, to Invincible Rock, in the bay of San Francisco, near the entrance of the straits of San Pablo; thence, in a direct line, to northwestern point of Red Rock; thence southerly to the extreme southerly point of Angel Island; thence southwesterly to the extreme end of Point Cavallo at low-water mark; thence on the line of low-water mark along the northern shore of the bay to Point Bonita, and three miles into the Pacific Ocean, to the northwestern corner of San Francisco, as established in section three thousand nine hundred forty-six; thence northwesterly by ocean shore to the place of beginning."

[8]*Statutes,* 1861 : 351.
[9]*Political Code* (1919), § 3929; (1923), § 3929.

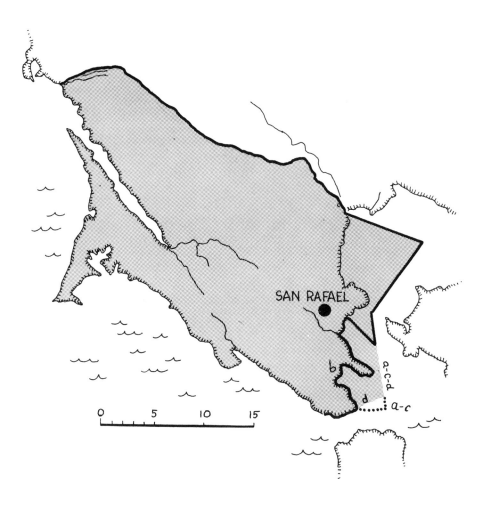

Marin County

Solid	Stats.	1850: 60; 1851: 177.
a	Stats.	1854: 121.
b	Stats.	1857: 209.
c	Stats.	1860: 269; 1861: 351.
d	Stats.	1867-8: 347; Pol. Code (1872), Sec. 3957.
Shaded	Pol. Code (1919), Sec. 3929.	

Solid bold line designates original boundary. Changes are lettered (a, b, c, etc.). Shading denotes present county boundaries.

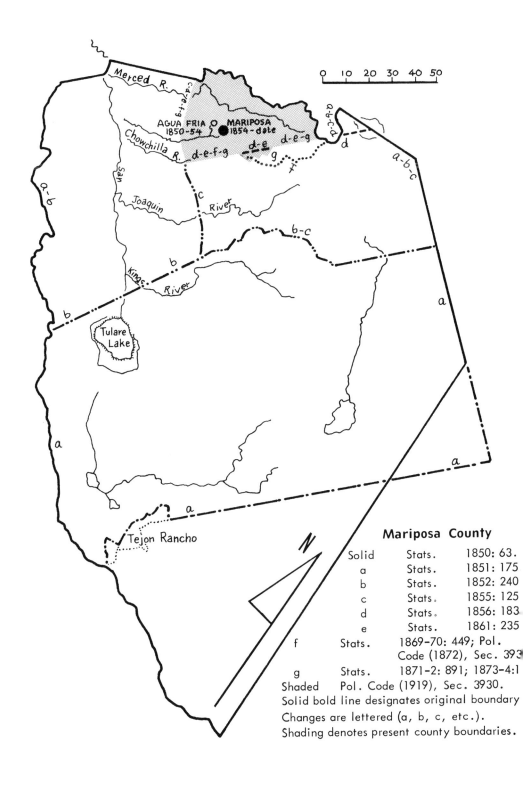

Mariposa County

Solid	Stats.	1850: 63.
a	Stats.	1851: 175
b	Stats.	1852: 240
c	Stats.	1855: 125
d	Stats.	1856: 183
e	Stats.	1861: 235
f	Stats.	1869-70: 449; Pol. Code (1872), Sec. 393
g	Stats.	1871-2: 891; 1873-4:1
Shaded	Pol. Code (1919), Sec. 3930.

Solid bold line designates original boundary
Changes are lettered (a, b, c, etc.).
Shading denotes present county boundaries.

MARIPOSA COUNTY

Original Boundaries, 1850. At the time the first legislature, in 1850, divided the state into counties Mariposa shared with San Diego the distinction of being the largest of those counties, its boundaries being somewhat indefinitely described as follows:[1]

> "Beginning on the summit of the Coast Range at the southwest corner of Tuolumne County, and running thence along the southern boundary of said county, to the summit òf the Sierra Nevada; thence along the summit of the Sierra Nevada to the parallel of thirty-eight degrees of north latitude; thence due east, on the said parallel, to the boundary of the state; thence in a southeasterly direction, following said boundary, to the northwest corner of San Diego County; thence due south, along the boundary of San Diego County, to the northeast corner of Los Angeles County; and thence in a northwesterly direction, along the summit of the Coast Range, to the place of beginning."

In order to understand the location of these boundaries it is necessary to consider what the boundaries of the adjacent counties were at this time. The southwest corner of Tuolumne County in 1850 was located on the summit of the Coast Range at a point due southwest of the mouth of the Merced River.[2] The northern boundary of Mariposa County then ran northeasterly along the present southern boundaries of Stanislaus and Tuolumne counties to the summit of the Sierra Nevadas. The northwest corner of San Diego County, mentioned in the section above quoted, was located upon the state line at a point due north of the source of San Mateo Creek, which creek is located at what is now approximately the northwestern boundary of San Diego County.[3] The western and southern boundary of Mariposa County went along the summit of the Coast Range from the northeast corner of Los Angeles County, which in 1850[4] was located at the point where the Coast Range mountains intersected the western boundary of San Diego County.

[1]*Statutes*, 1850 : 63, § 28.
[2]*Ibid.*, 1850 : 263.
[3]*Ibid.*, 1850 : 58.
[4]*Ibid.*, 1850 : 59.

In other words, Mariposa County originally contained the whole of that portion of the state which is now included in the boundaries of Mariposa, Merced, Madera, Fresno, Kings, Tulare and Kern counties and, in addition, included a large portion of Mono and Inyo and small parts of San Bernardino, Los Angeles and San Benito counties. The subsequent changes in the boundaries of Mariposa County have almost without exception tended to diminish its territory.

The Southern Boundary, 1851. In 1851 the southern boundary of the county was modified by a change in the boundaries of San Diego and Los Angeles counties, the northern boundary of Los Angeles County now being placed further north and becoming the southern line of Mariposa County.[5] The portion of the boundary affecting Mariposa County is described in the statute as running from

> "the Rancho of Casteque and Lejon and along their northern line to the northeastern corner, and from thence in a northeast line to the eastern boundary of the state."

Tulare County Line, 1852. The first great loss in the territory of Mariposa County came in the year 1852 when more than half of the southern part of its area was detached and formed into a separate county called Tulare.[6] The northern boundary of this county, which became the new southern line of Mariposa County, is described in the statute as follows:

> "Beginning at the summit of the Coast Range at the corner of Monterey and San Luis Obispo counties, thence running in a northeasterly direction to the ridge dividing the waters of the San Joaquin and Kings rivers, thence along said ridge to the summit of the Sierra, thence in the same direction to the state line."

The chief point in question here is the proper location of the corner of Monterey and San Luis Obispo counties. This was described in the statutes of 1851[7] as being on the summit of the Coast Range at a point "due east of the mouth of the Nacisniento River."

Creation of Merced County, 1855. The next change in the boundary of Mariposa County was due to the formation

---

[5]*Statutes*, 1851: 172.
[6]*Ibid.*, 1852: 240.
[7]*Ibid.*, 1851: 173, § 5.

of Merced County, which included the western or valley portion of Mariposa County and comprised approximately one-half of its area. The Mariposa-Merced county line, as it was established in 1855, ran northward from the Tulare County boundary at a point where it was crossed by

> "the road leading from Converse's Ferry on the San Joaquin River to Visalia in Tulare County, thence in a straight line to * * * a place on the San Joaquin River known as Converse's Ferry, thence along the main road leading to a place on the Merced River known as Phillips' Upper Ferry, thence in a straight line to the southeast corner of Stanislaus and southwest of Tuolumne counties."[8]

Fresno County Line, 1856. The last great reduction in the area of Mariposa County was due to the formation of Fresno County from the southern part of Mariposa and a portion of Merced County in 1856. That part of the Fresno line which affected Mariposa County, is described as beginning at a point "where the Stockton road to Millertown crosses the Chowchilla, known as Newton's Crossing"[9] and ran from here due northeast to the state boundary line.

Upon examination of the map it is noted that this line detached from the remainder of Mariposa County a triangular piece of territory lying south of latitude 38° north and between Mono Lake and the Sierra Nevada Mountains. Since this was not included within the bounds of any other county it must be considered as belonging to Mariposa County until, in 1861,[10] it was incorporated in the territory of Mono County at the time of the creation of that county.

Later Changes. In 1870 the line between Fresno and Mariposa was redefined and a portion of it amended as follows:[11]

> "The line at present known as the boundary line between Mariposa and Fresno counties, from the westerly point of junction of said counties, running easterly to the southwest corner of section eleven (11) and the northwest corner of section fourteen (14), in township six (6) south, range twenty (20) east, of Mount Diablo Meridian, shall hereafter be known as the established boundary line

[8]*Statutes,* 1855 : 125.
[9]*Ibid.,* 1856 : 183.
[10]*Ibid.,* 1861 : 235.
[11]*Ibid.,* 1869–70 : 449.

between the said counties. From the southwest corner of section eleven (11) and the northwest corner of section fourteen (14), in township six (6) south, range twenty (20) east, of Mount Diablo Meridian, a new line shall be surveyed and established as follows: Running east, following the section lines to the top of the main ridge between the waters of Big Creek and the Fresno; thence eastwardly on the main ridge which divides the waters of the Merced and the San Joaquin rivers, to the eastern boundary of Fresno County.''

This is the line subsequently followed in section 3938 of the Political Code as adopted in 1872.

At this same session of the legislature a further change was made in the boundary. Although the legislature of 1872 failed to incorporate this into the code it was reënacted by the subsequent legislature and still remains the boundary between the two counties.[12] This line is described as follows:

''The line at present known as the boundary line between Mariposa and Fresno counties, from the westerly point of junction of said counties, running easterly to the southwest corner of section eleven, and the northwest corner of section fourteen, in township six south, range twenty east, of Mount Diablo Meridian; thence east to the northwest corner of section fourteen, in township six south, range twenty-one east; thence north to the northwest corner of section thirty-five, in township five south, range twenty-one east; thence east to the southwest corner of section thirty, in township five south, range twenty-two east; thence north to the southwest corner of the Mariposa Big Tree Grant; thence east along the line of said grant to the southeast corner of said grant; thence north along the line of said grant to the northeast corner of the same; thence north to the original boundary line between the counties of Mariposa and Fresno; thence along said line to the present boundary line of Tuolumne County; is hereby declared and constituted the boundary line between said counties.''

---

[12]*Statutes*, 1871–72 : 891; 1873–74 : 100.

The Present Boundary, 1923. This change was incorporated in section 3930 of the Political Code when it was amended in 1923.[13]

"3930. *Mariposa.* Beginning on the boundary line of Madera County, where the Stockton road to Millerton crosses the Chowchilla Creek, known as Newton's crossing; thence north, forty-six degrees east, to the southwest corner of section eleven, and the northwest corner of section fourteen, in township six south, range twenty east, of Mount Diablo Meridian; thence east to the northwest corner of section fourteen, in township six south, range twenty-one east; thence north to the northwest corner of section thirty-five, township five south, range twenty-one east; thence east to the southwest corner of section thirty, in township five south, range twenty-two east; thence north to the southwest corner of the Mariposa Big Tree Grant; thence east, along the line of said grant to the southeast corner of said grant; thence north, along line of said grant to the northeast corner of the same; thence north to the original boundary line between the counties of Mariposa and Fresno; thence northeasterly along said line to the boundary line of Tuolumne County; thence westerly, by the southerly boundary of Tuolumne, to the southwest corner thereof, being common corner of Stanislaus, Merced, Tuolumne, and Mariposa; thence southeasterly, on the eastern line of Merced, as established in section three thousand nine hundred thirty-two, to the place of beginning."

[13]*Political Code* (1923), § 3930; (1919), § 3930.

MENDOCINO COUNTY

Mendocino holds the distinction of having been created almost a decade before it was finally organized as a separate county. For, although it was one of the original counties created in 1850, it remained attached to Sonoma County until 1859, when it was given an independent existence. In the meanwhile many changes had been made in its boundaries.

The Original Boundary, 1850. The original boundaries of Mendocino County are in some parts uncertain, but are capable of location when compared with the boundaries of other counties and with the topography of the region. As defined in the act of 1850 they were as follows:[1]

> "Beginning on the parallel of forty degrees of north latitude, at a point in the ocean three English miles from land, and running due east on said parallel to the summit of the Coast Range; thence in a southerly direction following the summit of the Coast Range and passing Cache Creek, to Puto Creek; thence following up said creek to its source in the mountain called Mayacmas; thence along the summit of said mountain to the head of Russian River; thence down the middle of said river to its mouth, and three English miles into the ocean; and thence in a northerly direction, parallel with the coast, to the point of beginning."

Difficulty arises here through the reference to "Cache" and "Puto" creeks, which a study of the map shows to lie east of Clear Lake, whereas the real summit of the Coast Range lies west of the lake. To the east of Clear Lake there are two ridges either of which might be accepted as the "summit of the Coast Range" if the western ridge is excluded: one of these is the present accepted boundary between Lake and Colusa counties; the other lies further west and forms the watershed between Clear Lake and Long Valley on the north fork of Cache Creek. A study of later legislation seems to support the belief that the latter ridge was the one meant by these early statutes.[2]

---

[1] *Statutes*, 1850 : 61. The description is virtually the same in *Statutes*, 1851 : 178.

[2] This point is more fully discussed in considering the western boundary of Colusa and the northern line of Napa.

The Napa Boundary, 1852, 1855. The northern boundary of Napa County was very unsatisfactorily defined in the statutes before 1852, a condition which resulted in much confusion regarding jurisdiction. In that year, however, the description was made more definite and it becomes possible to locate with some degree of accuracy the line between Napa and Mendocino counties. That part of the Napa boundary which affected Mendocino ran from the northern end of "Berryellessa Valley"

> "thence in a northwesterly direction to the outlet of Clear Lake; thence up the middle of said lake to its head; thence in a westerly direction to the northeast corner of Sonoma County."[3]

This line through Clear Lake was observed for a period of three years, when another change was made giving to Napa all the territory draining into Clear Lake, for as may be seen the act of 1852 left to Mendocino a narrow strip of territory lying along the eastern shore of the lake. Since this act placed the Napa line on

> "the top of the mountains dividing Clear Lake Valleys from Sacramento Valley; thence northerly along the top of said mountains to the head of Clear Lake; thence westerly to the top of the mountains that divide Clear Lake Valleys from the Russian River Valley,"[4]

the eastern boundary of Mendocino was very much shortened. The line there followed the watershed between Clear Lake and Eel River, a ridge which was in reality the "summit of the Coast Range."

The Sonoma-Mendocino Line, 1855, 1859. Before 1859 the line between Sonoma and Mendocino is of little importance in view of the fact that the two counties were together for all administrative and judicial purposes. There were, however, during these years changes in the boundary between the two counties. The boundary originally was located along Russian River to its source. In 1855 the line was shifted further northward by a change in the Sonoma boundary, the Mendocino-Sonoma boundary being described as follows:[5]

---

[3]*Statutes*, 1852 : 192.
[4]*Ibid.*, 1855 : 77.
[5]*Ibid.*, 1855 : 150.

"Beginning at a point in the Pacific Ocean opposite to and three miles from a point on the coast one mile north-westerly from Fort Ross, and running thence in a direct line to the northwest corner of Napa County."

In 1859 a further change was made at the time of the organization of Mendocino County. This was the observed boundary for many years and only in 1917 was it replaced by a new line. It will be discussed more fully in the consideration of the boundary of 1859.

The Line of 1859, 1860. When Mendocino County was finally separately organized in 1859 its boundaries were redefined in full and in some places modifications were made. As stated in the act the boundaries were as follows:[6]

"Beginning at a point in the Pacific Ocean, three miles due west of the mouth of Gualale River, thence east to the middle of the mouth of said stream, and up the middle of the channel of said stream, two miles; thence in a direct line to the most northern and highest peak or summit of the Redwood Mountain, immediately north of Cloverdale, and Oat Valley; thence due east to the western boundary of Napa County, on the summit of the Mayacmas Ridge; thence northerly, and easterly, along the west and north boundary of Napa County, to the western boundary of Colusa County; thence northerly along the western boundaries of the counties of Colusa and Tehama, to a point on the line of the fifth standard north of the Mount Diablo Meridian; thence along the said standard parallel due west, to a point in the Pacific Ocean three miles west from the shore; thence southerly, parallel with the coast, to the point of beginning."

The changes made were at the southern and northern ends of the county, respectively.

The northern boundary had, up to 1859, been located upon the fortieth degree of north latitude. By this act it was placed upon the "fifth standard north of the Mount Diablo Meridian." When the fifth standard was found to be some five miles north of the fortieth degree Humboldt and Trinity counties immediately raised a protest against this

---

[6]*Statutes*, 1859 : 98.

change with the result that in 1860 the boundary was once again placed

"on the line of the fortieth parallel of north latitude."[7]

Lake County Boundary, 1864. In 1864 the area of Lake County was extended by annexing to it a large district north of Clear Lake which had previously been within the limits of Mendocino. This territory is drained by the upper waters of Eel River. After excluding this territory the eastern or Lake County boundary of Mendocino ran

> "thence along the summit [of the Coast Range] to Hull's Mountain; thence west on a direct line to Mount St. Hedson; thence southerly on the ridge dividing the waters of Russian River on the west, and Clear Lake on the east"[8]

Although this description is not entirely free from fault it may be traced upon the map. If the summit of the Coast Range be strictly followed it would lie to the east of any of the tributaries of Eel River and it would be necessary to follow a ridge westward in order to arrive at Mount Hull. South from this last mentioned mountain the description is faulty, for it is necessary to cross south Eel River in order to reach the ridge between Russian River and Clear Lake.

The Northern Boundary, 1872. Notice has already been taken of the northern boundary which, in 1859, was changed from its original location upon the fortieth degree north latitude to the fifth standard parallel north of Mount Diablo and again changed to the fortieth degree the following year. At the session of the legislature in 1872 two acts were passed defining the northern boundary of Mendocino. The first of these was the act adopting the Political Code, section 3918 of which defined the line as lying along the fortieth parallel. The other was a special act relating to Mendocino, Trinity, Humboldt and Klamath counties and provided that the counties named were to appoint a commission to see that the boundary lines between these counties were surveyed and marked. It was specified that the surveyor "must accurately run, thoroughly mark, and place monuments on" the lines between the counties "in accordance with the boundaries as now designated

---

[7]*Statutes*, 1860 : 334.
[8]*Ibid.*, 1863–64 : 112; 1867–8 : 269. St. Hedson is here used for San-hedrin.

by statute.'' It also provided that ''the lines run out, marked, and defined as required by this act are hereby declared to be the true boundary lines of the counties named herein.''[9]   In accordance with this act the northern line of Mendocino was surveyed by Wm. H. Fauntleroy in August, 1872, and became the established line. Some twenty years later the line was again surveyed by the surveyor general's office, with the result that the Fauntleroy survey was found to be defective in that it ran the line some distance south of the fortieth degree. Mendocino claimed to the line of the later survey but Trinity maintained that the Fauntleroy line was the legal boundary and was sustained by a decision of the supreme court.[10] Humboldt, on the other hand, did not dispute the Rice survey which places the boundary on the fortieth degree.

Recent Changes, 1907, 1917.   During recent years there has been a growing tendency to define county boundaries in reference to established township and section lines.   In accordance with this idea the greater part of Mendocino's boundaries have been changed since 1907.   The first change was by an act passed in 1907 defining the boundary northward from Mount Hull to the southwest corner of Tehama County.[11]   By this act a small portion of Mendocino was transferred to Glenn County.

In 1917 similar changes were made in the description of the Lake-Mendocino line west and south of Mount Hull[12] and in the Sonoma-Mendocino boundary.[13]

Present Boundary, 1923.   Section 3931 of the Political Code defines the boundaries of Mendocino County as they now stand in the following language:[14]

''3931. *Mendocino.* Beginning at the southwest corner of Humboldt, as established in section three thousand nine hundred twenty; thence east on the southern line of Humboldt to the west boundary of Trinity County as established in section three thousand nine hundred sixty-one; thence southerly along said west boundary of Trinity County two miles more or less to the southwest corner of said county as described in said section three thousand

[9]*Statutes,* 1871–72 : 766.
[10]151 *Calif. Reports,* 279.
[11]*Statutes,* 1907 : 135.
[12]*Ibid.,* 1917 : 1396.
[13]*Ibid.,* 1917 : 1635.
[14]*Political Code* (1923), §3931. *See also Ibid.* (1919), § 3931.

nine hundred sixty-one; thence east along the southern boundary of Trinity County to the summit of the Coast Range mountains, forming the southeast corner of Trinity and the northeast corner of Mendocino county and being the western boundary of Tehama County as established in section three thousand nine hundred sixty; thence southerly along the said western boundary of Tehama County to the southwest corner of the said county which is also the northwest corner of Glenn County; thence south along the half-section line running south through sections two, eleven, fourteen, and twenty-three to the middle of said section twenty-three in township twenty-two north, range ten west, Mount Diablo Base and Meridian; thence east along the half section line through sections twenty-three and twenty-four to the southeast corner of the northeast quarter of section twenty-four; thence south on the range line between ranges nine and ten west, to the southwest corner of section thirty-two in township twenty-two north, range nine west; thence east along the line between and dividing sections five and thirty-two to the southeast corner of said section thirty-two; thence south on the line between and dividing sections four and five, eight and nine, sixteen and seventeen, twenty and twenty-one, twenty-eight and twenty-nine, thirty-two and thirty-three, all in township twenty-one north, range nine west, Mount Diablo Base and Meridian to the southeast corner of section thirty-two; thence east on the line dividing townships twenty and twenty-one north, range nine west, the same being the fourth standard parallel line north, seven hundred seventy-five feet, more or less, to the northeast corner of section five in township twenty north, range nine west; thence south along the line between and dividing sections four and five, eight and nine, sixteen and seventeen, twenty and twenty-one, twenty-eight and twenty-nine, thirty-two and thirty-three, all of township twenty north, range nine west; thence continuing south along the line between and dividing sections four and five of township nineteen north, range nine west to the southeast corner of the northeast quarter of section five, township nineteen north, range nine west; thence west along the said half section line through section five and then through sections one and two in township nineteen north, range ten west, Mount Diablo Base and Meridian, to a point on said line due north from the monument on top of Mount Hull, established by T. P. Smythe and R. P. Hammond and party on October 20, 1885, and approved by H. J. Willey, surveyor general of the State of California, on December 23, 1885; thence due south to said monument; thence due south to the half section line running east and west through section eleven, township nineteen north, range ten west, Mount Diablo Base and Meridian; thence west along said half section line through sections eleven, ten, nine, eight, and seven of said township, range, base and meridian; and thence through section twelve, township nineteen north, range eleven west Mount Diablo Base and Meridian; to the center of said section twelve; thence south one-half mile to the quarter section corner on the south boundary of said section twelve; thence west one mile to the quarter section corner between sections eleven and fourteen, said last mentioned township and range; thence south one-half mile to the center of said section fourteen; thence west one mile to the center of section fifteen, said township and range; thence south along the half section line running through sections fifteen, twenty-two, twenty-seven, and thirty-four, to the quarter section corner on the south line of section thirty-four, said township nineteen north, range eleven west, Mount Diablo Base and Meridian; thence west along tne township line between townships eighteen and nineteen north, range eleven west, Mount Diablo Base and Meridian, to the northwest corner of lot three, section three, township eighteen north, range eleven west, Mount Diablo Base and Meridian; thence south along the line dividing the east half of the west half from the west half of the west half of said section three, a distance of one mile to the south boundary line of said section three; thence west along the south boundary of said section three to the corner common to sections three, four, nine, and ten, said township and range; thence south along the section line between sections nine and ten and fifteen and sixteen, a distance of two miles to the corner of sections fifteen, sixteen, twenty-one and twenty-two, said last mentioned township and range; thence east along the line between sections fifteen and twenty-two to the corner of sections fourteen, fifteen, twenty-two and twenty-three, said township nineteen north, range eleven west; thence south along the section line between sections twenty-two and twenty-three, and twenty-six and twenty-seven, a distance of two miles to the corner of sections twenty-six, twenty-seven, thirty-four, and thirty-five, said township and range; thence east along the section line between sections twenty-six and thirty-five, a distance of one-half mile to the quarter section corner between last mentioned sections; thence south along the half section line one mile to the quarter section corner on the south boundary of section thirty-five, township eighteen north, range eleven west, Mount Diablo Base and Meridian; thence east along the township line on the north boundary of township seventeen north, range eleven west, Mount Diablo Base and Meridian, to the northeast corner of section two, said township and range; thence south along the section line between sections one and two, and eleven and twelve, a distance of two miles to the corner of sections eleven, twelve, thirteen, and fourteen; thence east along the section line between sections twelve and thirteen, a distance of one-half mile to the quarter section corner between said sections; thence south along the half section line a distance of one mile to the quarter section corner between sections thirteen and twenty-four; thence east along the section line between said sections thirteen and twenty-four, a distance of one-half mile to the line between townships seventeen north, ranges ten and eleven west, Mount Diablo Base and Meridian; thence south along said line a distance of three miles to the corner of townships sixteen and seventeen north, ranges ten and eleven west, Mount Diablo Base and Meridian; thence east along the north line of township sixteen north, range ten west, Mount Diablo Base and Meridian, to the northeast corner of section six, said township and range; thence south along the section line between sections five and six and seven and eight, a distance of one and one-half miles to the quarter section corner between sections seven and eight; thence east along the half section line a distance of one-half mile to the center of said section eight; thence south along the half section line a distance of one and one-half miles to the quarter section corner between sections seventeen and twenty, said township and range; thence west along the section line a distance of one mile to the quarter section corner between sections eighteen and nineteen; thence south along the half section line a distance of one mile to the quarter section corner between sections nineteen and thirty; thence west one-half mile more or less, to the corner of sections nineteen, twenty-four, twenty-five, and thirty, township sixteen north, ranges ten and eleven west, Mount Diablo Base and Meridian; thence south along the range line between said ranges ten and eleven, a distance of one-half mile to the quarter section corner on the east boundary of section twenty-five, township sixteen north, range eleven west; thence west along the north line of lot three, section twenty-five, said township and range, a distance of one-quarter mile, more or less, to the northwest corner of said lot three; thence south along the west line of lots three and four, said section twenty-five, a distance of one-half mile to the south boundary of said section twenty-five; thence west along the south line of said section twenty-five to the quarter section corner between sections twenty-five and thirty-six, said township and range; thence south along the half section line, a distance of one-half mile to the center of said section thirty-six; thence west along the half section line a distance of one-fourth mile to the northwest corner of the northeast quarter of the southwest quarter of said section thirty-six, thence south along the west line of the northeast quarter of the southwest quarter and the west line of lot six of said section thirty-six, to the north boundary of township fifteen north, range eleven west, Mount Diablo Base and Meridian; thence west along said township line to the quarter section corner on the north boundary of section two, township fifteen north, range eleven west, Mount Diablo Base and Meridian; thence south along the half section line to the quarter section corner between sections two and eleven, said township and range; thence west along the section line between sections two and eleven one-quarter mile to the northwest corner of the east half of the northwest quarter of said section eleven; thence south along the west line of the said east half of the northwest quarter of section eleven, a distance of one-half mile to the half section line running east and west through said section eleven; thence west along said half section line one and three-quarters miles to the center of section nine, said township and range; thence south along the half section line a distance of two and one-half miles to the quarter section corner between sections twenty-one and twenty-eight; thence west along the section line a distance one-half mile to the corner of sections twenty, twenty-one, twenty-eight, and twenty-nine; thence south along the section line a distance of two miles to the line on the north boundary of township fourteen north, range eleven west, Mount Diablo Base and Meridian; thence east along said township line a distance of three and sixty-five hundredths chains to the northwest corner of section four, township fourteen north, range eleven west, Mount Diablo Base and Meridian; thence south along the section line a distance of one mile to the corner of sections four, five, eight, and nine, said township and range; thence west along the section line a distance of one-half mile to the quarter section corner between sections five and eight; thence south along the half section line to the quarter section corner on the south boundary of section eight; thence east along the section line between sections eight and seventeen, a distance of five and ninety-hundredths chains, more or less, to the quarter section corner on the north boundary of section seventeen; thence south along the half section line a distance of one-half mile to the center of said section seventeen; thence east along the half section line a distance of one-half mile to the quarter section corner between sections sixteen and seventeen; thence south along the section line a distance of one-half mile to the corner of sections sixteen, seventeen, twenty, and twenty-one; thence east along the section line a distance of one mile to the corner of sections fifteen, sixteen, twenty-one and twenty-two; thence south along the section line a distance of one mile to the corner of sections twenty-one, twenty-two twenty-seven, and twenty-eight; thence east along the section line a distance of one-half mile to the quarter section corner between sections twenty-two and twenty-seven; thence south along the half section line two miles to the north boundary of township thirteen north, range eleven west, Mount Diablo Base and Meridian; thence east along the township line one-half mile to the northwest corner of section two, said township and range; thence south along the section line a distance of one-half mile to the quarter section corner between sections two and three; thence east along the half section line a distance of one-half mile to the center of said section two; thence south along the half section line a distance of one-half mile to the quarter section corner between sections two and eleven; thence east along the section line a distance of one-half mile to the corner of sections one, two, eleven, and twelve; thence south along the section line a distance of one-half mile to the quarter section corner between sections eleven and twelve; thence east along the half section line a distance of one-half mile to the center of said section twelve; thence south along the half section line a distance of one-quarter mile to the corner of lots two, three, six, and seven, said section twelve; thence east along the south line of lots one and two of said section twelve, a distance of one-half mile to the line between townships thirteen north, ranges eleven and twelve west, Mount Diablo Base and Meridian; thence north along said range line a distance of nine and twenty-five hundredths chains to the southwest corner of section five, township thirteen north, range ten west, Mount Diablo Base and Meridian; thence east along the section line a distance of eighty-nine chains to the corner of sections four, five, eight, and nine; thence south along the section line a distance of one mile to the corner of sections eight, nine, sixteen, and seventeen; thence east along the section line a distance of one-half mile to the quarter section corner between sections nine and sixteen; thence south along the half section line a distance of two and one-half miles to the center of section twenty-eight; thence east along the half section line a distance of one-half mile to the quarter section corner between sections twenty-seven and twenty-eight; thence south along the section line a distance of one mile to the quarter section corner between sections thirty-three and thirty-four; thence east along the half section line, a distance of one-half mile to the center of section thirty-four; thence south along the half section line a distance of one-half mile to the north boundary of township twelve north, range ten west, Mount Diablo Base and Meridian; thence east along said township line a distance of fifty-five chains to the northeast corner of section three, township twelve north, range ten west; thence south along the section line a distance of one and one-half miles to the quarter section corner between section ten and eleven; thence east along the half section line a distance of two miles to the line between townships twelve north, ranges nine and ten west, Mount Diablo Base and Meridian; thence south along the line between said ranges nine and ten a distance of one-half mile to the corner of sections seven, twelve, thirteen, and eighteen, said townships and ranges; thence east along the section line a distance of one mile to the corner of sections seven, eight, seventeen, and eighteen, township twelve north, range nine west, Mount Diablo Base and Meridian; thence south along the section line a distance of one mile to the corner of sections seventeen, eighteen, nineteen, and twenty; thence east along the section line a distance of one mile to the corner of sections sixteen, seventeen, twenty, and twenty-one; thence south along the section line a distance of one-half mile to the quarter section corner between sections twenty and twenty-one; thence east along the half section line a distance of one mile to the quarter section corner between sections twenty-one and twenty-two; thence south along the section line a distance of one-half mile to the corner of sections twenty-one, twenty-two, twenty-seven, and twenty-eight; thence east along the section line a distance of one mile to the corner of sections twenty-two, twenty-three, twenty-six, and twenty-seven; thence south along the section line a distance of one-half mile to the quarter section corner between sections twenty-six and twenty-seven; thence east

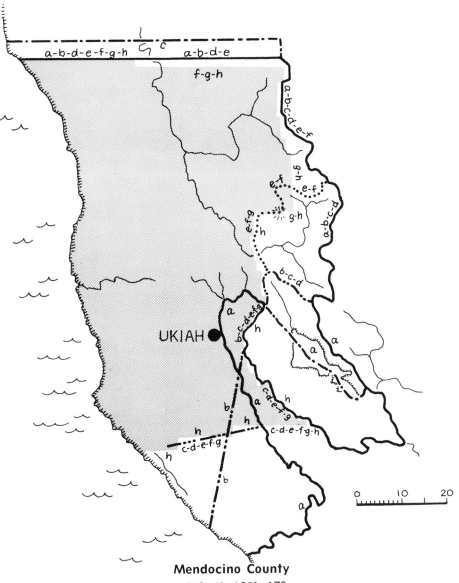

Mendocino County

Solid	Stats.	1850: 61; 1851: 178.
a	Stats.	1852: 192.
b	Stats.	1855: 77, 150.
c	Stats.	1859: 98.
d	Stats.	1860: 334.
e	Stats.	1863–4: 111; Pol. Code (1872), Sec. 3918.
f	Stats.	1871–2: 766.
g	Stats.	1907: 135.
h	Stats.	1917: 1396, 1635.
Shaded	Pol. Code (1919), Sec. 3931.	

Solid bold line designates original boundary. Changes are lettered (a, b, c, etc.). Shading denotes present county boundaries.

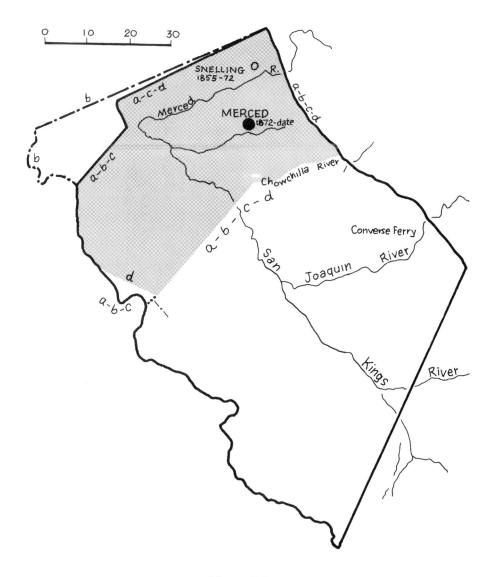

Merced County

Solid	Stats.	1855: 125.
a	Stats.	1856: 183.
b	Stats.	1865–6: 172.
c	Stats.	1867–8: 56; Pol. Code (1872), Sec. 3934.
d	Stats.	1887: 103.
Shaded	Pol. Code (1919), Sec. 3932.	

Solid bold line designates original boundary. Changes are lettered (a, b, c, etc.). Shading denotes present county boundaries.

along the half section line a distance of one mile to the quarter section corner between sections twenty-five and twenty-six; and thence south along the section line a distance of one-half mile to the corner of sections twenty-five, twenty-six, thirty-five, and thirty-six, township twelve north, range nine west, Mount Diablo Base and Meridian, said point being the southeast corner of Mendocino and the northeast corner of Sonoma county; thence westerly on the northern line of Sonoma to the Pacific Ocean; thence northerly along the ocean shore to the place of beginning.''

MERCED COUNTY

Original Boundary, 1855. Merced County was created on April 19, 1855, from the western portion of Mariposa County, its original boundaries being as follows:[1]

> "Beginning at a place on the San Joaquin River known as Converse's Ferry, thence along the main road leading to a place on the Merced River known as Phillips' Upper Ferry, thence in a straight line to the southeast corner of Stanislaus and southwest of Tuolumne counties, thence along the line dividing Mariposa and Stanislaus counties to the most western corner of the same, thence southeastwardly along the western boundary of Mariposa County to the corner of Tulare and said county of Mariposa, thence along the dividing line of Tulare and Mariposa counties to the road leading from Converse's Ferry on the San Joaquin River to Visalia in Tulare County, thence in a straight line to the place of beginning."

As will be seen from the act just quoted and a subsequent act of the following year,[2] the eastern boundary of the county followed what seems to have been the main traveled road between Stockton and Visalia, crossing the Merced River at Phillips' Upper Ferry, the Chowchilla at Newton's Crossing and the San Joaquin at Converse's Ferry. The latter of these places, which forms the initial point in the description of the boundaries of Merced County, does not appear upon any of the maps which are now at hand. Since, however, the other two points are definitely fixed, inasmuch as they lie on the present eastern boundary of Merced County, it is not difficult to locate the general course of the road which determined the location of the boundary line and consequently gives us the position of Converse's erry. It has, therefore, been placed upon the San Joaquin River near Millerton.

The northern boundary of the county, which followed the southern line of Stanislaus, ran as it does at the present time, while the western boundary followed for its entire course the summit line of the Coast Range mountains as far as the then northwestern corner of Tulare County. By statute this point

[1]*Statutes,* 1855 : 125.
[2]*Ibid.,* 1856 : 183.

was determined as being at the summit of the Coast Range of mountains, due east of the Nacisniento River.[3]

The southeastern boundary is here described in the terms of Tulare County, which ran northeasterly from the corner of Tulare County as above mentioned to the ridge dividing the waters of San Joaquin and Kings rivers.

Fresno Boundary Line, 1856. In 1856 Merced County was greatly decreased in area through the organization of Fresno County, to which was given all that part of Merced County lying south and east of the line which is described in the statute as follows:[4]

"Beginning at a point where the Stockton road to Millertown crosses the Chowchilla, known as Newton's Crossing; thence down said stream, on the north side, with the high water mark to the sink of the same at the lower molt of cottonwood timber; thence south, forty-five degrees west to the south boundary of Merced County."

The line as then established, has since that time remained essentially the southeastern boundary of Merced County.

The Northern Boundary, 1866, 1868. At the session of the legislature held in 1865–66 the line between Stanislaus and Merced counties was redefined as follows:[5]

"Commenc [ing] at the southwest corner of Tuolumne County, and southeast corner Stanislaus County, and the northwest corner of Mariposa County, and run[ning] south seventy (70) degrees west to the summit of the Coast Range of hills."

This act does not seem, however, to have given satisfaction for, at the next session of the legislature, the line was again placed as it originally stood in 1855 and since that time no change has been made.[6]

Code Line of 1872. At the time of the adoption of the Political Code in 1872 the boundaries of Merced County were described without change as they were after the passage of

[3]*Statutes,* 1852:240; 1851:173. See also the description of Monterey County boundaries.
[4]*Statutes,* 1856:183.
[5]*Ibid.,* 1865–66:172, § 3.
[6]*Ibid.,* 1867–68:56.

the act of 1868 just referred to. The section of the code reads as follows:[7]

"Beginning at northwest corner, being southwest corner of Stanislaus, as shown on survey and map of A. J. Stakes, eighteen hundred and sixty-eight; thence northeasterly, on southern line of Stanislaus, as described in section 3933, to common corner of Tuolumne, Mariposa, Merced, and Stanislaus, as established in said section; thence southeasterly, by direct line, being western line of Mariposa, to Phillips' Ferry, on Merced River; thence southeasterly, on line of Mariposa, being line shown on 'Map of Mariposa County,' to Newton's Crossing on Chowchilla Creek, forming southeast corner; thence down the northern side and on high water mark, being on line of Fresno, to the lower clump of cottonwood timber at the sink of said creek; thence south, forty-five degrees west, to the eastern line of Monterey, on summit of Coast Range, forming southwest corner; thence northwesterly, by said summit and line of Monterey and Santa Clara, to the place of beginning."

San Benito-Merced Boundary, 1887. By an act passed in 1887 the eastern boundary of San Benito County was changed from the summit of the Coast Range mountains to a position further east and placed upon township and section lines.[8]

Present Boundaries, 1923. The present boundaries are described in the Political Code as follows:[9]

"3932. *Merced.* Beginning at northwest corner, being southwest corner of Stanislaus as shown on survey and map of A. J. Stakes, 1868; thence northeasterly, on southern line of Stanislaus, as described in section three thousand nine hundred fifty-eight, to common corner of Tuolumne, Mariposa, Merced, and Stanislaus, as established in said section; thence southeasterly, by direct line, being western line of Mariposa, to Phillips' Ferry, on Merced River; thence southeasterly, on line of Mariposa, being line shown on 'map of Mariposa County,' to Newton's Crossing on Chowchilla Creek, forming southeast corner; thence down the northern side and on highwater mark, being on line of Madera to the lower clump of cottonwood timber at the sink of said creek; thence south, forty-five degrees west, to the eastern line of San Benito, forming southwest corner; thence northwesterly, by said line of San Benito and Santa Clara, to the place of beginning."

[7]*Political Code* (1872), § 3934.
[8]*Statutes,* 1887: 103.
[9]*Political Code* (1923), § 3932. *See Ibid.* (1919), § 3932.

MODOC COUNTY

Modoc County, located in the northeastern corner of the state, was created on February 17, 1874.[1] Previous to its organization this territory had been a part of Siskiyou County. Its boundaries as originally adopted have not been modified. A slight change was made in the wording of the statute when it was incorporated in the code as adopted in 1923, so that the present description of the boundary reads as follows:[2]

"3933. *Modoc.* Commencing at the northeast corner of the State of California; thence west, along the northern boundary line of said state, to the range line between ranges numbers four and five east, of Mount Diablo Base and Meridian; thence due south, on said range line, to the southern boundary line of Siskiyou County; thence east along an extension of said southern boundary line, to the state line; and thence north to the place of beginning."

[1] *Statutes,* 1873–74:124.
[2] *Political Code* (1919), § 3933; (1923), § 3933.

MONO COUNTY

The development of the mines to the east of the Sierra Nevadas, during the early sixties, led to the development of that region and to the consequent formation of new counties. The first of these to be created was Mono, which was composed of territory taken from Calaveras and Fresno counties. The boundaries as they were originally are described as follows:[1]

> "Commencing at the point where the southern boundary line of Amador County is intersected by the main summit of the Sierra Nevada mountains; thence running due east to the eastern boundary of the state; thence, in a southeasterly direction, along the said boundary line to the southern boundary line of Fresno County; thence along said line, in a westerly direction, to the summit of the Sierra Nevada Mountains; thence, in a northwesterly direction, along the said summit to the place of beginning."

The eastern boundary of the state was for many years undetermined with the result that for the period from 1861–1864 the county seat was located at Aurora, discovered in 1864 to be in the state of Nevada.

Alpine Boundary, 1864, 1866. As other counties were created in the region east of the Sierras, Mono was called upon to yield some of its territory. The first of these changes came with the organization of Alpine County. This county was made up almost entirely from the eastern parts of Amador and El Dorado, but a small piece of territory came from Mono. The southeastern boundary of Alpine County is described as running from the point where the Sonora trail strikes the summit of the Sierra Nevadas;

> "thence northerly along said summit to the dividing ridge between the West Walker and the Carson rivers; thence northeasterly along said dividing ridge to the state line."[2]

When this line is considered in connection with the map it is observed that, although Alpine was formed very largely

---

[1] *Statutes,* 1861: 235.
[2] *Ibid.,* 1863–64: 178.

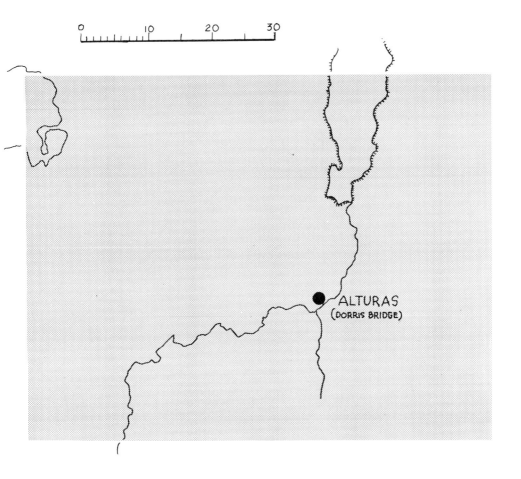

Modoc County

Statutes   1873-4: 124.
Political Code (1919), Sec. 3933.
Solid bold line designates original boundary. Changes are
lettered (a, b, c, etc.). Shading denotes present county
boundaries.

Mono County

Solid   Stats.   1861: 235.
   a   Stats.   1863–4: 178.
   b   Stats.   1865–6: 144, 355.
   c   Stats.   1869–70: 421; Pol. Code (1872), Sec. 3935.
Shaded   Pol. Code (1919), Sec. 3934.
Solid bold line designates original boundary. Changes are
lettered (a, b, c, etc.). Shading denotes present county
boundaries.

from the eastern portion of Amador County, it did not include the whole of the part detached. The next session of the legislature added this to Mono County, whose northwestern line was then made to coincide with the eastern line of Alpine.[3]

Inyo Line, 1866, 1870. In 1866 another county, named Inyo, was organized east of the Sierras. Since this county took a part of its territory from Mono it affected the southern boundary of that county. The line between the two counties ran from the summit of the Sierra Nevada Mountains at

> "the headwaters of Big Pine Creek; thence in an easterly direction down the middle of the channel of said Big Pine Creek to its mouth; thence due east to the state line."[4]

In 1870 this boundary was shifted further north and located as follows:

> "Beginning at the point where the main summit of the Sierra Nevada mountains is intersected by the line between townships numbered five and six south, of Mount Diablo Base Line; thence running due east in said township line to the eastern boundary of the State of California. All the territory lying between the line herein established and the line heretofore dividing said counties is hereby declared to form a portion of and be included in the county of Inyo."[5]

Present Line, 1923. Since 1870 the boundaries of Mono County have not been changed. They are described in the Political Code as adopted in 1923 as follows:[6]

> "3934. *Mono.* Beginning at north corner on state line, being east corner of Alpine, as established in section three thousand nine hundred ten; thence southwesterly, on the easterly line of Alpine, as established in section three thousand nine hundred ten, to the main summit of the Sierra Nevada mountains; thence southerly, along said summit, on easterly line of Alpine, Tuolumne, Madera, and Fresno, to a point where the northern line of township six south, Mount Diablo Base, intersects said summit line, forming southwest corner; thence east, on said township line, being the northern line of Inyo, to the eastern line of the state, forming southeast corner; thence northwest, on the state line, to the place of beginning."

[3]*Statutes,* 1865–66: 144.
[4]*Ibid.,* 1865–66 : 355.
[5]*Ibid.,* 1869–70 : 421.
[6]*Political Code* (1923), § 3934. This is based upon the former section 3935, and is identical with the section adopted in 1919.

MONTEREY COUNTY

Original Boundary, 1850. Monterey was created in 1850, being one of the original counties. At that time its boundaries were defined as follows:[1]

"Beginning at the mouth of Pajaro River, on the bay of Monterey, and running thence up the middle of said stream to its source in the small lake called San Felipe; thence along the northern and western banks of said lake to the creek San Felipe; thence on a line due east to the summit line of the Coast Range; thence along the summit of the Coast Range to the northeast corner of San Luis Obispo County; thence following the northern boundary of San Luis Obispo County to the Pacific Ocean, and three English miles therein; and thence parallel with the coast to the place of beginning."

The southern boundary is here defined in terms of the northern line of San Luis Obispo, which, it should be noted, ran from a point on the coast

"due east to the source of said river [Nacimiento]; thence down the middle of said river to its confluence with Monterey River; thence up or down, as the case may be, the middle of Monterey River to the parallel of thirty-six degrees of north latitude; thence due east, following said parallel to the summit of the Coast Range."[2]

The Nacimiento River here mentioned is the same as the Sierra River on the recent maps of the Department of the Interior; the Monterey River is now known as the Salinas.

The Southern Boundary, 1851, 1861, 1863. The southern line of Monterey was changed several times before its position became permanently located. In 1851 the area of Monterey County was enlarged by the shifting of the line further south. It was described in the terms of San Luis Obispo County as running from a point on the summit of the Coast Range

"due east to the mouth of the Nacisniento River; thence west to * * * the junction of the Monterey, or Salinas and Nacisniento rivers; thence up the Nacisniento ten miles, following the meanderings of said river; thence due west to the ocean, and three miles therein."[3]

[1]*Statutes*, 1850:59.
[2]*Ibid.*, 1850:59.
[3]*Ibid.*, 1851:173.

Ten years later in an effort to straighten the boundary it was placed as follows:[4]

"Beginning at the summit of the Monte Diablo Range of mountains, three miles north of the sixth standard line, south of the Monte Diablo Base and Meridian, and thence due west to the Pacific Ocean."

In 1863 the boundary was finally fixed as an east and west line located upon the sixth standard south, Mount Diablo Meridian.[5] Since that date it has not been changed.

The Line Adopted by the Political Code, 1872. In 1872, section 3948 of the Political Code defined the boundary of Monterey County as follows:[6]

"Beginning in Pacific Ocean, at southwest corner of Santa Cruz, as established in section 3949; thence west to the mouth of Pajaro River, on the bay of Monterey; thence up said stream to its source, the small Lake San Felipe; thence along the northern and western banks of said lake to the Creek San Felipe; thence east to the summit line of the Coast Range, forming northeastern corner; thence southeasterly along the summit of the Coast Range to the sixth standard south, Mount Diablo Base, being the common corner of San Luis Obispo, Kern, Tulare, and Monterey; thence following the northern boundary of San Luis Obispo County, on said standard line and extension thereof, to the Pacific Ocean; thence along the shore northerly to the place of beginning."

San Benito County, 1874. In 1874 that portion of Monterey County lying north and east of the Gabilan Mountains was separately organized as San Benito County. The western boundary of this county is described in the statutes as follows:[7]

"Commencing at a point in the center of Pajaro River, said point being the northwest corner of the Rancho las Arromitas y Agua Caliente, and being on the northern boundary line of Monterey County, and running thence in a southerly direction along the southwest boundary of said rancho to the southwest corner thereof; thence southerly in a direct line to the northwest corner of the Rancho las Vergelos; thence southerly in a direct line to the summit of the Gavilan range of mountains; and thence southeasterly along the summit of said Gavilan Mountains to the

[4]*Statutes,* 1861 : 349.
[5]*Ibid.,* 1863 : 358.
[6]*Political Code* (1872), § 3948.
[7]*Statutes,* 1873–74 : 95.

Chalon Peak; thence southeasterly in a direct line to the division line of the parts of the San Lorenzo Sobrantes owned respectively by Breen and Dunn; thence along said dividing line of said rancho to the southern boundary thereof; thence due south to the San Lorenzo Creek; thence southeasterly up said San Lorenzo or Lewis Creek, and up the north fork thereof, to the summit of the divide between the waters of said Lewis Creek and San Benito Creek; thence, following said divide southerly, to the eastern boundary of Monterey County, and the summit of the Coast Range of mountains.''

Present Line, 1923. In 1923 this change was incorporated in the Political Code, section 3935 of which defines the present boundaries of Monterey County as follows:

''3935. *Monterey.* Beginning in Pacific Ocean, at southwest corner of Santa Cruz, as established in section three thousand nine hundred fifty-two; thence east to the mouth of Pajaro River, on the bay of Monterey; thence up said stream to a point in its center, said point being the northwest corner of the Rancho las Arromitas y Agua Caliente, and being also the northwest corner of San Benito County, and running thence in a southerly direction along the southwest boundary of said rancho to the southwest corner thereof; thence southerly in a direct line to the northwest corner of the Rancho las Vergeles; thence southerly in a direct line to the summit of the Gavilan range of mountains; and thence southeasterly along the summit of said Gavilan Mountains to the Chalone Peak; thence southeasterly in a direct line to the division line of the parts of the San Lorenzo Sobrantes owned respectively by Breen and Dunn; thence along said dividing line of said rancho to the southern boundary thereof; thence due south to the San Lorenzo Creek; thence southeasterly up said San Lorenzo or Lewis Creek, and up the north fork thereof, to the summit of the divide between the waters of said Lewis Creek and San Benito Creek; thence following said divide southerly, to the summit of the Coast Range of mountains, this being the common corner of Monterey, San Benito and Fresno counties; thence southeasterly along the summit of the Coast Range to the sixth standard south, Mount Diablo Base, being the common corner of San Luis Obispo, Kern, Tulare, and Monterey; thence following the northern boundary of San Luis Obispo County, on said standard line and extension thereof, to the Pacific Ocean; thence along the shore northerly to the place of beginning.''

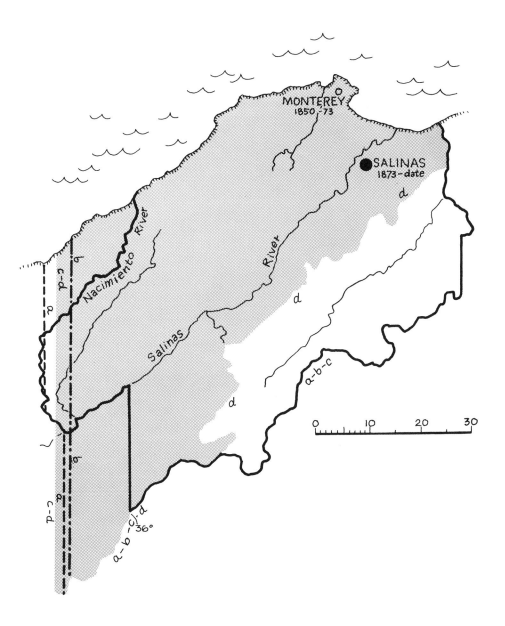

Monterey County

Solid	Stats.	1850: 59.
a	Stats.	1851: 173.
b	Stats.	1861: 349.
c	Stats.	1863: 358; Pol. Code (1872), Sec. 3948.
d	Stats.	1873-4: 95.
Shaded	Pol. Code (1919), Sec. 3935.	

Solid bold line designates original boundary. Changes are
lettered (a, b, c, etc.). Shading denotes present county
boundaries.

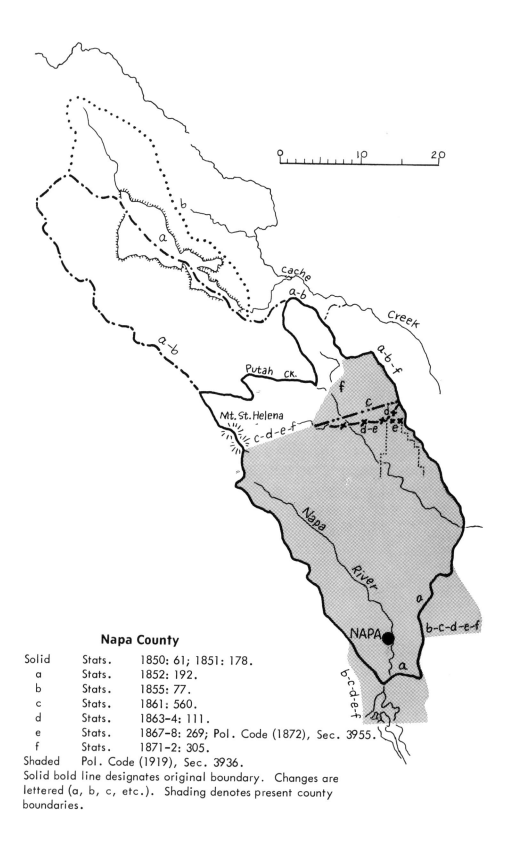

Napa County

Solid	Stats.	1850: 61; 1851: 178.
a	Stats.	1852: 192.
b	Stats.	1855: 77.
c	Stats.	1861: 560.
d	Stats.	1863-4: 111.
e	Stats.	1867-8: 269; Pol. Code (1872), Sec. 3955.
f	Stats.	1871-2: 305.
Shaded	Pol. Code (1919), Sec. 3936.	

Solid bold line designates original boundary. Changes are lettered (a, b, c, etc.). Shading denotes present county boundaries.

NAPA COUNTY

Original Boundary, 1850 and 1851. Napa was one of the counties created at the first session of the legislature. Its boundaries, as described then and redefined in 1851, were as follows:[1]

> "Commencing in the Napa River, at the mouth of Soscol Creek, and running up said creek to the point of said creek nearest to the range of mountains dividing Napa Valley from Suisun Valley; and thence in a direct line to the nearest point of said range; thence along the summit of said range northwardly to its northern extremity; thence due north to the fortieth parallel of north latitude; thence due west twenty miles; thence southwardly to the nearest point of the range of mountains dividing Napa Valley from Sonoma Valley; thence southwardly along said range of mountains to its termination in Carnero Mountain; thence in a direct line to the nearest point of Carnero Creek; thence down said creek to its junction with Napa River; and thence to the place of beginning."

A study of the map, together with the boundaries of the adjacent counties, shows at once that, except for the southern part of the county, the lines here described can not be made to conform to the topography of the country and conflict most radically with the well-defined boundaries of surrounding counties. It is, therefore, necessary to approximate the location of these boundaries very largely from the boundaries of adjacent counties.

The first portion of the description is definite and can be followed without great difficulty. This reads

> "Commencing in the Napa River, at the mouth of Soscol Creek, and running up said creek to the point of said creek nearest to the range of mountains dividing Napa Valley from Suisun Valley; and thence in a direct line to the nearest point of said range; thence along the summit of said range."

No difficulty is encountered in locating the ridge between Napa and Suisun valleys, but as the line extends northward it becomes less definitely fixed for the mountain ridges are more

---

[1] *Statutes,* 1850 : 61 ; 1851 : 178.

broken and the Suisun Valley soon ends. To take the ridge immediately east of Napa Valley to Atlas Peak was seen to limit Napa County too narrowly, in view of the later boundary; furthermore, it is possible to follow another ridge further east to the Vaca Mountains and thence northward. Since later statutes have accepted these mountains as the boundary line, it seems reasonable that they may have been the ridge referred to in these acts. Having located the ridge described, another difficulty presents itself in determining the point mentioned as being its northern extremity. To follow this ridge to its northern extremity would be to carry the Napa boundary line far north of any point contemplated in the act; on the other hand it is seen that Putah Creek, flowing from west to east, cuts through these mountains. It may be, therefore, that the "northern extremity" of the ridge was at Putah Creek.

It is, however, of little practical importance where this point was located, as the portion of the act following this can not be made to conform with the known boundaries of other counties, for to go north to the fortieth parallel would be to include large sections of both Yolo and Colusa counties and would place the northeast corner of Napa County in the Sacramento Valley not far from the town of Tehama. That the legislators really intended to include this territory in Napa County can not be considered. Similar difficulties would arise if the line were to be run north to the fortieth parallel from any other point along the described eastern boundary of Napa County.

On the other hand, the boundaries of these other counties, with the possible exception of Solano, are definite and, if the confused description of Napa's boundaries is set aside, furnish fairly definite lines which are furthermore in accord with later legislation, and hence indicate more probably the real intent of the legislators. The western boundary of Yolo County was described in both 1850 and 1851 as running from the northern boundary of Solano County, at Putah Creek "northerly following the summit of the Coast Range."[2] If, then, Napa is

---

[2] *Statutes,* 1851: 179.

adjacent to Yolo County, it follows that Napa's eastern boundary must also be along the "summit of the Coast Range."[3]

This then brings the Napa line to the southern boundary of Mendocino County, which is described as running

"in a southerly direction, following the summit of the Coast Range and passing Cache Creek to Puta Creek."[4]

That Mendocino County extended south as far as the northwestern corner of Solano County is, of course, possible, in which case Napa County would be confined to the region west of Putah Creek. This is improbable, however, in view of the fact that it would give Mendocino County a long strip of country far detached from the other territory belonging to that county; and especially since this area included the Los Putos Rancho which would hereby be separated by several mountain ranges and a great extent of unpopulated region from the remaining settled part of Mendocino County. Furthermore, since Mendocino County itself was not organized until 1859, it seems unlikely that it should have been the intention of the lawmakers to place the Los Putos Rancho, or Berryessa Valley, in Mendocino County. It was, therefore, most probably included in Napa County. The line dividing Napa from Mendocino in 1850 and 1851 has therefore been considered to approach Putah Creek from the "summit of the Coast Range" along a ridge near the present northern boundary of Napa County, as being the most probable and natural location of the line. The remainder of the northern boundary then follows the course of Putah Creek "to its source in the mountain called Mayacmas." At this point it strikes the ridge of hills which has subsequently become the western boundary of Napa and the eastern boundary of Sonoma. This may be followed southward to Carnero Creek and the Napa River, the place of beginning.

Boundary of 1852. In 1852 the boundary of Napa County was defined in a manner which permits it to be mapped more nearly in accordance with the act. In general the limits of the county are presumably the same as previously described.

---

[3]There is still the possibility that Mendocino County extended along the western side of Yolo County as far as Putah Creek. This, however, has been set aside as being out of harmony with the general division of counties. It is improbable that the Los Putos Rancho belonged to any other than either Yolo or Napa counties. See discussion of the Colusa-Mendocino boundary.

[4]*Statutes,* 1851:178.

There was, however, an important change in the north, whereby the line between Mendocino and Napa was made to run from "the outlet of Clear Lake; thence up the middle of said lake to its head." The full section reads as follows:[5]

"Commencing in Napa River, at the mouth of Suscol Creek, and running up said creek to the point of said creek nearest to the range of mountains dividing Napa Valley from Suisun Valley; thence in a direct line to the nearest point of said range; thence in a northerly direction to the east side of Chimilles or Corral Valley; thence in a direct line to the east side of Berryellessa Valley, thence along the eastern side of said valley to the northern end of said valley; thence in a northwesterly direction to the outlet of Clear Lake; thence up the middle of said lake to its head; thence in a westerly direction to the northeast corner of Sonoma County; thence south along the eastern line of said county to the place of beginning."

Line of 1855. In 1855 the boundaries of Napa were again amended. At this time important changes were made both at the northern end of the county, giving to Napa the whole of Clear Lake; another change at the southern extremity, fixed the boundaries there approximately as they are at present. The section reads as follows:[6]

"* * * commencing at a point in Guichica Creek where the said creek empties into San Pablo Bay; thence running in a direct line due east to the top of the ridge of mountains dividing Napa Valley from Suisun Valley; thence in a northerly direction along the top of said mountains to a point parallel with the southern boundary line of the ranch known as the Chimilas Rancho; thence easterly along said line to the top of the mountains known as the Vacca Mountains, which divide the Vacca Valleys from the Chimilas Rancho; thence northerly along the top of the main ridge of said Vacca Mountains to the Puta Creek; thence northerly across said creek to the top of the mountains dividing Berriessa Valleys from Sacramento Valley; thence northerly along the top of said ridge to the outlet of Clear Lake; thence easterly to the top of the mountains dividing Clear Lake Valleys from Sacramento Valley; thence northerly along the top of said mountains to the head of Clear Lake; thence westerly to the top of the mountains that divide Clear

[5]*Statutes*, 1852 : 192.
[6]*Ibid.*, 1855 : 77.

Lake Valleys from the Russian River Valley; thence southerly along the top of said mountains to a point on the top of said mountains one mile east of the eastern boundary line of the rancho known as Fitch's Rancho on Russian River; thence in a direct line southerly to the westerly branch of the headwaters of the Guichica Creek; thence westerly to the top of the main ridge that divides the Guichica Valley from the Sonoma Valley; thence in a southerly direction along the said dividing ridge to the tule bordering on San Pablo Bay; thence southerly to the centre of the Guichica Creek; thence following the centre of said creek to its mouth, the place of beginning.''

Lake County Line, 1861, 1864 and 1868. The next change was made in 1861 by the act creating Lake County from the northern part of Napa County. The southern boundary of Lake and hence the northern boundary of Napa was made to run from

"the highest point of Mount St. Helena; thence easterly in a direct line to the point where the second standard line north * * * crosses the line dividing Yolo and Napa counties.''[7]

This line was modified in 1864 to read from

"the highest point of Mount St. Helena; thence along the present line to the Butts' Cañon road; thence eastwardly to the most northern point of the Los Putas Rancho, commonly known as the 'Berryessa Rancho'; thence easterly in a direct line to a point where the second standard line north (United States survey) crosses the line dividing Yolo and Napa counties.''[8]

Another slight change was made in 1868 when, instead of running from the Los Putos Ranch to the second standard north, it was continued

"easterly, along the northern line of said rancho, to the northeast corner thereof; thence east to the line between Yolo and Napa counties.''[9]

---

[7]*Statutes*, 1861: 560.
[8]*Ibid.*, 1863–64: 111.
[9]*Ibid.*, 1867–68: 269.

In 1872 the Political Code redefined the boundaries approximately as they were at that time. The section reads as follows:[10]

> "Beginning at southwestern corner, at a point in Huichica Creek where the said creek empties into San Pablo Bay; thence east to the mountains dividing Napa Valley from Suisun Valley, forming southeastern corner; thence northerly along the summit line of said mountains to its intersection with the first standard north, Mount Diablo Base, marked by a rock monument erected by Ralph Norris; thence east along said standard line seven and three-fourth miles to Vaca Mountains, which divide the Vaca and Suisun valleys; thence northerly along the main ridge of said Vaca Mountains to Putah Creek, at a point called the Devil's Gate; thence northerly across said creek to and along the mountains dividing Berryessa Valley from Sacramento Valley to the southeast corner of Lake County on the western line of Yolo; thence westerly along the southern line of Lake, as established in section 3917, to its intersection with the eastern line of Sonoma; thence southeasterly on said line of Sonoma to the western branch of the headwaters of the Huichica Creek; thence westerly to the main ridge that divides the Huichica Valley from the Sonoma Valley; thence southerly along the said dividing ridge to the tule bordering on San Pablo Bay; thence southerly to the center of the Huichica Creek; thence down said creek to its mouth, the place of beginning."

At the same session of the legislature an act was passed amending the Lake-Napa boundary. This was not incorporated in the code section just given. By this act considerable territory, including the Knoxville district, was re-annexed to Napa County. The section in question reads as follows:[11]

> "The northern boundary line of Napa and the southeasterly boundary line of Lake counties shall commence at the highest point of the Mount St. Helena; thence running in an easterly direction along the present boundary line between said counties to the Buttes Cañon road; thence northeasterly in a direct line to the junction of Jericho and Putah creeks; thence up Jericho Creek to the junction of Hunting Creek, in Jericho Valley; thence up Hunting Creek to a large pile of rocks on the southeasterly side of the county road, at the lower and most

[10]*Political Code,* 1872, § 3958.
[11]*Statutes,* 1871–72: 305.

easterly end of Hunting Valley; thence in a straight line in the direction of the intersection of Bear and Cache creeks to the county line of Yolo County; thence along the line of Yolo County in a southeasterly direction to the present county line dividing Yolo and Napa counties.''

Present Boundary, 1923. As revised in 1919 the Political Code incorporated these changes. The section reads as follows:[12]

''3936. *Napa.* Beginning at southwestern corner at a point in Huichica Creek where the said creek empties into San Pablo Bay; thence east to the mountains dividing Napa Valley from Suisun Valley, forming southeastern corner; thence northerly along the summit line of said mountains to its intersection with the first standard north, Mount Diablo Base, marked by a rock monument erected by Ralph Norris; thence east along said standard line seven and three-fourth miles to Vaca Mountains, which divide the Vaca and Suisun valleys; thence northerly along the main ridge of said Vaca Mountains to Putah Creek, at a point called the Devil's Gate; thence northerly across said creek to and along the mountains dividing Berryessa Valley from Sacramento Valley to the southeast corner of Lake County on the western line of Yolo; thence southwesterly along the southern line of Lake, as established in section three thousand nine hundred twenty-five, to its intersection with the eastern line of Sonoma; thence southeasterly on said line of Sonoma to the western branch of the headwaters of Huichica Creek; thence westerly to the main ridge that divides the Huichica Valley from the Sonoma Valley; thence southerly along the said dividing ridge to the tule bordering on San Pablo Bay; thence southerly to the center of the Huichica Creek; thence down said creek to its mouth, the place of beginning.''

[12]*Political Code* (1919), § 3936; (1923). § 3936.

NEVADA COUNTY

Original Boundary. Nevada County was created on April 25, 1851, from the south and eastern part of Yuba County. Its boundaries at that time were described in these words:

> "Beginning at the point in the middle of Yuba River, opposite the mouth of Deer Creek, and running thence up the middle of Yuba River to a point opposite the mouth of the middle branch of Yuba, thence up the middle of said middle branch ten miles from its mouth; thence easterly in a straight line to the boundary of the state; thence south along the boundary line of the state to the northeast corner of Placer County; thence westerly on the northerly line of Placer County to the source of Bear Creek; thence down Bear Creek to a point due south of the junction of Deer Creek and Yuba River; thence north to the place of beginning."[1]

The north boundary of Placer here referred to was located as at present upon a line running from the state line due west to the source of Bear River.

The Northern Line, 1852 and 1856. Two changes were made in the north boundary during the next few years. The first of these was in 1852 when Sierra County was formed, the line dividing the two counties being defined as running

> "up the middle of said middle branch [of Yuba River] to a point opposite the mouth of Wolf Creek; thence easterly in a straight line to the boundary of the state."[2]

Another shift was made in this line in 1856 when it was once again moved further north, running this time

> "up said Middle Yuba River to the mouth of the south fork of the same; thence up said south fork to its source; thence due east to the eastern line of the state."[3]

Present Boundary, 1923. Since 1856 no important change has been made in the boundaries of Nevada County. At the time of the adoption of the Political Code in 1872 the limits were defined practically as they were after the change of 1856.[4] In 1909, however, in order to settle a dispute as to

---

[1]*Statutes*, 1851 : 177.
[2]*Ibid.,* 1852 : 191.
[3]*Ibid.,* 1856 : 143.
[4]*Political Code* (1872), § 3923.

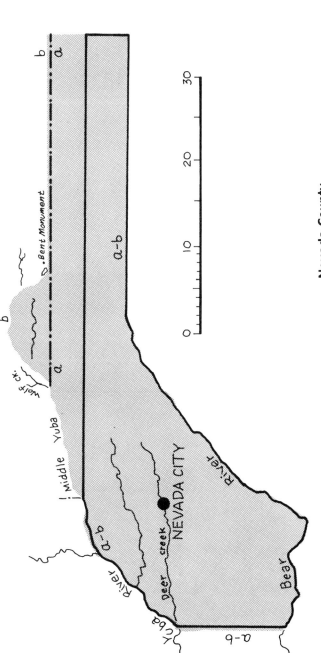

Nevada County

Solid   Stats.   1851: 177.
a   Stats.   1852: 190.
b   Stats.   1856: 143; Pol. Code (1872), Sec. 3923; (1909), Sec. 3923.
Shaded   **Pol. Code** (1919), Sec. 3937.
Solid bold line designates original boundary. Changes are
lettered (a, b, c, etc.). Shading denotes present county
boundaries.

Orange County

Statutes   1889: 123.
Political Code (1923), Sec. 3938.
Solid bold line designates original boundary. Changes are
lettered (a, b, c, etc.). Shading denotes present county
boundaries.

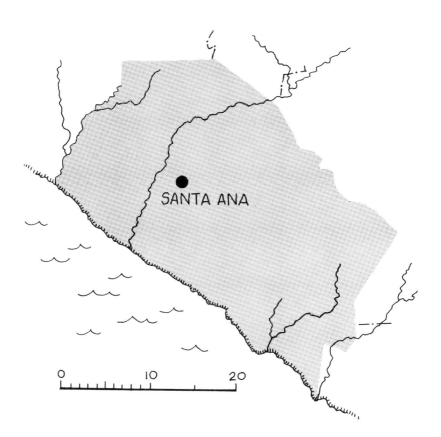

the exact location of the line described in the code, an act was passed defining the northern boundary more definitely in the terms of a recent survey.[5] These boundaries were incorporated into the code in 1923 as they have been described. They are as follows:[6]

"3937. *Nevada.* Beginning at the northwest corner, at a point in the main Yuba River, at the mouth of Deer Creek; thence up the main Yuba to the mouth of the middle Yuba; thence up the latter to the mouth of the south fork of the same; thence up the south fork to the Bent monument situated at the falls of said south fork, in the northwest quarter of section ten, township eighteen north, range thirteen east, Mount Diablo Meridian, and being one thousand feet, or thereabouts, southwest from the quarter-section corner between sections three and ten, township and range aforesaid; thence to the eastern line of the state, all on the southeastern and southern lines of Yuba and Sierra; then south, along the state line to the northeast corner of Placer as established in section three thousand nine hundred thirty-nine; thence westerly, on the northern line of Placer, as established in said section, to the source of Bear River; thence down Bear River, to a point south of the junction of Deer Creek and the main Yuba, forming southwest corner, thence north, to the place of beginning."

[5]*Statutes,* 1909 : 86.
[6]*Political Code* (1923), §3937. *See also Ibid.* (1919), § 3937.

ORANGE COUNTY

Orange County was created on March 11, 1889, from that part of Los Angeles County lying south and east of a line running approximately along the Coyote Creek. Since the organization of the county the boundaries have not been changed. They were described in the statute creating the county as follows:[1]

"Beginning at a point in the Pacific Ocean three miles southwest of the center of the mouth of Coyote Creek, proceeding up said creek in a northeasterly direction until it intersects the township line between township three south of ranges ten and eleven west; thence north on said township line to the northwest corner of section six, township three south, range ten west; thence east on said township line until it intersects the boundary line between

[1]*Statutes,* 1889 : 123.

Map removed

San Bernardino and Los Angeles counties; thence along said boundary southeasterly until it intersects the boundary line of San Diego County; thence along said line southwest until it reaches the Pacific Coast; thence in the same direction to a point three miles in said Pacific Ocean; thence in northwesterly line parallel to said coast to the point of beginning.''

In 1919 the boundaries of Orange County were redefined and the description incorporated in section three thousand nine hundred and thirty-eight of the Political Code. The new description reads as follows:[2]

"3938. *Orange.* Beginning at the northwest corner of San Diego County at a point in the Pacific Ocean opposite San Mateo point; thence northerly along the northwestern boundary of San Diego County, as defined in section three thousand nine hundred forty-five, to the southwest corner of Riverside County; thence northerly along the western boundary of said county, as defined in section three thousand nine hundred forty-one, to the corner common to Riverside, San Bernardino and Orange counties; thence northwesterly along the southwest boundary of San Bernardino County to the point of intersection of said boundary with the southerly line of township two south, range nine west; thence westerly along the township line between townships two and three south, San Bernardino Base and Meridian, to the corner common to townships two and three south, ranges ten and eleven west, San Bernardino Base and Meridian; thence southerly along the range line between ranges ten and eleven west, San Bernardino Base and Meridian, to the southeast corner of section thirteen, township three south, range eleven west, in the Rancho Los Coyotes; thence in a general southwesterly direction along section lines, quarter section lines and quarter quarter section lines in the Rancho Los Coyotes, as follows: westerly along section line to the quarter corner on the south line of said section thirteen; thence southerly along quarter section line to the center of section twenty-four, township three south, range eleven west; thence westerly along quarter section line to the quarter corner on the west line of said section twenty-four; thence southerly along section line to the southwest corner of said section twenty-four; thence westerly along section line to the quarter corner on the north line of section twenty-six,

[2]*Political Code* (1919), § 3938; (1923), § 3938.
14—21936

township three south, range eleven west; thence southerly along quarter section line to the center of said section twenty-six; thence westerly along quarter section line to the quarter corner on the west line of said section twenty-six; thence southerly along section line to the southwest corner of said section twenty-six; thence westerly along section line to the northeast corner of section thirty-three, township three south, range eleven west; thence southerly along section line to the quarter corner on the east line of said section thirty-three; thence westerly along quarter section line to the center of said section thirty-three; thence southerly along quarter section line to the northeast corner of the southeast one-quarter of the southwest one-quarter of said section thirty-three; thence westerly along quarter quarter section line to the center of the southwest one-quarter of said section thirty-three; thence southerly along quarter quarter section line to the south line of said section thirty-three; thence westerly along the township line between townships three and four south, to the northeast corner of section five, township four south, range eleven west; thence southerly along section line to the northeast corner of the southeast one-quarter of said section five; thence westerly along quarter section line to the northwest corner of the northeast one-quarter of the southeast one-quarter of said section five; thence southerly along quarter quarter section line to the center of the southeast one-quarter of said section five; thence westerly along quarter quarter section line to the westerly line of the southeast one-quarter of said section five; thence southerly along quarter section line to the quarter corner on the south line of said section five; thence westerly along section line to the northeast corner of the northwest one-quarter of the northwest one-quarter of section eight, township four south, range eleven west; thence southerly along quarter quarter section lines to the northeast corner of the southwest one-quarter of the southwest one-quarter of said section eight; thence southwesterly in a straight line to the northeast corner of section eighteen, township four south, range eleven west; thence south zero degrees, eleven minutes, fifty seconds east, along section line to the boundary line between Rancho Los Coyotes and Rancho Los Alamitos; thence south fifty-nine degrees, seven minutes, forty seconds west, a distance of three thousand three hundred ninety-one and forty-eight hundredths feet; thence south thirty-nine degrees, forty-eight minutes, twenty seconds west, a distance of five thousand six hundred fifty and ninety-seven hundredths feet; thence south eleven degrees, thirty-six minutes, fifty-five seconds west, a distance of two thousand two hundred forty-one and forty-one hundredths feet; thence south twenty-seven degrees, fifty-five minutes, fifty-five seconds west, a distance of eight thousand three hundred seventy-five and forty hundredths feet; thence south thirty-one degrees, twenty-two minutes, fifty seconds east, a distance of one thousand two hundred ninety-six and twenty-one hundredths feet; thence south twenty-seven degrees, twelve minutes, zero seconds east, a distance of two thousand one hundred six and ten hundredths feet; thence south sixteen degrees, forty-six minutes, forty-five seconds east, a distance of one thousand four hundred forty-four and eighty-two hundredths feet; thence south two degrees, forty-eight minutes, thirty-five seconds east, a distance of two thousand two hundred seven and ninety-four hundredths feet; thence south fifty-seven degrees, ten minutes, forty seconds west, a distance of eight thousand two hundred thirty-eight and seventy-eight hundredths feet; thence south thirty-three degrees, zero minutes, zero seconds west, a distance of six hundred twenty-two and forty-three hundredths feet to a point on the northeasterly line of block fifty-nine, Alamitos Bay tract, as shown on map recorded in map book 5, page 137, on file in the office of the recorder of the county of Los Angeles, distant thereon south fifty-seven degrees, fifty minutes, forty-five seconds east, a distance of four hundred twenty-eight and ninety-one hundredths feet from the most northerly corner of said block fifty-nine; thence continuing south thirty-three degrees, zero minutes, zero seconds west, a distance of three miles, more or less, to the southwesterly boundary line of the State of California (the boundary line between Los Angeles and Orange counties hereinabove described and hereby established being shown on county surveyor's map No. 8175 on file in the office of the surveyor of the county of Los Angeles; and likewise on map No. 300 on file in the office of the surveyor of Orange County); thence southeasterly by state line to point of beginning.''

PLACER COUNTY

Original Boundary, 1851. Placer County was created in 1851. This territory had previously been portions of Yuba and Sutter counties. Auburn, which became the county seat of the new county, was at the time of the creation of Placer County the seat of justice of Sutter County. The boundary of the county as originally defined ran as follows:[1]

"Beginning on the Sacramento River at the northwest corner of Sacramento County, and running thence up the middle of said river, to a point ten miles below the junction of Sacramento and Feather rivers; thence in a northerly direction in a straight line to a point in the middle of Bear Creek opposite Camp Far West; thence up the middle of said creek to its source; thence due east to the state line; thence southerly on the state line to the northeasterly corner of El Dorado County; thence westerly on the northerly line of El Dorado County to the junction of the north and south forks of the American River; thence westerly on the northerly line of Sacramento County to the place of beginning."

In this description two points require further explanation. The first is in reference to the western line which, from the description, would seem to run along the Sacramento River for some distance from the northern line of Sacramento County. Observation, however, shows clearly that, unless some remarkable changes have taken place in the river courses, it was impossible to proceed up the river to a point ten miles below the junction of the Feather and Sacramento rivers. In view of this condition, which was probably not evident to the lawmakers, it is likely that the line ran directly from the northwest corner of Sacramento County to a point on Bear River opposite Camp Far West. The second line in question is the southern boundary, or that common to El Dorado. This line is defined elsewhere in the act as running up the north fork of the American River to the middle fork, thence up that fork to its source and thence due east to the state boundary.[2] Because of the vague reference to the middle fork, which has more than one branch, it is impossible from the text of this act to locate the line with accuracy. Fortunately later legislation helps to determine this boundary.

---

[1]*Statutes*, 1851:176.
[2]*Ibid.*, 1851:176, § 16.

Placer-El Dorado Boundary, 1863. As just stated the line between Placer and El Dorado counties as defined in 1851 was open to dispute. By an act passed in 1863, entitled ''An act to define the boundary of El Dorado County,'' this line was more definitely located as shown by the following description :[3]

"Beginning at the junction of the north and south fork of the American River, running thence up the middle of the north fork to the mouth of the middle fork; thence up the middle of the middle fork to Junction Bar; thence up the middle of the main south fork of the said middle fork to the point where the same south fork is intersected by the Georgetown and Lake Bigler trail; thence along said trail to Sugar Pine Point, on the western shore of Lake Bigler; and thence due east to the boundary of the state."

In general this act merely defined the existing boundary. It did, however, make a slight change at the eastern end of the line by passing east on the Georgetown-Lake Bigler [Tahoe] trail rather than running to the source of the stream as heretofore.

Sutter-Placer Line, 1866, 1872 and 1889. The next change in boundary came in 1866 when the line between Sutter and Placer was more definitely located, the description being given in terms of township lines rather than by metes and bounds as previously. The description of this line reads as follows :[4]

"Beginning on the northern boundary line of Sacramento County at a point due south of the southwest corner of township eleven (11) north, range five (5) east, Mount Diablo Base and Meridian; thence due north to the northwest corner of township twelve (12) north, range five (5) east, Mount Diablo Base and Meridian; thence due east to the southwest corner of section thirty-four, (34,) township thirteen (13) north, range five (5) east, Mount Diablo Base and Meridian; thence due north to the middle of Bear Creek or River."

In 1872 at the time of the adoption of the Political Code a further slight change was made in this portion of the boundary,[5] the southwest corner being defined as lying at

"a point where the west line of range five east, Mount Diablo Meridian, intersects the northern line of Sacramento County."

[3] *Statutes,* 1863 : 349.
[4] *Ibid.,* 1865–66 : 223.
[5] *Political Code* (1872), § 3924.

On account of the irregularity of the range line at this
point this change added to Placer County a small piece of territory amounting to about three-quarters of a square mile.   In
1889 a further change in wording defined this line as it is now
given in the Political Code.   This, however, was a change in
description and not a change in the location of the line.[6]

El Dorado Line, 1913.   The latest change in the boundaries of Placer County was made in 1913 when the eastern
part of the line between that county and El Dorado was redefined and placed upon definite township and section lines.
By this act Placer County received between 800 and 900 square
miles of territory lying south of the Rubicon River.   The line
between the two counties as defined in the act of 1913 still
remains the boundary between the two counties.[7]

The Present Boundary, 1923.   Section 3939 of the Political Code as amended in 1919 defines the present boundaries of
Placer County as follows:[8]

> "3939.   *Placer.*   Beginning at a point where the west
> line of township ten north, range five east, Mount Diablo
> Meridian, intersects the northern line of Sacramento
> County, as established in section three thousand nine hun-
> dred forty-two; thence north on range line to the north-
> west corner of section six, in township ten, north, range
> five east; thence east on township line to the southwest
> corner of section thirty-one, township eleven north, range
> five east; thence north on range line to the northwest cor-
> ner of township twelve north, range five east; thence east
> to the southwest corner of section thirty-four, township
> thirteen north, range five east; thence north to Bear
> River; thence on the southern line of Yuba and Nevada
> counties, up said river to its source; thence east in a direct
> line to the eastern line of the State of California, form-
> ing the northeast corner; thence southerly along said line
> to the northeast corner of El Dorado County, as established
> in section three thousand nine hundred seventeen; thence
> westerly, on the northern lines of El Dorado and Sacra-
> mento counties, as established in section three thousand
> nine hundred seventeen, and section three thousand nine
> hundred forty-two, to the place of beginning."

[6]*Statutes,* 1889 : 402.
[7]*Political Code* (1913), § 3924.
[8]*Ibid.,* (1919), § 3939; (1923), § 3939.

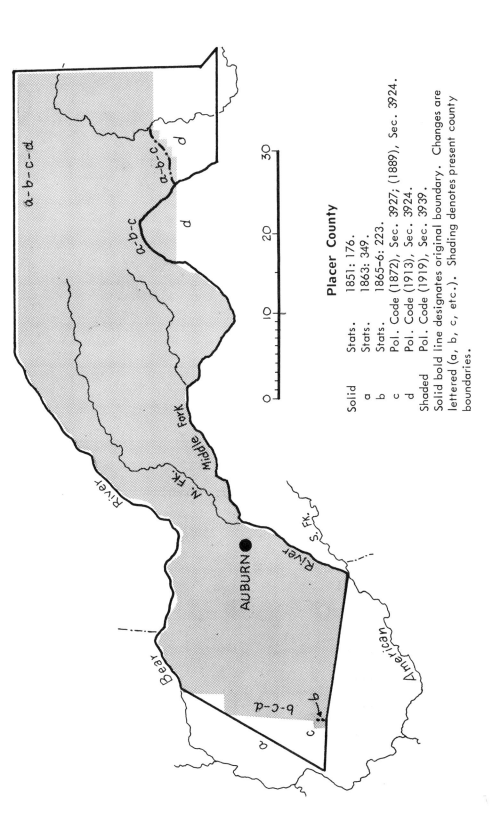

Placer County

Solid	Stats.	1851: 176.
a	Stats.	1863: 349.
b	Stats.	1865-6: 223.
c	Pol. Code (1872), Sec. 3927; (1889), Sec. 3924.
d	Pol. Code (1913), Sec. 3924.
Shaded	Pol. Code (1919), Sec. 3939.

Solid bold line designates original boundary. Changes are
lettered (a, b, c, etc.). Shading denotes present county
boundaries.

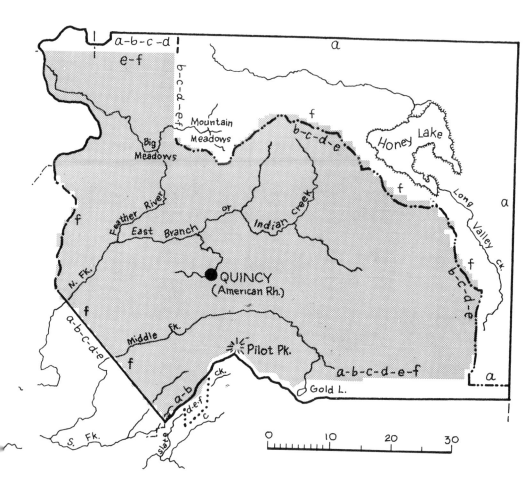

Plumas County

Solid	Stats.	1854: 129.
a	Stats.	1863: 114.
b	Stats.	1863–4: 264.
c	Stats.	1865–6: 605.
d	Stats.	1867–8: 462.
e	Pol. Code (1872), Sec. 3920.	
f	Stats.	1901: 76, 549.
Shaded	Pol. Code (1919), Sec. 3940.	

Solid bold line designates original boundary. Changes are lettered (a, b, c, etc.). Shading denotes present county boundaries.

PLUMAS COUNTY

Creation of Plumas County, 1854. Butte County originally included within its boundaries practically all of the present Plumas County as well as a portion of Lassen. In 1854 the development of the mountain region in the eastern part of the county led to a division of Butte, the eastern portion being separately organized as Plumas County with the county seat at American Ranch, a name later changed to Quincy. The original boundaries of Plumas County were described as follows:[1]

"Commencing at the Buckeye House on the line between Yuba and Butte, and running in a right line crossing the southern portion of Walker's Plains and Feather River, to the summit of the dividing ridge, dividing the waters of the west branch and the main Feather River; thence following the said divide, to the summit of the main divide, separating the waters of the Sacramento and the main north Feather; thence following said divide to the line of Shasta County, dividing Shasta and Butte; thence along said line to the boundary of the state; thence along the eastern boundary of the state to the northeast corner of Sierra County; thence following the northwestern boundary of Sierra and Yuba to the place of beginning."

The southern boundary, since it is defined in terms of Sierra and Yuba counties, requires further consideration. In the act of 1852 creating Sierra County[2] this line is described as running from

"a point on the dividing ridge between the waters of Feather and Yuba Rivers, known as the Lexington House; leaving said house in Yuba County; thence northerly following out said ridge; thence easterly in a straight line to the boundary line of the state."

The Sierra Boundary, 1863. In 1863 an attempt was made to fix more definitely the boundary between Sierra and Plumas counties. In general the boundary was much the same as it had been, but its eastern portion was placed further north, thus giving to Sierra a narrow strip of territory

---

[1]*Statutes*, 1854 (Redding): 129.
[2]*Ibid.*, 1852: 230.

(203)

which had formerly been a part of Plumas. The new line ran from

> "a point on the dividing ridge between the waters of Feather and Yuba rivers, known as the Lexington House, leaving said house in Yuba County; thence northerly along the centre of said ridge to a point known as Pilot's Peak; thence southeasterly along the centre of said ridge to a point due west from a point about one mile below the outlet of Gold Lake, known as the Falls; thence due east to the eastern boundary line of the state."[3]

Separation of Lassen, 1864. The same tendency that caused the segregation of Plumas County from Butte led to the further separation of Lassen from Plumas. In so far as they affected Plumas County the boundaries of Lassen were as follows:[4]

> "Commencing on the boundary line dividing Sierra and Plumas counties, at a point on the summit of the ridge which crosses said boundary line, and which divides Long Valley from Sierra Valley; thence following the summit of said ridge (northwesterly) which separates the waters of Feather River from those which flow into the Great Basin and Honey Lake Valley, to a point due south from the town of Susanville; thence due south to the summit of the ridge separating the waters which flow into the east branch of the north fork of Feather River, running through Indian Valley, from those which flow into the north fork of Feather River, running through the Mountain Meadows; thence following the summit of said ridge to a point due south from a point where the old and present travelled road from the Big Meadows, via Hamilton's Ranch, first crosses the said north fork of Feather River; thence due north to the southern boundary line of Shasta County."

Sierra-Plumas Line, 1866, 1868. In 1866 the boundaries of Plumas were redefined in full. In general the lines ran as in earlier acts except that Plumas was given a small piece of territory included in the valley of Slate Creek. The southern boundary of Plumas was described as follows:[5]

> "thence along said northern boundary line of Sierra County to a point on said lines six miles in a northeast-

---

[3]*Statutes*, 1863 : 114.
[4]*Ibid.*, 1863–64 : 264.
[5]*Ibid.*, 1865–66 : 605.

erly direction from the Lexington House; thence south
five miles; thence southwest five miles; thence north three
miles; thence in a direct line to said Buckeye House.''

This annexation to Plumas was met by a protest from Sierra
County and as a result the legislature at the next session
effected a compromise by passing an act which declared that:[6]

> ''All that portion of the territory of Plumas County
> lying south of Slate Creek is re-annexed to the county of
> Sierra and hereby declared to be a part of Sierra
> County.''

The boundary as it was amended at this time was incorporated into the Political Code in 1872.[7]

The Present Boundaries.   In keeping with the general
tendency of recent years to place boundaries upon township
and section lines rather than describe them by natural
features the northeastern or Lassen-Plumas boundary and a
portion of the Butte-Plumas boundary were redefined in 1901.[8]
These changes, with some revision in wording, were incorporated in the act of 1919 amending the Political Code.   The
present description of the boundaries of Plumas County reads
as follows:[9]

> ''3940.   *Plumas.*   Beginning at the corner common to
> Plumas, Butte and Yuba counties, situated in the north-
> west quarter of section fifteen, township twenty north,
> range eight east, Mount Diablo Base and Meridian and
> indicated by a large spruce tree standing in front of the
> Buckeye House marked 'Corner of Plumas, Butte and
> Yuba' and running thence northeasterly by direct line
> to the corner common to Plumas, Sierra and Yuba coun-
> ties in Slate Creek situated in the northeast quarter of
> section thirty-one, township twenty-one north, range nine
> east, Mount Diablo Base and Meridian at a point where
> the third course or terminating north and south line of
> survey of Keddie and Church, made June 19, 1866, crosses
> said creek; thence northeasterly up said creek to its inter-
> section with the first north and south line of said survey
> in the northeast quarter of section eleven, township
> twenty-one north, range nine east, Mount Diablo Base and
> Meridian; thence north along said line to the initial point
> thereof, being the summit line of the ridge dividing the

[6]*Statutes,* 1867–68 : 462.
[7]*Political Code* (1872), § 3920.
[8]*Statutes,* 1901 : 76, 549.
[9]*Political Code* (1919), § 3940; (1923), § 3940.

waters of the Feather River from the waters of the Yuba River, situate in the southeast quarter of section twenty-six, township twenty-two north, range nine east, Mount Diablo Base and Meridian; thence easterly, on said summit line, and east to 'The Falls' about one mile below the outlet of Gold Lake; thence east to the range line between township twenty-one north, range thirteen east, and township twenty-one north, range fourteen east, Mount Diablo Meridian; thence north on said range line, to the northwest corner of township twenty-one north, fourteen east, Mount Diablo Base and Meridian; thence east on the line between townships twenty-one and twenty-two north, Mount Diablo Base, to the corner common to Plumas, Lassen and Sierra counties, said corner being the southeast corner of Plumas County and the southwest corner of Lassen County, said point also being the corner common to sections one and two, township twenty-one north, range sixteen east, Mount Diablo Base and Meridian, and sections thirty-five and thirty-six, township twenty-two north, range sixteen east, Mount Diablo Base and Meridian; thence northwesterly, on the southwestern irregular line of Lassen, as established in section three thousand nine hundred twenty-six, to the corner common to Shasta, Lassen and Plumas, as established in said section; thence west nine miles more or less on the southern line of Shasta to the northeast corner of Tehama, as established in section three thousand nine hundred sixty; thence southerly, on the ridge, being eastern line of Tehama, to the common corner of Tehama, Butte and Plumas counties, as established in section three thousand nine hundred twelve; thence southerly along the eastern boundary of Butte County, as established in said section, to the place of beginning.''

RIVERSIDE COUNTY

On March 11, 1893, Riverside County was created from territory which had previously belonged to San Diego and San Bernardino counties, 6044 square miles being taken from the former, and 590 from the latter county. The boundaries of the county as then adopted were as follows:[1]

"Beginning at the common corner of the counties of Orange and San Bernardino and the westerly line of San Diego County; thence southwesterly along the line between Orange and San Diego counties to the point of intersection of said line with the township line between township seven south and township eight south, San Bernardino Base and Meridian; thence easterly along said township line to its intersection with western boundary of Santa Rosa Rancho; thence southerly along the boundary of said rancho to where said boundary of said rancho intersects the range line between the townships eight south, three west, and eight south, four west; thence south on said range line to the point of intersection of the said line with the second standard parallel south; thence east along said parallel to the eastern boundary of the State of California; thence northerly along the said eastern boundary of the State of California to the northeast corner of the county of San Diego; thence westerly along the northerly line of San Diego County to a point where the line between townships one and two south, of San Bernardino Base Line, intersects such northerly line of San Diego County; thence west along such township line to the northwest corner of township two south, of range one east, San Bernardino Base and Meridian; thence south two miles to the northeast corner of section thirteen, in township two south, of range one west; thence west seventeen miles to the southwest corner of section eight, in township two south, of range three west; thence north one mile to the northwest corner of said section eight; thence west eight and one-half miles to the quarter corner on the south line of section two, in township two south, of range five west; thence north one mile to the quarter corner on the north line of said section two; thence west ten and one-half miles to the northwest corner of section six, in township two south, of range six west; thence south to the northern boundary of the Jurupa Rancho; thence west-

[1]*Statutes,* 1893:159.

erly along the north boundary of Jurupa Rancho to the northwest corner of said rancho; thence south along the west boundary of Jurupa Rancho to the quarter corner on the west line of section ten, in township three south, of range seven west; thence west to the center of section seven, in township three south, of range seven west; thence south to the quarter corner on the south line of section nineteen, in township three south, of range seven west; thence west to the intersection with the eastern boundary of El Cañon de Santa Ana Rancho; thence southerly along the eastern boundary of said rancho to intersection with the boundary line between Orange and San Bernardino counties; thence southeasterly along the southern boundary of San Bernardino County to the place of beginning; all of said townships and ranges being from San Bernardino Base and Meridian.''

Present Boundary, 1923.   In 1919 the boundaries of Riverside County were for the first time incorporated into the Political Code. Because of the fact that the former description carried over references to San Diego boundaries where these had been superseded by those of Riverside it became necessary to revise the wording in some places. It should be also noted that a slight change was made in the northeastern boundary in an effort to establish it in a definite manner, the former description having been given in terms of the San Diego County boundary which was itself not only not defined but practically incapable of determination. The boundary description is as follows:[2]

"3941. *Riverside.* Beginning at the corner common to Orange, San Bernardino and Riverside counties, being located at the point of intersection of the easterly boundary of the El Cañon de Santa Ana Rancho with course number seven of the boundary line, established by joint survey in December, 1876, and January, 1877, as the line between Los Angeles and San Bernardino counties; thence southeasterly along said line of survey to the point of beginning of said joint survey, it being upon the northern boundary of San Diego County, as it was then established; thence southwesterly to a point on the eastern line of Rancho Mission Viejo or La Paz two miles north of the south boundary of township seven south, San Bernardino Base and Meridian; thence south along said boundary to the point of intersection of said line with the township

---

[2]*Political Code* (1919), § 3941; (1923), § 3941.

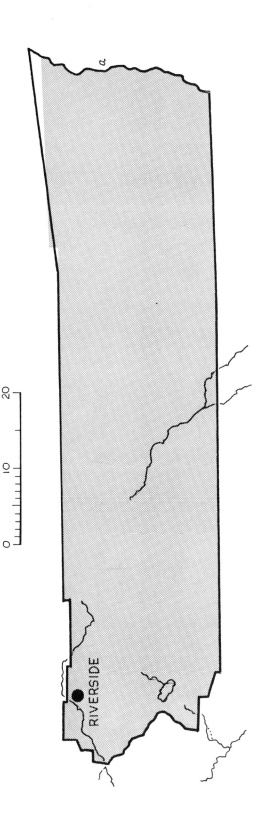

Riverside County

Solid   Stats.   1893: 159.
Shaded   Pol. Code (1919), Sec. 3941.
a   See Addendum, Page 340
Solid bold line designates original boundary. Changes are
lettered (a, b, c, etc.). Shading denotes present county
boundaries.

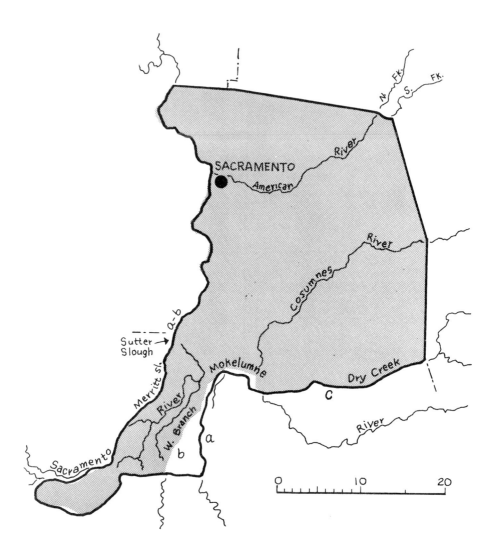

Sacramento County

Solid	Stats.	1850: 61; 1851: 174; 1857: 132; 1861: 221; 1865-6: 223.
a	Stats.	1869-70: 294; Pol. Code (1872), Sec. 3928.
b	Pol. Code (1878), Sec. 3928; (1905), Sec. 3928.	
Shaded	Pol. Code (1919), Sec. 3942.	
c	See Addendum, Page 340	

Solid bold line designates original boundary. Changes are
lettered (a, b, c, etc.). Shading denotes present county
boundaries.

line between township seven south and township eight
south, San Bernardino Base and Meridian; thence easterly along said township line to its intersection with
western boundary of Santa Rosa Rancho; thence southerly
along the boundary of said rancho to where said boundary
of said rancho intersects the range line between the townships eight south, three west, and eight south, four west;
thence south on said range line to the point of intersection of the said line with the second standard parallel
south; thence east along said parallel to the eastern boundary of the State of California; thence northerly along the
said eastern boundary of the State of California to its
point of intersection with the east and west center line of
township one south, range twenty-four east, San Bernardino Base and Meridian, or the prolongation thereof;
thence westerly along section lines to the southeast corner
of section seventeen, township one south, range sixteen
east, San Bernardino Base and Meridian; thence south to
the southeast corner of section thirty-two, same township
and range, said point being on the township line between
townships one and two south, San Bernardino Base and
Meridian; thence west on said township line to the northeast corner of township two south, range one west, San
Bernardino Base and Meridian, thence south to the southeast corner of section twelve, township two south, range
one west, San Bernardino Base and Meridian; thence
west to the southwest corner of section eight, township
two south, range three west, San Bernardino Base and
Meridian; thence north to the northwest corner of said
section eight; thence west to the quarter corner of the
south line of section two, township two south, range five
west, San Bernardino Base and Meridian; thence north
to the quarter corner on the north line of said section
two; thence west to the southwest corner of section thirty-
one, township one south, range six west; thence south
along section lines to the northern boundary of the Jurupa
Rancho; thence southwesterly along said north boundary
to the northwest corner of said rancho; thence south along
the west boundary of said Jurupa Rancho to the quarter
corner on the east line of section nine, township three
south, range seven west; thence west in a direct line to
center of section seven, same township and range; thence
south in a direct line, to the quarter corner on the south
line of section nineteen, township three south, range seven
west, thence west to the east boundary of the El Cañon
de Santa Ana Rancho; thence southerly along the easterly
boundary of said rancho to the place of beginning.''

SACRAMENTO COUNTY

Original Boundary, 1850. Sacramento was one of the original counties created on February 18, 1850, although unlike most of the older counties, it has had no important changes in its territory. As defined by the act creating the county its limits were as follows:[1]

> "Beginning at a point ten miles due north of the mouth of the American River, and running thence in an easterly direction to the junction of the north and south forks of said river; thence up the middle of the principal channel of the south fork to a point one mile above the head of Mormon Island, so as to include said island in Sacramento County; thence in a southerly direction to a point on the Cosumne River eight miles above the house of William Daylor; thence due south to Dry Creek; thence down the middle of said creek to its entrance into the Moquelumne River, or into a large slough in the tule marsh; thence down the middle of said slough to its junction with the San Joaquin River; thence down the middle of said river to the mouth of the Sacramento River, at the head of Suisun Bay; thence up the middle of the Sacramento to the mouth of Merritt's Slough; thence up the middle of said slough to its head; thence up the middle of the Sacramento River to a point due west of the place of beginning, and thence east to the place of beginning."

In view of the fact that these lines conform so nearly to the present boundaries as described in a subsequent paragraph it will not be necessary to explain points which might otherwise be left in doubt. Although the boundaries were redefined in 1851 and 1857 these descriptions were practically identical with the act of 1850.[2]

In 1861 the boundaries were once again defined. At this time a slight change is to be found in the description of the southern or San Joaquin boundary. The new description reads as follows:[3]

> "thence down the middle of said Mokelumne River to a point where said river divides into its east and west branches; thence down the middle of the east branch of

[1]*Statutes*, 1850:61.
[2]*Ibid.*, 1851: 174; 1857: 132.
[3]*Ibid.*, 1861: 221.

said Mokelumne River to its junction with the west branch of said Mokelumne River; thence down the middle of said river to its junction with the San Joaquin River.''

Although at first reading it would appear from the reference to the east branch of the Mokelumne River that this was a change of boundary to that branch of the river, a further study of previous acts and of old maps of the region indicates that this was originally the main channel of the river and not until a new channel began to be cut further west was it necessary thus to define it more closely. In 1866 the boundaries were again redefined, but with slight verbal changes they remained the same as previously.[4]

The Western Boundary, 1870. Changing river channels have necessitated the only boundary changes made in Sacramento County. The first of these was made in 1870 when the western boundary, instead of following up the Sacramento River and Merritt's Slough to the head of that slough, was made to run

"up the middle of said Merritt's Slough to the mouth of Sutter Slough; thence up the middle of said Sutter Slough to the Sacramento River.''[5]

This change placed the line slightly further west than it had previously been. At the time of the adoption of the Political Code in 1872 this description was incorporated in that code.[6]

San Joaquin-Sacramento Line, 1878. The formation of a new western channel by the Mokelumne River had earlier required more definite reference to the channels of that river when describing the boundary between Sacramento and San Joaquin counties. By 1878 the development of the western channel had become so marked that it had become the main channel. Under these conditions it was felt desirable to make the boundary conform to this change. By an amendment to the Political Code the line was made to run as follows:[7]

"down the Mokelumne River to a point where said river divides into east and west branches; thence down the west branch to its junction with the east branch; thence down said river to its junction with the San Joaquin River.''

[4]*Statutes*, 1865–66 : 223.
[5]*Ibid.*, 1869–70 : 295.
[6]*Politcal Code* (1872), § 3928.
[7]*Ibid.* (1878), § 3928.

This same description was re-enacted by an amendment to the code in 1905.[8]

Present Boundary, 1923. At the time of the revision of this part of the code in 1919 the section referring to Sacramento County was incorporated practically as it stood. It reads in full as follows:[9]

"3942. *Sacramento.* Beginning on the northern line of the county, at a point ten miles north of a point which was, on the thirtieth of March, 1857, the mouth of the American River; thence easterly to the junction of the north and south forks of said river; thence up the principal channel of the south fork to a point one mile above Mormon Island, so as to include said island in Sacramento County, forming the northeast corner; thence southerly to a point on the Cosumnes River, eight miles above the house of William Daylor; thence south to Dry Creek, forming southeast corner; thence down said Dry Creek to its entrance into Mokelumne River; thence down the Mokelumne River to a point where said river divides into east and west branches; thence down the west branch to its junction with the east branch; thence down said river to its junction with the San Joaquin River; thence down the San Joaquin River to the mouth of the Sacramento River, at the head of Suisun Bay, forming southwest corner; thence up the Sacramento River to the mouth of Steamboat Slough, formerly called Merritt Slough; thence up said slough to the mouth of Sutter Slough; thence up said Sutter Slough to the Sacramento River; thence up the Sacramento River to a point west of the place of beginning, forming the northeast corner of Sacramento County; thence east to the place of beginning."

[8]*Political Code* (1905), § 3928.
[9]*Ibid.,* (1919), § 3942; (1923), § 3942.

SAN BENITO COUNTY

Original Line, 1874. San Benito County was created on February 12, 1874, out of that portion of Monterey County lying east and north of the Gabilan Mountains. Its original boundaries were defined as follows:[1]

"Commencing at a point in the center of Pajaro River, said point being the northwest corner of the Rancho las Arromitas y Agua Caliente, and being on the northern boundary line of Monterey County, and running thence in a southerly direction along the southwest boundary of said rancho to the southwest corner thereof; thence southerly in a direct line to the northwest corner of the Rancho las Vergelos; thence southerly in a direct line to the summit of the Gavilan range of mountains; and thence southeasterly along the summit of said Gavilan mountains to the Chalon Peak; thence southeasterly in a direct line to the division line of the parts of the San Lorenzo Sobrantes owned respectively by Breen and Dunn; thence along said dividing line of said rancho to the southern boundary thereof; thence due south to the San Lorenzo Creek; thence southeasterly up said San Lorenzo or Lewis Creek, and up the north fork thereof, to the summit of the divide between the waters of said Lewis Creek and San Benito Creek; thence, following said divide southerly, to the eastern boundary of Monterey County, and the summit of the Coast Range of mountains; thence northerly, following the summit of said mountains, to the southern boundary line of Santa Clara County; thence westerly, following the southern boundary line of Santa Clara County, to the place of beginning."

Amended Boundary, 1887. In 1887 the eastern boundary was changed from the summit of the Coast Range, which had since 1850 served as the eastern boundary of Monterey and, later, San Benito County, and was placed further east upon lines described in terms of the United States surveys. The eastern boundary as modified at that time ran as follows:[2]

"thence northerly, following the summit of said mountains to where the range line between townships eighteen south, of ranges twelve and thirteen east, Mount Diablo Meridian, crosses the same; thence northerly along said

[1] *Statutes,* 1873–74 : 95.
[2] *Statutes and Amendments to the Code,* 1887 : 103.

range line to the northeast corner of township eighteen
south, range twelve east; thence northerly along said
township line to the southeast corner of township sixteen south, range twelve east, Mount Diablo Base and
Meridian; thence northwest in a straight line to the northeast corner of township fourteen south, range nine east;
thence in a straight line northwesterly, running toward
the northeast corner of township thirteen south, range
seven east, to a point where said line intersects the present boundary line between the counties of San Benito
and Merced; thence along the present boundary line between the counties of San Benito and Merced to the northeast corner of San Benito County and southeast corner of
Santa Clara County.''

Present Boundary, 1923. The boundaries of 1887 with
slight verbal changes were incorporated into the Political Code
by the act of 1919. The description is as follows:[3]

''3943. *San Benito.* Commencing at a point in the
center of the Pajaro River, said point being the northwest
corner of the Rancho las Arromitas y Agua Caliente, and
being on the northern boundary line of Monterey County,
and running thence in a southerly direction along the
southwest boundary of said rancho to the southwest corner thereof; thence southerly in a direct line to the summit of the Gabilan range of mountains, and thence southeasterly along the summit of said Gabilan mountains to
the Chalone Peak; thence southeasterly in a direct line to
the division line of the parts of the San Lorenzo Sobrantes
Rancho owned respectively by Breen and Dunn; thence
along said dividing line of said rancho to the southern
boundary thereof; thence due south to the San Lorenzo
Creek; thence southeasterly up the center of said San
Lorenzo or Lewis Creek, and up the north fork thereof, to
the summit of the divide between the waters of said
Lewis Creek and San Benito Creek; thence following said
divide southerly to the eastern boundary of Monterey
County and the summit of the Coast Range mountains;
thence northerly, following the summit of said mountains
to where the range line between townships eighteen south,
of ranges twelve and thirteen east, Mount Diablo Meridian,
crosses the same; thence northerly along said range line to
the northeast corner of township eighteen south, range
twelve east; thence northerly along said township line to the
south line of township sixteen south, range thirteen east,

[3]*Political Code* (1919), § 3943; (1923), § 3943.

Mount Diablo Base and Meridian; thence west to the southeast corner of township sixteen south, range twelve east, Mount Diablo Base and Meridian; thence northwest in a straight line to the northeast corner of township fourteen south, range nine east; thence in a straight line northwesterly, running toward the northeast corner of township thirteen south, range seven east, to a point where said line intersects the present boundary line between the counties of San Benito and Merced; thence along the present boundary line between the counties of San Benito and Merced to the northeast corner of San Benito County and southeast corner of Santa Clara County; thence following the present county line between the counties of Santa Clara and San Benito, and Santa Cruz and San Benito, to the place of beginning."

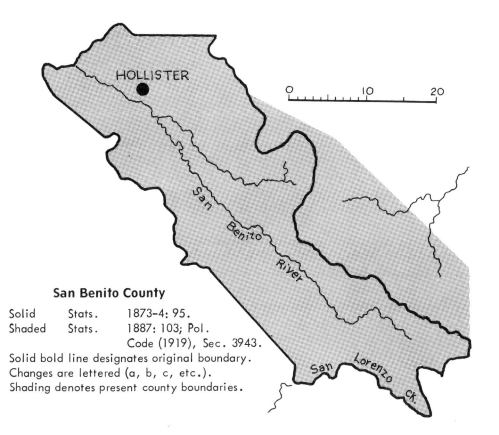

San Benito County

Solid   Stats.   1873-4: 95.
Shaded   Stats.   1887: 103; Pol.
                    Code (1919), Sec. 3943.
Solid bold line designates original boundary.
Changes are lettered (a, b, c, etc.).
Shading denotes present county boundaries.

SAN BERNARDINO COUNTY

San Bernardino County was created from the eastern portion of Los Angeles County by an act of April 26, 1853. The county seat was fixed at San Bernardino and its boundaries defined as follows:[1]

> "Beginning at a point where a due south line drawn from the highest peak of the Sierra de Santiago intersects the northern boundary of San Diego County; thence running along the summit of said Sierra to the Santa Ana River, between the ranch of Sierra and the residence of Bermardo Yorba; thence across the Santa Ana River along the summit of the range of hills, that lie between the Coyotes and Chino, (leaving the ranches of Ontiveras and Ybana to the west of this line,) to the southeast corner of the ranch of San Jose; thence along the eastern boundaries of said ranch and of San Antonio, and the western and northern boundaries of Cucaimonga Ranch to the ravine of Cucaimonga; thence up said ravine to its source in the Coast Range; thence due north to the northern boundary of Los Angeles County; thence northeast to the state line; thence along the state line to the northern boundary line of San Diego County; thence westerly along the northern boundary of San Diego to the place of beginning."

Since that part of this line which separated San Bernardino from Los Angeles County has remained essentially unchanged as the western boundary of San Bernardino County it would seem to require but little or no comment. Upon studying the definition together with the maps, however, it is found that the line as surveyed in 1878 and subsequently observed does not in all places conform to the statute provision. In the first place it is difficult to see by what process the southwest corner of the county was determined, for while this and later statutes[2] have spoken of this point as "due south" or "south" of the "highest peak of the Sierra de Santiago [Santiago Peak]" the line as surveyed seems to follow along the ridge of the Sierra northward from its point of intersection with the

---

[1]*Statutes*, 1853 : 119.
[2]*Ibid.*, 1857 : 165. *Political Code* (1872), § 3943.

San Diego-Los Angeles line, now the northern line of Riverside County.[3]

Further north there is even greater disparity between the
survey and the statute line, due to the fact that the surveyors
failed to take into consideration that part of the description
which relates to Cucaimonga Rancho and ravine, viz: instead
of going along ''the western and northern boundaries of Cucaimonga Ranch to the ravine of Cucaimonga'' as defined in the
act, the line was run along the western boundary of the ranch,
thence directly to the summit of the peak of Mount San Antonio (Old Baldy). Cucaimonga Ravine is shown upon the
maps to intersect the northern boundary of the rancho about
two miles east of the northwestern corner of the rancho. The
line as surveyed lies, therefore, that distance west of the
statute line.[4]

By a legislative error in 1856 the boundary of Los Angeles
County was confused and apparently made to include once
again the territory of San Bernardino County.[5] This necessitated another act of 1857[6] which once again defined the boundaries as they had been fixed in 1853.

The Political Code, 1872. At the time of the adoption
of the code in 1872 the boundaries on the north and south were
modified, the principal change being made in the north where
the line was fixed along the sixth standard meridian south of
Mount Diablo, thereby giving to Inyo County a large triangular piece of territory formerly in San Bernardino. On the
south a slight change was made in that part of the boundary
common to San Diego County, for in the section defining San
Diego boundaries its northern line was reestablished and
placed a short distance further south.[7]

Survey of 1878. In 1878 the line between Los Angeles
and San Bernardino counties was definitely surveyed and
marked. As stated in a previous paragraph there seems to
have been much carelessness in reference to the location of
this line for it was not made to conform to the terms of the
statutes. This is particularly true in two places, viz., the be-

[3]See discussion under Los Angeles County.
[4]For more complete discussion see Los Angeles County.
[5]*Statutes*, 1856 : 53.
[6]*Ibid.*, 1857 : 165.
[7]*Political Code* (1872), § 3943. For more complete discussion see San
Diego County.

ginning point in the survey and the location of Cucaimonga Ravine.[8]

Riverside County Created, 1893. In 1893 Riverside County was created by dividing San Diego County, giving to the new county also a part of San Bernardino County, including the town of Riverside which became the new county seat. The creation of Riverside County affected the southern boundary of San Bernardino County, causing it to take approximately the position which it now occupies.[9]

Western Boundary, 1917. Due to a dispute in jurisdiction along the line between Kern and San Bernardino, an attempt was made in 1917 to determine more definitely the location of the western boundary of San Bernardino in so far as it related to Kern County. By this act it was straightened and made to follow more closely the original act of 1853. The act defining the line of 1917 reads as follows:[10]

> "Beginning at the northwest corner of township eight north, range seven west, San Bernardino Meridian, being the northeast corner of Los Angeles County; thence east along the township line to the section line between sections thirty-two and thirty-three, township nine north, range seven west, San Bernardino Meridian; thence north, following section lines, to the eighth standard parallel south of Mount Diablo Base; thence east along said standard parallel to the southwest corner of township thirty-two south, range forty-one east, Mount Diablo Meridian; thence north along township lines to the seventh standard parallel south of Mount Diablo Base; thence along said standard parallel to the southwest corner of section thirty-six, township twenty-eight south, range forty east, Mount Diablo Meridian; thence north along section lines to the northwest corner of section one, township twenty-five south, range forty east, Mount Diablo Meridian, said point being hereby established as the northeast corner of Kern County and the northwest corner of San Bernardino County."

Boundary of 1923. In 1919 a further attempt was made to obtain a clear definition of these boundaries. The line between San Bernardino and Los Angeles had never been laid down in accordance with existing law, while furthermore the

[8]See previous discussion of these points.
[9]*Statutes*, 1893 : 159.
[10]*Ibid.*, 1917 : 301.

eastern extremity of the southern boundary was open to dispute due to the uncertain manner in which it was defined. Two bills were introduced affecting the boundaries of San Bernardino County, one of which was adopted and defines the boundaries as follows:[11]

"3944. *San Bernardino*. Beginning at the northwest corner of section one, township twenty-five south, range forty east, Mount Diablo Base and Meridian; thence east along the township line between townships twenty-four and twenty-five south of the Mount Diablo Base Line, to the San Bernardino Meridian Line; thence along said San Bernardino Meridian Line to the quarter section corner on the west line of section thirty, township twenty north, range one east, San Bernardino Base and Meridian; thence east following the one-half section line to the eastern boundary of the State of California; thence southeasterly and southerly along said state line to its intersection with the east and west center line of township one south, range twenty-four east, San Bernardino Base and Meridian, or the prolongation thereof; thence westerly along the northern boundary of Riverside County as defined in section three thousand nine hundred forty-one to the corner common to Orange, Riverside and San Bernardino counties; thence northwesterly along the boundary line established by joint survey in December, 1876, and January, 1877, as the line between Los Angeles and San Bernardino counties to the corner common to San Bernardino, Los Angeles and Orange counties as defined in section three thousand nine hundred twenty-seven; thence northerly along the eastern boundary of Los Angeles County as defined in said section to the corner common to Los Angeles, Kern and San Bernardino counties, situated at the northeast corner of township eight north, range eight west, San Bernardino Base and Meridian; thence east on township line between townships eight and nine north of San Bernardino Base Line to the section line between sections thirty-two and thirty-three, township nine north, range seven west, San Bernardino Base and Meridian; thence north following section lines to the eighth standard parallel south of Mount Diablo Base Line; thence east along said eighth standard parallel to the southwest corner of township thirty-two south, range forty-one east, Mount Diablo Base and Meridian; thence north along township line to the seventh standard parallel south of Mount Diablo Base Line; thence along

[11]*Political Code* (1919), § 3944; (1923), § 3944.

said standard parallel to the southwest corner of section thirty-six, township twenty-eight south, range forty east, Mount Diablo Base and Meridian; thence north along section lines to the northwest corner of section one, township twenty-five south, range forty east, Mount Diablo Base and Meridian, said point being the place of beginning.''

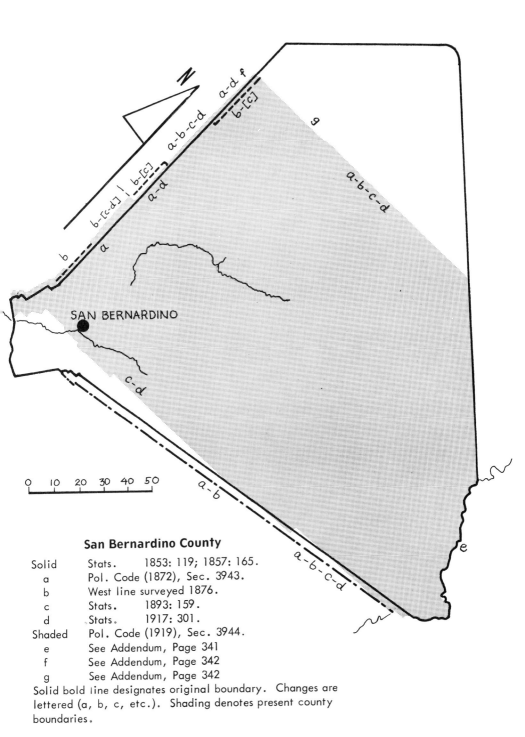

San Bernardino County

Solid	Stats. 1853: 119; 1857: 165.
a	Pol. Code (1872), Sec. 3943.
b	West line surveyed 1876.
c	Stats. 1893: 159.
d	Stats. 1917: 301.
Shaded	Pol. Code (1919), Sec. 3944.
e	See Addendum, Page 341
f	See Addendum, Page 342
g	See Addendum, Page 342

Solid bold line designates original boundary. Changes are
lettered (a, b, c, etc.). Shading denotes present county
boundaries.

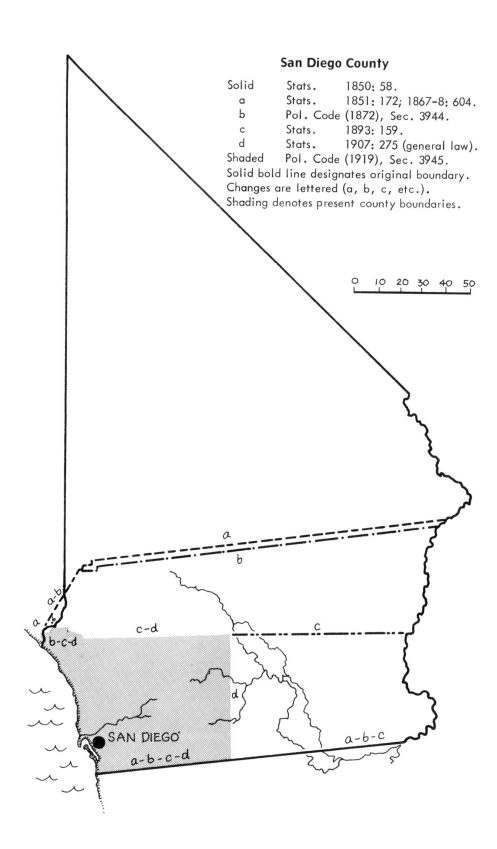

San Diego County

Solid	Stats.	1850: 58.
a	Stats.	1851: 172; 1867–8: 604.
b	Pol. Code (1872), Sec. 3944.
c	Stats.	1893: 159.
d	Stats.	1907: 275 (general law).
Shaded	Pol. Code (1919), Sec. 3945.

Solid bold line designates original boundary.
Changes are lettered (a, b, c, etc.).
Shading denotes present county boundaries.

0 10 20 30 40 50

a

b

a-b

a

b-c-d

c-d

c

d

SAN DIEGO

a-b-c

a-b-c-d

SAN DIEGO COUNTY

San Diego was one of the original counties created by the first legislature on February 18, 1850. The territory given to it at that time made it one of the largest counties in the state, for it included all that portion of the state south and east of a line commencing in the Pacific Ocean at the mouth of San Mateo Creek, running up this creek to its source, and thence due north to the state line.[1] This, therefore, included practically all of the present counties of San Diego, Imperial, Riverside, and San Bernardino.

The next session of the legislature, however, saw fit to reduce its size by annexing that territory which is now San Bernardino County to Los Angeles, the northern line of the county being then defined as follows:

> "Commencing on the coast of the Pacific at San Mateo Point and running thence in a direction so as to include the ranchos of Santa Margaurita and Lajuna Ternacala [Temecula] to the rancho of San Jacinto, and along its northern line to the northeast corner"

and from thence eastward in a line parallel with the southern boundary of the state.[2]

The line here described remained the northern boundary of the county until the adoption of the Political Code in 1872. However, in 1868 an attempt was made "more clearly to define" the boundaries of the county, with the result that the line was very much confused, for, according to the reading of the statute, the northern boundary was to run from

> "the southwest corner of the Rancho of San Jacinto Nuevo; thence, along the western and northern line of said rancho to the Rancho of San Jacinto Viejo; thence along the western and northern line of said last named rancho to the northeast corner thereof to township three (3) south, range two (2) west, San Bernardino Meridian."[3]

---

[1] *Statutes*, 1850:58.
[2] *Ibid.*, 1851:172. The difficulty of locating the points mentioned is greatly increased on account of the fact that the ranchos at that time had not been surveyed and their limits were more or less variable. *Report of Surveyor General*, 1855, pp. 223–224. On the map we have run the line from the northwest corner of the Rancho Santa Margarita to the extreme western corner of the Rancho San Jacinto Nuevo, since this seems to fulfill the requirements and conforms with the later lines. This seems to be the point described in the code as the southwest corner.
[3] *Statutes*, 1867–1868:604.

If an attempt is made to trace this line it is found to present insurmountable difficulties because of the confusion of ideas. A probable explanation of this seems to be that when the bill was first drawn up it included two alternative propositions, the first, that the line was to proceed from the southwest corner of the Rancho San Jacinto Nuevo "along the western and northern line of said rancho to the Rancho of San Jacinto Viejo." If this had been adopted the line would have proceeded in a southeasterly direction for a distance of six or eight miles and thence easterly, parallel with the Mexican boundary. The second alternative specified that the line was to run along the western and northern boundary of the said rancho (San Jacinto Nuevo) to its northeast corner, a point now more definitely specified by township and section. This alternative would be strictly in keeping with the purpose of the act, "more clearly to define the boundaries," and is in accordance with the line adopted in 1851. Instead of one or the other of these alternatives being adopted, both seem to have been included in the act as finally passed by the legislature.

At the time of the adoption of the Political Code in 1872 the boundaries of this county, in common with those of the other counties, were redefined, the northern line running from the same place in the Pacific Ocean, opposite San Mateo Point;

> "thence northerly along the western line of Rancho Santa Margarita to the southern line of Mission Viejo or La Paz; thence along the southern and eastern line of La Paz to a point two miles north of the south boundary line of township seven south, range six west, San Bernardino Base and Meridian; thence northeasterly, to the southwest corner of San Jacinto Nuevo, in township four south, range four west; thence north along west boundary of said rancho to line between townships three and four south; thence east to line between ranges two and three west; thence north on range line to a point where a line parallel with the southern boundary between the United States and Mexico will just clear the Rancho San Jacinto Viejo; thence northeasterly along such parallel line to the Colorado River."[4]

By this act, then, the line from the northwest corner of Santa Margarita Rancho to the southwest corner (extreme western cor-

----

[4]*Political Code* (1872), § 3944.

ner) of San Jacinto Nuevo[5] was modified. That portion from the coast to the northeast corner of Orange County is still accepted as the line between the contiguous counties, the remainder having been obliterated by the formation of Riverside County. Eastward from this western corner of San Jacinto Nuevo a further modification was made to remedy the difficulties presented by the law of 1868. If, however, an attempt were made to run this line in accordance with the present survey of the ranchos, the new line would be as impossible as the old one, because of the fact that the corners of the San Jacinto ranchos had not been determined until they were surveyed in 1876. Instead of following the code literally, we have run the line directly east from the western corner of San Jacinto Nuevo to the range line between townships two and three west, thence eastward parallel with the southern boundary of the state.[6] This is apparently in agreement with the old maps showing the northern boundary of San Diego County.[7]

The next change in the boundaries of San Diego County was made in the year 1893, at the time of the organization of Riverside County. The northern boundary of the county still follows the line which was at that time adopted.[8]

With the formation of Imperial County in 1907, the modifications of San Diego County up to the present time were completed. By this action the eastern boundary of the county was placed upon a line running north and south between ranges eight and nine of the San Bernardino Meridian.[9]

Present Boundaries, 1923. When the Political Code was amended in 1919 the boundaries of San Diego County were redefined so as to include the provisions of these later acts. Sec-

---

[5]We have taken the extreme western point to be the point described as the southwest corner of San Jacinto Nuevo, because of the fact that this is the only corner of the rancho which is in, or touches, township four south, range four west, and since it seems to have been the point which was followed in the early maps of the county.

[6]While not strictly in accordance with the wording of the code, this seems to be the only reasonable interpretation of the section. The difficulty arises, as before explained, on account of the ignorance as to the location of the points described. First, the southwest corner of San Jacinto Nuevo coincides exactly with the northeast corner of township four south, four west. It would, therefore, be impossible to run north from this corner to the line between townships three and four south. Second, the Rancho San Jacinto Viejo does not extend north of, nor even to, the line between townships three and four south, hence to "just clear" this rancho the line would have to go south on the range line between two and three west, rather than north along the range line as stated in the code.

[7]Official Map of San Diego County by Beasley & Schuyler, 1889.

[8]*Statutes*, 1893:159.

[9]Imperial County was created August 15, 1907, under general act passed by the legislature. *Statutes*, 1907:275.

tion 3945, the new section for San Diego County, reads as follows :[10]

"3945. *San Diego*. Beginning at the southwest corner of the State of California as described in article twenty-one of the constitution of the State of California; thence easterly along the international boundary line between the United States and Mexico to its intersection with the range line between ranges eight east and nine east of San Bernardino Meridian; thence northerly along the range lines between said ranges eight east and nine east, which is also the westerly boundary of Imperial County, as established by section three thousand nine hundred twenty-one, to the northeast corner of township nine south, range eight east, which point is also on the southerly boundary line of Riverside County, as established by section three thousand nine hundred forty-one; thence west along the second standard parallel south, San Bernardino Base, which is also the south boundary line of Riverside County, to the range line between township eight south, range three west and township eight south, range four west; thence north along said range line to the southerly boundary of the Rancho Santa Rosa; thence northwesterly and northerly along the boundary line of said Rancho Santa Rosa to the township line between township seven south and township eight south, San Bernardino Base and Meridian; thence west along said township line to the easterly line of the Rancho Mission Viejo or La Paz, which is also the southeasterly boundary line of Orange County, as established by section three thousand nine hundred thirty-eight; thence following said southeasterly boundary of Orange County southerly and westerly along the easterly and southerly line of said Rancho Mission Viejo or La Paz to the most westerly line of the Rancho Santa Margarita y Las Flores; thence southerly along said westerly line of said Rancho Santa Margarita y Las Flores to the shore line of the Pacific Ocean and continuing in the same direction to a point three English miles in said Pacific Ocean, which point is on the westerly boundary line of the said State of California; thence southerly along said westerly boundary line of the State of California to the place of beginning."

[10]*Political Code* (1919), § 3945; (1923), § 3945.

SAN FRANCISCO COUNTY

Boundary of 1850. San Francisco County, created in 1850, was originally much larger than it is at the present time, for it then included, in addition to its present area, practically three-fourths of the territory of what is now San Mateo County. Two attempts were made in 1850 to define the boundaries of San Francisco County, the second act describing them as follows:[1]

> "Beginning at low water mark on the north side of the entrance of the bay of San Francisco, and following the line of low water mark along the northern and interior coast of said bay to a point due northwest of Golden Rock; thence due southeast to a point within three miles of high water mark of Contra Costa County; thence in a southerly direction to a point three miles from and opposite the mouth of Alameda Creek; thence in a direct line to the mouth of San Francisquito Creek; thence up the middle of said creek to its source in the Santa Cruz mountains; thence due west to the ocean and three English miles therein; thence in a northwesterly direction, parallel with the coast, to a point opposite the mouth of the bay of San Francisco; and thence to the place of beginning; including the islands of Alcatraces, Yerba Buena, and the rock islands known as the Farrallones."

As will be seen from the description, the northern line of San Francisco County skirted the Marin coast at low water mark to a point on the shore near San Rafael, then it turned southeast to Golden Rock, or Red Rock, as it is now known.[2] The further description of the line in the bay is less definite. The point southeast of Red Rock, located three miles from the Contra Costa shore, appears to have been used as a boundary point down to the present time—hence is easily found by consulting the maps. From there the line went southward down the bay to a point three miles off the mouth of Alameda Creek and on to the mouth of San Francisquito Creek, where it joined the northern boundary of Santa Clara County. It then ran west up this creek "to its source in the Santa Cruz mountains" and "thence due west to the ocean." A question may arise

---

[1]*Statutes*, 1850:156.
[2]See Code Commissioners' Notes to § 3950 in their report of 1872.

in reference to the *source* of the San Francisquito Creek. Although present-day maps would seem to indicate that this lies in Searsville Lake, other evidence places it further south at the source of Los Trancos Creek, or the south branch of the San Francisquito Creek.[3] From this point the boundary runs west to the ocean and thence north to the place of beginning. This line was reaffirmed in 1851.[4]

The Marin Line, 1854, 1868. In 1854 the line of Marin was redefined and modified in that part which affects the northern boundary of San Francisco County. The portion of the act reads as follows:[5]

> "to the 'Invincible Rock' situated in the bay of San Francisco, near the entrance of the straits of San Pablo; thence southwardly by a direct line so as to include the island of Los Angelos, to a point in the bay of San Francisco, equi-distant between said island and Bird[6] Island; thence by a direct southwestwardly line to its intersection with the present line of the county of San Francisco."

This line was redefined in an act of 1860 defining in full the boundaries of Marin County, however, in the meanwhile through what appears to be an error in legislation the act of 1857 defining the boundaries of San Francisco County, ostensibly to give a clear definition of the new San Mateo line, did not incorporate in its provisions the change in the San Francisco-Marin line of 1854. This portion then is from 1857 to 1860 defined as running along the low water line of the Marin shore. The Marin County act of 1860 would take precedence over the act of 1857 and therefore restored the line of 1854. In 1868 the description of the Marin County line was once again amended to read:[7]

> "thence, running from the northwest point of said Red Rock in a direct southeasterly course, to the extreme south-easterly point of Angel Island; thence, in a direct course southwesterly, to the extreme end of Point Cavallo at

---

[3]Head of San Francisquito Creek is better defined by referring to the Santa Clara line, for this creek has since 1850 been the northwestern boundary of Santa Clara County. The point in question would seem therefore to be on the Santa Clara line. This idea is confirmed in the act of 1857 defining the southern boundary of San Mateo County. *Statutes*, 1857 : 222.
[4]*Statutes*, 1851 : 174.
[5]*Ibid.*, 1854 (Redding) :121.
[6]Alcatraz (Pelican) Island meets these terms so well that there seems little room for doubt that this was the island referred to.
[7]*Statutes*, 1867–68 : 347.

low water mark; thence along the line of low water mark, along the western shore of the bay, to Point Bonita and three miles into the Pacific Ocean.''

With a slightly different wording this line is the one followed in the present code section.

San Mateo Line, 1856. The act providing for the formation of San Mateo County in 1856 declared that the boundary between the two counties should be as follows:[8]

''Beginning in the boundary line of the county of San Francisco, as it now exists at a point due east from a rock in the bay of San Francisco, southwesterly from Point Divisidero or Hunter's Point, which rock is designated on Wheeler's map of said county as Shag Rock; thence running due west to said Shag Rock; thence running westerly to a point in the county road, one-fourth of a mile, northeasterly in a straight line from the house known as the County House, kept and occupied by C. E. Lilly; thence in a straight line to the southeastern extremity of the southern arm of the Laguna de la Merced; thence due west to the Pacific Ocean, and thence due west to the western boundary of the county of San Francisco as it now exists.''

Since this act defined merely the boundary between San Francisco and San Mateo counties, and was not in itself entirely satisfactory, the whole of the county boundary was again defined in 1857.[9] It is unnecessary to quote the whole act, but its main feature was that the San Francisco-San Mateo boundary was placed upon the line between townships two and three south of Mount Diablo Base Line, rather than upon the irregular line described in the former act. A portion of this act referring to the northern boundary has already been considered in connection with the Marin County line, it being pointed out that the act failed to take into consideration the change in the Marin County line made in 1854.

[8]*Statutes*, 1856: 146.
[9]*Ibid.*, 1857: 209. In the part defining the boundary common with Marin, this act followed the description of 1850 and 1851 rather than the amended description of 1854. By the act of 1854 Marin had been given jurisdiction out into the bay.

Code Line, 1872. In the Political Code adopted in 1872, the boundaries of San Francisco County were defined as follows:[10]

"Beginning at the southwest corner, being northwest corner of San Mateo, in Pacific Ocean, on the extension of northern line of township three south, of Mount Diablo Base; thence northerly along the Pacific Coast, to its point of intersection with westerly extension of low water line on northern side of the entrance to San Francisco Bay, being southwest corner of Marin and northwest corner of San Francisco; thence easterly, through Point Bonita and Point Caballo, to the most southeastern point of Angel Island, all on the line of Marin, as established in section 3957; thence northerly, along the easterly line of Marin, to the northwest point of Golden Rock (also known as Red Rock), being a common corner of Marin, Contra Costa, and San Francisco; thence due southeast four and one-half miles, more or less, to a point distant three statute miles from the natural high water mark on the eastern shore of San Francisco Bay, being a common corner of Contra Costa, Alameda, and San Francisco; thence southeasterly, in a direct line, to a point three miles from said eastern shore, and on the line first named (considered as extending across said bay); and thence west along said first named line to the place of beginning. The islands known as the Farralones shall be attached to and be a part of said city and county."

Amended Alameda County Line, 1873. The eastern line of San Francisco County had run from a point in the bay forming the common corner of Contra Costa, Alameda and San Francisco, located three miles from the eastern shore "southeasterly" in a direct line to a point on its southern boundary three miles from the eastern shore. This gave Yerba Buena Island to San Francisco and caused no difficulty until the building of the Oakland mole by the Central Pacific Railroad Company. The length to which this pier extended into the bay raised the question as to county jurisdictions at its western end. The line between San Francisco and Alameda was therefore amended to run from[11]

"the common corner of San Francisco, Contra Costa, and Alameda, as established by section three thousand nine hundred fifty; thence southerly to a point in the bay of

---

[10]*Political Code* (1872), § 3950.
[11]*Amendments to the Codes,* 1873–74: 169.

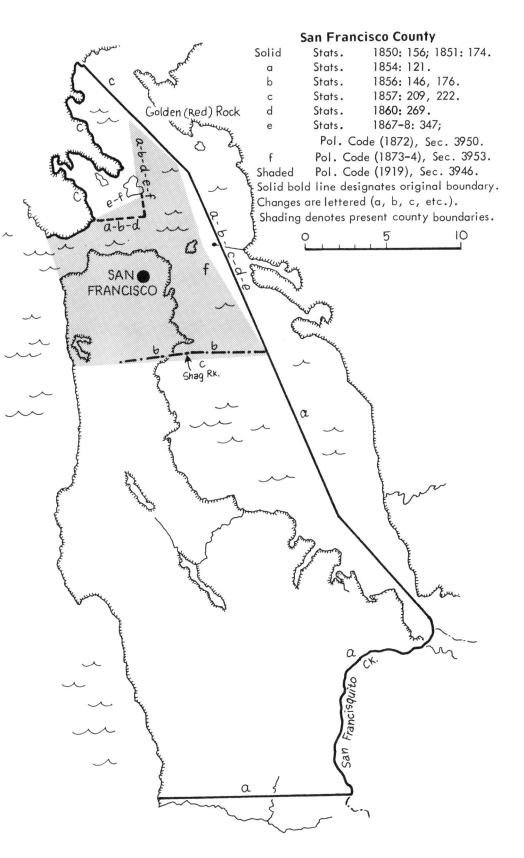

San Francisco County

Solid	Stats.	1850: 156; 1851: 174.
a	Stats.	1854: 121.
b	Stats.	1856: 146, 176.
c	Stats.	1857: 209, 222.
d	Stats.	1860: 269.
e	Stats.	1867–8: 347;
		Pol. Code (1872), Sec. 3950.
f	Pol. Code (1873–4), Sec. 3953.
Shaded	Pol. Code (1919), Sec. 3946.

Solid bold line designates original boundary.
Changes are lettered (a, b, c, etc.).
Shading denotes present county boundaries.

Golden (Red) Rock

SAN FRANCISCO

Shag Rk.

San Francisquito Ck.

0   5   10

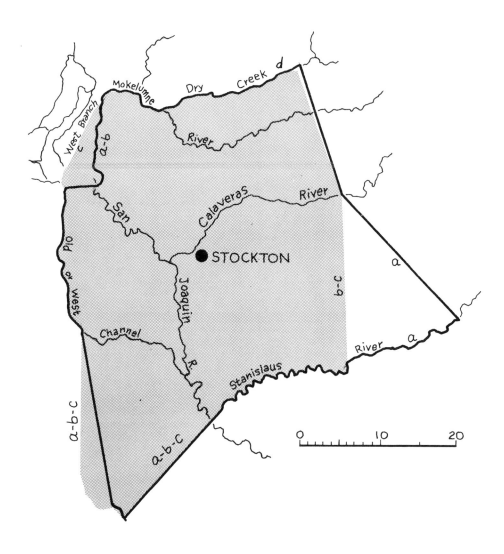

San Joaquin County

Solid   Stats.   1850: 63; 1851: 175.
  a   Stats.   1852: 178, 180.
  b   Stats.   1860: 34; Pol. Code (1872), Sec. 3932.
  c   Pol. Code (1878), Sec. 3928.
Shaded   Pol. Code (1919), Sec. 3947.
  d   See Addendum, Page 342
Solid bold line designates original boundary. Changes are
lettered (a, b, c, etc.). Shading denotes present county
boundaries.

San Francisco that would intersect a line parallel with the north line of the Central Pacific Railroad Company's wharf (as it now is), if extended westerly five hundred feet towards Yerba Buena Island; thence southeasterly in a line parallel with the east line of the city and county of San Francisco (which is the line now dividing said city and county from the county of Alameda), to its intersection with the south line of said city and county, as established in section three thousand nine hundred and fifty.''

Present Boundary, 1923. As they are at present, the boundaries of San Francisco County are defined in the Political Code as amended in 1919 in the following manner:[12]

"3946. *San Francisco.* Beginning at the southwest corner of San Mateo, in Pacific Ocean, on the extension of northern line of township three south, of Mount Diablo Base; thence northerly along the Pacific Coast, to its point of intersection with westerly extension of low-water line on northern side of the entrance to San Francisco Bay, being southwest corner of Marin and northwest corner of San Francisco; thence easterly, through Point Bonita and Point Cavallo, to the most southeastern point of Angel Island, all on the line of Marin, as established in section three thousand nine hundred twenty-nine; thence northerly, along the easterly line of Marin, to the northwest point of Golden Rock (also known as Red Rock), being a common corner of Marin, Contra Costa, and San Francisco; thence due southeast four and one-half statute miles to a point hereby established as the corner common to Contra Costa, Alameda, and San Francisco; thence southeasterly, on the western line of Alameda County to a point on the north line of township three south, range four west, Mount Diablo Base and Meridian; thence westerly on township lines and an extension thereof to the place of beginning. The islands known as the Farralones (Farrallons) shall be attached to and be a part of said city and county.''

12*Political Code* (1919), § 3946; (1923), § 3946.

SAN JOAQUIN COUNTY

Original Boundaries, 1850. San Joaquin County, lying just south of Sacramento County at the lower or northern end of the San Joaquin River Valley, was one of the original counties, it being created in 1850. The county seat was located at Stockton, the metropolis of that region, where it has always remained. The original boundaries were defined as follows:[1]

"Beginning at the junction of the San Joaquin River, and the large slough which is the outlet of the Moquelumne River and Dry Creek; thence following up the middle of said slough to the mouth of Dry Creek; thence up Dry Creek to the corner of Sacramento County; thence south to a point one mile north of Lemon's Ranch; thence south to a point one mile north of Knight's Ferry on the Stanislaus River; thence down the middle of the Stanislaus River to its confluence with the San Joaquin River; thence due southwest to the summit of the Coast Range; thence in a northwesterly direction, following the summit of said range, to the southern boundary of Contra Costa County; thence in a northeasterly direction, following the boundary of Contra Costa County, to the San Joaquin River; thence down the middle of said river to the place of beginning."

In 1852 owing to a change in the eastern boundary of Contra Costa County, a slight change was made in the western line of San Joaquin County. The amended description of this boundary read as follows:[2]

"thence up the middle of said west channel [of the San Joaquin River] to a point about ten miles below Moore and Rhodes's Ranch, at a bend where the said west channel running downward, takes a general course north; thence due south in a direct line to the summit of the Coast Ranges."

Annexation to Stanislaus, 1860. The only important change in the boundary of San Joaquin County was made in 1860 when a triangular piece of territory lying north of the Stanislaus River was detached from San Joaquin and annexed to Stanislaus County. The chief town in this district was Knight's Ferry which two years later became the county seat

[1]*Statutes*, 1850: 63; 1851: 175.
[2]*Ibid.*, 1852: 178.

of Stanislaus County. The act making this change read as follows:[3]

"Commencing on the Stanislaus River, at the corner of Tuolumne and Stanislaus counties; thence running along the boundary line between Calaveras and San Joaquin counties to McDermott's Bridge, on the Calaveras River, where the range line, between ranges nine and ten, east, intersects the easterly boundary of San Joaquin County; thence along said range line due south to the Stanislaus River; thence up said river to the place of beginning."

Political Code Line, 1872. The boundary as amended in 1860 was incorporated into the Political Code in 1872. The description at that time read as follows:[4]

"Beginning at the junction of the San Joaquin and Mokelumne rivers, on the line of Sacramento County; thence up the latter to the mouth of Dry Creek; thence up Dry Creek to the southeast corner of Sacramento, as established in section 3928; thence southeasterly, to a point on Mokelumne River, being the point of beginning of survey of Boucher and Wallace of line between San Joaquin and Calaveras counties, May, eighteen hundred and sixty-four; thence southeasterly, on the line of said survey, to the extreme northern corner of Stanislaus County, on north side of and near to Calaveras River, at a point on western line of range ten east, Mount Diablo Meridian, as established by survey of George E. Drew, approved May, eighteen hundred and sixty, shown on map of said survey; thence south, on said range line, to Stanislaus River; thence down said river to its confluence with the San Joaquin; thence southwest to the summit of the Coast Range, as shown on survey and map of Wallace and Stakes, May, eighteen hundred and sixty-eight, and forming the common corner of San Joaquin, Stanislaus, Santa Clara, and Alameda, as shown also on map of Boardman and Stakes, July, eighteen hundred and sixty-eight; thence northwesterly, following the summit of the said Coast Range to a post near the middle of section thirty-two, township four south, range four east; thence north to the southeast corner of Contra Costa, being a point on the west channel of the San Joaquin River, as laid down on Gibbe's map, at a bend where the said west channel, running downward, takes a general course north, which point is shown on map of Boardman and Stakes, July, eighteen hundred and sixty-eight; thence down the said west channel to its confluence with the main river; thence down said river to the place of beginning."

[3]*Statutes*, 1860: 34.
[4]*Political Code* (1872), § 3932.

Sacramento-San Joaquin Boundary, 1878. By an amendment to the code in 1878 a slight change was made in the northwest boundary of thè county along the Mokelumne River. This change was due to the shifting channels of that river whereby the main bed of the stream was transferred to a channel further west. The new line was made to run as follows:[5]

> "down the Mokelumne River to a point where said river divides into east and west branches; thence down the west branch to its junction with the east branch; thence down said river to its junction with the San Joaquin River."

Present Boundary, 1923. The part of the Political Code dealing with county boundaries was revised in 1919, the section referring to San Joaquin County being incorporated practically as it stood. It reads as follows:[6]

> "3947. *San Joaquin.* Beginning at the junction of the San Joaquin and Mokelumne rivers, on the line of Sacramento County; thence up the latter to the mouth of Dry Creek; thence up Dry Creek to the southeast corner of Sacramento, as established in section three thousand nine hundred forty-two; thence southeasterly, to a point on Mokelumne River, being the point of beginning of survey of Boucher and Wallace of line between San Joaquin and Calaveras counties, May, 1864; thence southeasterly, on the line of said survey, to the extreme northern corner of Stanislaus County, on north side of and near to Calaveras River, at a point on western line of range ten east, Mount Diablo Meridian, as established by survey of George E. Drew, approved May, 1860, shown on map of said survey; thence south, on said range line, to Stanislaus River; thence down said river to its confluence with the San Joaquin; thence southwest to the summit of the Coast Range, as shown on survey and map of Wallace and Stakes, May, 1868, and forming the common corner of San Joaquin, Stanislaus, Santa Clara, and Alameda, as shown also on map of Boardman and Stakes, July, 1868; thence northwesterly and northerly along the eastern boundary of Alameda County as established in section three thousand nine hundred nine to the corner common to Alameda, Contra Costa and San Joaquin; thence due east to the center of the west channel of the San Joaquin River; thence down the said west channel to its confluence with the main river; thence down said river to the place of beginning."

[5]*Political Code* (1877–78), § 3928.
[6]*Political Code* (1919), § 3947; (1923), § 3947.

SAN LUIS OBISPO COUNTY

Original Boundary, 1850. San Luis Obispo was one of the original counties created in 1850, its county seat being at the town of San Luis Obispo. The boundaries were defined as follows:[1]

> "Beginning three English miles west of the coast, at a point due west of the source of the Nacimiento River, and running due east to the source of said river; thence down the middle of said river to its confluence with Monterey River; thence up or down, as the case may be, the middle of Monterey River to the parallel of thirty-six degrees of north latitude; thence due east, following said parallel to the summit of the Coast Range; thence following the summit of said range in a southeasterly direction to the northeast corner of Santa Barbara County; thence following the northern boundary of Santa Barbara County to the ocean, and three English miles therein; and thence in a northwesterly direction, parallel with the coast, to the place of beginning. The seat of justice shall be at San Luis Obispo."

By another section the north boundary of Santa Barbara is defined as follows:[2]

> "Beginning on the sea coast, at the mouth of the creek called Santa Maria, and running up the middle of said creek to its source; thence due northeast to the summit of the Coast Range, the farm of Santa Maria falling within Santa Barbara County."

The Southern Boundary, 1851-72. In 1851 the act redefining the county boundaries changed both the northern and southern boundaries of San Luis Obispo County. In the south it was a question regarding the jurisdiction over the ranches on either side of Santa Maria River. This act gave to San Luis Obispo County the whole of Guadalupe Rancho lying at the mouth of the river.[3] In 1852 the river was again made the boundary, the Guadalupe rancho being divided.[4] Another change was made in 1854 whereby the whole of this rancho was

[1] *Statutes*, 1850 : 59.
[2] *Ibid.*, 1850 : 59.
[3] *Ibid.*, 1851 : 173, § 4.
[4] *Ibid.*, 1852 : 218.

given to Santa Barbara County and in return the Santa Maria Rancho along the headwaters of the stream was given to San Luis Obispo County.[5] The act of 1854 reads as follows:

> "The rancho of Guadalupe and Oso Placo, now lying partly in the county of Santa Barbara, and partly in that of San Luis Obispo, shall be considered as being and lying wholly in the county of Santa Barbara; and the rancho of Santa Maria, now lying in the county of Santa Barbara, shall be considered as being and lying in the county of San Luis Obispo."

When the Political Code was adopted in 1872 the line was fixed at the bed of the river and there it has since remained.[6]

The Northern Boundary, 1851-63. A number of changes were also made in the northern boundary of the county before a satisfactory location was reached. In 1851 the boundaries of the county were defined thus:[7]

> "Beginning at the junction of the Monterey, or Salinas and Nacisniento rivers; thence up the Nacisniento ten miles, following the meanderings of said river; thence due west to the ocean, and three miles therein; thence in a southeasterly direction, parallel with the coast, to the northwest corner of Santa Barbara County; thence along the northern line of said county, to the northeast corner thereof, on the summit of the Coast Range; thence in a northwesterly direction, following the summit of the Coast Range to a point due east of the mouth of the Nacisniento River; thence west to the place of beginning."

For ten years the boundary remained as just defined, but in 1861 an attempt was made to locate it with reference to the United States survey lines. The act prescribed that it should run from a point on[8]

> "the summit of the Monte Diablo range of mountains, three miles north of the sixth standard line, south of the Monte Diablo Base and Meridian, and thence due west to the Pacific Ocean."

[5]*Statutes,* 1854 : 148.
[6]*Political Code* (1872), § 3947.
[7]*Statutes,* 1851 : 173, § 5.
[8]*Ibid.,* 1861 : 349.

Two years later, 1863, this line was placed upon the sixth standard south, the act reading as follows :[9]

"Beginning at a point on the summit of the Monte Diablo range of mountains (which is the range of mountains between the Salinas and Tulare valleys) where the sixth standard parallel line south of the Monte Diablo Base Line (as laid down on the map of United States surveys) crosses said summit, and running thence, due west, along said line to the Pacific Ocean, and three miles therein."

This line was incorporated into the Political Code in 1872 and has since that time remained the county boundary.

The Eastern Boundary, 1885. For many years the range of mountains had been accepted as the eastern boundary of the county, but in 1885 it was felt that this was too indefinite. The line was therefore carefully redefined and placed upon township and section lines as now observed.[10]

Present Boundaries. The act of 1919 revising the Political Code redefined the boundaries of San Luis Obispo County in terms of the existing laws in the following words :[11]

"3948. *San Luis Obispo.* Beginning in Pacific Ocean, at northwestern corner of Santa Barbara, as established in section three thousand nine hundred fifty; thence easterly, on the northern line of Santa Barbara, up the Santa Maria River, to intersection of southern line of township ten north, San Bernardino Base; thence east on said line to the southeast corner of section thirty-one, in township ten north, of range twenty-four west, of San Bernardino Base and Meridian; thence north on dividing section lines between thirty-one and thirty-two, thirty and twenty-nine, nineteen and twenty, eighteen and seventeen, seven and eight, six and five, to the northeast corner of section six, in the said township ten north, range twenty-four west of San Bernardino Base and Meridian; thence continuing north through township eleven north, range twenty-four west of San Bernardino Base and Meridian, on section lines between sections thirty-one and thirty-two, thirty and twenty-nine, nineteen and twenty, eighteen and seventeen, seven and eight, six and five, to the northeast corner of section six in said township eleven north, of range twenty-four west, of San Bernardino Base and Meridian; thence west on township line between townships eleven and twelve north, range twenty-four west, of San Bernardino Base and Meridian, and along the north boundary of section six to the northwest corner of said township eleven

---

[9]*Statutes*, 1863 : 358.
[10]*Statutes*, 1885 : 139.
[11]*Political Code* (1919), § 3948; (1923), § 3948.

north, range twenty-four west, of San Bernardino Base
and Meridian; thence north, between sections thirty-one
(in fractional township twelve north, range twenty-four
west), and section thirty-six (in fractional township
twelve north, range twenty-five west), to the eighth standard parallel south of Mount Diablo Base and Meridian;
thence westerly on the said eighth standard parallel south
to the corner common to township thirty-two south, range
twenty-two east, and thirty-two south, range twenty-three
east, of Mount Diablo Meridian; thence northerly, as per
the United States survey, on line between said townships
and ranges last above named, to the northeast corner of
the said township thirty-two south, range twenty-two
east, of Mount Diablo Meridian; thence westerly on the
north boundary of said last above named township and
range to the corner common to township thirty-one south,
range twenty-one east, and thirty-two south, range twenty-
one east of Mount Diablo Meridian; thence north to the
northeast corner of said township thirty-one south, range
twenty-one east, of Mount Diablo Meridian; thence west
eight miles to the southwest corner of section thirty-five,
in township thirty south, range twenty east; thence north
on section line between sections thirty-four and thirty-
five, twenty-seven and twenty-six, twenty-two and twenty-
three, fifteen and fourteen, ten and eleven, and three and
two, to the northeast corner of section three in said township thirty south, range twenty east, of Mount Diablo
Meridian; thence west four miles to the northwest corner of
said last above named township and range; thence north to
the northeast corner of township twenty-nine south, range
nineteen east; thence west to the northwest corner of said
township twenty-nine south, range nineteen east, of Mount
Diablo Meridian; thence west one mile to the southeast
corner of section thirty-five, in township twenty-eight
south, range eighteen east, of Mount Diablo Meridian;
thence north to the northeast corner of section twenty-six,
in said township twenty-eight south, range eighteen east;
thence west to the northwest corner of said section twenty-
six; thence north to the northeast corner of section twenty-
two; thence west to the northwest corner of said section
twenty-two; thence north to the northeast corner of section sixteen; thence west to the northwest corner of said
section sixteen; thence north to the northeast corner of
section eight; thence west to the northwest corner of said
section eight; thence north to the township line at the
northeast corner of section six; thence west to the northwest corner of said township twenty-eight south, range

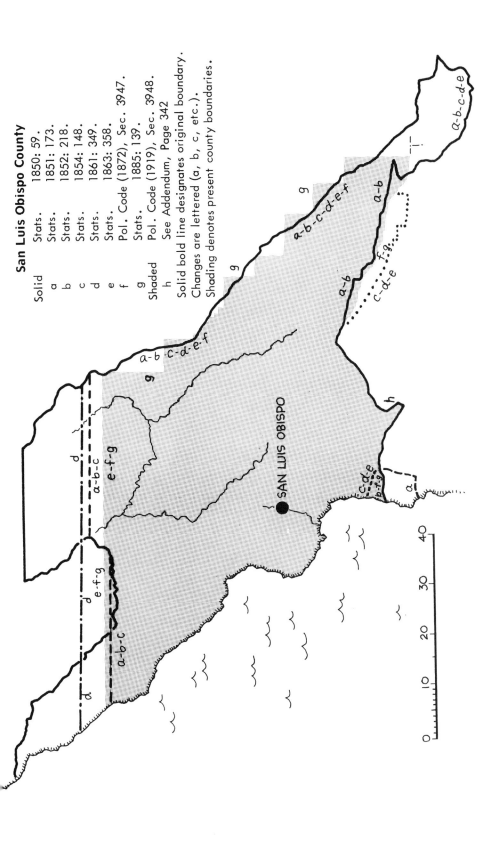

San Luis Obispo County

Solid	Stats.	1850: 59.
a	Stats.	1851: 173.
b	Stats.	1852: 218.
c	Stats.	1854: 148.
d	Stats.	1861: 349.
e	Stats.	1863: 358.
f	Pol. Code (1872), Sec. 3947.
g	Stats.	1885: 139.
Shaded	Pol. Code (1919), Sec. 3948.
h	See Addendum, Page 342

Solid bold line designates original boundary.
Changes are lettered (a, b, c, etc.).
Shading denotes present county boundaries.

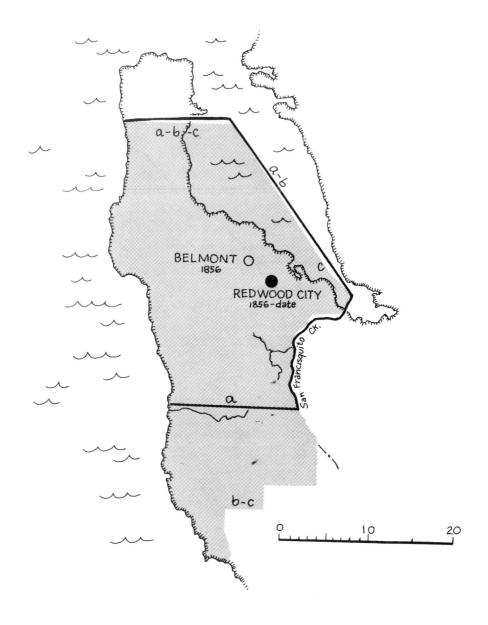

San Mateo County

Solid	Stats.	1856: 146, 176.
a	Stats.	1857: 209, 222.
b	Stats.	1867-8: 174; Pol. Code (1872), Sec. 3951.
c		Pol. Code (1878), Sec. 3951; (1901), Sec. 3951.
Shaded		Pol. Code (1919), Sec. 3949.
d		See Addendum, Page 342

Solid bold line designates original boundary. Changes are lettered (a, b, c, etc.). Shading denotes present county boundaries.

eighteen east; thence north on range line to northeast corner of township twenty-seven south, range seventeen east, of Mount Diablo Meridian; thence west on township line to the northwest corner of said last above named township; thence north, on range line between township twenty-six south, range sixteen east, and township twenty-six south, range seventeen east, to the northeast corner of said township twenty-six south, range sixteen east; thence north on said range line between township twenty-five south, range sixteen east, and township twenty-five south, range seventeen east, of Mount Diablo Meridian, to the northeast corner of said township twenty-five south, range eighteen east, on the sixth standard parallel south of Mount Diablo Base; thence west on said standard parallel and extension thereof to the Pacific Ocean; thence southerly along the shore to the place of beginning.''

SAN MATEO COUNTY

Original Boundary, 1856. In 1856 the southern portion of San Francisco County was detached and organized separately as San Mateo County. According to the act the boundaries of the new county were to be the same as those of San Francisco except on the north[1] where the line between San Francisco and San Mateo counties was defined as follows:[2]

"Beginning in the boundary line of the county of San Francisco, as it now exists at a point due east from a rock in the bay of San Francisco, southwesterly from Point Divisidero or Hunter's Point, which rock is designated on Wheeler's map of said county as Shag Rock; thence running due west to said Shag Rock; thence running westerly to a point in the county road, one-fourth of a mile, northeasterly in a straight line from the house known as the County House, kept and occupied by C. E. Lilly; thence in a straight line to the southeastern extremity of the southern arm of the Laguna de la Merced; thence due west to the Pacific Ocean, and thence due west to the western boundary of the county of San Francisco as it now exists."

The Line of 1857. In 1857 the boundaries were redefined in full and a slight change was made in the line common to San Francisco. The description reads as follows:[3]

"Beginning at a point in the Pacific Ocean, three miles from shore and on a line with the line of the United States survey, separating townships two and three, south, (Mount Diablo Mountain,) thence running east along said line separating the said townships, to the eastern boundary of the county of San Francisco, as established by an act entitled 'An act dividing the state into counties and establishing seats of justice therein,' passed April twenty-fifth, one thousand eight hundred and fifty-one; thence in a direct line to the middle of the bay of San Francisco, opposite the mouth of San Francisquito Creek; thence to and up the middle of said creek, following the middle of the south branch thereof to its source in the Santa Cruz Mountains; thence due west to the Pacific Ocean, and three miles therein; thence in a northwesterly direction parallel with the coast to the place of beginning."

[1] *Statutes,* 1856 : 176. These boundaries have been discussed fully under San Francisco County.
[2] *Ibid.,* 1856 : 146.
[3] *Ibid.,* 1857 : 222.

Annexation from Santa Cruz, 1868. In 1868 San Mateo County was increased to its present size through annexation of territory originally in Santa Cruz County. The line thus established between San Mateo and Santa Cruz counties ran as follows :[4]

"Commencing at a point in the Pacific Ocean, south, forty-five degrees west, three miles from the intersection of the east line of Rancho Punta del Año Nueva with said ocean; thence north, forty-five degrees east, to said point of intersection; thence northerly, following the eastern boundary line of said Rancho Punta de Año Nueva, to its intersection with the south boundary line of township eight south, range four west, Mount Diablo Meridian; thence east to the southeast corner of said township; thence north to the northeast corner of section twenty-five of said township; thence east to the corner of sections twenty-three, twenty-four, twenty-five and twenty-six, township eight south, range three west; thence north to the line between the counties of Santa Clara and Santa Cruz."

The boundaries as thus adopted were incorporated into the Political Code in 1872.[5]

The Eastern Boundary, 1878. In 1878 a slight change was made in the line separating San Mateo from Alameda County, which through its whole course is located in San Francisco Bay. By the earlier acts it went from a point in the bay opposite the mouth of San Francisquito Creek in a direct line to the southeast corner of San Francisco City and County, but by a change in 1878 the line was made to run from the initial point in the bay[6]

"to a point in the center of ship channel in the bay of San Francisco, west of and opposite to Dumbarton Point; thence in a direct line to the southeast corner of San Francisco City and County."

San Francisco Line Redefined, 1901.[7] In 1901 the line separating San Francisco from San Mateo County having been definitely surveyed was redescribed without change in the location. This description was incorporated in the redefinition of the boundaries in 1919.

---

[4]*Statutes*, 1867–8 : 174.
[5]*Political Code* (1872), § 3951.
[6]*Political Code* (1877–78), § 3951.
[7]*Ibid.*, (1901), § 3951. *Statutes,* 1901 : 291.

Present Boundaries, 1923. As described in the Political Code as amended in 1923, the boundaries of San Mateo County are as follows:[8]

"3949. *San Mateo.* Beginning at the southwest corner, being the west corner of Santa Cruz County as established in section three thousand nine hundred fifty-two; thence on the northwestern line of Santa Cruz County as established in said section, to the southwestern line of Santa Clara County, being the summit line of the Santa Cruz mountains; thence northwesterly by said summit line to the source of San Francisquito Creek; thence down the south branch thereof, and down said creek to its mouth; thence to a point in the middle of San Francisco Bay, opposite said mouth, forming a common corner of San Mateo, Santa Clara, and Alameda counties; thence in a direct line to a point in the center of ship channel in the bay of San Francisco west of and opposite to Dumbarton Point; thence in a direct line to the southeast corner of San Francisco City and County; thence westerly on the boundary line between the counties of San Mateo and San Francisco (said line being the north boundary of San Mateo County, between San Mateo County and San Francisco County and the south boundary of San Francisco County between the counties of San Mateo and San Francisco), as the same was surveyed, established and marked by Charles S. Tilton, city and county surveyor of the city and county of San Francisco, William B. Gilbert, county surveyor of the county of San Mateo, and D. Bromfield, assistant civil engineer of the county of San Mateo, between August 28 and December 28, 1898, and being the north boundary line of the county of San Mateo, and the south boundary line of the county of San Francisco, and marked by granite monuments eight inch by eight inch square set three feet in the ground in a bed of concrete three feet square and three feet in the ground, on section and quarter-section corners, on township line between townships two and three south, ranges five and six west, Mount Diablo Meridian, and the line being marked on each monument by a copper nail in a plug of lead which has been countersunk into the top of the monument, and on the dressed faces the letters 'S. F.' being cut into the stone on the San Francisco side of the line, and the letters 'S. M.' being cut into the stone on the San Mateo side of the line, and the bearing of the said line being determined by stellar observation as north

[8]*Political Code* (1919), § 3949; (1923), § 3949.

eighty-nine degrees forty-nine and one-half minutes east, to the southwest corner of the said boundary line of San Francisco City and County in the Pacific Ocean, and thence southerly along the ocean shore to the point of beginning. The eastern boundary of San Mateo County shall be the western boundary of Alameda County, in so far as the same borders on San Mateo County.''

SANTA BARBARA COUNTY

Original Limits, 1850. Santa Barbara was one of the original counties created by the act of February 18, 1850, the seat of government being fixed at Santa Barbara. The boundaries of the county were defined as follows:[1]

> "Beginning on the sea coast, at the mouth of the creek called Santa Maria, and running up the middle of said creek to its source; thence due northeast to the summit of the Coast Range, the farm of Santa Maria falling within Santa Barbara County; thence following the summit of the Coast Range to the northwest corner of Los Angeles County; thence along the northwest boundary of said county to the ocean, and three English miles therein; and thence in a northwesterly direction, parallel with the coast, to a point due west of the mouth of Santa Maria Creek; thence due east to the mouth of said creek, which was the place of beginning, including the islands of Santa Barbara, San Nicholas, San Miguel, Santa Rosa, Santa Cruz, and all others in the same vicinity. The seat of justice shall be at Santa Barbara."

The northwest boundary of Los Angeles County as here referred to is elsewhere defined, running from south to north as follows:[2]

> "Beginning on the coast of the Pacific at the southern boundary of the farm called Trumfo, and running thence along the summit of the ridge of hills called Santa Susana to the northwestern boundary of the farm called San Francisco; thence along the northern and northeastern boundary of said farm of San Francisco to the farm called Piro; thence in a line running due northeast to the summit of the Coast Range."

The Northern Boundary. For several years the question of jurisdiction over the ranches along the Santa Maria River, forming the boundary between Santa Barbara and San Luis Obispo counties caused the boundary line to be shifted back and forth. In 1851 the boundary act gave to San Luis Obispo County the whole of Guadalupe Rancho lying at the mouth of

---

[1] *Statutes*, 1850 : 59, § 4.
[2] *Ibid.*, § 3.

(242)

the river. By the earlier act it had been divided between the two counties.[3] The next year, however, the original line was restored and the boundary defined as dividing ''that part of the Rancho of Guadalupe, called La Larga, from that part called Oso Flaco.''[4] In 1854 this line was again shifted, the whole of the Guadalupe Rancho being given to Santa Barbara, and Santa Maria Rancho, further up the river, given to San Luis Obispo. The wording of the act is as follows:[5]

> ''The rancho of Guadalupe and Oso Placo, now lying partly in the county of Santa Barbara, and partly in that of San Luis Obispo, shall be considered as being and lying wholly in the county of Santa Barbara; and the rancho of Santa Maria, now lying in the county of Santa Barbara, shall be considered as being and lying in the county of San Luis Obispo.''

At the time of the adoption of the Political Code in 1872 the northern boundary was fixed at the Santa Maria River as it is at present.[6]

The Eastern Boundary. Through changes in the boundaries of Los Angeles County and the creation of Ventura in 1872 the eastern boundary of Santa Barbara County has been changed several times. The first of these was in 1851 when the Los Angeles boundary was redefined, that portion contiguous to Santa Barbara being described as follows:[7]

> ''Beginning on the coast of the Pacific, at a point parallel with the northern boundary of the rancho, called Malaga; thence in a direction so as to include said rancho, to the northwest corner of the rancho, known as Triumpo, running on the northerly line of the same to the northeast corner; thence to the summit of the ridge of hills called Santa Susanna; thence in a direct line to the rancho of Casteque and Lejon.''

This line is fully discussed in the description of the boundary of Los Angeles County,[8] and since the line here described is practically identical with the present observed Los Angeles-Ventura line it need not be described further here.

---

[3]*Statutes*, 1851 : 173, § 4.
[4]*Ibid.*, 1852 : 218.
[5]*Ibid.*, 1854 : 148.
[6]*Political Code* (1872), § 3946.
[7]*Statutes*, 1851 : 172.
[8]*See* Los Angeles County.

In 1872 two legislative acts affected the eastern boundary of Santa Barbara County. By the adoption of the Political Code one change was made[9] but the effect of this upon Santa Barbara was entirely eliminated by a subsequent act whereby the whole eastern part of Santa Barbara was detached and organized as Ventura County. The line between Ventura and Santa Barbara counties was defined as follows:[10]

> "Commencing on the coast of the Pacific Ocean, at the mouth of the Rincon Creek; thence following up the center of said creek to its source; thence due north to the northern boundary line of Santa Barbara County."

Present Boundaries. In the act of 1919 an attempt was made to codify the existing statutes, which was done by replacing the old with a new section which reads as follows:[11]

> "3950. *Santa Barbara.* Beginning at the western corner of Ventura as established in section three thousand nine hundred sixty-four; thence northerly, on westerly line of Ventura, as described in said section, to point of intersection with the southern line of township ten north, San Bernardino Base; said point being on the southern boundary of Kern and being the common corner of Santa Barbara and Ventura counties; thence west on said township line, to the Santa Maria River; thence down said river to a point in the Pacific Ocean opposite the mouth of said river, forming northwest corner; thence southeasterly, by the ocean shore, to the place of beginning; including the islands of Santa Barbara, San Miguel, Santa Rosa, and Santa Cruz."

[9]*See* Los Angeles County.
[10]*Statutes,* 1871–72 : 484.
[11]*Political Code* (1919), § 3950; (1923), § 3950.

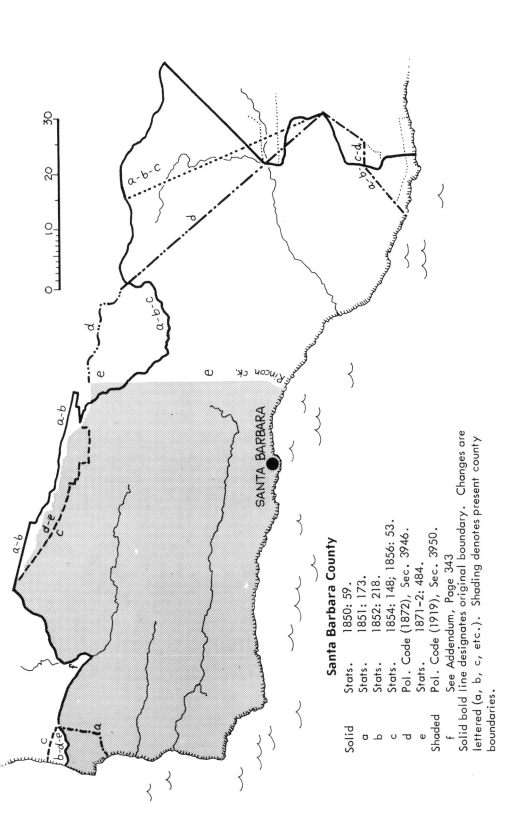

Santa Barbara County

Solid   Stats.   1850: 59.
a   Stats.   1851: 173.
b   Stats.   1852: 218.
c   Stats.   1854: 148; 1856: 53.
d   Pol. Code (1872), Sec. 3946.
e   Stats.   1871–2: 484.
Shaded Pol. Code (1919), Sec. 3950.
f   See Addendum, Page 343

Solid bold line designates original boundary. Changes are lettered (a, b, c, etc.). Shading denotes present county boundaries.

SANTA BARBARA

Rincon ck.

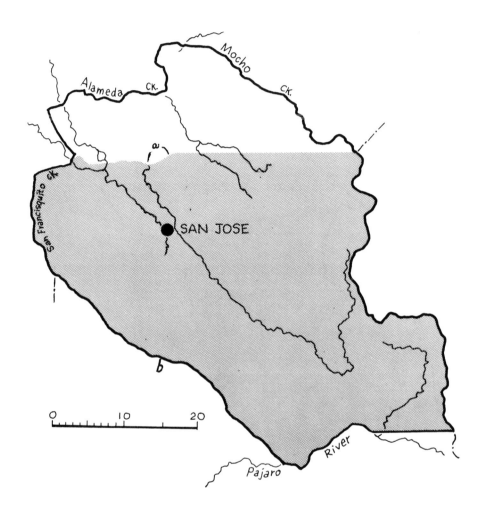

Santa Clara County

Solid	Stats.	1850: 156; 1851: 174; 1852: 178.
Shaded	Stats.	1853: 56; 1855: 288; Pol. Code (1872), Sec. 3952; (1919), Sec. 3951.
a	See Addendum, Page 343	
b	See Addendum, Page 343	

Solid bold line designates original boundary. Changes are lettered (a, b, c, etc.). Shading denotes present county boundaries.

SANTA CLARA COUNTY

Original Boundary, 1850. Santa Clara County was created in 1850, and was therefore one of the original twenty-eight counties. At that time its boundaries ran as follows:[1]

> "Beginning at the mouth of Alameda Creek, and running up the middle of said creek to its source in the Coast Range; thence in a southeasterly direction, following the summit of the Coast Range, to the northeast corner of Monterey County; thence in a westerly direction, following the northern boundary of Monterey County to the southeast corner of Santa Cruz County; thence in a northwesterly direction, following the summit of the Santa Cruz mountains, to the head of San Francisquito Creek; thence down the middle of said creek to its mouth; and thence in a direct line to the mouth of Alameda Creek, which was the place of beginning."

In 1852 the southern line of Contra Costa, and consequently the northern boundary of Santa Clara, was more clearly defined as running westward to

> "the head of Mocho Creek, in a direct line; thence down the middle of said creek to its confluence with Alameda Creek; thence down the middle of said creek."[2]

Since the Mocho Creek is the longest branch of the Alameda Creek and is the only branch which does meet the requirements of the acts of 1850 and 1851, it is considered that it must have been the stream referred to in those earlier acts.

Alameda County Line, 1853. The only change in the boundaries of Santa Clara County was made in 1853 when the northern portion of the county was detached to contribute to the territory of the newly-organized Alameda County. The boundary between these counties was at that time defined as follows:[3]

> "Beginning at a point at the head of a slough which is an arm of the bay of San Francisco, making into the mainland in front of the Gegara ranches; thence to a lone sycamore tree that stands in a ravine between the dwell-

---

[1] *Statutes,* 1850 : 156 ; 1851 : 174.
[2] *Ibid.,* 1852 : 178.
[3] *Ibid.,* 1853 : 56.

ings of Fluhencia and Valentine Gegara; thence up said ravine to the top of the mountains; thence on a direct line eastwardly, to the junction of the San Joaquin and Tuolumne counties."

Political Code Boundaries, 1872. The boundaries of Santa Clara County as defined in section 3952 of the Political Code of 1872 are as follows:[4]

"Beginning at a point opposite the mouth of San Francisquito Creek, being common corner of Alameda, San Mateo, and Santa Clara, as established in section 3951; thence easterly, to a point at the head of a slough, which is an arm of the bay of San Francisco, at its head, making into the main land in front of the Gegara Ranches; thence easterly, to a lone sycamore tree that stands in a ravine between the dwellings of Fluhencia and Valentine Gegara; thence easterly, up said ravine, to the top of the mountains, and as surveyed by Horace A. Higley, and shown on survey and map of Alameda County, eighteen hundred and fifty-seven; thence on a direct line easterly, to the common corner of San Joaquin, Stanislaus, Alameda, and Santa Clara, on the summit of the Coast Range, as established in section 3932; thence southeasterly, following the summit of the Coast Range, to the northeast corner of Monterey County, as established in section 3948; thence westerly, following the northern boundary of Monterey County to the southeast corner of Santa Cruz County, as established in section 3949; thence northwesterly, following the summit of the Santa Cruz mountains, to the head of San Francisquito Creek; thence down said creek, to its mouth; thence in a direct line to the place of beginning."

Present Boundaries, 1923. Because of uncertainties in the description of some of the boundary lines they were defined anew at the time of the revision of this part of the Political Code in 1919. The description is as follows:[5]

"3951. *Santa Clara.* Beginning at a point distant north thirty degrees west, one thousand two hundred fifty-four feet from the southwest corner of section twenty-two, township five south, range two west, Mount Diablo Base and Meridian; said point being hereby established as the corner common to San Mateo, Santa Clara and Alameda counties; thence southeasterly in a direct line to the south-

---

[4]*Political Code* (1872), § 3952.
[5]*Ibid.*, (1919), § 3951; (1923), § 3951.

west corner of section twenty-six, township five south, range two west, Mount Diablo Base and Meridian; thence easterly in a direct line to the point where the center of the Coyote River is intersected by the west line of township five south, range one west, Mount Diablo Base and Meridian; thence easterly along the center of the Coyote River to a point from which a sandstone monument set on the southwesterly side of the county road leading from San Jose to Oakland, or state highway, as described in the field notes of the survey of the boundary line between the counties of Alameda and Santa Clara, filed June 2, 1873, in the office of the clerk of Santa Clara County, California, bears north fifty-seven degrees, thirty-five minutes east, four thousand three hundred forty feet distant, more or less; thence north fifty-seven degrees, thirty-five minutes east, four thousand three hundred forty feet, more or less, to said sandstone monument; thence northeasterly and easterly along the boundary line between Alameda and Santa Clara counties, as described in the field notes of said survey, to the corner common to Alameda, San Joaquin, Stanislaus and Santa Clara counties; thence southeasterly following the summit of the Coast Range to the corner common to San Benito, Merced and Santa Clara counties, situated in section twenty-one, township eleven south, range seven east, Mount Diablo Base and Meridian, as established by Charles T. Healy, deputy surveyor general of California in September, 1858; thence westerly on the present surveyed line between Santa Clara and San Benito counties to a point on the San Felipe Creek, near San Felipe Lake; thence around the eastern and northern side of said lake to the Pajaro River; thence down said river to the southwest corner of Santa Clara County and the southeast corner of Santa Cruz County, as established in section three thousand nine hundred fifty-two; thence northwesterly, following the summit of the Santa Cruz mountains, being northeasterly boundary of Santa Cruz County, to the head of the south fork of the San Francisquito Creek; thence down said creek to its mouth; thence in a direct line to the place of beginning.''

SANTA CRUZ COUNTY

Original Boundary. Santa Cruz was one of the original counties created in 1850. It was first known as Branciforte, but a subsequent amendment passed during the first session gave it the name of Santa Cruz. With the exception of its northern boundary, the limits of the county were the same as they are now. They were defined as follows:[1]

"Beginning in the ocean three English miles from land, at a point due west of the head of San Francisquito Creek, and running due east to the summit of the Santa Cruz Mountains; thence in a southeasterly direction, along the summit of said mountains, to the Pajaro River, thence along the middle of said river to the bay of Monterey, and three English miles into the ocean, and thence in a northwesterly direction, parallel with the coast, to the point of beginning."

Annexation to San Mateo, 1868. In 1868 the northern line of the county was moved further south, a portion of what had been Santa Cruz County being annexed to San Mateo County, which had been created in 1856. The dividing line between the two counties was described as follows:[2]

"Commencing at a point in the Pacific Ocean, south, forty-five degrees west, three miles from the intersection of the east line of Rancho Punta del Año Nueva with said ocean; thence north, forty-five degrees east, to said point of intersection; thence northerly, following the eastern boundary line of said Rancho Punta de Año Nueva, to its intersection with the south boundary line of township eight south, range four west, Mount Diablo Meridian; thence east to the southeast corner of said township; thence north to the northeast corner of section twenty-five of said township; thence east to the corner of sections twenty-three, twenty-four, twenty-five and twenty-six, township eight south, range three west; thence north to the line between the counties of Santa Clara and Santa Cruz."

---

[1]*Statutes*, 1850: 155. In *Ibid.*, 1851: 173, they were redefined as in 1850.
[2]*Ibid.*, 1867–68: 174.

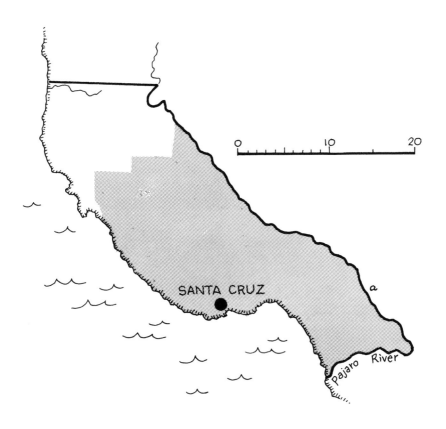

Santa Cruz County

Solid   Stats.   1850: 155; 1851: 173.
Shaded   Stats.   1867-8: 174; Pol. Code (1872), Sec. 3949;
                     (1919), Sec. 3952.

   a   See Addendum, Page 345
Solid bold line designates original boundary. Changes are
lettered (a, b, c, etc.). Shading denotes present county
boundaries.

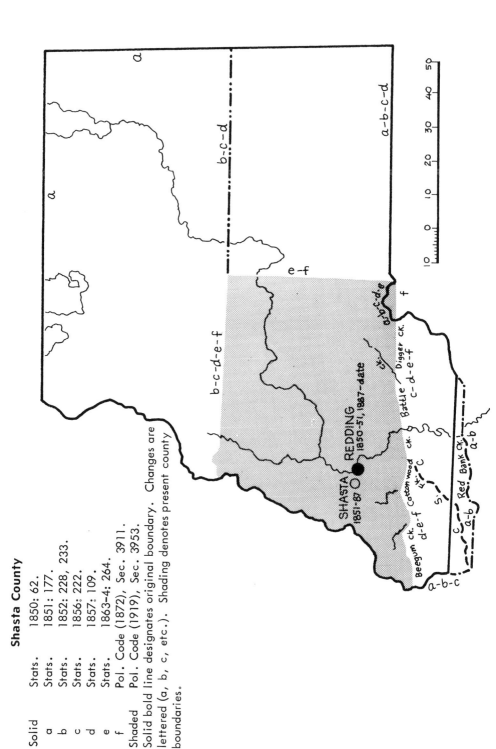

Shasta County

Solid		
a	Stats.	1850: 62.
b	Stats.	1851: 177.
c	Stats.	1852: 228, 233.
d	Stats.	1856: 222.
e	Stats.	1857: 109.
f	Stats.	1863-4: 264.
Shaded	Pol. Code (1872), Sec. 3911.
	Pol. Code (1919), Sec. 3953.

Solid bold line designates original boundary. Changes are lettered (a, b, c, etc.). Shading denotes present county boundaries.

Present Boundary, 1923. Since 1868 there has been no change in the boundaries of Santa Cruz County, the present northern line being the same as that adopted in 1868, while the others are identical with the original boundary. The following description, taken from the Political Code as amended in 1923, is the same as that given in section 3949 of the Political Code for 1872, except for a few minor changes in wording:[3]

"3952. *Santa Cruz.* Beginning at the south corner of San Mateo County, at a point in the Pacific Ocean south forty-five degrees west, three nautical miles from the intersection of the east line of Rancho Punta del Año Nuevo with said ocean, forming western corner; thence north, forty-five degrees east, to said point of intersection; thence northerly, following the eastern line of said rancho, to its intersection with the south line of township eight south, range four west, Mount Diablo Base and Meridian; thence east to the southeast corner of said township; thence north to the northeast corner of section twenty-five of said township; thence east to the northeast corner of section twenty-six, township eight south, range three west; thence north to the summit of Santa Cruz mountains, being western line of Santa Clara County; thence southeasterly along the summit of said mountains, on the western line of Santa Clara, to the Pajaro River, forming southeast corner, on northern line of San Benito; thence westerly along said river, on northern line of San Benito and Monterey, to the bay of Monterey, and three miles westerly into the ocean, forming southwest corner; thence northwesterly along a course three nautical miles distant from the shore to the point of beginning."

[3]*Political Code* (1923), § 3952. *See also Ibid.,* (1919), § 3952.

SHASTA COUNTY

Original Boundary, 1850. Shasta was one of the original counties created in 1850. It then included that great region but little known lying at the northeast corner of the state. The county seat was first established at Reading's Ranch. From there it was moved to Shasta City in 1851 and to Redding, its present location, in 1887. For the first year Trinity County although separately created was attached to Shasta County for administrative and judicial purposes. The original boundaries of Shasta County were as follows:[1]

> "Beginning on the summit of the Coast Range in latitude forty-two degrees north, and running thence due east to the northeast corner of the state; thence due south, following the boundary of the state, to the northeast corner of Butte County; thence, following the northwestern and northern boundaries of Butte County, to the Sacramento River; thence in a due west direction along the summit of the Coast Range; thence in a northeasterly direction, following the summit of said range, to the place of beginning."

In the section defining the boundaries of Butte County it is seen that the northern line of Colusa and Butte and therefore the southern line of Shasta ran from the Coast Range due east to Red Bluff[2] and thence "due east to the dividing ridge which separates the waters flowing into the Sacramento River below the Red Bluffs, and into Feather River, from those flowing into the Sacramento above the Red Bluffs; thence following the top of said ridge to the Sierra Nevada; thence due east to the boundary of the state."[3]

The Southern Boundary, 1851, 1857. Several changes were made in the southern boundary before it was established at its present location. In 1851, the line which had run east and west through the Red Bluffs was shifted south to the mouth of Red Bluff Creek, the amended description reading:[4]

> "Beginning at a point in the middle of Sacramento River opposite the mouth of Red Bluff Creek below the

[1]*Statutes*, 1850 : 62.
[2]*Ibid.*, 1850 : 62, § 21.
[3]*Ibid.*, 1850 : 62, § 21.
[4]*Ibid.*, 1851 : 177.

Red Bluffs, and running thence up the middle of said creek to its source in the Coast Range; thence west in a straight line to the summit of the Coast Range."

In 1856 the boundary was placed further north, giving territory to the newly created Tehama County. This change took place west of the Sacramento River, the new line reading as follows:[5]

"Beginning at the mouth of Cottonwood Creek, in Shasta County; running up the middle of said creek, to the mouth of the south fork of Cottonwood; up the middle of the south fork, to the summit of the Coast Range."

The south branch of Cottonwood Creek served as the county limits for one year only. In 1857 the boundaries of Tehama were redefined, the statute placing the Shasta-Tehama line along the middle fork of Cottonwood Creek where it has since remained.[6]

Siskiyou Detached, 1852. The first great loss of territory suffered by Shasta was when its northern half was separately organized as Siskiyou County. This change took place in 1852. The southern line of Siskiyou which became the northern boundary of Shasta is described in the act creating that county as beginning on the Coast Range at[7]

"a point known as the Devil's Castle, near and on the opposite side from Soda Springs, on the upper Sacramento River; from said point or place of beginning, to run due east to the eastern boundary of the State of California."

With the substitution of the name "Castle Rock" for "Devil's Castle" the description was adopted in the Political Code and has since remained the boundary between the two counties.

Lassen County Cut Off, 1864. In 1864 Shasta was again divided, about one-half of its remaining territory being

---

[5]*Statutes*, 1856 : 222.
[6]*Ibid.*, 1857 : 109.
[7]*Ibid.*, 1852 : 233.

attached to the newly-organized Lassen County. The line
between Lassen and Shasta as then defined ran from[8]

> "a point due south of the Black Butte Mountain;
> thence due north to the southern boundary line of Siskiyou
> County."

The Present Boundaries. At the time of the adoption of
the code in 1872 the section defining the boundaries of Shasta
County without noticeable change was based upon the lines
as already described,[9] as was also the case when this part of the
code was revised in 1919. The section referring to Shasta
County reads as follows:[10]

> "3953. *Shasta.* Beginning at the northern line of
> Tehama, at the head of Bloody Island, in Sacramento
> River; thence to and down the eastern channel to the
> mouth of Battle Creek; thence easterly, up Battle Creek,
> by the main channel, to the mouth of the middle fork,
> known as Digger Creek; thence up Digger Creek to its
> head; thence east to a point south of Black Butte Moun-
> tain, forming southeast corner; thence north, on western
> line of Lassen, to a rock mound forming northeast cor-
> ner, on southern line of Siskiyou; thence west, on said
> southern line, to Castle Rock, forming northwest corner;
> thence southerly along Trinity Mountain to the head of
> Bee Gum Creek, forming southwest corner; thence east-
> erly down Bee Gum, Middle Fork, and Cottonwood creeks
> to the western channel of Sacramento River; thence, by
> direct line, to the point of beginning."

[8] *Statutes,* 1863–64 : 264.
[9] *Political Code* (1872), § 3911.
[10] *Ibid.,* (1919), § 3953; (1923), § 3953.

SIERRA COUNTY

Creation of Sierra County, 1852. The development of the mining region around Downieville in the early fifties coupled with the difficulty of communication between that region and the county seat at Marysville led in 1852 to the founding of a separate county from the eastern portion of Yuba County. The seat of justice was fixed at Downieville and has remained there since that time. Originally the boundaries were as follows:[1]

> "Beginning at a point in the middle of the middle branch of Yuba River, ten miles from its mouth, running thence in a northwesterly direction to a point on the north branch of Yuba River, known as Cut Eye Foster's Bar; thence westerly to a point on the dividing ridge between the waters of Feather and Yuba rivers, known as the Lexington House; leaving said house in Yuba County, thence northerly following out said ridge; thence easterly in a straight line to the boundary line of the state; thence south along said boundary line to a point east of the middle branch of Yuba River, and the northeast corner of Nevada County; thence west following the northerly line of Nevada County to the place of beginning."

That the courses of the lines here set down are not properly defined in this section becomes evident when a study of the region is made. In the first place the direction from the point of beginning to Cut Eye Foster's Bar is not "northwesterly" as given in the act, but north, and it is so defined in the Political Code in 1872.[2] From that point the line is defined as running "westerly" to the Lexington House on the ridge between the Feather and Yuba rivers. Here again the direction is entirely misleading, as the Lexington House is not west of Cut Eye Foster's Bar, but north. As before, the present line helps to locate the early boundary as it in general follows the same course.

---

[1] *Statutes*, 1852 : 230.
[2] *Political Code* (1872), § 3921. There can be no question regarding the location of Cut Eye Foster's Bar as it has remained in the statutes defining the boundaries down to the present date. Furthermore, early county maps of Yuba and Butte show clearly the location of this bar. This must not be confused with Foster's Bar which lies in the northwesterly direction defined in the act.

The southern line is common to Nevada County and was elsewhere defined as running

"up the middle of said middle branch to a point opposite the mouth of Wolf Creek; thence easterly in a straight line to the boundary of the state."[3]

The Nevada-Sierra Line. The first change in boundary was made in 1856 when the Nevada line was shifted further north at the expense of Sierra County. The new Nevada boundary was defined as running from the mouth of the Middle Yuba River,[4]

"thence up said Middle Yuba River to the mouth of the south fork of the same; thence up said south fork to its source; thence due east to the eastern line of the state."

With a slight change in wording this was incorporated into the Political Code in 1872.[5]

On account of a dispute between the two counties in reference to the survey of that part of the line lying east of the source of the river an act was passed in 1909 definitely locating the point theretofore referred to only as the source of the south fork of the Middle Yuba River. This point was marked by the monument referred to in the statutes and code as Bent's Monument.[6] This is the present boundary between the two counties.

The Northern Boundary. In 1863 an attempt was made to define the boundaries more clearly, by giving a better description of the northern line which previously had been very inadequately described. This line was then defined anew after striking the ridge just east of the Lexington House as follows:[7]

"thence northerly along the centre of said ridge to a point known as Pilot's Peak; thence southeasterly along the centre of said ridge to a point due west from a point about one mile below the outlet of Gold Lake, known as the Falls; thence due east to the eastern boundary line of the State."

A study of the map shows that this not only is a more definite boundary description but that it also gave to Sierra

[3]*Statutes*, 1852 : 191.
[4]*Ibid.*, 1856 : 143.
[5]*Political Code* (1872), § 3921.
[6]*Statutes*, 1909 : 86.
[7]*Ibid.*, 1863 : 114.

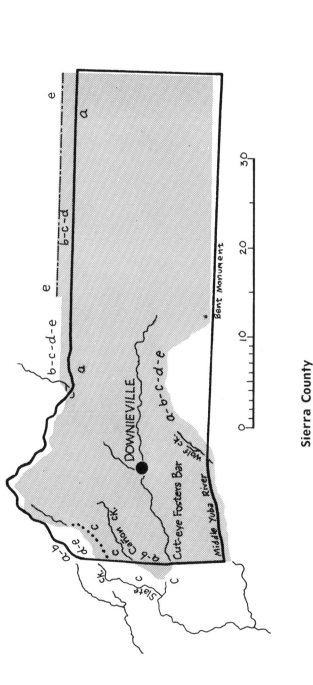

Sierra County

Solid	Stats.	1852: 230.
a	Stats.	1856: 143.
b	Stats.	1863: 114.
c	Stats.	1865–6: 228, 605.
d	Stats.	1867–8: 462; Pol. Code (1872), Sec. 3921.
e		Pol. Code (1874), Sec. 3921; (1909), Sec. 3921.
Shaded		Pol. Code (1919), Sec. 3954.

Solid bold line designates original boundary. Changes are
lettered (a, b, c, etc.). Shading denotes present county
boundaries.

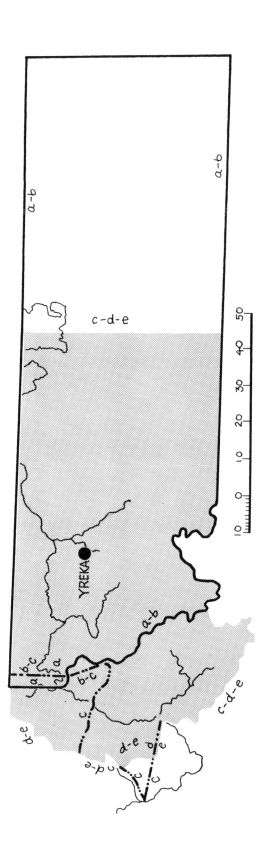

Siskiyou County

Solid	Stats.	1852: 233.
a	Stats.	1857: 35; 1858: 21.
b	Pol. Code (1872), Sec. 3913.
c	Stats.	1873-4: 124, 755.
d	Stats.	1887: 106.
e	Stats.	1901: 600.
Shaded	Pol. Code (1919), Sec. 3955.

Solid bold line designates original boundary. Changes are lettered (a, b, c, etc.). Shading denotes present county boundaries.

a small strip of territory along its northern border. The line as adopted in 1863 has been accepted in subsequent legislation, the only change being in 1874, when by a code amendment the line was placed upon township and section lines.[8]

Present Boundary, 1923. In the revision of the Political Code in 1919 these various acts were incorporated into section 3954 of the revised code. The present boundaries are there described as follows:[9]

"3954. *Sierra*. Beginning at the south corner of Plumas, in the center of Slate Creek, as established in section three thousand nine hundred forty; thence easterly on southern line of Plumas, as established in said section, to the range line between township twenty-one north, range thirteen east, and township twenty-one north, range fourteen east, Mount Diablo Meridian; thence north on said range line, to the northwest corner of township twenty-one north, fourteen east, Mount Diablo Base and Meridian; thence east on the line between townships twenty-one and twenty-two north, Mount Diablo Base, to the state line forming the northeast corner; thence south on said state line to the northeast corner of Nevada County, a point east of the Bent monument, situated as described in section three thousand nine hundred thirty-seven; thence west to the said Bent monument; thence down the south fork of the middle Yuba River and down the middle Yuba River to a point ten miles above the mouth of the latter; thence in a straight line northerly to a point on the north fork of the Yuba River known as Cuteye Foster's Bar; down said river to the mouth of Big Cañon Creek, and then up said creek four miles; thence in a straight line to the point of beginning."

[8] *Political Code* (1874), § 3921.
[9] *Ibid.*, (1923), § 3954. *See also Ibid.*, (1919), § 3954.

SISKIYOU COUNTY

Original Boundary, 1852. Siskiyou County was created in 1852 by detaching the northern portion of Shasta County and adding thereto a part of Klamath County. The seat of justice has always been located at Yreka. As originally defined the boundaries were as follows:[1]

> "At a point known as the Devil's Castle, near and on the opposite side from Soda Springs, on the upper Sacramento River; from said point or place of beginning, to run due east to the eastern boundary of the State of California, and thence north to the Oregon line, and from thence running west along the boundary line of the Territory of Oregon and the State of California, to a point on said line due north of the mouth of Indian Creek, (being the first large creek adjoining the Indian Territory, at a place known as Happy Camp, which empties into the Klamath River, on the opposite side below the mouth of Scott's River,) and from thence across Klamath River, running in a southeasterly course along the summit of the mountains, dividing the waters of Scott's and Salmon Rivers, to the place of beginning."

With the exception of slight changes in that portion of the boundary joining upon Del Norte County created in 1857, no changes were made before the adoption of the code in 1872. The changes in the line adjoining Del Norte were of little importance and resulted from an attempt to define a line in a region practically unknown rather than a conscious effort to change the boundary.[2] In 1872 the Political Code defined the boundaries as follows:[3]

> "Beginning at southwest corner, being common corner of Trinity, Klamath, and Siskiyou, as established in section 3910; thence easterly, on northern line of Trinity, to northwest corner of Shasta, as established in section 3911; thence east, on northern line of Shasta and Lassen, to western line of the State of Nevada; thence north, on the line of said state, to the southern line of the State of Oregon; thence west, on Oregon line, to the northeast corner of Del Norte, as established in section 3909; thence south-

---

[1]*Statutes*, 1852 : 233.
[2]See the description of Del Norte boundaries for discussion of the acts defined in *Statutes*, 1857 : 35 ; 1858 : 21.
[3]*Political Code* (1872), § 3913.

easterly, on the eastern lines of Del Norte and Klamath, as established in sections 3909 and 3910, to the place of beginning.''

Modoc Detached, 1874. During the session of the legislature in 1873–4 two changes in the boundaries of Siskiyou County were made: one on the east, the other on the west. The first came as the result of the creation of Modoc from that part of Siskiyou County lying east of

> "the range line between ranges Nos. four (4) and five (5) east, of Mount Diablo Base and Meridian;"[4]

this range line becoming, as it now is, the eastern boundary of Siskiyou.

Annexation from Klamath, 1874-5. The other change above mentioned added to Siskiyou County about one-half of what had previously been in Klamath County, which by the statute was then abolished. The line dividing Klamath County, a portion of which was given to each of Siskiyou and Humboldt counties, was defined as follows:[5]

> "Commencing at the point where the present boundary of Klamath and Del Norte crosses the Klamath River; thence running easterly in a direct line to where the Salmon River enters the Klamath River; thence in a southerly direction, following the ridge of the mountain that divides the waters of the Salmon and its tributaries from the waters of Klamath and Trinity rivers, and their tributaries, to the northern boundary line of Trinity County.''

Since this act placed the extreme western corner of Siskiyou County at the point where the Del Norte-Klamath boundary crossed the Klamath River it also made a large part of the Del Norte boundary the western boundary of Siskiyou. That part of the Del Norte line then common to Siskiyou was defined in the code as running from a point[6]

> "one mile south of the mouth of the Klamath River, forming southeast corner; thence easterly, on a line parallel with Klamath River, to a point one mile south of the mouth of Blue Creek; thence northeasterly to Siskiyou Mountains; thence easterly, following the ridge that divides the waters of Clear Creek from the waters of Dil-

[4]*Statutes,* 1873–4 : 124.
[5]*Ibid.,* 756.
[6]*Political Code* (1872), § 3909.

lon's Creek, to Klamath River, at a point equidistant from the mouths of said creeks; thence across Klamath River and east to the summit of Salmon Mountains, forming the southeast corner; thence northerly in a direct line to the head of the cañon of said river, about five miles above the mouth of Indian Creek; thence north, crossing Klamath River, to a point on the forty-second parallel of north latitude."

Del Norte Boundary, 1887, 1901. Two later acts changing the boundaries of Del Norte affect the lines of Siskiyou. The more important of these was the act of 1887 which added to Siskiyou considerable territory along the Klamath River in the region of Happy Camp, the summit of the mountains to the west being made the dividing line between the two counties.[7] A change in 1901 placing the boundary of Humboldt and Del Norte on section lines made a slight change in one portion of the Siskiyou boundary.[8]

Present Boundaries, 1923. As defined in the Political Code as amended in 1919 these recent changes were incorporated in section three thousand nine hundred and fifty-five which describes these boundaries as follows:[9]

"3955. *Siskiyou.* Commencing on the northern line of the State of California at the northeast corner of Del Norte, as described in section three thousand nine hundred sixteen, being on the summit of a spur of the Siskiyou range of mountains; thence southerly along the eastern line of Del Norte County to the northern line of Humboldt County, as defined in section three thousand nine hundred twenty; thence easterly and southerly along the northern and eastern line of Humboldt County to the northwest corner of Trinity County; thence along the northern boundary of Trinity County, as defined in section three thousand nine hundred sixty-one, to the northwest corner of Shasta County, at Castle Rock, as defined in section three thousand nine hundred fifty-three; thence due east to the range line between ranges four and five east of Mount Diablo Base and Meridian; thence north along said range line to the northern boundary of the State of California; thence due west along said state boundary line to the place of beginning."

[7]*Statutes,* 1887:106.
[8]*Ibid.,* 1901:600.
[9]*Political Code* (1919), § 3955; (1923), § 3955.

SOLANO COUNTY

Solano County was another of the original counties, it being created by an act of the first legislature. Since the time of its organization none but minor changes have been made in its boundaries, in fact the only change of any significance was the transfer of Mare Island from Sonoma County in 1853. The original boundaries of Solano were defined as follows:[1]

"Beginning at the mouth of Napa Creek, and running up the middle of its channel to the mouth of Suscol Creek; thence following up said creek to the eastern boundary line of Napa County; thence along said boundary line to the northeast corner of Napa County; thence in a direct line to the nearest point of Puto Creek; thence down the middle of said creek to its termination in the tule marsh; thence in a direct line to the head of Merritt's Slough; thence down the middle of said slough to its mouth; thence down the middle of Sacramento River to its mouth; thence down the middle of Suisun Bay to the Straits of Carquinez; and thence through the middle of said straits to the place of beginning."

The eastern boundary of Napa County here referred to is elsewhere defined as "the range of mountains dividing Napa Valley from Suisun Valley."[2]

Mare Island Annexed, 1853. Since Mare Island lies in such proximity to Vallejo, one of the chief centers of population in Solano County, it was but natural that it should look to that county for supervision rather than to Sonoma under whose jurisdiction it had been placed by the acts of 1850 and 1851. In 1852 two acts were passed evidently seeking to exclude the island from Sonoma and include it within the limits of Solano County. Through an error the word "exclude" was used in both acts whereas it was intended that it should be included in Solano.[3] It therefore required another act, passed in 1853, to complete the change.[4]

Napa-Solano Boundary, 1855. In the year 1855 Napa County's boundaries were redefined and minor changes made

---

[1] *Statutes*, 1850: 61, § 13.
[2] *Ibid.*, 1850: 61, § 15.
[3] *Statutes*, 1852: 192, 236.
[4] *Ibid.*, 1853: 20.

in that part common with Solano. The boundary line as then determined is as follows:[5]

> "Commencing at a point in Guichica Creek where the said creek empties into San Pablo Bay; thence running in a direct line due east to the top of the ridge of mountains dividing Napa Valley from Suisun Valley; thence in a northerly direction along the top of said mountains to a point parallel with the southern boundary line of the ranch known as the Chimilas Rancho; thence easterly along said line to the top of the mountains known as the Vacca Mountains, which divide the Vacca Valleys from the Chimilas Rancho; thence northerly along the top of the main ridge of said Vacca Mountains to the Puta Creek."

Yolo-Solano Line, 1857. In 1857 a slight change was made in the northeastern corner of Solano County along the boundary common to Yolo County and Solano County, the new description reading as follows:[6]

> "The boundary line of Yolo County shall commence at a point in the middle of Sacramento River, near the head of Merritt's or Steamboat Slough, at a point where the township line between township number five and township number six, north of the Monte Diablo base line, intersects said river; thence running due west with said township line to the range line between range number two and range number three, east of the meridian of Monte Diablo; thence due north with said range line to the south branch or old bed of Putah Creek."

Present Boundary, 1923. No changes in the boundary of Solano County have been made since 1857. At the time of the adoption of the code in 1872 the boundaries were redescribed and more clearly defined but without introducing any material change in location.[7] In 1923 the code was revised and the boundaries of Solano described anew, but using practically the identical language. The description is as follows:[8]

> "3956. *Solano.* Beginning at southwest corner, in San Pablo Bay, at common corner of Contra Costa, Sonoma, Marin, and Solano, as established in section three thousand nine hundred fifteen; thence north, twenty-six and one-half degrees west, about six and one-quarter miles on

---

[5]*Statutes,* 1855 : 77.
[6]*Ibid.,* 1857 : 108.
[7]*Political Code* (1872), § 3956.
[8]*Ibid,* (1923), § 3955. *See also Ibid.,* (1919), § 3956.

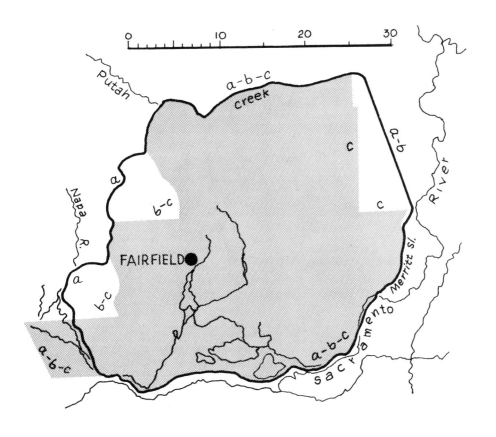

Solano County

Solid   Stats.   1850: 61; 1851: 179; 1852: 192.
a   Stats.   1853: 20.
b   Stats.   1855: 77.
c   Stats.   1857: 108; Pol. Code (1872), Sec. 3956.
Shaded   Pol. Code (1919), Sec. 3956.
Solid bold line designates original boundary. Changes are
lettered (a, b, c, etc.). Shading denotes present county
boundaries.

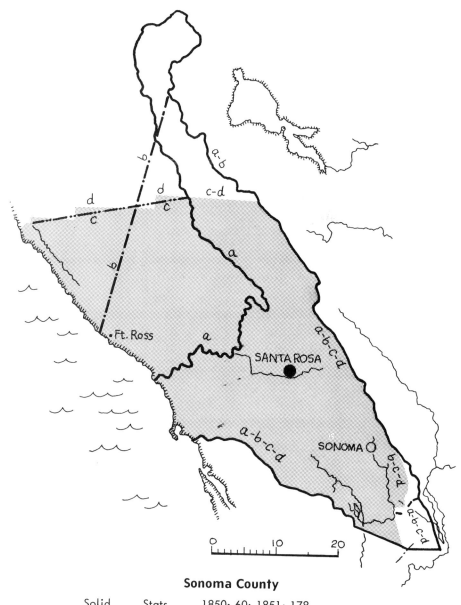

Sonoma County

Solid	Stats.	1850: 60; 1851: 178.
a	Stats.	1852: 236; 1853: 20.
b	Stats.	1855: 150, 77.
c	Stats.	1859: 98.
d	Stats.	1859: 98.
Shaded	Pol. Code (1919), Sec. 3957.	

Solid bold line designates original boundary. Changes are
lettered (a, b, c, etc.). Shading denotes present county
boundaries.

the western line of Sonoma, as established in section three
thousand nine hundred fifty-seven, to the southwest corner of Napa at the mouth of the Huichica Creek; thence
east, on southern line of Napa, to the southeast corner
thereof, as established in section three thousand nine hundred thirty-six; thence north, on line of Napa, as established in said section, to the first standard north; thence
east along said standard, on said Napa line, to the summit
of Vaca Mountains; thence northerly, on said summit and
Napa line, to Devil's Gate, on Putah Creek, which point
forms the northwest corner of Solano and southwest corner of Yolo; thence easterly, on line of Yolo, down said
creek and old bed thereof, to its intersection with western
line of range three east, Mount Diablo Meridian, forming
the northeast corner of Solano, with exterior angle in
Yolo; thence south, along line of Yolo, on said range line,
two and seven-tenths miles, to the north line of township
seven north, Mount Diablo Base; thence east, nine and
seventy-two one-hundredths chains, to northeast corner of
said township; thence south, to the first standard north,
Mount Diablo Base; thence east, on said standard line, to
the center of Sutter Slough; thence down said slough to
Steamboat Slough, formerly called Merritt Slough, down
said slough to the Sacramento River, down the Sacramento River about thirteen miles to Suisun Bay; thence
down the bay, along the center of the main ship-channel,
in a westerly course about eighteen miles, to the Straits
of Carquinez; thence down the middle of said straits, and
down San Pablo Bay, to the place of beginning; all these
courses and lines being as shown by map and notes of
William Wayne Fitch and E. H. Marshall, surveyor and
deputy suveyor of Solano County.''

SONOMA COUNTY

Original Boundaries, 1850. Sonoma was one of the original counties created by the legislature in 1850. Its boundaries at that time were described as follows:[1]

> "Beginning on the sea coast at the mouth of Russian River and following up the middle of said river to its source in the range of mountains called Mayacmas; thence in a direct line to the northwestern corner of Napa County; thence down and along the western boundary of Napa County to its termination in Carnero Mountain; thence in a direct line to the nearest point of Carnero Creek; thence down said creek to its entrance into Napa River; thence down the middle of Napa River to its mouth, thence due south to the north line of Contra Costa County, thence down the middle of said bay[2] to the corner of Marin County; thence following the boundary of said county to Petaluma Creek; thence up said creek following the boundary of Marin County to the ocean, and three English miles therein; thence in a northerly direction parallel with the coast to a point opposite the mouth of Russian River, and thence to said river, which was the place of beginning, including the islands called Segua, or Mare Island."

The lines described in this act are not clear at all points. The sources of the Russian River can not definitely be identified from the description here given. In the absence of other information, Alder Creek has been taken as the stream which most nearly meets the requirements of the act.

Still greater difficulty was encountered in locating the northwest corner of Napa County. In fact, there is a serious doubt whether in 1851 Napa County can be considered as reaching as far north along this range of mountains as is here described, for the sections defining the boundaries of Mendocino County clearly indicate that the Mayacmas range of mountains formed the boundary between Mendocino and Sonoma counties, Mendocino extending as far south as Putah Creek. The line, however, may without serious question be run south along the

---

[1]*Statutes,* 1850 : 60 ; 1851 : 178. The text is quoted from the act of 1851. The act of 1850 gives the name of Mare Island as Yegua, which is the correct spelling of the Spanish word meaning mare. This name is also spelled Signa (1852), and Signor (1853).
[2]San Pablo Bay.

range of mountains from the head waters of Alder Creek
until it reaches the northern end of the western boundary of
Napa County.

Exclusion of Mare Island, 1852, 1853. In 1852 an amendment was made to the boundaries of Sonoma County "excluding the island called Signa, or Mare Island." The legislature, however, failed to attach this island to any other county,
so it was not until 1853 that it was separated from Sonoma
and made a part of Solano County.[3]

Northern and Eastern Boundary, 1855. In the year 1855
two acts were passed affecting the boundaries of Sonoma
County. One of these referred directly to Sonoma County,
the other indirectly by modifying the west line of Napa, which
was of course the east line of Sonoma. The first mentioned
act reads as follows:[4]

> "* * * beginning at a point in the Pacific Ocean oppo-
> site to and three miles from a point on the coast one mile
> northwesterly from Fort Ross, and running thence in a
> direct line to the northwest corner of Napa County; thence
> southerly along the Napa County boundary in the Mayaca-
> mas mountains to the westerly branch of Guichica Creek;
> thence southerly along said county boundary to its initial
> point in the mouth of Guichica Creek; thence in a direct
> line to the northwest corner of Contra Costa County in
> San Pablo Bay; thence down the middle of said bay to
> the northeast corner of Marin County; thence following
> the boundary of Marin County to Petaluma Creek; thence
> up the centre of said creek to the mouth of San Antonio
> Creek; thence up the centre of said creek to its head;
> thence in a direct line to the head of the Estero Ameri-
> cano; thence following the centre of said estero to its
> mouth; thence in a direct line three miles to a point in
> the Pacific Ocean opposite to the mouth of said Estero;
> thence northerly to the place of beginning."

It will be noted that this act makes a radical change in the
northern line which now runs from a point one mile northwest
from Fort Ross to the northwest corner of Napa County, from
which point it follows south along the western boundary of
Napa County.

---

[3] *Statutes,* 1852 : 236 ; 1853 : 20.
[4] *Ibid.,* 1855 : 150.

By another act passed in 1855 the western boundary of Napa was also changed. It will therefore be necessary to notice the location of that line in order to determine the eastern boundary of Sonoma. The act in question[5] describes this line as running from

> "the top of the mountains that divide Clear Lake Valleys from the Russian River Valley; thence southerly along the top of said mountains to a point on the top of said mountains one mile east of the eastern boundary line of the rancho known as Fitch's Rancho on Russian River; thence in a direct line southerly to the westerly branch of the headwaters of the Guichica Creek."

Inasmuch as the line between Napa and Sonoma has never been accurately defined since this act of 1855,[6] difficulty arises in trying to locate the line. This is due mainly to the fact that the summit of the mountains mentioned in the act lies no nearer than seven miles from Fitch's Rancho (Sotoyome Rancho), the Rancho Mallacomes lying almost wholly between the two points. It is, therefore, impossible to locate a point on the mountains "one mile from Fitch's Rancho." The nearest plausible point would be at the southern end of the Rancho Mallacomes from which a direct line might be run to the Guichica Creek. This would run along the hills and not intersect any rancho boundaries. This, however, does not at best comply strictly with the statute. As stated above, this line has not been clearly defined since the act of 1855, each county leaving its boundary to be determined by the line of the adjacent county. It may, therefore, be of assistance in determining the proper location of the line to work back from its later history. Now, all recent maps show the summit of the mountains to be the boundary, as it was during the period before 1855. No authority can be found for following the summit other than the acts of 1855 and preceding. It seems, therefore, that it may be proper to interpret the line as defined in that act in terms of earlier acts and later surveys as lying along the summit of the mountains. On the other hand, an official map of Napa County, 1876, shows the west line of Napa to be a straight line from the northeast corner of Sonoma

---

[5]Statutes, 1855: 77.
[6]Later acts and both the Napa and Sonoma sections of the Political Code define this line for each of these counties in the terms of the boundary of the other county.

to the Guichica Creek. This gives weight to the idea of a straight line between Sonoma and Napa, but there is no authority for beginning the line at any point north of one mile east of Fitch's Rancho, which is only about two-thirds as far north as the line runs. In view of the difficulties involved in the legal interpretation of the line, and since all later maps and most of the earlier ones follow the mountain ridge, and since this seems the most reasonable location of the line, which would otherwise disregard settlements, the line has been shown on the map to follow the ridge.

Sonoma-Marin County Line. No important change has been made in the southern line of Sonoma since it was firśt organized. In the earlier statutes this line has been determined by the description of the line in the Marin County boundary acts,[7] in which the line goes from the head of the Estero Americano by the Bodega-San Rafael road to the Laguna San Antonio. In the act of 1855 a change was made in the description at this point, the line now being made to run from the head of San Antonio Creek ''in a direct line to the head of the Estero Americano.''

No great change was involved in this amendment, but the line was now more easily determined. Since 1855 there has been no change in that line between Marin and Sonoma counties. In 1856 the line here described was surveyed by Wm. Mock, under the direction of the surveyor general, and the survey confirmed in a statute of 1861, and in later legislation.[8]

Mendocino Line. In 1859 Mendocino County, which had been joined to Sonoma County for administrative purposes since 1850, was separately organized. The boundary with Sonoma was then redetermined in the following language:[9]

> ''Beginning at a point in the Pacific Ocean, three miles due west of the mouth of Gualale River, thence east to the middle of the mouth of said stream, and up the middle of the channel of said stream, two miles; thence in a direct line to the most northern and highest peak or summit of the Redwood Mountain, immediately north of Cloverdale, and Oat Valley; thence due east to the western boundary of Napa County, on the summit of the Mayacmas Ridge.''

[7] *Statutes,* 1850 : 60 ; 1851 : 177 ; 1854 : 121.
[8] *Statutes,* 1861 : 351 ; 1867–68 : 347. *Political Code,* 1872, § 3955.
[9] *Statutes,* 1859 : 98.

There is little difficulty in locating the points mentioned on this line as it remained the boundary between the two counties until changed by the legislature in 1917. In 1917 the line was made more definite by being placed upon township and section lines.

Present Boundary, 1923. These changes were incorporated in the Political Code as amended in 1919, section 3957, which defines the boundaries of Sonoma County as follows:[10]

"3957. *Sonoma.* Commencing at a point in the Pacific Ocean, three miles due west of a point in the center of the channel at the mouth of the Gualala River, thence due east three miles to said point in the center of the channel at the mouth of said Gualala River; thence up the center of the channel of said Gualala River to a point where the center of said channel intersects the section line running east and west between sections twenty-three and twenty-six, township eleven north, range fifteen west, Mount Diablo Meridian; thence east on said section line and its continuation between sections twenty-four and twenty-five, said township and range, to the range line between ranges fourteen and fifteen west, Mount Diablo Meridian; thence continuing east on the section line between sections nineteen and thirty, twenty and twenty-nine, twenty-one and twenty-eight, twenty-two and twenty-seven, twenty-three and twenty-six, and twenty-four and twenty-five, township eleven north, range fourteen west, Mount Diablo Meridian, to the range line between ranges thirteen and fourteen west, Mount Diablo Meridian; thence north on said range line between said ranges thirteen and fourteen two miles more or less, to the section corner common to sections twelve and thirteen, township eleven north, range fourteen west, Mount Diablo Meridian, and sections seven and eighteen, township eleven north, range thirteen west, Mount Diablo Meridian; thence east on the section line between sections seven and eighteen, eight and seventeen, nine and sixteen, ten and fifteen, eleven and fourteen, and twelve and thirteen, township eleven north, range thirteen west, Mount Diablo Meridian, to the intersection of said section line with the range line between ranges twelve and thirteen west, Mount Diablo Meridian; thence continuing east on the section line between sections seven and eighteen, eight and seventeen, nine and sixteen, ten and fifteen, eleven and fourteen, and twelve and thirteen, township eleven north, range twelve west, Mount Diablo

[10]*Political Code* (1919), § 3957; (1923), § 3957.

Meridian, to the intersection of said section line with the range line between ranges eleven and twelve west, Mount Diablo Meridian; thence north on said range line between ranges eleven and twelve, two miles, more or less, to the southwest corner of township twelve north, range eleven west, Mount Diablo Meridian; thence east on the south boundary line of said township twelve north, range eleven west, three miles, more or less, to the southeast corner of section thirty-three township twelve north, range eleven west; thence north on the section line between sections thirty-three and thirty-four, one mile, more or less, to the northwest corner of said last named section thirty-four; and thence east on the section line between sections twenty-seven and thirty-four, twenty-six and thirty-five, and twenty-five and thirty-six, township twelve north, range eleven west, Mount Diablo Meridian, and continuing east on the section line between sections thirty and thirty-one, twenty-nine and thirty-two, twenty-eight and thirty-three, twenty-seven and thirty-four, twenty-six and thirty-five, and twenty-five and thirty-six, township twelve north, range ten west, Mount Diablo Meridian, and continuing east on the section line between sections thirty and thirty-one, twenty-nine and thirty-two, twenty-eight and thirty-three, twenty-seven and thirty-four, and twenty-six and thirty-five to the corner common to sections twenty-five, twenty-six, thirty-five, and thirty-six, township twelve north, range nine west, Mount Diablo Meridian, said point lying upon the summit of the Mayacamas ridge and constituting the common corner of Mendocino, Lake and Sonoma counties; thence southerly along the Mayacamas mountains, and on the western lines of Lake and Napa counties, to the westerly branch of headwaters of Huichica Creek; thence westerly on the line of Napa County to the top of the main ridge that divides the Huichica Valley from the Sonoma Valley; thence southerly along the said dividing ridge to the tule bordering on San Pablo Bay; thence southerly to the center of Huichica Creek; thence down said creek to its mouth, which is the southwest corner of Napa; thence on the line of Solano south, twenty-six and one-half degrees east, about six and one-quarter miles distant from the mouth of Huichica Creek, to the point of intersection with the westerly line of Contra Costa County, forming common corner of Marin, Solano, Contra Costa, and Sonoma, as described in section three thousand nine hundred fifteen; thence following the northern boundary of Marin westerly to the mouth of Petaluma Creek; thence up said creek to the mouth of San Antonio Creek; thence up said San Antonio Creek to its head; thence in a direct line to the head of the Estero Americano, on the line surveyed and established by William Mock, under the direction of the surveyor general, in the year 1856, thence down said Estero Americano to its mouth; thence due west three miles to a point in the Pacific Ocean; thence northwesterly by ocean shore to the point of beginning.''

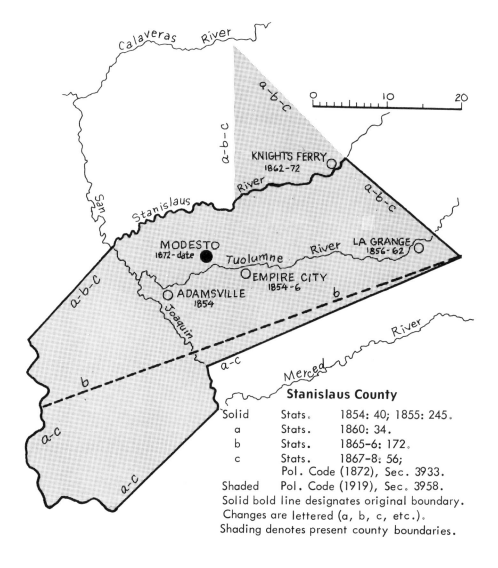

Stanislaus County

Solid	Stats.	1854: 40; 1855: 245.
a	Stats.	1860: 34.
b	Stats.	1865–6: 172.
c	Stats.	1867–8: 56;
		Pol. Code (1872), Sec. 3933.
Shaded	Pol. Code (1919), Sec. 3958.	

Solid bold line designates original boundary.
Changes are lettered (a, b, c, etc.).
Shading denotes present county boundaries.

STANISLAUS COUNTY

Stanislaus County was created on April 5, 1854, from territory which had previously been a portion of Tuolumne County. Because of the indefinite description of the boundaries in the original act another was passed and approved within the month. This act describes the boundaries as follows:[1]

"Commencing on the Stanislaus, at the corner of Calaveras and San Joaquin counties, thence running in a southeast course to Spark's Ferry, on the Tuolumne River, thence to the boundary line between Tuolumne and Mariposa counties, thence west along said line, to the San Joaquin River, thence up said river to the mouth of the Merced River, thence in a due southwest direction, to the summit of the Coast Range, thence in a northwesterly direction, following the summit of the said range, thence to the southwest corner of San Joaquin County, thence northeasterly along the line of said county to the place of beginning."

The following year the line between Stanislaus and Tuolumne was redefined without material change. The description was as follows:[2]

"Beginning at the southeast corner of San Joaquin County, at the corner where said county adjoins the county of Calaveras, and running in a southeasterly course on a direct line to the Big Falls on the Tuolumne River, in the mouth of the large cañon one mile north of Dye's Sawmill, (near Spark's old ferry) crossing the Tuolumne River at the point above described, and continuing the same parallel direction to the line separating the counties of Tuolumne and Merced."

Annexation from San Joaquin, 1860. During the year 1860 a triangular piece of territory including Knights Ferry was added to Stanislaus County at the expense of San Joaquin County. It is not improbable that local ambition had something to do with this change of allegiance, for in 1862 Knights Ferry became the county seat of the county. The territory

---

[1]*Statutes,* 1854 : 40. The wording is taken from the act of May 3, 1854.
[2]*Ibid.,* 1855 : 245.

in question is that part of Stanislaus County lying north of the Stanislaus River. The act of 1860 describes it thus:[3]

"Commencing on the Stanislaus River, at the corner of Tuolumne and Stanislaus counties; thence running along the boundary line between Calaveras and San Joaquin counties to McDermott's Bridge, on the Calaveras River, where the range line, between ranges nine and ten, east, intersects the easterly boundary of San Joaquin County; thence along said range line due south to the Stanislaus River; thence up said river to the place of beginning."

Merced-Stanislaus Line, 1866-68. By an act of March 8, 1866, a material change was made in the boundary between Stanislaus and Merced counties making it a straight line running as follows:[4]

"Commenc[ing] at the southwest corner of Tuolumne County, and southeast corner Stanislaus County, and the northwest corner of Mariposa County, and run[ning] south seventy (70) degrees west to the summit of the Coast Range of hills."

This change does not, however, seem to have been satisfactory as the legislature at its next session restored the line of 1855[5] and it has not since been changed.

The Present Boundary. As defined in the code of 1872 and reincorporated in the act of 1923 the description of the boundaries of Stanislaus is as follows:[6]

"3958. *Stanislaus.* Beginning at common corner of Stanislaus, Santa Clara, Alameda, and San Joaquin, on the summit of **Mount Boardman**, of the Mount Diablo range, as shown on survey and map of Wallace and Stakes, May, 1868; thence southeasterly, on the summit line of said range, being eastern line of Santa Clara, to the northwest corner of Merced, forming the southwest corner of Stanislaus, as established by survey and map of A. J. Stakes, July, 1868; thence northeasterly, on line as established by said last-named survey, to the junction of the Merced and San Joaquin rivers; thence down the San Joaquin seven miles; thence in a direct line a little north of east to a monument established by survey of A. J.

---
[3]*Statutes*, 1860 : 34.
[4]*Ibid.*, 1865–6 : 172.
[5]*Ibid.*, 1867–8 : 56.
[6]*Political Code* (1872), § 3933; (1919), § 3958; (1923), § 3958.

Stakes, being on the summit of the ridge between Merced and Stanislaus, and marking common corner of Tuolumne, Merced, Mariposa, and Stanislaus; thence northwesterly, in a direct line, and crossing the Stanislaus River, to monument established by survey and map of George E. Drew, May, 1860, on the north bank of said last-named river; thence northwesterly, on line of said survey, to its intersection with western line of range ten east, Mount Diablo Meridian, which point is marked by a monument establishing the north corner of Stanislaus County; then south, on said range line, to Stanislaus River; thence down the latter to its mouth in San Joaquin River; thence southwesterly on line as surveyed and mapped by Wallace and Stakes, May, 1868, to the place of beginning.''

SUTTER COUNTY

Sutter was one of the counties created in 1850 by the first legislature. During the first two years, four towns, Oro, Nicolaus, Auburn, and Vernon, each in turn claimed the county seat. Later it was removed to Yuba City, where it has remained. The original boundaries were as follows:[1]

"Beginning on the Sacramento River at the northwest corner of Sacramento County, and running thence up the middle of said river to a point due west of the mouth of Honcut Creek; thence due east to the mouth of said creek; thence down the middle of Feather River to the mouth of Bear Creek; thence up Bear Creek to a point six miles from its mouth; thence in a direct line to the junction of the north and middle forks of the American River; thence down the north fork to the junction of the south fork; and thence in a westerly direction, following the northern boundary of Sacramento County, to the place of beginning."

The northern boundary of Sacramento County here referred to is elsewhere defined as running from[2]

"a point ten miles due north of the mouth of the American River, and running thence in an easterly direction to the junction of the north and south forks of said river."

This is approximately the present boundary of the county.

The Placer-Sutter Boundary, 1851, 1866. The only great change in the territory of Sutter County was made in 1851 when approximately one-third of its area including the county seat was given to the newly created Placer County. The line between the two counties was declared to run from a point in the Sacramento River[3]

"ten miles below the junction of Sacramento and Feather rivers; thence in a northerly direction in a straight line to a point in the middle of Bear Creek opposite Camp Far West."

The line here described remained the boundary between the two counties until 1866, when the line was shifted further east

[1]*Statutes,* 1850: 62.
[2]*Ibid.,* 1850: 61.
[3]*Statutes,* 1851: 176.

(272)

and placed upon the United States survey lines. As defined in the section describing the boundaries of Placer County it then ran as follows:[4]

> "Beginning on the northern boundary line of Sacramento County at a point due south of the southwest corner of township eleven (11) north, range five (5) east, Mount Diablo Base and Meridian; thence due north to the northwest corner of township twelve (12) north, range five east, Mount Diablo Base and Meridian; thence due east to the southwest corner of section thirty-four (34,) township thirteen (13) north, range five (5) east, Mount Diablo Base and Meridian; thence due north to the middle of Bear Creek or River."

In 1891 a further change was made in the wording of the description of this line but without change in its location.[5] It is this description that is now followed in the Political Code.

The Butte-Sutter Boundary, 1851, 1856. Several changes were made before the northern boundary was located in a permanent manner, although none of the changes involved either much or valuable territory. The first of these changes was in 1851, when the boundary was run from a point in the middle of the Sacramento River[6]

> "due west of the north point of the three buttes; thence due east to the middle of Feather River."

The following year, 1852, the second shift was made. At this time the boundary ran from the same point in the Sacramento River[7]

> "thence in a southeasterly direction to a point at the base of the buttes, due west of the south point of the same; thence in a northeasterly direction to a point in the middle of Feather River, opposite the mouth of Honcut Creek."

In 1854 this line was once again changed. The same point in the Sacramento River was taken as the northwest corner, but there it ran[8]

> "due east to the said north point of the three buttes; thence in a straight line to a point in the middle of Feather River opposite the mouth of Honcut Creek."

---

[4]*Statutes*, 1865–66: 223.
[5]*Ibid.*, 1891: 455.
[6]*Ibid.*, 1851: 176.
[7]*Ibid.*, 1852: 237.
[8]*Ibid.*, 1854: 26.

In 1856 a more decided change was made, the line being placed upon Butte Creek rather than the Sacramento River and the whole line pushed farther north. It is described in the act as running up the middle of the Sacramento River[9]

> "to the mouth of Butte Creek; thence up the middle of said creek to a point due west of a point of timber half a mile north of James E. Edwards' house; thence due east to said point of timber; thence in a straight line to a point in the middle of Feather River opposite the mouth of Honcut Creek."

After the extension of the United States survey this line was redescribed and placed upon a section line where it has since remained.[10]

Present Boundary, 1923. When the Political Code was adopted in 1872 the boundaries as they had been amended in 1866 were incorporated into the code. This in turn with the changes of 1891 in describing the Placer County line formed the basis for section 3959 of the code as amended in 1919 with the exception that because of a shifting of the channel of Bear River during the years since the code was enacted, 1872, it became necessary to specify definitely the old channel of that stream. The section as adopted in 1923 reads as follows:[11]

> "3959. *Sutter.* Beginning at the northwest corner of Sacramento County, as established in section three thousand nine hundred forty-two; thence up the Sacramento River to the mouth of Butte Slough; thence down said slough to the dividing line between sections thirty-five and thirty-six, township sixteen north, range one west, Mount Diablo Base and Meridian; thence north, on the line between sections thirty-five and thirty-six, and sections twenty-five and twenty-six in said township and range to Butte Creek; thence following said Butte Creek to its intersection with the south line of section nineteen, township seventeen north, range one east, Mount Diablo Base and Meridian; then east on section lines to Feather River; thence down Feather River to mouth of Bear River; thence up the original or old channel of Bear River as the same was established by official government meander line

---

[9]*Statutes,* 1856:231. The Edwards House referred to is found to have been located in Sec. 25 (T17N,R1E) M. D. B. & M. See Henning Map of Butte County, 1862.
[10]*Ibid.,* 1863–64:301.
[11]*Political Code* (1919), § 3959; (1923), § 3959.

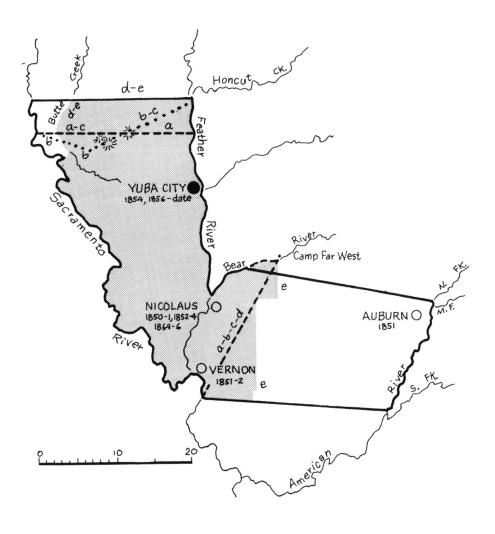

Sutter County

Solid	Stats.	1850: 62.
a	Stats.	1851: 176.
b	Stats.	1852: 237.
c	Stats.	1854: 26.
d	Stats.	1856: 231; 1863–4: 301.
e	Stats.	1865–6: 223; Pol. Code (1872), Sec. 3926.
Shaded	Pol. Code (1919), Sec. 3959.	

Solid bold line designates original boundary. Changes are lettered (a, b, c, etc.). Shading denotes present county boundaries.

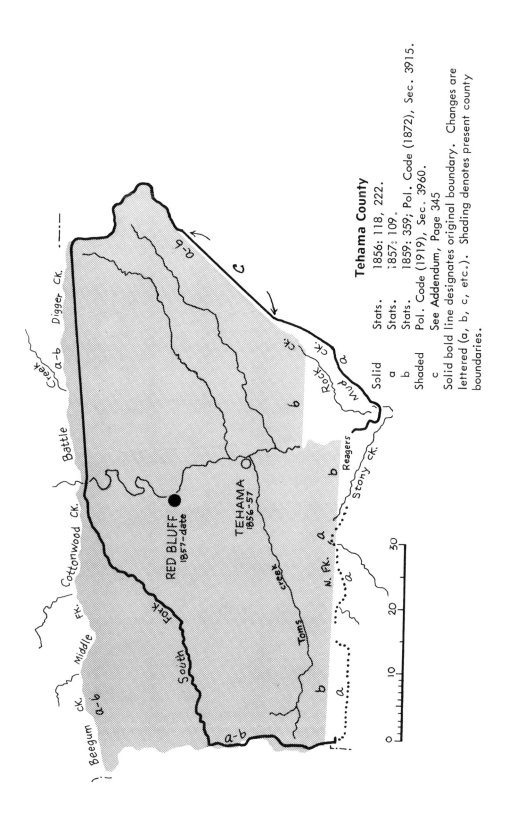

Tehama County

Stats.   1856: 118, 222.
Stats.   1857: 109.
Stats.   1859: 359; Pol. Code (1872), Sec. 3915.
Pol. Code (1919), Sec. 3960.
See Addendum, Page 345

Solid
a
b
Shaded
c

Solid bold line designates original boundary. Changes are lettered (a, b, c, etc.). Shading denotes present county boundaries.

surveys made by E. Dyer and others prior to 1870, of record in the office of the United States surveyor general for the state of California, to the northwest corner of Placer County as established in section three thousand nine hundred thirty-nine; thence along the western boundary of Placer County to the southwest corner thereof; thence westerly along the northern boundary of Sacramento County to the place of beginning.''

TEHAMA COUNTY

In 1856 Tehama County was created from territory which previous to that date had belonged to Colusa, Butte and Shasta counties. The county seat was placed at Tehama, where it remained for one year, when it was removed to Red Bluff, its present location. The original boundaries are given in the act creating the county as follows:[1]

> "Beginning at the mouth of Cottonwood Creek, in Shasta County; running up the middle of said creek, to the mouth of the south fork of Cottonwood; up the middle of the south fork, to the summit of the Coast Range; down the summit of said range, to a point five miles below Thom's Creek; thence easterly, to a point one hundred yards south of Regan's Ranch, on the Sacramento River; thence down the middle of the Sacramento, to the mouth of Mud Creek; thence up the middle of Mud Creek, to the line which divides the counties of Butte and Plumas; up said line, to the line of Shasta County; thence westerly, to the place of beginning."

Two portions of this description are apt to cause difficulty in locating these boundaries. The first is in reference to the location of "Regan's Ranch, on the Sacramento River." This is located just south of the present Tehama-Glenn County line, namely the south line of township twenty-three north of Mount Diablo Base Line.[2] The other difficulty is in that part which places the line along Mud Creek "to the boundary line that divides the counties of Butte and Plumas." A study of the maps shows that in 1856 the line between Butte and Plumas did not approach Mud Creek. It has been necessary therefore to await the description of a later statute to determine the course of the line from the source of Mud Creek.[3]

Changes in Boundary, 1857. By action of the legislature in 1857 the area of Tehama County was increased by boundary changes both on the northwest and the southwest. That portion of the act describing the boundaries west of the Sacra-

[1] *Statutes,* 1856 : 222.
[2] Shown upon Plat of Capay Rancho (April-May, 1858) in Archives of United States Surveyor General for California, San Francisco. It is variously referred to in the statutes as "Regan's Ranch" (1856), "Ragers' House" (1857) and "Rogers' House" (1859). It is shown upon the plat as "Reagan's Ranch."
[3] In 1859 this boundary was run in a direct line to the headwaters of Rock Creek, a stream heading near and running parallel to Mud Creek. It may be proper then to presume that this eastern line took a similar course.

mento River, where both of these changes were made, reads as follows:[4]

"Beginning at the first section line north of Rager's House, on the Sacramento River, and running west on that line to where it is crossed by Stony Creek; thence up the middle channel of said creek, to the mouth of the north fork of said creek; up the middle channel of the said north fork, to the summit of the Coast Range; thence up the Coast Range to the middle fork of Cottonwood Creek, and down the center channel of said creek, to where it empties into the Sacramento River."

The change here made in the northern or Shasta-Tehama line was to locate it practically the same as it now stands. The southern boundary remained as described for two years, when it was restored approximately to its former location.

The Present Boundaries, 1923. In 1859 the limits of Tehama County were fixed about as they are at present, whatever changes appear in the subsequent acts being but attempts to define already existing lines in a more precise manner.[5] The boundaries of Tehama as they are at present are defined by the Political Code as follows:[6]

"3960. *Tehama.* Beginning at the point of intersection of Sacramento River with south line of township twenty-three north, Mount Diablo Base; thence west, on said line, being northern line of Glenn to the summit of the Coast Range, being southwest corner; thence northerly, on said summit line, to the southwest corner of Shasta, as established in section three thousand nine hundred fifty-three; thence easterly, on the southern line of Shasta, as established in said section, to the northwest corner of Plumas, being the point of intersection of southern line of Shasta with the summit line of the dividing ridge between the waters of Mill and Deer creeks, tributaries of the Sacramento River, and Rice's and Warner's creeks, tributaries of the north fork of Feather River, forming northeast corner of Tehama; thence southerly, along said summit line, to the north point of Butte County, it being the point where the northern road from Big Meadows to Butte Meadows, by Dye's house, crosses the said summit line; thence southwesterly, in a direct line, to the head of Rock Creek; thence southwesterly, down Rock Creek, to the south line of township twenty-four north, Mount Diablo Base; thence west on said line to the Sacramento River; thence along said river to the place of beginning."

---

[4]*Statutes,* 1857 : 109.
[5]*Statutes,* 1859 : 359 ; *Political Code* (1872), § 3915.
[6]*Political Code* (1923), § 3960. See also *Ibid.,* (1919), § 3960.

TRINITY COUNTY

Original Boundary. Trinity was one of the original counties, created on February 18, 1850. It, however, was not organized until 1851, being joined to Shasta for judicial and administrative purposes. The original boundaries were defined in the statute as follows:[1]

> "Beginning on the parallel of forty-two degrees north latitude at a point in the ocean three English miles from shore, and running due east on said parallel to the summit of the Coast Range; thence in a southerly direction to the parallel of forty degrees north latitude; thence due west to the ocean, and three English miles therein; and thence in a northwesterly direction, parallel with the coast, to the point of beginning."

The only point in this description that could cause difficulty is in locating the northeast corner, which is described as the point where the forty-second parallel crosses the "summit of the Coast Range," a difficulty due to the fact that the Klamath River here runs about from east to west. Evidence, however, shows that this line, which in 1851 became the eastern boundary of Klamath County, ran east of Shasta River Valley,[2] probably giving to Trinity County all the area drained by the Klamath River.

Klamath County Line, 1851. In 1851 Trinity County was separately organized, but not with its original boundaries, for more than half of her territory was detached to form Klamath County. The new boundary is described thus:[3]

> "Beginning at a point in the ocean three miles due west from the mouth of Mad River, and running thence due east to the summit of the Coast Range; thence in a southerly direction along the summit of said Coast Range, to the parallel of forty degrees north latitude; thence due west to the ocean, and three miles therein; thence in a northwesterly direction parallel with the coast to the place of beginning."

Humboldt County Detached, 1853. In 1853 Trinity County was once again reduced in size, this time the western

---

[1]*Statutes*, 1850 : 62, § 24.
[2]See Klamath County description.
[3]*Statutes*, 1851 : 179.

half being separately organized as Humboldt County. The boundary separating the two counties ran from the Klamath County line on the Trinity River, due east from the mouth of Mad River,

> "thence up the Trinity River to the mouth of the south fork of said Trinity River, running along the eastern side of the said south fork, one hundred feet above high water mark, to the mouth of Grouse Creek; and thence in a due south direction to the fortieth degree of north latitude."[4]

Reannexation from Klamath, 1855. It was soon seen that the eastern half of the Trinity-Klamath boundary was unfortunately located in that it cut off from Trinity County a large portion of territory naturally belonging to that county, whereas it was far detached from the remainder of Klamath County. In consequence an act was passed in 1855 placing the head waters of the Trinity River once again in Trinity County. The section of the act making this change is as follows:[5]

> "Beginning at the northeast corner of Humboldt County, on the Trinity River, at the point where the boundary line between said county of Humboldt and the county of Klamath crosses said river; thence northeasterly up the principal ridge to the summit of the range of mountains dividing the waters of the Trinity River from the waters of Salmon River; thence following the said summit in an easterly direction to the summit of the range that divides the waters of the Sacramento from the waters that flow westwardly through the Klamath into the Pacific; thence southerly following the summit of said range to its intersection with the fortieth degree of parallel of north latitude; thence due west along said parallel of latitude to the eastern boundary of Humboldt County; thence in a northerly direction along said eastern boundary to the place of beginning."

Southern Boundary, 1859, 1860. Due to an unintentional change in the description of the northern boundary of Mendocino County at the time of its separate organization in 1859,[6]

---

[4] *Statutes*, 1853:161.
[5] *Ibid.*, 1855:200.
[6] Mendocino County had been created in 1850, but until 1859 was joined to Sonoma County.

the southern line of Trinity was moved northward a distance of approxmiately four miles to "the fifth standard north of Mount Diablo Meridian."[7]

This change affected both Trinity and Humboldt counties and immediately gave rise to a protest from these counties with the result that the following year the boundary was once again placed "on the line of the fortieth parallel of north latitude."[8]

Since 1860 it has presumably remained upon this line, but through an error in survey it was placed some few miles further south. This came about through a survey made under the act of March 30, 1872,[9] which authorized that the line between Trinity and Mendocino counties be surveyed and that the line as surveyed under the provisions of the act should constitute the legal boundary. The line was surveyed by Wm. H. Fauntleroy in 1872 and thus became the authorized boundary. In 1891 a later survey revealed the fact that the Fauntleroy survey had been in error in that the fortieth degree of latitude does in reality run farther north. Mendocino County therefore laid claim to the territory north to the fortieth degree of latitude. By a decision of the supreme court of the state the line as surveyed by Fauntleroy was maintained as the legal boundary notwithstanding the technical error.[10]

Code Line, 1872. After 1860 no changes in the boundary of Trinity County were made before the adoption of the Political Code in 1872, section 3919 of which defined the limits of the county in the following manner:[11]

> "Beginning at the northeast corner of Mendocino, as established in section 3918, on the summit line of the Coast Range; thence northerly on said range and the western line of Tehama and Shasta, to the point of intersection with the southern line of Siskiyou, being northeast corner of Trinity and northwest corner of Shasta; thence westerly, on the ridge dividing the waters flowing south and west into Trinity and Salmon rivers from the waters flowing north and east into Scott's and Sacramento rivers, to common corner of Klamath, Siskiyou, and Trinity, as established in section 3910; thence southwesterly, on the line of Scott's Mountain, being the southern line of

---

[7]*Statutes*, 1859 : 98.
[8]*Ibid.*, 1860 : 334.
[9]*Ibid.*, 1871–2 : 766.
[10]*County of Trinity* vs. *County of Mendocino.*   151 California Reports, 279.
[11]*Political Code* (1872), § 3919.

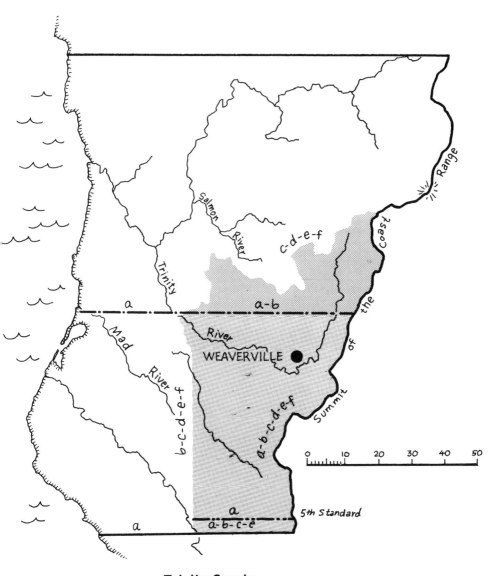

Trinity County

Solid	Stats.	1850: 62.
a	Stats.	1851: 179.
b	Stats.	1853: 161.
c	Stats.	1855: 200.
d	Stats.	1859: 98.
e	Stats.	1860: 334; Pol. Code (1872), Sec. 3919.
f	Stats.	1871-2: 766.
Shaded	Pol. Code (1919), Sec. 3961.	

Solid bold line designates original boundary. Changes are lettered (a, b, c, etc.). Shading denotes present county boundaries.

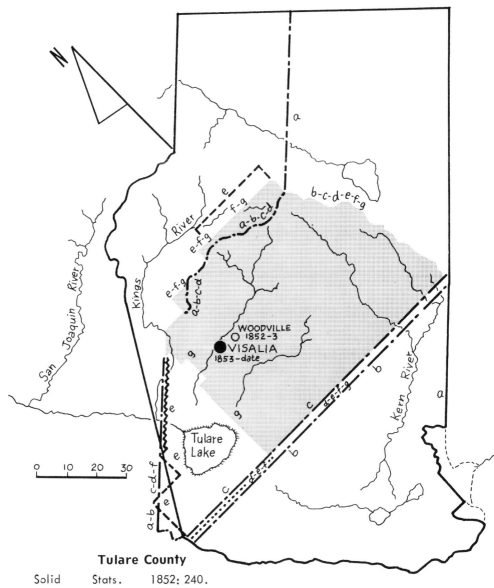

Tulare County

Solid	Stats.	1852: 240.
a	Stats.	1856: 183.
b	Stats.	1865-6: 355, 796.
c	Stats.	1867-8: 40.
d	Pol. Code (1872), Sec. 3940.
e	Stats.	1873-4: 700.
f	Stats.	1875-6: 397.
g	Stats.	1893: 176.
Shaded	Pol. Code (1919), Sec. 3962.

Solid bold line designates original boundary. Changes are
lettered (a, b, c, etc.). Shading denotes present county
boundaries.

Klamath, to common corner of Trinity, Klamath, and Humboldt, as established in section 3909; thence southerly, by the eastern line of Humboldt, to the fortieth parallel of latitude, being the northern line of Mendocino, forming southwest corner; thence east, to the place of beginning."

Present Boundary, 1923. In 1919 this section was revised and reincorporated into the Political Code as section 3961. In the revised section the description is given as follows:[12]

"3961. *Trinity.* Beginning at the northeast corner of Mendocino County and southeast corner of Trinity County as established and marked by Wm. H. Fauntleroy in 1872, on the summit of the Coast Range at or near the quarter section corner on east line of section thirty-four in township twenty-five north, range ten west, Mount Diablo Meridian; thence northerly along the summit of said range and the line of Tehama County to the northwest corner of Tehama County; thence northeasterly and northerly along the summit of the mountain dividing the waters flowing into Sacramento River and the waters flowing into Trinity River on the west line of Shasta and Siskiyou counties to a point in the southern line of Siskiyou County located in section twenty-six, township forty-one north, range six west, Mount Diablo Meridian; thence southwesterly and westerly along the summit of the mountain dividing the waters flowing into Trinity River from the waters flowing into Scott and Salmon rivers to intersection of east line of Humboldt on what is known as Salmon summit, being northwest corner of Trinity near the corner to sections four, five, eight and nine, township nine north, range seven east, Humboldt Meridian; thence southwesterly and southerly by the eastern line of Humboldt to the southwest corner of Trinity County as surveyed and marked by Wm. H. Fauntleroy in August, 1872, the same being in the southeast quarter of section thirty-one, township five south, range six east, Humboldt Meridian; thence east along the line between Trinity and Mendocino as surveyed and marked by Wm. H. Fauntleroy in 1872 to the point of beginning."

[12] *Political Code* (1919), § 3961; (1923), § 3961.

TULARE COUNTY

Original Boundaries, 1852. Tulare County was created in 1852 from the southern portion of Mariposa County. Its boundaries at that time were defined as follows:[1]

> "Beginning at the summit of the Coast Range at the corner of Monterey and San Luis Obispo counties, thence running in a northeasterly direction to the ridge dividing the waters of the San Joaquin and Kings rivers, thence along said ridge to the summit of the Sierra, thence in the same direction to the state line, thence southeasterly along said line to the county of Los Angeles, thence southwesterly along the line of Los Angeles County, to Santa Barbara, thence along the summit of the Coast Range to the place of beginning."

The point of beginning was here described in terms of Monterey and San Luis Obispo counties. It is therefore necessary to note that the corner here mentioned was fixed by statute of 1851[2] as lying on the summit of the Coast Range at "a point due east of the mouth of the Nacisniento River."

The southeast boundary of the county, as noted in the section quoted above, is defined in the terms of the northern boundary of Los Angeles County. This line was defined in 1851[3] as running along the northern line of the "Rancho of Casteque and Lejon * * * to the northeastern corner, and from thence in a northeast line to the eastern boundary of the state." Reference is evidently made in this section to the ranchos now known as Castac and El Tejon. Although the boundaries of these ranchos were not clearly defined at the time of the passage of this act, it is possible to point out a definite line based upon the later survey of the ranchos.

Fresno County Line, 1856. In 1856 the formation of Fresno caused a considerable reduction in the size of Tulare County and changed its northern boundary to read as follows:[4]

> "[Beginning at] a point in the southwestern boundary of Tulare County south, forty-five degrees west from the point on Kings River, where the line dividing townships

[1]*Statutes*, 1852 : 240.
[2]*Ibid.*, 1851 : 173.
[3]*Ibid.*, 1851 : 172.
[4]*Ibid.*, 1856 : 183.

fifteen and sixteen south, crosses the same; thence north, forty-five degrees east to said point on Kings River; thence east with the line dividing townships fifteen and sixteer south, to the dividing ridge between the waters of Kings River and the Kawdah; thence with the said dividing ridge to the summit of the Sierra Nevada; thence north, forty-five degrees east to the eastern boundary of the State of California.''

Inyo and Kern Counties Detached, 1866. During the session of the legislature, 1865–66, two new counties were organized from territory which had been portions of Tulare County. The first of these was Inyo, to which was given that portion lying east of ''the summit of the Sierra Nevada Mountains.''[5] The second was Kern County, whose northern boundary was described as[6]

> ''Commencing at a point on the western boundary line of Tulare County, two miles due south of the sixth standard south of the Mount Diablo Base Line; thence due east to the western boundary line of Inyo County.''

In 1868 the Kern County line was shifted northward to a position ''one-half mile due north of the sixth standard south of the Mount Diablo Base Line.''[7]

Redefinition of Boundaries, 1872, 1874, 1876. At the time of the adoption of the code in 1872 the boundaries of Tulare County, in common with those of all the other counties of the state, were redefined, as follows:[8]

> ''Beginning at southwest corner, being common corner of Monterey, San Luis Obispo, Kern, and Tulare, and being the point where the line of the sixth standard south crosses the summit line of the Mount Diablo range of mountains; thence east, on said standard, to the point of intersection with summit line of the Sierra Nevada Mountains, forming the southeast corner of Tulare and southwest corner of Inyo; thence northwesterly, on said summit, being on the western line of Inyo, to the east corner of Fresno, as established in section 3939; thence on the southern line of Fresno to the eastern line of Monterey; thence southerly, on the line of Monterey, as established in section 3948, to the place of beginning.''

---

[5]*Statutes*, 1865–66: 355.
[6]*Ibid.*, 796.
[7]*Ibid.*, 1867–68: 40.
[8]*Political Code* (1872), § 3940.

A comparison with the early statutes shows that this legislation followed the earlier acts except in reference to the southern boundary which was moved one-half mile south to the sixth standard south.

The next session of the legislature in 1873–74 amended the Fresno-Tulare County line which is described in the act as follows:[9]

> "Commencing on the sixth standard south from Mount Diablo Meridian, at the southwest corner of township number seventeen (17) east, and running from thence north on the range line between townships sixteen and seventeen east, to the northwest corner of township number twenty-two south, range seventeen east; thence east on the township line between townships twenty-one and twenty-two south, to the southeast corner of township number twenty-one south, range eighteen east; thence north on the range line between townships eighteen and nineteen east to the northwest corner of township number twenty south, range number nineteen east; thence east on the township line between townships number nineteen and twenty south, to the southeast corner of section thirty-three, in township nineteen (19) south, range nineteen (19) east; thence north on section lines one mile, east one mile, north one mile and east one mile, north one mile and east one mile, to the southwest corner of section eighteen (18) in township nineteen (19) south, range twenty east; thence north one mile and east to the northeast corner of said section eighteen, township nineteen south, range twenty east; thence north one mile, east one mile, north one mile and east one mile to the southeast corner of section thirty-three, in township number eighteen south, range number twenty east; thence north one mile, east one mile, north one mile, east one mile, north one mile, east one mile, north one mile, and east to the southeast corner of section seven (7) in township eighteen south, range twenty-one east; thence north one mile, east one mile, north one mile, east one mile, to the southwest corner of section thirty-four (34), in township seventeen (17) south, range twenty-one east; thence north one mile, east one mile, north one mile, east one mile, north one mile, east one mile, north one mile and east to the southeast corner of section seven (7), in township number seventeen (17) south, range number twenty-two (22) east; thence north one mile, east one mile, north one mile and east to the southwest corner of section thirty-three (33), in township number sixteen (16) south, range number twenty-

[9]*Statutes,* 1873–74: 700.

two east; thence north one mile, east one mile, north one mile, east one mile; thence north one mile, east one mile, north one mile and east to the northeast corner of section eighteen (18), in township number sixteen (16) south, range number twenty-three (23) east; thence north one mile, east one mile, and north on section line to the township line between townships fifteen and sixteen south; thence east on said township line to the southeast corner of township number fifteen south, range twenty-four east; thence north on the range line between ranges twenty-four and twenty-five east, to the northwest corner of township number fifteen south, range twenty-five east; thence east on the township line between townships fourteen and fifteen south, to the northeast corner of township number fifteen south, range number twenty-seven east; thence north six miles to the northwest corner of township number fourteen south, of range number twenty-eight east; thence east to the southeast corner of township number thirteen (13) south, range number twenty-eight east; thence north on the range line to the third standard line south from Mount Diablo Meridian, and from thence east on township line between townships thirteen and fourteen south to the present county line of Inyo County.''

The complicated description here given seems to have been unsatisfactory, for at the next session of the legislature, 1875–76, the line was again changed and described in the following words:[10]

''Commencing at a point on the eastern boundary line of Monterey County, as described in section three thousand nine hundred and forty-eight of Political Code, being on the summit of Coast Range, which point is south forty-five degrees west from the point on Kings River where the northern line of township sixteen south crosses the same; thence north forty-five degrees east to said point on Kings River; thence east along northern line of township sixteen south and continuing on said line to the northwest corner of township sixteen south, range twenty-five (25) east; thence north to the northwest corner of township fifteen (15) south, range twenty-five (25) east; thence east to the northeast corner of township fifteen south, range twenty-seven (27) east; thence north to the northeast corner of township fourteen south of range twenty-seven east; thence east on the line between township thirteen and fourteen south to the summit of Sierra Nevada, being the western line of Inyo County.''

---

[10]*Statutes,* 1875–76 : 397.

This line, with the exception of that portion which was later taken over by Kings County, still forms the northern boundary of Tulare County.

Kings County Line, 1893. The latest change in the boundaries of the county was made in 1893 when the western section, including the region around Tulare Lake, was detached from Tulare and organized as Kings County. Its eastern boundary, which is also the western line of Tulare County, is described in the act as follows:[11]

> "Beginning at the point where the fourth standard line south of Mount Diablo Base Line intersects or crosses the boundary line as now established by law between Tulare and Fresno counties; thence east to the northeast corner of section one, in township seventeen south, of range twenty-two east, Mount Diablo Base and Meridian; thence south six miles; thence east three miles; thence south nine miles to the southeast corner of section sixteen, in township nineteen south, range twenty-three east, Mount Diablo Base and Meridian; thence west three miles to the southeast corner of section thirteen, township nineteen south, range twenty-two east, Mount Diablo Base and Meridian; thence south nine miles to the southeast corner of township twenty south, range twenty-two east, Mount Diablo Base and Meridian; thence west to the northeast corner of township twenty-one south, range twenty-two east, Mount Diablo Base and Meridian; thence south twenty-four miles to the boundary line between Kern and Tulare counties as now established by law."

Present Boundary, 1923. At the time when the revision of the code sections dealing with county boundaries was made in 1919 the limits of Tulare County were redescribed in accordance with the recent legislation creating Kings County. The boundaries of Tulare County are defined as follows:[12]

> "3962. *Tulare.* Beginning at the southwest corner, being the common corner of Kings, Kern and Tulare, and being located on the sixth standard south at the southwest corner of township twenty-four south, range twenty-three east, Mount Diablo Base and Meridian; thence east, on said standard, to the point of intersection with summit line of the Sierra Nevada mountains, forming the southeast

---

[11]*Statutes,* 1893 : 176.
[12]*Political Code* (1919), § 3962; (1923), § 3962.

corner of Tulare and southwest corner of Inyo; thence northwesterly, on said summit, being on the western line of Inyo, to the east corner of Fresno, as established in section three thousand nine hundred eighteen; thence on the southern line of Fresno to the eastern line of Kings; thence southerly, on the line of Kings, as established in section three thousand nine hundred twenty-four, to the place of beginning.''

TUOLUMNE COUNTY

Original Boundary, 1850. Tuolumne County was organized in 1850 and is therefore one of the original counties. With the exception of the loss of the territory of Stanislaus County in 1854 and a small contribution to Alpine in 1864, its boundaries remain the same as when it was created. The original boundaries were defined thus:[1]

> "Beginning on the summit of the Coast Range at the southwest corner of Calaveras County, and following in an easterly direction the southern boundary of said county to the summit of the Sierra Nevada; thence in a southeasterly direction, following the summit of the Sierra Nevada, to the dividing ridge between the Tuolumne and Merced rivers; thence following the top of said ridge down to the plains at a point equally distant between the said rivers; thence in a direct line to the San Joaquin River, at a point seven miles below the mouth of the Merced River; thence up the middle of the San Joaquin River to the mouth of the Merced River; thence in a due southwest direction to the summit of the Coast Range, and thence in a northwesterly direction, following the summit of said range, to the place of beginning."

The description given here is inaccurate and confusing in reference to the northern boundary, for in order to reach the summit of the Sierra Nevada it is necessary that the line follow not only the eastern boundary of San Joaquin but also Calaveras as well, the line running up the Stanislaus River to the source of its north fork.

In 1851 the boundaries of all the counties were redefined. At this time the section referring to Tuolumne County was altered, through the omission of some rather important clauses. That no change was intended, and none recognized at that time seems to be indicated by available evidence.[2]

Stanislaus Line, 1854, 1855. In 1854 the valley portion of Tuolumne County was separately organized as Stanislaus County. The line between the two counties then ran from

> "the Stanislaus, at the corner of Calaveras and San Joaquin counties, thence running in a southeast course to

---

[1] *Statutes*, 1850: 63.
[2] See discussion under Stanislaus County.

Sparks' Ferry on the Tuolumne River, thence to the boundary line between Tuolumne and Mariposa counties."[3]

The next year the line between the two counties was "permanently established" as follows:[4]

"Beginning at the southeast corner of San Joaquin County, at the corner where said county adjoins the county of Calaveras, and running in a southeasterly course on a direct line to the Big Falls on the Tuolumne River, in the mouth of the large cañon one mile north of Dye's Saw Mill, (near Spark's old ferry) crossing the Tuolumne River at the point above described, and continuing the same parallel direction to the line separating the counties of Tuolumne and Merced."

The boundaries as they were after the act of 1855 were redefined without change in a statute of 1859.[5]

Alpine County, 1864. In 1864 Alpine County was created out of portions of several of the older counties. Tuolumne was one of these, contributing that portion of the county lying south and west of the north fork of the Stanislaus and the Sierras and north and east of the present Alpine-Tuolumne line.[6]

Present Boundary. Since the formation of Alpine County no changes have been made in the limits of Tuolumne County. At the time of the adoption of the Political Code in 1872 the boundaries of Tuolumne, in common with those of all the other counties, were defined in full.[7] When the code was amended in 1919 the description of Tuolumne County was adopted as given in 1872, save for a few changes in wording. The boundaries, however, remain as they were. This description reads as follows:[8]

"3963. *Tuolumne.* Beginning at the most western corner, being the southern corner of Calaveras, as established in section three thousand nine hundred thirteen, in Stanislaus River; thence southeasterly to common corner of Merced, Mariposa, Stanislaus, and Tuolumne, as

---

[3]*Statutes*, 1854 (Redding) : 40, or 1854 (Kerr) : 148. This is the wording of the amended act, approved May 3, 1854.
[4]*Ibid.*, 1855 : 245.
[5]*Ibid.*, 1859 : 213.
[6]*Ibid.*, 1863–64 : 178.
[7]*Political Code* (1872), § 3937.
[8]*Ibid.*, (1919), § 3963; (1923), § 3963.

established in section three thousand nine hundred fifty-eight; thence easterly on the northern line of Mariposa and Madera, following summit line of the dividing ridge between Tuolumne and Merced Rivers, to Mount Lyell, as marked on Warren Holt's map, one thousand eight hundred sixty-nine, and the summit of the Sierra Nevada mountains, being on the western line of Mono and common corner of Tuolumne, Madera and Mono; thence northerly by the line of Mono, being the summit line of the Sierra Nevada mountains, to the southern corner of Alpine, as established in section three thousand nine hundred ten; thence northwesterly by the line of Alpine to the southeastern corner of Calaveras; thence westerly on the line of Calaveras and down the Stanislaus river to the place of beginning.''

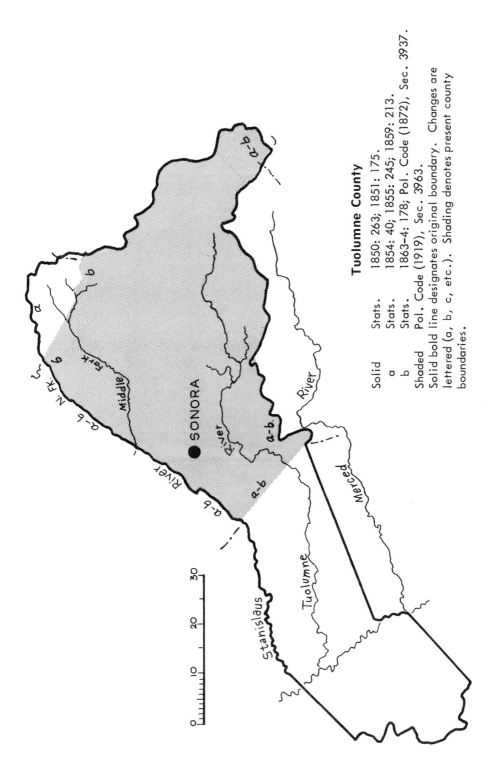

Tuolumne County

Solid	Stats.	1850: 263; 1851: 175.
a	Stats.	1854: 40; 1855: 245; 1859: 213.
b	Stats.	1863-4: 178; Pol. Code (1872), Sec. 3937.
Shaded	Pol. Code (1919), Sec. 3963.	

Solid bold line designates original boundary. Changes are lettered (a, b, c, etc.). Shading denotes present county boundaries.

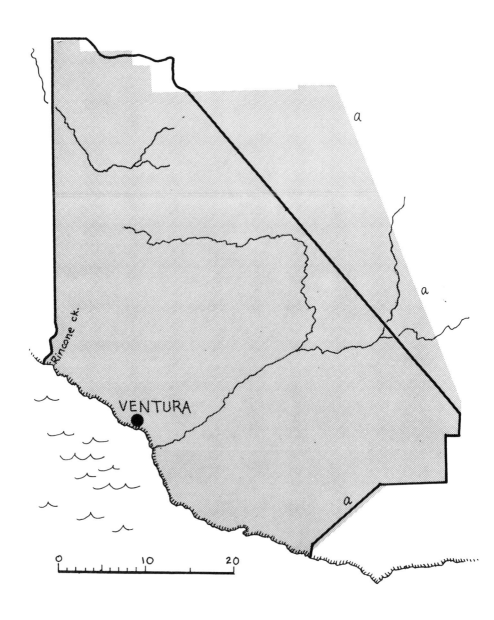

Ventura County

Solid   Stats.   1871–2: 484.
  a   Survey of 1881.
Shaded   Boundary as observed, 1922.
Solid bold line designates original boundary. Changes are
lettered (a, b, c, etc.). Shading denotes present county
boundaries.

VENTURA COUNTY

Original Boundary, 1872. Ventura was created in 1872 from the eastern portion of Santa Barbara County. The act creating the county defined its boundaries as follows:[1]

"Commencing on the coast of the Pacific Ocean, at the mouth of the Rincon Creek; thence following up the center of said creek to its source; thence due north to the northern boundary line of Santa Barbara County; thence in an easterly direction along the said boundary line of Santa Barbara County to the northeast corner of the same; thence southerly along the line between the said Santa Barbara County and Los Angeles County to the Pacific Ocean and three miles therein; thence in a northwesterly direction to a point due south of and three miles distant from the center of the mouth of Rincon Creek; thence north to the point of beginning, and including the islands of Anacapa and San Nicholas."

Since this act defines the northern and eastern boundaries by reference to the boundaries of Santa Barbara and Los Angeles counties it becomes necessary to consider the location of those lines in order to determine the limits of Ventura County.

The same legislative session that created Ventura County also adopted the Political Code, sections 3945 and 3946 of which defined, with some changes, the boundaries of Los Angeles and Santa Barbara counties.[2] The western line of Los Angeles County was there defined in part as follows:[3]

"Beginning at southeast corner of Santa Barbara, in the Pacific Ocean, at a point on extension line of the northern boundary of the rancho called Malaga, western corner; thence northeasterly, so as to include said rancho, to the northwest corner of the rancho called Triumfo, running on northerly line of the same to the northeast corner thereof; thence to the summit of the ridge of hills called Santa Susanna; thence in a direct line northwesterly, to the southwest corner of Kern, as established in Section 3941, forming the northwest corner of Los Angeles."

---

[1] *Statutes*, 1871–2: 484.
[2] The code, however, did not take cognizance of the creation of Ventura County.
[3] *Political Code* (1872), § 3945.

The northern line of Santa Barbara, which became the line of Ventura, was defined in the other section as running from the northwest corner of Los Angeles County,

> "on the summit of the Coast Range, being also the south-west corner of Kern, as established in section 3941; thence northwesterly, on the summit line, being also on western boundary of Kern, to a point of intersection with the southern line of township ten north, San Bernardino base; thence west, on said township line."[4]

The boundaries here described are fairly definite and can be determined without great difficulty. The Los Angeles line presents one point the location of which becomes certain only after a study of the history of the boundary. Other than this the description can be readily followed. This is in reference to the location of the point described as the summit of the Santa Susanna Hills. In the location of this point we are aided by the many early maps which show this line from early dates. From them it is clearly shown that the point here referred to lies in the near vicinity of the Santa Susanna Pass on the road leading from San Fernando Valley westward through Simi Valley.[5]

Eastern Boundary Survey, 1881. Notwithstanding the definite manner in which the boundaries had been defined in the code and statutes of 1872, the line as marked by a joint survey made in 1881 did not follow the line as defined in the code, but was located along a line which had been the Los Angeles-Santa Barbara boundary from 1856 to 1872.[6] In spite of the fact that this line gave to Ventura County a triangular piece of territory some 275 square miles in area, the line as surveyed was approved by the supervisors of the two counties.

Boundary of 1919. In 1919 a new section was placed in the Political Code defining the boundaries of Ventura County, which before that time had not had a place in the code. Two

---

[4]*Political Code* (1872), § 3946.
[5]For a more complete discussion of the location of this line see history of Los Angeles County boundary.
[6]The line of 1856 went from the summit of the Santa Susanna Hills "in a direct line to the northwesternmost corner" of the Castac Rancho, whereas the line of 1872 was defined as going from the summit of the Santa Susanna Hills "to the southwest corner of Kern as established in section 3941," which defines the corner as lying at the point where the southern line of Kern strikes the summit of the Coast Range of mountains. For more complete description see the history of the Los Angeles County boundary.

bills were introduced during the session of the legislature: one merely legalizing by statute the *de facto* boundary limits as observed since 1881; the other was proposed by the representatives of Ventura and Los Angeles counties and sought a modification of the line. The latter of these two was incorporated into the code.[7]

Present Boundary, 1923. As stated, the act as adopted made a modification in the boundary line. A test case was taken to the supreme court and by that body the new line was declared to be unconstitutional, upon the ground that the legislature did not have the power to alter a county boundary. In 1923 another act was adopted which defines the boundary with Los Angeles County as lying along the line surveyed in 1881. The description reads as follows:[8]

"3964. *Ventura.* Commencing on the coast of the Pacific Ocean, at the mouth of the Rincon Creek; thence following up the center of said creek to its source; thence due north to the corner common to Kern, Santa Barbara and Ventura located on the township line between townships nine and ten north, range twenty-four west, San Bernardino base and meridian, and running thence east with said line between townships nine and ten north, to the northeast corner of township nine north, range twenty-four west, San Bernardino meridian; thence south with the range line to the quarter section corner in the west line of section seven, township nine north, range twenty-three west, San Bernardino meridian; thence east with the center line of sections seven, eight, nine, ten, eleven and twelve of said township nine, range twenty-three west, to the line between ranges twenty-two and twenty-three west, of said township; thence south with range line to the southwest corner of section eighteen, township nine, range twenty-two west; thence east to the corner of sections sixteen, seventeen, twenty and twenty-one of same township; thence south to the southwest corner of section thirty-three, of same township; thence east on line between townships eight and nine north, to the southeast corner of section thirty-six, township nine north, range twenty west, in the west line of range nineteen west; thence north to the northwest corner of section six, of township eight north, range nineteen west; thence east along the north line of said section six and section five of said township to the

---

[7]A full description of this line is given under Los Angeles County, *ante,* 152–3.

[8]*Political Code* (1923), § 3964. This is the same as § 3964 in the act of 1919. For a more complete discussion see under Los Angeles County.

20—21936

northeast corner of said section five of said township eight north, range nineteen west, San Bernardino meridian, forming the corner common to Los Angeles, Kern and Ventura; thence southerly along the western line of Los Angeles County to the Pacific Ocean and three miles therein; thence in a northwesterly direction to a point due south of and three miles distant from the center of the mouth of Rincon Creek; thence north to the point of beginning, and including the islands of Anacapa and San Nicholas.''

YOLO COUNTY

Yolo, originally spelled Yola, was one of the counties created by the act of February 18, 1850. Its territory was then approximately twice what it now has, for it included a large part of the present territory of Colusa.[1] The original boundaries as set forth in the act were as follows:[2]

> "Beginning on the summit of the Coast Range at a point due west from the northwest corner of Sutter County, and running thence due east to the Sacramento River; thence down the middle of said river to the head of Merrit's Slough; thence northwesterly and westerly, following the boundary of Solano County to the summit of the Coast Range; and thence northerly, following the summit of the Coast Range, to the place of beginning."

The northwest corner of Sutter here referred to is found elsewhere defined as being on the Sacramento River due west of the mouth of Honcut Creek.[3] In another section the northern line of Solano is found to be the middle of Putah Creek to its sink and thence a direct line to Merritt Slough.[4] The western line which follows the "summit of the Coast Range" is less easily determined, but a study of the history of the boundaries of the adjacent counties seems to fix the line at the summit of the first divide east of Clear Lake.[5]

Boundary of 1851. In 1851 the limits of Yolo County were changed to approximately their present position. The northern half of the county including Colusa City was given to the county of Colusa, the line being made to run west from the Sacramento River at a point "ten miles below the head of Sycamore Slough," otherwise the boundaries were about as described in 1850.[6] On account of the tendency of these sloughs to change their course or location it has not been possible to locate this line with certainty. A subsequent act (1856) gives it a definite location "on the line between townships twelve and thirteen north, in Yolo County."[7] Since there

---

[1]Colusa at that time was located still further north.
[2]*Statutes,* 1850 : 156.
[3]*Ibid.,* 62.
[4]*Ibid.,* 61. "Merritt Slough" is now called "Steamboat Slough."
[5]For full discussion of this line see Colusa County.
[6]*Statutes,* 1851 : 179.
[7]*Ibid.,* 1856 : 124.

was probably no intention to change this line, but merely to place it upon a definite survey line, it may be safe to assume that this was the nearest township line to the point described as "ten miles below the head of Sycamore Slough."

Southern Boundary, 1857. The line between Yolo and Solano was fixed in 1857 as it now stands. The act of that year describing the whole boundary is as follows:[8]

> "The boundary line of Yolo County shall commence at a point in the middle of Sacramento River, near the head of Merritt's, or Steamboat Slough, at a point where the township line between township number five and township number six, north of the Monte Diablo base line, intersects said river; thence running due west with said township line to the range line between range number two and range number three, east of the meridian of Monte Diablo; thence due north with said range line to the south branch or old bed of Putah Creek; thence westerly up the middle of the old bed, as well as the main Putah Creek, to a point in the cañon where the highest ridge of mountains, dividing the valleys of Sacramento and Berryessa; thence along the highest ridge of said mountains, north to the outlet of Clear Lake, or until it intersects a line dividing the counties of Yolo and Colusi, established by an act of the legislature approved April 19, 1856; thence east, with said line, to the middle of the Sacramento River; thence south along the middle of said river to the place of beginning."

In 1866 a slight modification in the line between Yolo and Napa specified that the west line of Yolo should run "west of the California and Occidental Quicksilver Mines" lying along the ridge dividing the two counties.[9]

The Present Boundary. At the adoption of the Political Code in 1872 the description of the boundaries was rewritten and more definitely given. This description was incorporated in the act of 1923 defining the county boundaries:[10]

> "3965. *Yolo.* Beginning on southeast corner, at the most easterly northeast corner of Solano, in Sutter Slough, at its intersection with the first standard north; thence west on said standard line to west line of range three east, Mount Diablo meridian; thence north on said range line to the northeast corner of township seven north, two east;

[8]*Statutes*, 1857 : 108.
[9]*Ibid.*, 1865–66 : 162.
[10]*Political Code* (1872), § 3929; (1919), § 3965; (1923), § 3965.

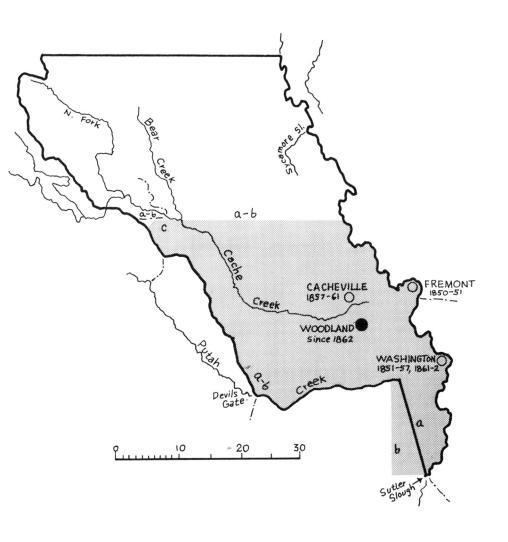

Yolo County

Solid	Stats.	1850: 156.
a	Stats.	1851: 179; 1856: 124.
b	Stats.	1857: 108.
c	Stats.	1865-6: 162; Pol. Code (1872), Sec. 3929.
Shaded	Pol. Code (1919), Sec. 3965.	

Solid bold line designates original boundary. Changes are
lettered (a, b, c, etc.). Shading denotes present county
boundaries.

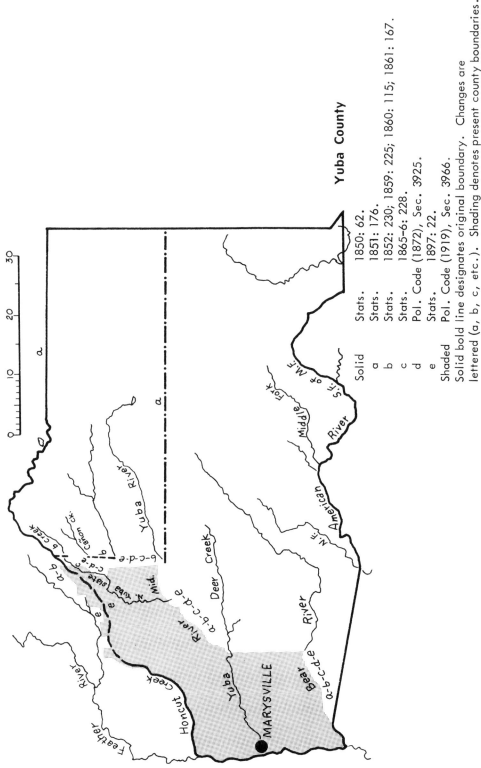

Yuba County

Solid   Stats. 1850: 62.
a   Stats. 1851: 176.
b   Stats. 1852: 230; 1859: 225; 1860: 115; 1861: 167.
c   Stats. 1865-6: 228.
d   Pol. Code (1872), Sec. 3925.
e   Stats. 1897: 22.
Shaded Pol. Code (1919), Sec. 3966.

Solid bold line designates original boundary. Changes are
lettered (a, b, c, etc.). Shading denotes present county boundaries.

thence west nine and seventy-two one-hundredths chains to southeast corner of township eight north, two east; thence north on easterly line of said township to the old bed of Putah Creek; thence westerly up the old bed and main Putah Creek to a point on eastern line of Napa, in the cañon, called Devil's Gate, where the highest ridge of mountains divides the waters of the Sacramento from Berryessa valley, forming the most westerly of the southwest corners of Yolo and northwest corner of Solano; thence northerly along the highest ridge of said mountains to Cache Creek; thence east to the summit of the spur of the Coast Range which divides the waters flowing east into Bear Creek and Stony Creek, and those flowing west into the north fork of Cache Creek; thence along the dividing ridge, to the southwest corner of Colusa, as established in section three thousand nine hundred fourteen; thence easterly on southern line of Colusa, as established in said section, to Sacramento River, forming the northeast corner at the point of intersection of the southern line of township thirteen north, Mount Diablo base; thence down said river to Sutter Slough; thence down said slough to the place of beginning.''

YUBA COUNTY

Original Boundaries, 1850. Yuba County was created by act of February 18, 1850, and was therefore one of the original counties. As created its territory included not only the present county but the greater portion of Placer, Nevada, and Sierra counties. The rapid development of the mining region, however, led to the cutting off of these districts at early dates. Since the organization of the county the seat of justice has remained at Marysville. The original limits of the county were defined in the act as follows:[1]

> "Beginning at the mouth of Honcut Creek, and running up the middle of the same to its source; thence following the dividing ridge between Feather and Yuba rivers to the summit of the Sierra Nevada; thence east to the boundary of the state; thence south following said boundary to the northeast corner of El Dorado County; thence in a westerly direction, following the northern boundary of said county, to the junction of the north and middle forks of the American River; thence in a northwesterly direction, following the boundary of Sutter County to the mouth of Bear Creek; thence running up the middle of Feather River to the mouth of Honcut Creek, which was the place of beginning."

The western and southern lines require further description since they were defined by the boundaries of Sutter and El Dorado counties. Running from west to east it should be noted that the southern line ran along the Sutter line from the mouth of Honcut Creek

> "down the middle of Feather River to the mouth of Bear Creek; thence up Bear Creek to a point six miles from its mouth; thence in a direct line to the junction of the north and middle forks of the American River."[2]

From this point the Yuba boundary was identical with the northern line of El Dorado County which was defined as running from the mouth of the Middle Fork of the American River

> "thence up the middle of said fork to its source; thence in a due easterly direction to the boundary of the state."[3]

[1]*Statutes,* 1850: 62, § 20.
[2]*Ibid.,* 1850: 62, § 19.
[3]*Ibid.,* 1850: 61, § 18.

By a subsequent act this line was defined more clearly as going up the Middle Fork and the South Fork of the Middle Fork to its source.[4]

Separation of Placer and Nevada Counties, 1851. After one year's existence Yuba County was forced to give up approximately one-half of its territory, the detached portion being formed into two new counties—Placer and Nevada. After the loss of this territory the southern boundary of Yuba was redefined as follows:[5]

> "Beginning at a point in the middle of Feather River, opposite the mouth of Bear Creek, and running thence east up the middle of said creek to a point due south from the mouth of Deer Creek; thence north to a point in the middle of Yuba River, opposite the mouth of said creek; thence up the middle of Yuba River to a point opposite the mouth of the middle branch of the Yuba; thence up the middle of the said branch ten miles from its mouth; thence easterly in a straight line to the boundary line of the state."

Loss of Sierra County, 1852. After the formation of Nevada and Placer counties at the expense of Yuba, but one year elapsed before her remaining territory was once again cut in two, the northeastern portion being separately organized as Sierra County. The line between Sierra and Yuba was defined in the act creating Sierra County in the following words:[6]

> "Beginning at a point in the middle of the Middle Branch of Yuba River, ten miles from its mouth, running thence in a northwesterly direction to a point on the North Branch of Yuba River, known as Cut Eye Foster's Bar; thence westerly to a point on the dividing ridge between the waters of Feather and Yuba Rivers, known as the Lexington House."

On account of the lack of knowledge of directions on the part of those who drew up this act, the directions indicated are misleading, since the location of Cut Eye Foster's Bar is almost due north of the point of beginning, and the Lexington House referred to is not "westerly," but a little east of north of Cut Eye Foster's Bar.[7]

---

[4] See El Dorado description.
[5] *Statutes*, 1851: 176.
[6] *Ibid.*, 1852: 230.
[7] See Westcoatt, *Official map of Yuba County, California, 1861.*

Butte-Yuba Boundary. Although the northwestern boundary common to Butte and Yuba counties has remained practically as it now is since the date of the foundation of these counties, several minor adjustments have been made. The first of these, adopted in 1860, explicitly placed Strawberry Valley in Yuba County. It reads as follows:[8]

> "Beginning at the highest point in the present county line, within three hundred yards east of the village of Strawberry Valley, and running thence in a right line to a point in the present county line two thousand feet distant from the place of beginning, and on the western and opposite side of said village of Strawberry Valley, so as to leave the said village of Strawberry Valley wholly in Yuba County."

The second of these acts, placing the Woodville House in Yuba County, describes the line as follows:[9]

> "Beginning at a station tree on the established line between said counties, about twenty-six chains easterly from the house known as the 'Woodville House,' thence, on a right line fifty chains, more or less, to the third station tree, westerly from the said Woodville House, on the said established line, said right line passing about three chains northerly of said house, and leaving the same, with all of the out-buildings, in Yuba County."

Inasmuch as the amount of territory here described is so small, and the effect of the acts was rather to define than amend the boundaries in question, these acts have not been indicated upon the map.

The line as set forth in these acts was, with slight modifications, incorporated into the Political Code in 1872 and remained the boundary between the two counties until 1897. During the latter year this line was in part redefined, it being described in terms of township and section lines. The change made by the act of 1897 caused this portion of the Butte-Yuba line to run as follows:[10]

> "Beginning at the intersection of the south line of section thirty-one, of township nineteen north, range six east, Mount Diablo base and meridian, with the west branch of

[8]*Statutes*, 1860: 115.
[9]*Ibid.*, 1861: 167.
[10]*Ibid.*, 1897: 22.

the Honcut Creek, the present line between the counties of Butte and Yuba, and running thence east to the southwest corner of the southeast one-quarter of the southeast one-quarter of section thirty-one, said township and range, thence north three-quarters of a mile, thence east one-quarter of a mile, thence north one-quarter of a mile, to corner common to sections twenty-nine, thirty, thirty-one, and thirty-two, said township and range; thence east one-half mile to the one-quarter section corner between sections twenty-nine and thirty-two, said township and range, thence north one-half mile to the center of section twenty-nine, thence east one-half mile to the one-quarter section corner between sections twenty-eight and twenty-nine, said township and range, thence north three-quarters of a mile, thence east one-quarter of a mile, thence north three-quarters of a mile, thence east one-quarter of a mile to the one-quarter section corner between sections sixteen and twenty-one, said township and range, thence north one and one-half miles to the center of section nine, said township and range, thence east one and one-half miles to the one-quarter section corner between sections ten and eleven, said township and range, thence south one-half mile to the corner common to sections ten, eleven, fourteen, and fifteen, said township and range, thence east two miles to the corner common to sections twelve and thirteen, township nineteen north, range six east, and sections seven and eighteen, township nineteen north, range seven east, Mount Diablo base and meridian, thence north one mile to the corner common to sections one and twelve, township nineteen north, range six east, and sections six and seven, township nineteen north, range seven east, Mount Diablo meridian, thence east three miles to the corner common to sections three, four, nine, and ten, township nineteen north, range seven east, Mount Diablo meridian, thence south one-half mile to one-quarter section corner between sections nine and ten, said township and range, thence east one and one-half miles to the center of section eleven, said township and range, thence north one-half mile to the one-quarter section corner between sections two and eleven, said township and range, thence east one-half mile to the corner common to sections one, two, eleven, and twelve, said township and range, thence north two miles to the corner common to sections twenty-five, twenty-six, thirty-five, and thirty-six, township twenty north, range seven east, Mount Diablo meridian, thence east one-half mile to one-qarter section corner between sections twenty-five and thirty-six, said township and range, thence north one-half mile to the center of section twenty-five, said township and range, thence east one and one-half miles to the one-quarter section corner between sections twenty-nine and thirty, township twenty north, range eight east, Mount Diablo meridian, thence north one-quarter of a mile, thence east one-half of a mile, thence north one' and one-quarter miles to the one-quarter section corner between sections seventeen and twenty, said township and range, thence east one and one-half miles to the corner common to sections fifteen, sixteen, twenty-one, and twenty-two, said township and range, thence north one mile to the corner common to sections nine, ten, sixteen, and fifteen, said township and range, thence east to the line between Plumas and Butte counties at its intersection with the northwest boundary line of Yuba County.''

Sierra and Plumas Boundary. In the meanwhile other changes had been made in the boundary with Sierra and Plumas counties. The Sierra line was changed in 1866, giving to Sierra County a small piece of territory lying north and east of the North Yuba River and Cañon Creek, the description of the line being given as follows:[11]

''Commencing at a point in the middle of the North Yuba River, (where the boundary line crosses said river,) opposite to a point called Cut Eye Foster's Bar, from thence running down the middle of said river to the mouth of Big Cañon Creek, thence up the middle of said Cañon Creek to a point where the present county line crosses said creek.''

Present Boundary, 1923. The section of the Political Code which defines the boundaries of Yuba County reads as follows:[12]

''3966. *Yuba.* Beginning at southwest corner, at junction of Feather and Bear rivers; thence up Bear River, on the line of Sutter and Placer, to the southwest corner of Nevada, as established in section three thousand nine hundred thirty-seven; thence north, on Nevada line, to the junction of Deer Creek and main Yuba; thence up the main to the middle Yuba and up the middle Yuba ten miles, to the southwest corner of Sierra, as established in section three thousand nine hundred fifty-four; thence in direct line northerly, and on line of Sierra, to Cut Eye Foster's Bar, on North Yuba River; thence down the river to the mouth of Big Cañon Creek; thence up said creek

---

[11]*Statutes,* 1865–66 : 228.
[12]*Political Code* (1923), § 3966.

four miles; thence in direct line to south corner of Plumas and northwest corner of Sierra, in Slate Creek, as established in sections three thousand nine hundred forty and three thousand nine hundred fifty-four; thence northwesterly in a direct line, to common corner of Plumas, Butte, and Yuba, in front of Buckeye House, as established in section three thousand nine hundred forty; thence on southwestern line of Butte, as established in section three thousand nine hundred twelve to the junction of Honcut Creek with Feather River; thence down Feather River, to the place of beginning.''

APPENDIX

Map of California with Key Showing Changes in
County Jurisdiction

MAP OF CALIFORNIA

SHOWING

CHANGES IN COUNTY JURISDICTION

MILES

FOR EXPLANATION SEE KEY

KEY TO MAP SHOWING CHANGES IN COUNTY JURISDICTION

ALAMEDA.
1. Contra Costa, 1850-53; Alameda, 1853-date.
2. Santa Clara, 1850-53; Alameda, 1853-date.

ALPINE.
1. El Dorado, 1850-64; Alpine, 1864-date.
2. El Dorado, 1850-1863; Amador, 1863-64; Alpine, 1864-date.
3. Calaveras, 1850-54; Amador, 1854-64; Alpine, 1864-date.
4. Calaveras, 1850-64; Alpine, 1864-date.
5. Calaveras, 1850-61; Mono, 1861-64; Alpine, 1864-date.
6. Tuolumne, 1850-64; Alpine, 1864-date.

AMADOR.
1. Calaveras, 1850-54; Amador, 1854-date.
2. El Dorado, 1850-55; Amador, 1855-date.
3. El Dorado, 1850-57; Amador, 1857-date.
4. El Dorado, 1850-63; Amador, 1863-date.

BUTTE.
1. Butte, 1850-date.
2. Butte, 1850-56; Tehama, 1856-59; Butte, 1859-date.
3. Butte, 1850-56; Colusa, 1856-72; Butte, 1872-date.

CALAVERAS.
Calaveras, 1850-date.

COLUSA.
1. Colusa, 1850-date.
2. Colusa, 1850-91; Glenn, 1891-93; Colusa, 1893-date.
3. Butte, 1850-56; Colusa, 1856-date.
4. Sutter, 1850-51; Butte, 1851-56; Colusa, 1856-date.
5. Sutter, 1850-56; Colusa, 1856-date.
6. Yolo, 1850-51; Colusa, 1851-date.

CONTRA COSTA.
Contra Costa, 1850-date.

DEL NORTE.
1. Trinity, 1850-51; Klamath, 1851-57; Del Norte, 1857-date.
2. Trinity, 1850-51; Klamath, 1851-75; Humboldt, 1875-1901; Del Norte, 1901-date.
3. Trinity, 1850-51; Klamath, 1851-75; Siskiyou, 1875-87; Del Norte, 1887-date.

EL DORADO.
1. El Dorado, 1850-date.
2. Placer, 1850-63; El Dorado, 1863-date.

FRESNO.
1. Mariposa, 1850-56; Fresno, 1856-date.
2. Mariposa, 1850-55; Merced, 1855-56; Fresno, 1856-date.
3. Mariposa, 1850-52; Tulare, 1852-56; Fresno, 1856-date.
4. Mariposa, 1850-52; Tulare, 1852-56; Fresno, 1856-74; Tulare, 1874-76; Fresno, 1876-date.

GLENN.
1. Colusa, 1850-91; Glenn, 1891-date.
2. Butte, 1850-56; Colusa, 1856-91; Glenn, 1891-date.
3. Colusa, 1850-57; Tehama, 1857-59; Colusa, 1859-91; Glenn, 1891-date.
4. Mendocino, 1850-1907; Glenn, 1907-date.

HUMBOLDT.
1. Trinity, 1850-53; Humboldt, 1853-date.
2. Trinity, 1850-51; Klamath, 1851-75; Humboldt, 1875-date.
3. Trinity, 1850-51; Klamath, 1851-57; Del Norte, 1857-1901; Humboldt, 1901-date.
4. Trinity, 1850-51; Klamath, 1851-75; Siskiyou, 1875-1887; Del Norte, 1887-1901; Humboldt, 1901-date.
5. Trinity, 1850-53; Humboldt, 1853-59; Mendocino, 1859-60; Humboldt, 1860-date.

IMPERIAL.
San Diego, 1850-1907; Imperial, 1907-date.

INYO.
1. Mariposa, 1850-56; Fresno, 1856-61; Mono, 1861-70; Inyo, 1870-date.
2. Mariposa, 1850-52; Tulare, 1852-56; Fresno, 1856-61; Mono, 1861-70; Inyo, 1870-date.

3. Mariposa, 1850-52; Tulare, 1852-56; Fresno, 1856-61; Mono, 1861-66; Inyo, 1866-date.
4. Mariposa, 1850-52; Tulare, 1852-61; Mono, 1861-70; Inyo, 1870-date.
5. Mariposa, 1850-52; Tulare, 1852-66; Inyo, 1866-date.
6. San Diego, 1850-51; Mariposa, 1851-52; Tulare, 1852-66; Inyo, 1866-date.
7. San Diego, 1850-51; Los Angeles, 1851-53; San Bernardino, 1853-72; Inyo, 1872-date.
8. Mariposa, 1850-51; Los Angeles, 1851-53; San Bernardino, 1853-72; Inyo, 1872-date.
9. Mariposa, 1850-51; Los Angeles, 1851-66; Kern, 1866-72; Inyo, 1872-date.

KERN.
1. Mariposa, 1850-52; Tulare, 1852-66; Kern, 1866-date.
2. Mariposa, 1850-51; Los Angeles, 1851-66; Kern, 1866-date.
3. San Luis Obispo, 1850-85; Kern, 1885-date.

KINGS.
1. Mariposa, 1850-52; Tulare, 1852-93; Kings, 1893-date.
2. Mariposa, 1850-52; Tulare, 1852-74; Fresno, 1874-76; Tulare, 1876-93; Kings, 1893-date.
3. Mariposa, 1850-56; Tulare, 1856-74; Fresno, 1874-76; Tulare, 1876-93; Kings, 1893-date.
4. Mariposa, 1850-56; Tulare, 1856-93; Kings, 1893-date.
5. Mariposa, 1850-56; Fresno, 1856-1909; Kings, 1909-date.
6. Mariposa, 1850-52; Tulare 1852-56; Fresno, 1856-1909; Kings, 1909-date.

LAKE.[1]
1. Napa, 1850-61; Lake, 1861-date.
2. Mendocino, 1850-52; Napa, 1852-61; Lake, 1861-date.
3. Mendocino, 1850-55; Napa, 1855-61; Lake, 1861-date.
4. Mendocino, 1850-64; Lake, 1864-date.
5. Yolo, 1850-51; Colusa, 1851-68; Lake, 1868-date.

---

[1]The northern boundary of Napa and the eastern boundary of Mendocino for 1850 and 1851 must not be accepted too literally. The Napa line was entirely inconsistent with other boundaries; and Mendocino was unorganized.

LASSEN.
1. Shasta, 1850-64; Lassen, 1864-date.
2. Butte, 1850-54; Plumas, 1854-64; Lassen, 1864-date.
3. Butte, 1850-54; Plumas, 1854-72; Lassen, 1872-date.

LOS ANGELES.
1. Los Angeles, 1850-date.
2. Mariposa, 1850-51; Los Angeles, 1851-date.
3. Santa Barbara, 1850-51; Los Angeles, 1851-date.

MADERA.
1. Mariposa, 1850-56; Fresno, 1856-93; Madera, 1893-date.
2. Mariposa, 1850-55; Merced, 1855-56; Fresno, 1856-93; Madera, 1893-date.
3. Mariposa, 1850-56; Fresno, 1856-70; Mariposa, 1870-72; Fresno, 1872-93; Madera, 1893-date.

MARIN.
Marin, 1850-date.

MARIPOSA.
1. Mariposa, 1850-date.
2. Mariposa, 1850-56; Fresno, 1856-70; Mariposa, 1870-date.

MENDOCINO.[2]
1. Mendocino, 1850-date.
2. Sonoma, 1850-55; Mendocino, 1855-date.
3. Sonoma, 1850-59; Mendocino, 1859-date.
4. Mendocino, 1850-55; Sonoma, 1855-59; Mendocino, 1859-date.

MERCED.
Mariposa, 1850-55; Merced, 1855-date.

MODOC.
Shasta, 1850-52; Siskiyou, 1852-74; Modoc, 1874-date.

MONO.
1 Calaveras, 1850-61; Mono, 1861-date.
2. Calaveras, 1850-54; Amador, 1854-64; unattached, 1864-66; Mono, 1866-date.
3. Calaveras, 1850-56; Fresno, 1856-61; Mono, 1861-date.

---

[2]Mendocino was unorganized before 1859, being joined to Sonoma County.

4. Mariposa, 1850-56; unattached, 1856-61; Mono, 1861-date.
5. Mariposa, 1850-56; Fresno, 1856-61; Mono, 1861-date.
6. Mariposa, 1850-52; Tulare, 1852-56; Fresno, 1856-61; Mono, 1861-date.

MONTEREY.

1. Monterey, 1850-date.
2. San Luis Obispo, 1850-51; Monterey, 1851-date.
3. San Luis Obispo, 1850-51; Monterey, 1851-61; San Luis Obispo, 1861-72; Monterey, 1872-date.
4. Monterey, 1850-61; San Luis Obispo, 1861-72; Monterey, 1872-date.
5. San Luis Obispo, 1850-63; Monterey, 1863-date.

NAPA.[3]

1. Napa, 1850-date.
2. Napa, 1850-64; Lake, 1864-72; Napa, 1872-date.
3. Napa, 1850-61; Lake, 1861-72; Napa, 1872-date.
4. Napa, 1850-68; Lake, 1868-72; Napa, 1872-date.
5. Solano, 1850-55; Napa, 1855-date.
6. Sonoma, 1850-55; Napa, 1855-date.

NEVADA.

1. Yuba, 1850-51; Nevada, 1851-date.
2. Yuba, 1850-52; Nevada, 1852-date.
3. Yuba, 1850-52; Sierra, 1852-56; Nevada, 1856-date.

ORANGE.

Los Angeles, 1850-89; Orange, 1889-date.

PLACER.

1. Sutter, 1850-51; Placer, 1851-date.
2. Yuba, 1850-51; Placer, 1851-date.
3. El Dorado, 1850-1913; Placer, 1913-date.

PLUMAS.

1. Butte, 1850-54; Plumas, 1854-date.
2. Yuba, 1850-52; Sierra, 1852-66; Plumas, 1866-date.

---

[3]The northern boundary of Napa for 1850 and 1851 is not considered since it is so inconsistent with the adjoining county boundaries.

RIVERSIDE.
1. San Diego, 1850-93; Riverside, 1893-date.
2. San Diego, 1850-51; Los Angeles, 1851-53; San Bernardino, 1853-93; Riverside, 1893-date.
3. Los Angeles, 1850-53; San Bernardino, 1853-93; Riverside, 1893-date.
4. Los Angeles, 1850-51; San Diego, 1851-93; Riverside, 1893-date.

SACRAMENTO.
Sacramento, 1850-date.

SAN BENITO.
1. Monterey, 1850-1874; San Benito, 1874-date.
2. Mariposa, 1850-55; Merced, 1855-56; Fresno, 1856-87; San Benito, 1887-date.
3. Mariposa, 1850-55; Merced, 1855-87; San Benito, 1887-date.

SAN BERNARDINO.
1. San Diego, 1850-51; Los Angeles, 1851-53; San Bernardino, 1853-date.
2. Mariposa, 1850-51; Los Angeles, 1851-53; San Bernardino, 1853-date.
3. Los Angeles, 1850-53; San Bernardino, 1853-date.
4. Mariposa, 1850-51; Los Angeles, 1851-78; claimed by San Bernardino since 1876.
5. Los Angeles, 1850-78; claimed by San Bernardino since 1876.

SAN DIEGO.
San Diego, 1850-date.

SAN FRANCISCO.
San Francisco, 1850-date.

SAN JOAQUIN.
1. San Joaquin, 1850-date.
2. Sacramento, 1850-78; San Joaquin, 1878-date.

SAN LUIS OBISPO.
1. San Luis Obispo, 1850-date.
2. San Luis Obispo, 1850-54; Santa Barbara, 1854-72; San Luis Obispo, 1872-date.

3. San Luis Obispo, 1850-51; Monterey, 1851-61; San Luis Obispo, 1861-date.
4. Monterey, 1850-61; San Luis Obispo, 1861-date.
5. Santa Barbara, 1850-54; San Luis Obispo, 1854-date.
6. Mariposa, 1850-52; Tulare, 1852-66; Kern, 1866-85; San Luis Obispo, 1885-date.

SAN MATEO.
1. San Francisco, 1850-56; San Mateo, 1856-date.
2. Santa Cruz, 1850-68; San Mateo, 1868-date.

SANTA BARBARA.
1. Santa Barbara, 1850-date.
2. Santa Barbara, 1850-51; San Luis Obispo, 1851-52; Santa Barbara, 1852-date.
3. Santa Barbara, 1850-54; San Luis Obispo, 1854-72; Santa Barbara, 1872-date.
4. San Luis Obispo, 1850-72; Santa Barbara, 1872-date.

SANTA CLARA.
Santa Clara, 1850-date.

SANTA CRUZ.
Santa Cruz, 1850-date.

SHASTA.
1. Shasta, 1850-date.
2. Butte, 1850-54; Plumas, 1854-72; Shasta, 1872-date.

SIERRA.
1. Yuba, 1850-52; Sierra, 1852-date.
2. Yuba, 1850-66; Sierra, 1866-date.
3. Yuba, 1850-52; Sierra, 1852-66; Plumas, 1866-68; Sierra, 1868-date.
4. Butte, 1850-54; Plumas, 1854-63; Sierra, 1863-date.

SISKIYOU.
1. Trinity, 1850-51; Klamath, 1851-52; Siskiyou, 1852-date.
2. Shasta, 1850-52; Siskiyou, 1852-date.
3. Trinity, 1850-51; Klamath, 1851-75; Siskiyou, 1875-date.
4. Trinity, 1850-51; Klamath, 1851-57; Del Norte, 1857-87; Siskiyou, 1887-date.

SOLANO.
1. Solano, 1850-date.
2. Mare Island: Sonoma, 1850-53; Solano, 1853-date.

SONOMA.
1. Sonoma, 1850-date.
2. Mendocino, 1850-55; Sonoma, 1855-date.
3. Mendocino, 1850-59; Sonoma, 1859-date.

STANISLAUS.
1. Tuolumne, 1850-54; Stanislaus, 1854-date.
2. Tuolumne, 1850-54; Stanislaus, 1854-66; Merced, 1866-68; Stanislaus, 1868-date.
3. San Joaquin, 1850-60; Stanislaus, 1860-date.

SUTTER.
1. Sutter, 1850-date.
2. Sutter, 1850-51; Placer, 1851-66; Sutter, 1866-date.
3. Sutter, 1850-51; Butte, 1851-56; Sutter, 1856-date.
4. Sutter, 1850-51; Butte, 1851-52; Sutter, 1852-date.
5. Sutter, 1850-52; Butte, 1852-54; Sutter, 1854-date.

TEHAMA.
1. Colusa, 1850-56; Tehama, 1856-date.
2. Colusa, 1850-51; Shasta, 1851-56; Tehama, 1856-date.
3. Colusa, 1850-51; Shasta, 1851-57; Tehama, 1857-date.
4. Shasta, 1850-57; Tehama, 1857-date.
5. Shasta, 1850-56; Tehama, 1856-date.
6. Butte, 1850-56; Tehama, 1856-date.
7. Butte, 1850-51; Shasta, 1851-56; Tehama, 1856-date.

TRINITY.
1. Trinity, 1850-date.
2. Trinity, 1850-51; Klamath, 1851-55; Trinity, 1855-date.
3. Trinity, 1850-59; Mendocino, 1859-60; Trinity, 1860-date.
4. Mendocino, 1850-72; Trinity, 1872-date.

TULARE.
1. Mariposa, 1850-52; Tulare, 1852-date.
2. Mariposa, 1850-52; Tulare, 1852-56; Fresno, 1856-74; Tulare, 1874-date.

TUOLUMNE.

     Tuolumne, 1850-date.

VENTURA.

    1. Santa Barbara, 1850-72; Ventura, 1872-date.

    2. San Luis Obispo, 1850-72; Ventura, 1872-date.

    3. Los Angeles, 1850-51; Santa Barbara, 1851-72; Ventura, 1872-date.

    4. Santa Barbara, 1850-72; Los Angeles, 1872-1881; claimed by Ventura since 1881.

    5. Los Angeles, 1850-51; Santa Barbara, 1851-72; Los Angeles, 1872-81; claimed by Ventura since 1881.

YOLO.

    1. Yolo, 1850-date.

    2. Solano, 1850-57; Yolo, 1857-date.

YUBA.

    Yuba, 1850-date.

CALIFORNIA COUNTY BOUNDARIES

INDEX

ADDENDUM

The continuing effect of the constitutional amendment voted by the people in 1894 has been to prevent the formation of any new counties and discourage any major realignment of the counties then existing. The changes since *California County Boundaries* was first printed in 1923 have in some instances involved the exchange of several thousand acres, but none of them have involved large numbers of people or major investments.

The requirements for the formation of a new county today make it almost impossible for one to be created in California. The petition calling for its formation must be signed by at least 65 per cent of the qualified electors (registered voters) in the proposed new county as well as 50 per cent of those residing in the county or counties from which the new one would be carved. The Board of Supervisors must then call an election, and an affirmative vote of 65 per cent of those cast in the separating district and 50 per cent of those cast in the county or counties affected would be necessary to ratify the creation of the new county. Population of the new county must be at least 10,000, and the existing county must not be reduced to a population of less than 20,000 or a territory of less than 1200 square miles. No boundary of a new county shall pass within five miles of the county seat of the existing county.

Boundary lines between counties may be changed by agreement of the Board of Supervisors of the counties concerned, provided that a line is not moved in excess of five miles, the area of a county is not reduced more than 5 per cent, and the population is not reduced more than 3 per cent. With the consent of a 4/5 majority of the Board of each county, the boundary line of one county may pass within five miles of the county seat of another.

Whenever a boundary change is desired, a petition must be filed with the Board of Supervisors of each county affected, signed by at least 25 qualified electors of that county and accompanied by a statement of consent signed by at least 50 per cent of the landowners in the area proposed to be transferred.

Another change made very unlikely by constitutional and statutory law is the relocation of a county seat. Such relocation requires the submission of a petition signed by a majority of the qualified electors of the county and calling for an election by the Board of Supervisors. Removal of the county seat to another location not only requires a 2/3 vote in favor of removal, but also a 2/3 vote in favor of removal to a particular place.

Sections of the Government Code dealing with county boundaries begin with Section 23000. Title 3, *Government of Counties,* was added by Statutes of 1947, C 424, p.1039, Section 1. Statutes dealing with the boundaries of counties are contained in Division 1, *Counties Generally,* which is divided into five chapters: 1 -- General, beginning with Section 23000; 2 -- Boundaries, Section 23070; 3 -- Creation of New Counties, Section 23300; 4 -- County Seats, Section 23600; and 5 -- County Charters, Section 23700.

The boundaries of the counties are redefined but not changed by the 1947 statutes. The descriptions are arranged alphabetically in Division 1, Article 2, Sections 23101 to 23158. The county seats are named in Chapter 4, Sections 23601 through 23658.

Many boundaries have had to be adjusted because they were based upon the creek or river between two counties. Phrases such as "down the San Joaquin" are interpreted to mean that the boundary line follows the middle of the natural deep water channel. This line may be changed due to accretion and avulsion. To solve these problems joint surveys are usually made to re-establish the county line, but the changes are usually minor and are not included in this volume.

Major changes since 1923 which have been reported to us are listed alphabetically by the counties affected.

ALAMEDA COUNTY

Two subdivisions, Park Hills and Berkeley Woods, containing 148.6 acres or 0.232 square miles, were annexed from Contra Costa County on January 14, 1958, by Resolution No. 85755 of the Board of Supervisors of Alameda County. The boundary was moved northeast from the former survey line to follow Wildcat Canyon Road from its intersection with Grizzly Peak Boulevard on the north to Shasta Road on the south.

Two narrow wedge-shaped parcels of land consisting of 6.5 acres were transferred to Santa Clara County by Ordinance No. 71-11, effective November 2, 1971. The two parcels were divided by an 80-foot right of way to the City and County of San Francisco and extended southwest from State Freeway No. 680 where it crosses the common boundary of the two counties.

BUTTE COUNTY

The diagonal northwest boundary of Butte County, which is the common boundary with Tehama County, was altered by action of the Board of Supervisors of Butte County on November 20, 1944. The former arbitrary diagonal boundary was changed to follow section lines and property lines. This resulted in no appreciable change in the direction of the boundary. About eight square miles of land were exchanged by the two counties.

CONTRA COSTA COUNTY

Two subdivisions known as Park Hills and Berkeley Woods, containing 148.6 acres or 0.232 square miles, were withdrawn from Contra Costa County and annexed to Alameda County on January 14, 1958 by action of the Contra Costa County Board of Supervisors. The boundary was moved northeast from the former survey line to follow Wildcat Canyon Road from its intersection with Grizzly Peak Boulevard on the north to Shasta Road on the south.

IMPERIAL COUNTY

The Colorado River has long served as a boundary line between the States of California and Nevada and also as the eastern boundary of Imperial County. Due to accretion or avulsion brought about by the meandering of the Colorado River, the interstate boundary and therefore the county boundary have been redefined. The statutes now describe the county boundary as being "a portion of the interstate boundary between the states of Arizona and California as described in *Interstate Compact Defining the Boundary Between the States of Arizona and California,*" a certified copy of which is recorded and filed in the office of the County Recorder of Imperial County. A true and complete copy of the *Compact* is on file for permanent public record in the office of the California Secretary of State and certified copies are on file in the California State Lands Commission office. Planimetric maps of the boundary appear as Exhibit A of the *Compact.* A redefinition of the boundary was enacted by the Legislature in 1967.

INYO COUNTY

Refer to San Bernardino County regarding changes in the boundary between Inyo and San Bernardino Counties.

KERN COUNTY

In 1963 the Board of Supervisors of Kern County and the Board of Supervisors of San Bernardino County agreed to the exchange of two sections or 1280 acres of land between the counties. San Bernardino County gave to Kern County Sections 13 and 24, Township 26 South Range 40 East, and Kern County gave to San Bernardino County Sections 2 and 11 of the same township. The northernmost section was six miles south of the northern boundary of Kern County.

Considerable uncertainty existed regarding the boundary line between Kern County and Ventura County, and it is generally recognized that it was the intent of the Legislature in enacting Sections 23177 and 23178 of the Government Code to resolve such problems and uncertainties. Passed in 1951, these sections provide for the validation of common boundaries used for tax purposes for 15 years, and the procedure to be followed upon the establishment of a common boundary.

RIVERSIDE COUNTY

The Colorado River has long served as a boundary line between the states of California and Nevada and also as the eastern boundary of Riverside County. Due to accretion or avulsion brought about by the meandering of the Colorado River, the interstate boundary and therefore the county boundary have been redefined. The statutes now describe the county boundary as being ''a portion of the interstate boundary between the states of Arizona and California as described in *Interstate Compact Defining the Boundary Between the States of Arizona and California,*'' a certified copy of which is recorded and filed in the office of the County Recorder of Riverside County. A true and complete copy of the *Compact* is on file for permanent public record in the office of the California Secretary of State and certified copies are on file in the California State Lands Commission office. Planimetric maps of the boundary appear as Exhibit A of the *Compact.* A redefinition of the boundary was enacted by the Legislature in 1967.

SACRAMENTO COUNTY

The county boundary between Sacramento County and San Joaquin County from the Mokelumne River to the Amador County line along Dry Creek was surveyed in 1969. The Board of Supervisors of each county authorized the survey which was completed by

Robert H. Leger and Curtis M. Brown. The survey was made to re-establish the existing County line, to monument it and to formulate an agreement between each County recognizing this as the official County line in this area. The map of the re-defined boundary was approved under Section 23171 of the Government Code by the Supervisors on May 9, 1969.

SAN BERNARDINO COUNTY

The Colorado River has long served as a boundary line between the states of California and Nevada and also as a portion of the eastern boundary of San Bernardino County. Due to accretion or avulsion brought about by the meandering of the Colorado River, the interstate boundary and therefore the county boundary have been redefined. The statutes now describe the county boundary as being "a portion of the interstate boundary between the states of Arizona and California as described in *Interstate Compact Defining the Boundary Between the States of Arizona and California,*" a certified copy of which is recorded and filed in the office of the County Recorder of San Bernardino County. A true and complete copy of the *Compact* is on file for permanent public record in the office of the California Secretary of State and certified copies are on file in the California State Lands Commission office. Planimetric

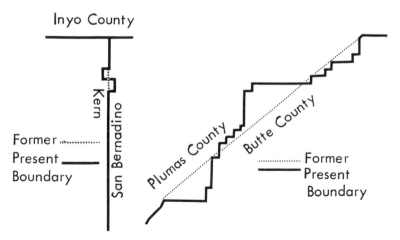

Change of common boundary between Kern and San Bernardino Counties.

Change of common boundary between Butte and Plumas Counties.

maps of the boundary appear as Exhibit A of the *Compact.* A redefinition of the boundary was enacted by the Legislature in 1967.

In 1963 the Board of Supervisors of San Bernardino County and the Board of Supervisors of Kern County agreed to the exchange of two sections or 1280 acres of land between the counties. San Bernardino County gave to Kern County Sections 13 and 24, Township 26 South Range 40 East, and Kern County gave to San Bernardino County Sections 2 and 11 of the same township. The northernmost section was six miles south of the northern boundary of San Bernardino County.

The northern boundary of San Bernardino County, which is the common boundary with Inyo County, has been in a state of conflict for many years. In 1872 the boundary was moved south to follow the Sixth Standard Parallel South, Mt. Diablo base (see page 114). In the redefinition of boundaries in 1947, a change established the boundary at the east and west center line of Sections 30 through 25 of all Townships 20 North and continuing East from Range 1 East to the interstate boundary. This was amended by Statutes 1957, Chapter 2382, Section 2, page 4119 to the Sixth Standard Parallel South, Mt. Diablo Base, approximately ½ mile south of the 1947 boundary.

SAN JOAQUIN COUNTY

See Sacramento County.

SAN LUIS OBISPO COUNTY

The county boundary between San Luis Obispo County and Santa Barbara County from the junction of the Cuyama and Sisquoc Rivers to the axis of Twitchell Dam was surveyed in 1959. The Board of Supervisors of each county authorized the survey which was completed by John B. Duff for Ferini Associates and maps filed on February 1, 1959. The survey was made to re-establish the existing County boundary. Approval under Section 23171 of the Government Code was voted by the Board of Supervisors of San Luis Obispo County on February 16, 1959 and of Santa Barbara County on February 17, 1959.

SAN MATEO COUNTY

The Board of Supervisors of the County of San Mateo authorized the alteration of the boundary lines between San Mateo County and Santa Clara County in October, 1963. The transfer involved approximately 800 acres, lying generally northeast of the point where San Francisquito Creek crosses the Bayshore Highway. The former boundary followed San Francisquito Creek. The new boundary goes north and east up along the line of the San Francisquito Creek Improvement Project No. 2 to the southern limits of the City of Menlo Park and then east and south to a point in San Francisco Bay where the Menlo Park boundary meets the former boundary between the two counties. The parcel transferred includes Sand Point and places all of the Palo Alto Yacht Harbor in Santa Clara County.

SANTA BARBARA COUNTY

See San Luis Obispo County. The boundaries of Santa Barbara County were defined by Statutes of 1968, Chapter 248, page 561, Section 1. It was specifically stated that "The amendment does not constitute a change but is a declaration of the pre-existing law."

SANTA CLARA COUNTY

The Board of Supervisors of Santa Clara County, by Ordinance No. NS-3.9, annexed a 6.5-acre parcel of land from Alameda County on November 2, 1971. This was in two parcels divided by an 80-foot right of way to the City and County of San Francisco. The narrow wedge-shaped parcels extended southwest from State Freeway No. 680 where it crosses the common boundary of the two counties.

Ordinance No. NS 3.13 was adopted November 17, 1971, by the Board of Supervisors of the County of Santa Clara adjusting the common boundary between Santa Clara County and Santa Cruz County.

The Board action was based on a report of a Joint Boundary Committee established September 23, 1969. The Committee was composed of six lay citizens from both counties and was headed by Co-Chairmen George Washington of Santa Cruz County and Edward Steffani of Santa Clara County.

When the Committee was formed the common boundary was legally defined as "Along the summit of the Santa Cruz Mountains." Since the establishment in 1850 of this vaguely stated boundary, several attempts had been made to more clearly and accurately define it. In 1886, when construction of a road along the summit was being considered, it was suggested that the road "should be adopted as a county boundary in place of the water divide." But no such action was taken. The question lay quiet for

over 60 years, until 1950, when problems of assessment, law en-
forcement, fire protection, and other legal matters began to mount.

The Committee appointed in 1969 made a thorough study of the
problem, interviewed department heads of both counties and state
officials. They also called meetings of the residents in the summit
area to determine their wishes in the matter.

In 1971 the Committee recommended that the boundary be
changed so that it would follow well-defined roads or other easily
recognizable landmarks near the summit of the mountains. They
proposed a transfer of 777 acres to Santa Clara County and 2184
acres to Santa Cruz County. The only major parcel of land transferred was a part of Mt. Madonna Park, which was annexed to
Santa Clara County so that all of that facility would be in the one
county.

The Committee also made certain recommendations based upon
their experience for changes in the state law. The three local senators
introduced Senate Bill No. 467, which was passed by the Legislature
and signed into law. The recommendations adopted were primarily
definitions, operational changes in circulation of petitions and
statements of consent, and the responsibility of various officials and
agencies when a boundary is altered and property transferred. The
Legislature rejected a recommendation for the reduction of con-
senting signatures from 50 to 35 per cent.

This boundary adjustment has been reported in considerable detail
because it is considered by officials to be one of the most extensive,
orderly and mutually satisfactory transfers made in recent years.

The new boundary was summarized in the report as follows:

"Briefly and in very general terms, the proposed boundary, with
a few minor exceptions, (1) runs along one edge or the other of the
recorded rights of way of the roads along the summit of the Santa
Cruz mountains where there are such recorded rights of way; (2)
along a line displaced a measured distance from the average center-
line of a traveled road where there is such a road but no recorded
right of way; (3) departing from the road to follow a parcel of land
forming part of Mt. Madonna Park and owned by the County of
Santa Clara so as to place all that parcel within the County of Santa
Clara; (4) along the summit of the mountains generally
southeasterly from the easterly end of Bella Vista Lane; (5)
departing from the summit to follow an old recorded property line to
and across Pescadero Creek to a section line and thence through
easily identifiable points on section lines and quarter section lines to

its end in the Pajaro River so as to place within the County of Santa Cruz the entire proposed Pescadero Creek Reservoir.

"The recommended boundary crosses the roads only seven times. It crosses Skyline Blvd. at the easterly side of the intersection with Black Road and at the westerly side of State Highway 17 to place the northwesterly half (approximately) of the State maintained road in the County of Santa Clara and the southeasterly half in the County of Santa Cruz. After crossing State Highway 17 the recommended boundary also crosses Summit Road adjacent to its intersection with the Old Santa Cruz-Los Gatos Highway, and crosses Loma Prieta Avenue at the southeastern end of the public road at its juncture with a fire control road. It also crosses Mt. Madonna Road at the southeastern end of Summit Road and crosses State Highway 152 (Hecker Pass Highway). Thus long continuous stretches of the road would be placed clearly within either County instead of repeatedly and very frequently crossing from one County to the other at places difficult for officials and the public to ascertain."

Ordinance No. NS 3.4 was adopted by the Supervisors of the County of Santa Clara on October 14, 1963, altering the boundary line between Santa Clara County and San Mateo County. The action annexed about 800 acres to Santa Clara County, which is more completely described under San Mateo County.

SANTA CRUZ COUNTY

Ordinance No. 1654 was adopted November 16, 1971, by the Board of Supervisors of the County of Santa Cruz, adjusting most of the common boundary of Santa Cruz and Santa Clara Counties. For details see Santa Clara County.

TEHAMA COUNTY

The southeast diagonal boundary of Tehama County, which is the common boundary with Butte County, was altered by action of the Board of Supervisors in 1944. The two counties exchanged about eight square miles of land. The former arbitrary diagonal boundary was eliminated, and the new boundary follows section lines and property lines. This resulted in no appreciable change in the direction of the boundary.